Y0-AGT-563

$2.00

10 -

The NEW ENCYCLOPEDIA *of* SOUTHERN CULTURE

VOLUME 6 : ETHNICITY

Volumes to appear in
The New Encyclopedia of Southern Culture
are:

The NEW

ENCYCLOPEDIA *of* SOUTHERN CULTURE

CHARLES REAGAN WILSON General Editor

JAMES G. THOMAS JR. Managing Editor

ANN J. ABADIE Associate Editor

Ethnicity

CELESTE RAY Volume Editor

Sponsored by

THE CENTER FOR THE STUDY OF SOUTHERN CULTURE

at the University of Mississippi

THE UNIVERSITY OF NORTH CAROLINA PRESS

Chapel Hill

© 2007 The University of North Carolina Press

All rights reserved

This book was published with the assistance of the Anniversary
Endowment Fund of the University of North Carolina Press.

Designed by Richard Hendel

Set in Minion types by Tseng Information Systems, Inc.

Manufactured in the United States of America

The paper in this book meets the guidelines for permanence and
durability of the Committee on Production Guidelines for Book
Longevity of the Council on Library Resources.

Library of Congress Cataloging-in-Publication Data

The new encyclopedia of Southern culture / Charles Reagan
Wilson, general editor ; James G. Thomas Jr., managing editor ;
Ann J. Abadie, associate editor.

p. cm.

Rev. ed. of: Encyclopedia of Southern culture. 1991.

"Sponsored by The Center for the Study of Southern Culture
at the University of Mississippi."

Includes bibliographical references and index.

Contents: — v. 6. Ethnicity.

ISBN 978-0-8078-3123-6 (cloth : v. 6 : alk. paper)

ISBN 978-0-8078-5823-3 (pbk. : v. 6 : alk. paper)

1. Southern States—Civilization—Encyclopedias. 2. Southern
States—Encyclopedias. I. Wilson, Charles Reagan. II. Thomas,
James G. III. Abadie, Ann J. IV. University of Mississippi.
Center for the Study of Southern Culture.

V. Encyclopedia of Southern culture.

F209.N47 2006

975.003—dc22

2005024807

The *Encyclopedia of Southern Culture*, sponsored by the Center for
the Study of Southern Culture at the University of Mississippi, was
published by the University of North Carolina Press in 1989.

cloth   11 10 09 08 07   5 4 3 2 1
paper   11 10 09 08 07   5 4 3 2 1

Tell about the South. What it's like there.

What do they do there. Why do they live there.

Why do they live at all.

WILLIAM FAULKNER

Absalom, Absalom!

CONTENTS

In 1989 years of planning and hard work came to fruition when the University of North Carolina Press joined the Center for the Study of Southern Culture at the University of Mississippi to publish the *Encyclopedia of Southern Culture*. While all those involved in writing, reviewing, editing, and producing the volume believed it would be received as a vital contribution to our understanding of the American South, no one could have anticipated fully the widespread acclaim it would receive from reviewers and other commentators. But the *Encyclopedia* was indeed celebrated, not only by scholars but also by popular audiences with a deep, abiding interest in the region. At a time when some people talked of the "vanishing South," the book helped remind a national audience that the region was alive and well, and it has continued to shape national perceptions of the South through the work of its many users—journalists, scholars, teachers, students, and general readers.

As the introduction to the *Encyclopedia* noted, its conceptualization and organization reflected a cultural approach to the South. It highlighted such issues as the core zones and margins of southern culture, the boundaries where "the South" overlapped with other cultures, the role of history in contemporary culture, and the centrality of regional consciousness, symbolism, and mythology. By 1989 scholars had moved beyond the idea of cultures as real, tangible entities, viewing them instead as abstractions. The *Encyclopedia*'s editors and contributors thus included a full range of social indicators, trait groupings, literary concepts, and historical evidence typically used in regional studies, carefully working to address the distinctive and characteristic traits that made the American South a particular place. The introduction to the *Encyclopedia* concluded that the fundamental uniqueness of southern culture was reflected in the volume's composite portrait of the South. We asked contributors to consider aspects that were unique to the region but also those that suggested its internal diversity. The volume was not a reference book of southern history, which explained something of the design of entries. There were fewer essays on colonial and antebellum history than on the postbellum and modern periods, befitting our conception of the volume as one trying not only to chart the cultural landscape of the South but also to illuminate the contemporary era.

When C. Vann Woodward reviewed the *Encyclopedia* in the *New York Review of Books*, he concluded his review by noting "the continued liveliness of interest in the South and its seeming inexhaustibility as a field of study." Research on the South, he wrote, furnishes "proof of the value of the *Encyclopedia* as a scholarly undertaking as well as suggesting future needs for revision or supplement to keep up with ongoing scholarship." The decade and a half since the publication of the *Encyclopedia of Southern Culture* have certainly suggested that Woodward was correct. The American South has undergone significant changes that make for a different context for the study of the region. The South has undergone social, economic, political, intellectual, and literary transformations, creating the need for a new edition of the *Encyclopedia* that will remain relevant to a changing region. Globalization has become a major issue, seen in the South through the appearance of Japanese automobile factories, Hispanic workers who have immigrated from Latin America or Cuba, and a new prominence for Asian and Middle Eastern religions that were hardly present in the 1980s South. The African American return migration to the South, which started in the 1970s, dramatically increased in the 1990s, as countless books simultaneously appeared asserting powerfully the claims of African Americans as formative influences on southern culture. Politically, southerners from both parties have played crucial leadership roles in national politics, and the Republican Party has dominated a near-solid South in national elections. Meanwhile, new forms of music, like hip-hop, have emerged with distinct southern expressions, and the term "dirty South" has taken on new musical meanings not thought of in 1989. New genres of writing by creative southerners, such as gay and lesbian literature and "white trash" writing, extend the southern literary tradition.

Meanwhile, as Woodward foresaw, scholars have continued their engagement with the history and culture of the South since the publication of the *Encyclopedia*, raising new scholarly issues and opening new areas of study. Historians have moved beyond their earlier preoccupation with social history to write new cultural history as well. They have used the categories of race, social class, and gender to illuminate the diversity of the South, rather than a unified "mind of the South." Previously underexplored areas within the field of southern historical studies, such as the colonial era, are now seen as formative periods of the region's character, with the South's positioning within a larger Atlantic world a productive new area of study. Cultural memory has become a major topic in the exploration of how the social construction of "the South" benefited some social groups and exploited others. Scholars in many disciplines have made the southern identity a major topic, and they have used a variety of methodologies to suggest what that identity has meant to different social groups. Literary critics have adapted cultural theories to the South and have raised the issue of postsouthern literature to a major category of concern as well as exploring the links between the literature of the American South and that of the Caribbean. Anthropologists have used different theoretical formulations from literary critics, providing models for their fieldwork in southern communities. In the past 30 years anthropologists have set increasing numbers of their ethnographic studies in the South, with many of them now exploring topics specifically linked to southern cultural issues. Scholars now place the Native American story, from prehistory to the contemporary era, as a central part of southern history. Comparative and interdisciplinary approaches to the South have encouraged scholars to look at such issues as the borders and boundaries of the South, specific places and spaces with distinct identities within the American South, and the global and transnational Souths, linking the American South with many formerly colonial societies around the world.

The first edition of the *Encyclopedia of Southern Culture* anticipated many of these approaches and indeed stimulated the growth of Southern Studies as a distinct interdisciplinary field. The Center for the Study of Southern Culture has worked for more than a quarter century to encourage research and teaching about the American South. Its academic programs have produced graduates who have gone on to write interdisciplinary studies of the South, while others have staffed the cultural institutions of the region and in turn encouraged those institutions to document and present the South's culture to broad public audiences. The center's conferences and publications have continued its long tradition of promoting understanding of the history, literature, and music of the South, with new initiatives focused on southern foodways, the future of the South, and the global Souths, expressing the center's mission to bring the best current scholarship to broad public audiences. Its documentary studies projects build oral and visual archives, and the New Directions in Southern Studies book series, published by the University of North Carolina Press, offers an important venue for innovative scholarship.

Since the *Encyclopedia of Southern Culture* appeared, the field of Southern Studies has dramatically developed, with an extensive network now of academic and research institutions whose projects focus specifically on the interdisciplinary study of the South. The Center for the Study of the American South at the University of North Carolina at Chapel Hill, led by Director Harry Watson and Associate Director and *Encyclopedia* coeditor William Ferris, publishes the lively journal *Southern Cultures* and is now at the organizational center of many other Southern Studies projects. The Institute for Southern Studies at the University of South Carolina, the Southern Intellectual History Circle, the Society for the Study of Southern Literature, the Southern Studies Forum of the European American Studies Association, Emory University's Southern-Spaces.org, and the South Atlantic Humanities Center (at the Virginia Foundation for the Humanities, the University of Virginia, and Virginia Polytechnic Institute and State University) express the recent expansion of interest in regional study.

Observers of the American South have had much to absorb, given the rapid pace of recent change. The institutional framework for studying the South is broader and deeper than ever, yet the relationship between the older verities of regional study and new realities remains unclear. Given the extent of changes in the American South and in Southern Studies since the publication of the *Encyclopedia of Southern Culture*, the need for a new edition of that work is clear. Therefore, the Center for the Study of Southern Culture has once again joined the University of North Carolina Press to produce *The New Encyclopedia of Southern Culture*. As readers of the original edition will quickly see, *The New Encyclopedia* follows many of the scholarly principles and editorial conventions established in the original, but with one key difference; rather than being published in a single hardback volume, *The New Encyclopedia* is presented in a series of shorter individual volumes that build on the 24 original subject categories used in the *Encyclopedia* and adapt them to new scholarly developments. Some earlier *Encyclopedia* categories have been reconceptualized in light of new academic interests. For example, the subject section originally titled "Women's Life" is reconceived as a new volume, *Gender*, and the original "Black Life" section is more broadly interpreted as a volume on race. These changes reflect new analytical concerns that place the study of women and blacks in broader cultural systems, reflecting the emergence of, among other topics, the study of male culture and of whiteness. Both volumes draw as well from the rich recent scholarship on women's life and black life. In addition, topics with some thematic coherence are combined in a volume, such as *Law and Politics* and *Agriculture and Industry*. One new topic, *Foodways*, is the basis of a separate volume, reflecting its new prominence in the interdisciplinary study of southern culture.

Numerous individual topical volumes together make up *The New Encyclopedia of Southern Culture* and extend the reach of the reference work to wider audiences. This approach should enhance the use of the *Encyclopedia* in academic courses and is intended to be convenient for readers with more focused interests within the larger context of southern culture. Readers will have handy access to one-volume, authoritative, and comprehensive scholarly treatments of the major areas of southern culture.

We have been fortunate that, in nearly all cases, subject consultants who offered crucial direction in shaping the topical sections for the original edition have agreed to join us in this new endeavor as volume editors. When new volume editors have been added, we have again looked for respected figures who can provide not only their own expertise but also strong networks of scholars to help develop relevant lists of topics and to serve as contributors in their areas. The reputations of all our volume editors as leading scholars in their areas encouraged the contributions of other scholars and added to *The New Encyclopedia*'s authority as a reference work.

The New Encyclopedia of Southern Culture builds on the strengths of articles in the original edition in several ways. For many existing articles, original authors agreed to update their contributions with new interpretations and theoretical perspectives, current statistics, new bibliographies, or simple factual developments that needed to be included. If the original contributor was unable to update an article, the editorial staff added new material or sent it to another scholar for assessment. In some cases, the general editor and volume editors selected a new contributor if an article seemed particularly dated and new work indicated the need for a fresh perspective. And importantly, where new developments have warranted treatment of topics not addressed in the original edition, volume editors have commissioned entirely new essays and articles that are published here for the first time.

The American South embodies a powerful historical and mythical presence, both a complex environmental and geographic landscape and a place of the imagination. Changes in the region's contemporary socioeconomic realities and new developments in scholarship have been incorporated in the conceptualization and approach of *The New Encyclopedia of Southern Culture*. Anthropologist Clifford Geertz has spoken of culture as context, and this encyclopedia looks at the American South as a complex place that has served as the context for cultural expression. This volume provides information and perspective on the diversity of cultures in a geographic and imaginative place with a long history and distinctive character.

The *Encyclopedia of Southern Culture* was produced through major grants from the Program for Research Tools and Reference Works of the National Endowment for the Humanities, the Ford Foundation, the Atlantic-Richfield Foundation, and the Mary Doyle Trust. We are grateful as well to the individual donors to the Center for the Study of Southern Culture who have directly or indirectly supported work on *The New Encyclopedia of Southern Culture*. We thank the volume editors for their ideas in reimagining their subjects and the contributors of articles for their work in extending the usefulness of the book in new ways. We acknowledge the support and contributions of the faculty and staff at the Center for the Study of Southern Culture. Finally, we want especially to honor the work of William Ferris and Mary Hart on the *Encyclopedia of Southern Culture*. Bill, the founding director of the Center for the Study of Southern Culture, was coeditor, and his good work recruiting authors, editing text, selecting images, and publicizing the volume among a wide network of people was, of course, invaluable. Despite the many changes in the new encyclopedia, Bill's influence remains. Mary "Sue" Hart was also an invaluable member of the original encyclopedia team, bringing the careful and precise eye of the librarian, and an iconoclastic spirit, to our work.

W. J. Cash's much-quoted observation that "there are many Souths" is as true today as it was when he made the claim in 1941, but then it always has been. During the Mississippian period (ca. 1000–1600 A.D.), native southerners shared the Southeastern Ceremonial Complex, built flat-topped pyramidal mounds, and used shell-tempered pottery and cane basketry, but they also had many local variations on regional themes. The prehistoric Southeast had major cultural subregions relating to environmental diversity: the Atlantic Coastal Plain, the Interior to the Mountains, Florida, the Mississippi Valley, and the Gulf Coastal Plain. Each of these subregions had distinct chiefdoms, a variety of ethnic groups, and numerous linguistic areas. In colonial and antebellum times, the Chesapeake, the Lowcountry, and the Backcountry were recognized regions whose residents had distinct identities, as did people in the Upper and Lower Souths. Enduring cultural subregions linked to environmental zones now include the Appalachian Blue Ridge Mountains, the Cumberland and Ozark Plateaus, the Carolina and Georgia Piedmont, the Mississippi Delta, the Bluegrass Country of Kentucky, the Wiregrass Country from southeastern Alabama through the Florida Panhandle to Savannah, and the Black Belt (the rich soil zone in parts of the Deep South). Historically and currently, each of these areas has attracted different immigrants and has fostered different cultural developments so that, while multiple traditions have blended over the centuries to create a southern regional culture, southerners still identify themselves in a variety of ways.

The "many Souths" are the creation of the many southerners from an array of ethnic backgrounds. Scholars of the South have traditionally examined the region's population in binary terms of "black" and "white" or have examined gender, class, and power through an antebellum cast of planters, the yeomanry, tenant farmers, and slaves. In 1949, as historians began to look beyond elites, Frank Lawrence Owsley advanced a novel approach in his *Plain Folk of the Old South*. Owsley drew on U.S. Census records to argue that the region had been composed predominantly of democratic yeoman rather than having been a planter's oligarchy. Today, scholars employ census data to ask if, representing various ethnic backgrounds as they did, Old South southerners were really so "plain"? As a cultural identity, ethnicity crosses and complicates categories of "race" and class and had been a relatively neglected aspect of southern studies when the first *Encyclopedia of Southern Culture* appeared.

An explosion of scholarship on ethnicity in the last two decades has begun to recover the ethnic diversity of the early South as well as to document the contemporary arrival of new cultural groups in the region. This volume reflects both tracks of scholarship that have enabled, and necessitated, the creation of a new volume quite unlike the original "Ethnic Life" section of the first *Encyclopedia of Southern Culture*. The 1989 edition of the *Encyclopedia* considered 30 ethnic groups. The current volume has expanded coverage to 88 specific ethnicities and includes more information on both the newest and oldest southerners. Only five original essays were retained with updates; 83 new entries on individual groups and eight completely new introductory essays shape this fresh collection.

The original edition provided eight entries on specific American Indian groups; this edition describes 34, including, for encyclopedic clarity, all federally recognized groups located in the contemporary South. Some tribes figure in this volume because of their southern origins and associations but, because of the 19th-century diaspora onto the Southern Plains, are now primarily located outside the South in Oklahoma. Many state-recognized tribes also appear, but dozens of other state-recognized and unrecognized tribes still await scholarly attention. During the nearly two decades since the publication of the *Encyclopedia*'s original edition, the term "Native American" replaced "Indian," and now the preferred self-referent "American Indian" has begun to replace, or appear interchangeably with, "Native American." Entries reflect this evolution in terminology.

The volume includes a sampling of new scholarship developing on African ethnicities in the South, but subsequent editions may be able to offer many more as this interesting field grows. In addition to considering just under 20 European groups, this volume features unique hybrid identities created within various southern subregions over the last four centuries and reflects the current immigration and settlement trends from Latin America and Asia that are shaping new southerners.

The NEW ENCYCLOPEDIA *of* SOUTHERN CULTURE

VOLUME 6 : ETHNICITY

ETHNICITY & CREOLIZATION

When Europeans arrived in the South, they entered a region that had been inhabited for perhaps 13,000 years and was, by the 16th century, well peopled by a diversity of protostates and chiefdoms. Africans joined the people of the South in 1619. Their status as slaves or indentured servants on arrival remains ambiguous. Accounts of southern history and experience onward from that time have conventionally, and simplistically, discussed the region's ethnic mix in terms of three broad categories relating to the three continents of colonial southerners' origins. Further obscured by late 19th- and 20th-century binary racial categorization of institutions and worldviews, the diverse ancestral origins of early southerners have only recently become a subject for recovery among scholars and in popular culture.

A social, political, and scholarly focus on racial categorization has denied the cultural (ethnic) differences within what have been called "racial" groups. The American Indians inhabiting the South at the beginning of the historic period included speakers of at least five major language families, within which there were long-standing ethnic divides that caused some to ally with outsider Europeans against other Native Americans. While the majority of the first European southerners came from England, Scotland, and Ireland, they did not share a culture or worldview, and some Catholic Irish and Highland Scots spoke their own versions of Gaelic rather than English. German, Swiss, French, and Spanish settlers early added to the religious, linguistic, and social mix of the new colonies. Africans came predominantly from the nations between Angola and Ghana (the Gold Coast), but also from the Gambia (Senegambia), Senegal, Sierra Leone, and Igbo country. Just as European colonists maintained their distinct identities from their particular nations (or regions of their home nations), Africans continued to think of themselves as Yoruba, Mandingo, Fon, or Wolof for several generations. Some ethnic groups were less likely to socialize or partner with members of others. Religious beliefs, song, folklore, and artistic traditions also perpetuated national and cultural affiliations within slavery on ethnically heterogeneous plantations.

Recent scholarship has begun to uncover the ethnic diversity of the early South as well as to document the contemporary arrival of new cultural groups in the region. This volume reflects both trends. Eliding the metonyms and stereotypes of the South in strictly black and white, this collection of essays attempts to represent the panoply of ethnicities that combined to shape the region. As culturally constructed notions, racial identities are imposed generally by those with whom one does not share a designation. Ethnic identity one traditionally learns at a grandparent's knee. Ethnicity lies in folktales, in tying fishing nets, in conceptions of the supernatural, in the music that delights multiple generations simultaneously, in the foods that mean home. Ethnic identities are cultural identities, and as such they are dynamic and renegotiated in different contexts and periods. Some consider southern identity, shared by black and white southerners (as opposed to "southern blacks and whites"), an ethnic identity within the United States. Since the 1700s the notion of the region as distinct has endured, although what is southern in any given period continues to evolve. Southern culture, or the multiple southern cultures of the South's many subregions, is a complex amalgamation of disparate ethnicities and traditions from around the globe. After centuries of blending, the sum is undoubtedly greater than its parts but is hardly a finished product.

Ethnicity. The concept of ethnicity comes from the Greek *ethnos*, meaning "people" or "nation." Herodotus flexibly described the Dorians, Kolophonians, Ephesians, and Ionians as *ethne* according to what festivals they celebrated, their language or dialect, their mythic genealogies tracing group origins to an eponymous ancestor, and sometimes their area of residence. Anthropologists today define ethnic groups similarly as having shared customs, linguistic traditions, religious practices, and geographical origins. Members of an ethnic group might also exhibit specific gender roles and inheritance patterns. Frederick Barth's groundbreaking work *Ethnic Groups and Boundaries: The Social Organization of Difference* (1969) led anthropologists to describe "ethnic boundary markers" (the possession of a distinctive language or dialect, a particular style of dress, music, and cuisine, and religious expression), although no one of these alone defines an ethnic group.

Membership in an ethnic group often relates to kinship and descent, but even when a belief in shared ancestry is involved in ethnic identity formation, it can be what anthropologists call "fictive kinship" and is often mythic. When ethnic identities are oriented to the past, those who claim them may have an emotional investment in legend and renegotiate history in more appealing forms as heritage. Ethnic identities evolve over time and are often quite voluntary. Those claiming an ethnic identity form an ethnic group in contrast to "ethnic categories," which are identities imposed from the outside (generally on a minority group). Occasionally an ethnic category goes through "ethnogenesis" and becomes an ethnic group—as with labels like "Hispanic."

Ethnic celebrations, heritage tourism to ancestral homelands, and an interest in ethnic music, foodways, and material culture have become an increasingly accepted part of American life. Spurred by America's bicentennial celebrations and popular books such as Alex Haley's *Roots* (1976), genealogy is now one of the fastest-growing hobbies in America. Even those whose families have been in the South for over 300 years are looking for origins and reclaiming what they perceive as ancestral traditions from nations where they would never be considered anything other than American.

While many people may reject a familial ethnicity, others actively embrace one their parents, grandparents, or more distant ancestors relinquished. How one values or emphasizes ethnicity may relate to the prestige (or lack thereof) that such an identity carries and to context (a religious holiday rather than an average worship service, within the home rather than the office). An individual may have more than one ethnicity simultaneously and play on overlapping sets of loyalties depending on the situation. The situational selection of ethnic identity can be different from "symbolic" or "convenience" ethnicity (embracing an ethnic identity self-consciously at festival occasions without living an ethnic existence daily). One may emphasize one's Mexican ancestry on Mexican Independence Day, and also acknowledge the Scottish branch of one's family by learning a song in Gaelic or competing in Scottish athletics, but otherwise live a nonethnic life. One might even dress for heritage events and festivals to signify a personal creole combining a sombrero and a kilt. Affiliating with an ethnic group voluntarily may involve acquiring ethnic shibboleths or rediscovering those devalued or discarded by one's ancestors.

Some scholars dismiss symbolic ethnicity as nostalgic yearning for a long-lost tradition and identity and as a superficial aspect of personal identity. However, such a perspective denies the deep emotional investment people make in voluntary or reclaimed identities. While individuals may not materially display their ethnicity to outsiders on a regular basis, scholars cannot simply assume it is not incorporated as part of their worldview or that it is detached, or even tangential, to their daily, nonfestival realities. Descendants of many of the groups in this volume may no longer be commonly identified as ethnic, but their origins and traditions (or invented traditions to commemorate those origins) may be quite significant in their family life and formative of a personal identity.

Many of the essays in this volume include information from the U.S. Census Bureau. In 1980 the census first included an "ancestry question" to collect selective information on ethnic origins and identity. In 1990 and 2000 the question simply read, "What is the person's ancestry or ethnic origin?" According to the Census Bureau, "ancestry" refers to a person's ethnic origins or descent, roots, heritage, or place of birth (although place of birth and ancestry are not always the same). The ancestry question does not measure to what extent a person is aware of ancestral origins. For example, a person reporting "German" on the census might be actively involved in the German American community or might only vaguely remember that ancestors centuries removed came from Germany. State-by-state census data is more useful than regional summaries in ascertaining which ethnic identities southerners claim, as the Census Bureau includes Oklahoma, West Virginia, Washington, D.C., Delaware, and Maryland within the southern region. Maryland was once culturally southern, and portions of Oklahoma and West Virginia still claim to be, but this inclusive mapping varies from both scholarly and popular specifications of the region.

Census data on ethnicity can be misleading, not only because numbers are based on a sample of the population, but also because ethnic identities and notions of "race" are conflated. Race categories on the census include both color designations and national origin groups. For example, Koreans are not listed on state ancestry charts because the census includes "Korean" as a choice under the "race" question. Tabulated numbers may often appear contradictory when, for example, more people specify "African American" in answering the census's race question than those answering the ancestry question who may then report nothing or a different, more specific identity (Nigerian, Haitian, Sudanese). To find figures for Mexicans and Spaniards, Panamanians or Guatemalans, for example, one must look to special Census Bureau national reports rather than state-by-state ancestry charts in which Central and South American nationalities are oddly not listed. The Census Bureau now couples a question on ethnicity ("Is this person Spanish/Hispanic/Latino?") with its question on race. The rationale as to why the bureau excludes specific Latino ethnicities from ancestry data—but collects information on Norwegians, Subsaharan Africans, Slovaks, and West Indians as ethnic groups—is not obvious, nor have such categorizations remained constant. Government definitions change with the evolving political and social implications of identities.

In the media and on government forms, ethnicity is incorrectly used interchangeably with "race," although ethnicity does not mean race. Ethnicity refers to cultural and social aspects of identity, not biological aspects or phenotype (physical appearance), which is the most common meaning of "race" in the United States. In the 19th and even early 20th centuries, "race" often denoted national or regional origins or referenced a particular cultural group, commonly in connection with the spurious notion that there could be any biological predisposition to cultural distinctiveness. Based on cultural assumptions about physical appearance, "race" is socially constructed rather than biologically valid. As a species, we are too evolutionarily recent to have discrete "racial" populations. The human genome carries only superficial markers relating to aspects of appearance such as hair form and melanin production for skin and eye color (characteristics that often relate to long-term environmental adaptation); it does not distinguish separate subspecies like "breeds." The continuum of human physical variation does not fall into three, five, nine, or more discrete groups, as scholars such as Johann Herder (1744–1803) and Johann Friedrich Blumenbach (1752–1840) proposed in the drive for Linnaean classification, and as popular culture continues to do in order to define difference for social and political expediency. Social classifications of "race" focus predominantly on phenotype and have done so since the Ancient Egyptians divided the world's people into "red" for Egyptian, "yellow" for people to the East, "white" for those to the north, and "black" for Africans from the south. However, since the writings of the ancient Greeks, "ethnicity" has properly referred to identity and culture.

The 20th-century conflation of "race" with ethnicity has led to the post–civil rights era racialization of distinct cultural groupings. The relatively recent category of "Asian Americans" provides a higher national profile for about 24 ethnic groups on the U.S. Census and on the American political scene. However, such a designation not only bundles East Asian groups such as Korean, Japanese, Malaysians, Vietnamese, and Chinese Americans into a shared grouping, it also absorbs Nepalese, Indian, and Pakistani Americans within one "racial" category despite their completely separate origins, histories, and cultural traditions.

While sociologist Max Weber had used the concept in work published in 1922 and other scholars had explored the notion in the 1940s, "ethnicity" did not enter public discourse and dictionary usage until the early 1960s. Today, the word is ubiquitous. Perhaps in reaction to globalization, scholars of many disciplines use "ethnic" or "ethnicity" when they might have employed "cultural" or "subculture" a quarter of a century ago. Ethnicity has come to mean distinctiveness, if variously defined. Many scholars view ethnicity as a political identity in relation to class, racial, or other potential social conflicts and discuss claims to ethnic identities as negative when embraced by a privileged group, but as a positive form of "resistance" when embraced by an unprivileged one.

However, class and power differentials exist within ethnic groups as well as between them. Ethnic identities are not necessarily exclusionary. Not only may one be a member of more than one ethnic group, one also may share an ethnic identity with those whom society designates as a different "race" from oneself. Increasingly, Americans are identifying themselves as multiethnic. Irish Americans not only celebrate their Irish roots; they may also claim to be German-, Mexican-, African-, or Italian-Irish Americans. Southerners may simultaneously feel southern *and* Chinese, or southern *and* Italian, and sometimes conflate the two. This is most obvious in expressive culture and at festivals, which are superb indicators of the evolution and recombination of ethnicities.

For those perceiving ethnicity as primarily political, the failure of the melting pot assimilationist ideal was considered a problem — an "ethnic problem." The 1960s and 1970s then witnessed a move from assimilationist models for immigrants to ideas of pluralism (a coexistence and toleration of difference). In the 1980s and 1990s, multiculturalism (a celebration of difference) replaced pluralism. Ethnicity is a much more comfortable, if not beatitudinous, concept than it was a quarter of a century ago. Americans now find ethnic food aisles in grocery stores, wear ethnic clothes, decorate their homes in "international ethnic pastiches," and often assume that multiculturalism means nonracism as if ethnicity meant race. While ethnicity may be "optional" for many Americans, the selection of identities and their renegotiation is revealing, not only of how Americans perceive each other, but also of our particular moment in history. Similarly, the recognition and study of ethnicities in the South communicates significant insights about the region's place historically and currently within both national and global frames.

Creolization and Creole Groups. Southern culture is a product of nearly 20 generations of creolization (a blending of cultures after long exposure, coexistence, and interaction of multiple social groups). W. J. Cash, Ralph Ellison, and historian Charles Joyner have remarked that every white southerner has an African heritage as well as a European one, and every black southerner has a European heritage as well as an African one. This idea continues to resonate because southern culture is a complex hybrid of varied traditions. Although southern society created well-bounded public hierarchies around difference, southern culture is the result of heterarchical relationships between individuals with regular and intimate interactions. Despite slavery and Jim Crow, the flow of ideas, customs, and worldviews was not solely top-down. Those with the least overt power in southern society created the infrastructure, erected the buildings, produced the cash crops that once made the South wealthy, and carried out a variety of skilled occupations essential to the smooth working of any urban settlement or rural community. Those enslaved — or, after slavery, in domestic service — cared for the children of the elite, taught them manners, and shaped their speech and tastes. Such formative relationships, and more subtle, ongoing exchanges, produced the cultural creoles we conceive of as southern traditions.

What we think of as typically "southern" is a product of centuries of cultural blending. Bluegrass is a mix of Irish and British fiddle traditions and African-derived banjo. Jimmie Rodgers, "the father of country music," combined Swiss yodeling with black field hollers in the 1920s to create his characteristic "blue yodels," which Chester Burnett of the Mississippi Delta blues tradition subsequently adapted to his own style and earned himself the moniker Howlin' Wolf. Southern spirituals merged the rhythm and structure of African music with elements of British text and melodies. Southern rock groups such as the Allman Brothers Band and Lynyrd Skynyrd produced fusions of rock and roll, blues slide guitar, jazz, soul, and rhythm and blues with southern dialect. Yale ethnomusicologist Willie Ruff has recently suggested that a distinct psalm-singing style in southern African American congregations called "presenting the line" derives from "line singing" or "precenting the line" in the Scottish Highlands. He argues that Gaelic-speaking enslaved Africans learned the singing style and notes a church in Alabama where their descendants worshipped in Gaelic as late as 1918. Employing an African American performance style and traditionally sung in French, zydeco music blends the blues with Afro-Caribbean rhythms and tone arrangements from Cajun music (the European American analogue to zydeco).

Cultural exchanges with American Indians transformed both Europeans and Africans in the South, yet such creolizations are perhaps less obvious today in part because of the colonial demographic revolution. As Peter Wood has noted, in 1690 approximately 250,000 people lived in the South (80 percent Native Americans, 19 percent Europeans, and perhaps 1 percent slaves). In 1790, after a century of introduced diseases and colonial expansion, just under 5 percent of the estimated 1.7 million southerners were Native Americans, 60 percent were Europeans, and 35 percent were of African descent (a large percentage despite historians' estimates that only 6 percent of Africans crossing the Atlantic in the 18th-century slave trade came to North America). While Europeans enslaved some Native Americans and intensive contact between enslaved American Indians and Africans took place in Charleston in the late 17th century, the Tuscarora War of 1711 and the Yamasee War four years later pointed to the dangers of a possible alliance between them. European colonists forfended this by hiring native peoples to capture escaping African slaves and by sending enslaved Africans into battle against American Indians. While such policies were common, intermarriage and cultural exchange did continue.

Mississippi Choctaws playing stickball
(Photograph courtesy of Mississippi Band of Choctaw Indians)

American Indians assisted initial European settlement by teaching new settlers to clear the foreign forest and grow native crops such as squash, maize, beans, and tobacco. They influenced early patterns and locations of colonial settlements in relation to their defense of their own and shaped the course of southern history through their military alliances. Newly arrived southerners borrowed indigenous architectural traditions, buckskin, and canoes in settling what they considered the frontier. Southern foodways draw from indigenous foodways; Native Americans made the first cornbread (or pone), grits, and succotash (a mix of corn kernels and beans). European Americans also adapted native crops to their own traditions (their use of maize to produce whiskey, for example). American Indians taught new southerners herbal remedies, and soft drinks like root beer and Coca-Cola had precursors in indigenous sassafras Indian tonics. Few indigenous languages remain extant in the Southeast, but many groups developed their own dialects of English (regional variants that are distinctive for their grammar, vocabulary, and pronunciation). For example, in North Carolina the vernacular English of the Lumbee employs unique vocabulary words such as *juvember* for "slingshot" and *ellick* for "coffee." Like other peripheral dialect areas with a long history of insularity, their speech also retains centuries-old English terms such as *mommuck* (mess) and *toten* (ghost). Native American linguistic contributions to southern culture include many loan words such as squash, hominy, hickory, opossum, skunk, and, of course, southern place names such as Tallahassee, Okefenokee, Santee, Mississippi, and Tullahoma.

American Indians' presence and impact on the southern cultural landscape decreased as that of African and African American populations increased. U.S. Census figures for 1860 indicate that European and enslaved African populations were very close in number in several southern states. That year, the population of Alabama was reported to be 54 percent "white" and 45 percent "slave"; similar estimates exist for Florida (55 percent and 44 percent), Georgia (56 percent and 43 percent), and Louisiana (50 percent and 46 percent). Two states had an enslaved population substantially larger than that of European Americans: in Mississippi "slaves" constituted 55 percent of the population while "whites" composed 44 percent, and in South Carolina the ratio was 57 percent to 41 percent. The increasing recognition of African influences on southern culture include linguistic contributions. Southern dialects evidence African contributions, including loan words such as goober (related to Kongo *n-guba*, or "peanut"), okra (a word of Bantu origin), yam (of West African origin), tote, gumbo, and boogie. Staples of southern foodways (including rice, types of squash, black-eyed peas, and okra) came from Africa, as did a preference for certain spices.

Foodways specific to enslaved African Americans — getting by on the less desirable cuts of meat and the vegetables they could grow on small plots — developed over time into "soul food," including chitlins, mustard greens, ham hocks, ham salad, pigs' feet, and hoppin' John (a dish featuring black-eyed peas, rice, and ham). Food items once considered soul food, such as barbecue, fried catfish, candied yams, hush puppies, coleslaw, and pot likker, have long been common to southern tables across ethnic divides.

Africans of many ethnic groups brought a strong reverence for ancestors, a belief in spirits, and folk-healing traditions that led to hoodoo and conjure (*ju-ju*) and the southern practice of voodoo (African traditions fused with folk practices of French Colonial Catholicism and the magicomedical knowledge and pharmacopeia of American Indians). Of the "queens," "doctors," or "workers" of voodoo, Marie Laveau was America's most famous, and her grave is still a site of pilgrimage in New Orleans. Africans adapted Christian beliefs to African expectations of the divine. African trickster characters and deities populate African American folktales in which the rabbit (shared with Native Americans) and the signifying monkey figure largely. Echoing earlier traditions of storytelling and performances of ritual insult, today's Mardi Gras Indians of New Orleans sing carefully crafted songs in mock battles that involve verbal competition and boasting about the reputation of individuals and neighborhoods.

Across the Deep South, the shotgun house stands as one of the most-cited examples of African-influenced architecture. The narrow, one-story buildings have a front porch, a gabled roof, and rooms aligned in single file. John Michael Vlach has convincingly argued that the shotgun house derives from those of the indigenous Arawak Indians of Haiti and modified by Africans brought there and then, in the early 19th century, to the South. The southern front porch may also find its origins in the vernacular precolonial architecture of West Africa and the West Indies. The Georgian "I houses" of Charleston, S.C., are a part of this tradition and feature a porch running the length of one side of the house that can be closed off from the street by a formal door.

Some of the most noted cases of syncretic Africanisms in the United States are the folkways and linguistic traditions of South Carolina's Gullah and Georgia's Geechee peoples. While enslaved Africans retained ethnic identities for generations, their interactions with Africans of other nationalities produced cultural creoles. Eventually, a racialized identity replaced ethnicities and Africans created an African *American* culture. In the Chesapeake and North Carolina, slaves and European Americans interacted on a regular basis, and slave populations there became more anglicized than in the Lowcountry and Sea Islands. South Carolina planters often lived in Charleston and left overseers to run their rice plantations. Having less interaction with European Americans, slaves there retained and exchanged more of their ethnic traditions.

The Gullah and Geechee peoples of the Lowcountry and Sea Islands maintain traditions that are a syncretism of those of several different West and Central African ethnic groups (including the Mende, Limba, Temne, Fante, Fon, and others). Their language is not African but African American, being a creole of various African languages and English influences. In Gullah-speaking communities, individuals still have African "basket names" (nicknames) such as Bala, Jah, or Jilo. Names indicate the day on which a child was born (for example, Yaa for a girl born on Thursday and Yao for a boy), reference physical features, or indicate a kinship relationship (*bubba* would equate with "brother" in English). Hand clapping and foot stomping replaced African drums and still accompany shouts in Christian worship (Methodist and Baptist) in Gullah churches. Today, the Gullah/Geechee Sea Island Coalition encourages cultural revitalization and aims to achieve international recognition as a nation with self-determination like a Native American tribe. This goal is contested since the Gullah/Geechee are not indigenous to the Sea Islands but formed a

Creole society there. Elsewhere, descendants of slaves from the Lowcountry and Sea Islands who joined a Native American tribe also find their status in question.

Perhaps as early as the late 1600s, Africans escaped plantations in what are now Gullah/Geechee communities and settled among the Florida Seminole, where they lived beyond the reach of British colonial administrators. Known as the Black Seminoles, they spoke Gullah and the Muskogee or Mikasuki languages of the Seminole, adopted many of their cultural attributes, and fought in the Seminole wars. Removed to Oklahoma with the Seminole, the Black Seminoles became known as "the Freedmen," and their status and rights as tribal members have varied over the last century and a half. As exogamy has led people without active ties to the Seminole Nation to enroll as tribal members (for the benefits and services membership entails), the Seminole Nation of Oklahoma adopted a resolution in 2000 requiring proof of one-eighth "Seminole Indian blood" for enrollment. Such a requirement excludes the majority of Black Seminoles from tribal membership and would seem to dim the multiple-centuries relationship that yielded social and political exchanges and cultural creolization.

The term "creole" has multiple meanings. A creole replaces a pidgin, the form of communication in first contact between two or more groups speaking different languages. The francophone dialect of south Louisiana is one example. Creole also has indicated a descendant of the original French or Spanish settlers of the southern states, or a person of African or Caribbean *and* European ancestry who speaks a creolized language, especially French or Spanish. Creole cuisine in the South refers to a New Orleans–style tomato, onion, and pepper sauce or a dish like filé gumbo (a union of Choctaw and West African foodways). Creole cuisine and culture have long been staples of the Louisiana tourism industry, but they also inspire the devoted work of local preservation and heritage societies. Northwestern State University in Natchitoches, La., has developed the Louisiana Creole Heritage Center and has initiated a Creole Studies Consortium. Although "Creole" can apply variously to people of European or African descent, for some the term distinguishes African Americans of French-speaking Louisiana from their European American Cajun neighbors in south Louisiana. However, some people of African descent self-identify as Cajun today.

Immortalized in Longfellow's *Evangeline*, Cajuns are descendants of Catholic French Acadians who settled in French Louisiana (some also went to Maine) after being expelled from Nova Scotia by the British in the mid-18th century. After centuries of mixing with other ethnic groups, Cajun surnames now include the German Hymel and Schexnider, the Spanish Castille and Romero, and the Scots-Irish McGee. Partly through interaction with southerners of African descent, Cajuns developed spicy dishes such as dirty rice, gumbo, and other foods reflecting their local resources and subsistence, such as boudin (Cajun sausage) and bouille (cane syrup pie).

Defining who is a "Creole" remains contentious. Most simply and inclusively put, the category of "Creole" may refer to anyone with African or European (but not Anglo-American) ancestry who was born in the Americas. The South has many creolized populations with ethnic identities original to the region, but it also has many populations that we would now call Creole groups that did have Anglo-American ancestry—some that were once called mulattos, triracial isolates, pardos, "mixed-bloods," and worse.

Across America, a practice called hypodescent assigns children of mixed unions the identity of the socially and economically disadvantaged group. Categorized as "colored" by the Louisiana Bureau of Vital Statistics because her great-great-great-great-grandmother was black, Susie Phipps garnered international attention in 1982 by trying to have herself declared "white." According to America's "one-drop rule," one black ancestor makes a person black, but one white ancestor does not make a person white. Following the death of over 600,000 combatants in the Civil War—the outcome of which made the abolition of slavery through the Thirteenth Amendment possible—"black codes" and then Jim Crow laws created a period of racial segregation across 29 states (the name "Jim Crow" originally applied to segregated facilities in the pre-Civil War North). In 1896 the U.S. Supreme Court approved the segregation of public facilities in *Plessy v. Ferguson*. In 1954 *Brown v. Board of Education* overturned that decision, but many "separate-but-equal" practices continued until the federal civil rights legislation of the mid-1960s. The biracial classification schemes of the New South replaced much more elaborate classification schemes from the colonial and antebellum periods.

Enslaved Africans and African Americans were sometimes freed, especially (but not always) when they were children of their mother's master. They occupied an ambivalent position, frequently owning slaves but at risk of being captured and returned to slavery themselves if they traveled or moved out of areas in which they were known. By 1800 the majority of free people of color in America lived in the South (60,000). By the time of the Civil War, their numbers had grown nationwide to 488,000, with the majority (262,000) still living in the southern region. In the 19th century, free persons of color (*gens de couleur libre*) living along the Gulf Coast began calling themselves "Creoles of Color." They maintained their identity and communities through the Jim Crow period in New Orleans, Mobile, Pensacola, and smaller enclaves throughout the Gulf South.

Creoles exemplify the complexity of ethnicity and how ethnic identities can cross and obfuscate social conceptions of racial categories. While long unused in academic circles, the word "mulatto" may still be heard among older generations in the South and still makes surprising appearances in popular films and music in the 21st century. Mulattos were regarded as a product of miscegenation, which referred to unions between whites and blacks, whites and mulattos, or blacks and mulattos and covered anything from single acts of intimacy to marriage. The first series of laws designed to discourage miscegenation passed the Virginia Assembly in 1662. Many Africans and their children were free before 1661, when the Virginia legislature passed laws making Africans slaves for life. By 1691 a European woman who gave birth to a mulatto child was required to pay a fine or, if unable, be sold into servitude for five years and thereafter banished to Barbados. European fathers of mulatto children needed only to do public penance one Sunday in their local churches, and even this practice was short lived as more and more white men sired mulatto children. By 1705 marriages between "white" and "black" persons invoked a jail sentence.

Strictly speaking, a mulatto was a person with one black parent and one white parent. Mulattos had different experiences depending upon the subregions in which they lived. In the Upper South their numbers were significant in the colonial period, and many were free, rural, and of poor or modest means. However, some, such as Sally Hemings, the half sister of Thomas Jefferson's wife, were tied to the most powerful people in the land. In the Lower South, mulatto populations grew later but had more varied classifications; for example, a "quadroon" was one-fourth black and an "octoroon" one-eighth black. They lived in communities in Charleston and New Orleans and also had considerably more freedom, financial prosperity, and social status than mulattos in the Upper South. Additionally, they more often had sponsorship from white fathers. In New Orleans, through a practice called *plaçage*, publicly known relationships between free black women and white men lasted long after the man married a white woman. Children took the father's surname, were supported by him, and could inherit from him. Sons were educated, sometimes abroad in France. Daughters born of *plaçage* often themselves became mistresses after debuting at "quadroon balls."

Also in Louisiana, someone who was three-fourths black was considered a "sambo" ("zambo") or a "griffe." These terms often referred to a child of a mulatto and a black person, or an American Indian and a black person. Elsewhere in the South, especially in South Carolina, a child of American Indian and black parentage was called "mustee," derived from the French *mestis* (*métis*) and Spanish *mestizo*. Occasionally, this also referred to combined Native American and European ancestries. Someone having seven out of eight great-grandparents who were black might be called a "sacatra" or a "mango." These terms emerged when people thought that culture and character were transmitted "in the blood," so that people of mixed descent posed a perceived social danger and often formed isolated and cohesive communities, some of which endure to the present.

Under Jim Crow, American Indian groups with mixed ancestry were variously unacknowledged, self-segregated, or classed with African Americans. Some such groups originated in the 17th and 18th centuries, when many American Indian chiefdoms had collapsed and towns and linguistically related groups tended to coalesce and gradually mingle with European and African populations. The Houma of the traditionally francophone areas of Terrebonne and Lafourche Parishes of Louisiana perhaps had this experience. They are one of many populations across the South that were neither "black nor white." during the Jim Crow era and are denied recognition by the federal government as American Indians today. The original Houma in Louisiana were displaced by the Tunica, and over the centuries they intermarried with European Americans and African Americans. Their ethnic identity now defies racial categorization. In the last census, almost 7,000 people self-identified as Houma.

Many similar groups (called "triple-mixes" by younger members) with American Indian, African, and European ancestries survive in pockets across the South, including the Melungeons of eastern Tennessee and western North Carolina; the Brass Ankles, Santees, and Turks of South Carolina; the Red Bones of Louisiana; the Guineas of Barbour and Taylor Counties in West Virginia; and the Ahoskie Blues of northeastern North Carolina's Hertford County. Not being black, white, or Indian, they often found themselves disdained by all three groups. Some "passed" as white or black and left their home areas. Many communities have long denied their ethnicity. However, in an age of multiculturalism, some members (usually those whose parents or grandparents had moved away from the original settlement areas) have begun to embrace a resurgent ethnicity and to claim a once-stigmatizing ethnonym as their own rather than as an imposed category.

Now identifying themselves as having American Indian, African American, and English, Scots-Irish, Tunisian, Portuguese, or other Mediterranean ancestry, Melungeons in the 1990s began holding reunions, publishing cookbooks, and promoting historic preservation efforts and heritage tourism to Turkey (another possible ancestral homeland). South Carolina's Turks, sometimes called Free Moors, have a more specific origin story, tracing their ancestry to one man "of Arab descent," Joseph Benenhaley, who fought with General Thomas Sumter in the American Revolution.

At times multiple ethnonyms existed for these groups—some more overtly disparaging than others, and some more comfortably euphemistic. Mountain people sometimes referred to their German neighbors as "Dutch" (for their language, *Deutsch*), so that Melungeons in eastern Tennessee and western North Carolina, where many Germans had settled, were also called "Black Dutch." Some Brass Ankle communities in South Carolina preferred to emphasize their American Indian roots and call themselves "Santees." These Creole groups problematize the usual binary categorization of "race." Their ethnonyms' self-ascription, or their application by outsiders, relates also to class and politics. Many communities and individuals lost more complex identities in the legal black/white caste system created by Jim Crow laws in the 1890s.

New South–Era Immigration. How did centuries of cultural creolization give way to the dichotomized society of the 20th century? After the Civil War and the end of slavery, social institutions and new laws prioritized "race" over class and ethnicity. The population of Brazil (where slavery lasted from the 16th century until 1888) has a far larger percentage of people with African ancestry than the United States. Brazilians also utilize over 500 recorded racial labels that are not applied through hypodescent, but are more flexibly related to a person's changing phenotype (one appears lighter or darker depending on recent exposure to the sun, standing in the shade, the time of day, etc.), so that even full siblings may belong to different "races." With so many intermediate categories, hypodescent rules did not develop in Brazil to keep "blacks" and "whites" separate. In the South, the antebellum color vocabulary (quadroon, octoroon, griffe, etc.), which reflected changing perceptions of difference as binary, passed mostly out of use in the 20th century. Segregation into "colored" and "white" carved separate domains in public facilities and buildings such as buses and trains, restaurants, restrooms, hotels, theaters, and even cemeteries. During Reconstruction, southern African Americans organized their own churches (which eventually fostered the civil rights movement). American Indians likewise set up their own churches and also church-sponsored schools rather than have their children attend segregated African American public institutions.

Despite such efforts to maintain their Indian identity, many groups faced legal attempts to abolish their peoplehood. Perhaps the most severe, and preposterous, actions were sponsored by Virginian eugenicists who wished to prevent miscegenation and limit access to white schools. The Racial Integrity Law of 1924 passed by the Commonwealth of Virginia (and not repealed until 1968) implemented a system of racial documentation to class all state residents as colored or white. Implementing the law meant denying the existence of any Indians in the state (despite their association with the oldest reservation lands in the country, granted in colonial treaties) and claiming that descendants of Pocahontas and John Rolfe were "white" and not Indians after all.

If indigenous peoples were denied their ancestral identity under Jim Crow–era legislation, what type of categorization did new immigrants face? Unlike Caribbean immigrants in the early 19th century who held a range of identities in relation to color and ancestry, "multiracial" immigrant groups, such as the Cubans, found themselves divided into separate categories in the South despite a shared nationality. As early as 1831, Cubans were making cigars in Key West. In the 1880s Vicente Martínez Ybor brought Cuban cigar manufacturing to Tampa, where Cubans founded Ybor City. More Cubans and Afro-Cubans arrived as exiles following the War of Independence from Spain (1895–98). Cuban writer José Martí had recruited support in Ybor City for that revolution (in which he died). Just over a century ago, Cuban immigrants founded the Martí-Maceo Society (a mutual aid, social, and Cuban independence group) in honor of both the Euro-Cuban Martí and an Afro-Cuban hero, the revolutionary general Antonio Maceo. The society quickly divided at the turn of the 20th century along color lines. About 15 percent of the Tampa Cuban community at the time was Afro-Cuban, and they faced different assimilation challenges than other Cubans. In Florida, Afro-Cuban immigrants found a society in which they were separated from Euro-Cubans by Jim Crow laws and from African Americans by culture, language, and religion. "White" Cubans joined the El Circulo Cubano (the Cuban Club), and the two groups have yet to reunite even though, today, cousins sharing the same great-grandparents have memberships in different societies.

For several decades after the Civil War, new immigrants to the South settled on one side or the other of a single color line, but they did not encounter the organized nativism that new immigrants did in the North. Nativism—the political or social expression of hostility toward immigrants based on ethnicity, religion, class, politics, economics, or social constructions of race—had never developed in the South during the antebellum era as it did in the North because new immigrants were few outside urban areas, and they assimilated quickly. In the early New South period, southerners rejected nativist movements because of their association with the Republican Party and because southern state governments actively sought new immigrant labor. While Germans and Irish were treated as different "races" in the North, they did not arrive in large enough numbers in the South to provoke a similar interpretation or negative response (nor did the small groups of Slavic or Polish immigrants who came south). Southern Italians, however, were sometimes deemed black, and 11 Sicilians were lynched in New Orleans in 1891. Some scholars have argued that early 20th-century southern nativism against Sicilians and Jews (including the 1915 Atlanta lynching of Leo Frank) was more class- and economic-based than ethnic, but with the post–World War I xenophobia that swept the nation, the 1920s South adopted religious and racial nativism. The reborn Ku Klux Klan played on anti-Catholic and anti-Jewish sentiments as well as color prejudice. However, remarkably few new Catholic or Jewish immigrants came to the South compared with other regions as the New South remained financially devastated well into the 20th century.

Despite efforts to attract new immigrants to the region, the vast majority chose the industrial urban areas of the North or the farmlands of the Midwest and West. Some Swiss, Slavonians, Czechs, and Hungarians settled together in ethnic communities in the South, and some Irish joined older Irish communities in New Orleans, Savannah, Memphis, Charleston, Mobile, Richmond, and Augusta. By 1905 Italians had arrived in Lambeth and Daphne, Ala., and had come to Tonitown, Ark., and Texas to work in cotton and rice cultivation. Italians also took work in the sugarcane and strawberry fields of Louisiana and Mississippi. Construction on the Texas railroads attracted Chinese, who also worked in the cotton fields of Mississippi and Louisiana. Those newcomers to the postwar South started fresh in a region with the lowest standard of living in the nation.

In 1936 famed regionalist Howard Odum published *Southern Regions of the United States*, in which he analyzed social and demographic characteristics of the South compared with other regions. The economic legacy of the Civil War meant that the gross annual income of the average southern farm in the 1920s was half or less (under $1,500) that of farms in Iowa, North Dakota, Wyoming, Nebraska, Montana, California, Nevada, or Arizona. In comparison with working wages across the country in 1929, Georgia, South Carolina, and North Carolina had the lowest annual income on average (under $800). Sixty-five years after the Civil War, southern farms were the smallest in the nation—most averaging under 75 acres. Georgia and Florida had a slightly higher average, closer to 75–100 acres, but only Texas had farms closer in size to those of the western and northwest central states (150–300 acres); this partly explains why Texas attracted a higher number of immigrants in the postwar period, including Czechs, Bohemians, and Italians. However, Texas was more like the rest of the

South in that fewer than 10 percent of its farms had tractors, and the percentage of its population living on farms (40 percent or more) was the greatest in the country. The South, then, had high percentages of its population living on the smallest and most underequipped farms, and making the lowest incomes from their farms, in the nation. Odum noted that between 50 and 90 percent of southern children suffered from inadequate diets leading to rickets, anemia, and the carious teeth found in about 50 percent of the schoolchildren examined. Such conditions were not what motivated immigrants to cross an ocean, and they kept European immigration to the region dramatically low.

Odum calculated that "foreign-born whites" constituted at least 17.5 percent of the population of the Northeast and between 12.5 and 17.5 percent of the populations of states such as California, Nevada, Washington, Montana, Minnesota, Wisconsin, Illinois, and Michigan, but that less than 2.5 percent of the white population of the southern states was foreign born in 1930. (Outside the South, only New Mexico and Oklahoma had a similar lack of new European immigrants.) Florida, such a magnet for Eastern Europeans in the late 20th century, had only 2.5 to 7.5 percent foreign-born whites, still making it the only state in the South with over 2.5 percent. Odum noted that the greatest numbers of African Americans were in the southern states, a statistic that remains true today. While seven cities in northern and midwestern states had African American populations of over 50,000, only southern states had black populations composing more than 10 percent of the state population in 1930. Mississippi's population in that year was over 50 percent African American, and Texas and Tennessee were the only southern states to have populations that were less than 26 percent African American.

Many southern states saw their percentage of African Americans decrease during the mid-20th century, in part because of exodus. However, this trend just as quickly began reversing with African Americans' return to the South. Since the mid-1990s, 8 of the top 10 metropolitan areas nationwide with black populations exceeding 200,000 are in the southern region. Florida was a favored destination of African American "returnees" to the South in the 1970s, attracting almost 16,000 new African American residents between 1975 and 1980, followed by a fourfold increase between 1985 and 1990. Orlando added 20,000 African American residents between 1995 and 2000 (a growth rate of over 60 percent in that segment of the city's population), slightly more than Atlanta. In the last two decades African Americans have been more likely than European Americans to resettle in the southern region, and Georgia and North Carolina have also had especially high growth rates.

Because the South did not receive the numbers of immigrants the rest of the country did after the Civil War, creolized southern identities are some of the oldest American identities. Many black and white southerners have ancestry in the region reaching back multiple centuries. This—coupled with the fact that the U.S. Census does not indicate a date range for answering its ancestry question—in part explains why southern states had the highest numbers of persons reporting their ancestry as "United States" or "American" on the 2000 census. This identification was more common for southern states than one of the three groups most frequently self-reported for ancestral origins across the nation (German, Irish, or English, in that order). California, Florida, Georgia, North Carolina, and Texas were the only states in the country in which more than 1 million people reported their ancestry as American. Perhaps because of Texas's border with Mexico, the influx of Mexican immigrants, and the accompanying emphasis on national identity, over 1,554,000 Texans claimed American ancestry alone on the 2000 census—more than in any other state (Texas also led the nation in this category in 1990). On the 2000 census, "American" was the most-reported ancestry group as a percentage of the total state populations in Tennessee, Arkansas, Kentucky, and nonsouthern West Virginia. Over 20 percent of Kentuckians listed "American" for their ancestry, as did 17.3 percent of Tennesseans and 15.7 percent of the population of Arkansas.

That said, the censuses also strongly reveal the panoply of ethnic groups (old and new) across the South. On the 1990 census, 47 percent of those self-identifying as "Scotch-Irish" (Scots-Irish) were from the South. Of the four states whose largest ancestry groups were Irish on the 2000 census, two were in the South (Arkansas and Tennessee). Nationally, the highest percentages of African Americans remain in the Deep South. In 2000, 36 percent of Mississippi's population was African American, followed by Louisiana (32.5 percent), South Carolina (29.5 percent), Georgia (28.7 percent), and Alabama (26 percent). The South has 69 percent of the nation's Cuban Americans, 91 percent of its Acadian/Cajuns, 40 percent of its Hondurans, and over 40 percent of its Haitian immigrants and Haitian Americans.

Late 20th- and 21st-Century New Southerners. The largest numbers of new immigrants to arrive since the colonial period have come to the dynamic and economically sound South of the latter 20th century. After President Lyndon B. Johnson's southern-focused War on Poverty, the South's economic boom, and national immigration reform, the South has become particularly attractive to new immigrants who reflect current processes of globalization. Greeks and Irish continue to settle across the South, and Sudanese and Somali immigrants fleeing civil war in their homelands are establishing communities in Nashville and

Atlanta; however, the bulk of the new southerners are not from Africa or Europe, but from South and Central America, the Middle East, and Asia. The 1965 Immigration Reform Bill abolished the national origins quota system and particularly favored Latin American and Asian immigration. Over the next decade almost 25 percent of new immigrants to the United States came from Asia and almost 40 percent came from Latin America (from 1980 to the mid-1990s, almost 35 percent came from Asia and over 45 percent came from Latin America).

The foreign-born population of the South quadrupled in the four decades prior to the year 2000. Atlanta is the nation's ninth-largest metro population and one of its fastest growing. When the first edition of the *Encyclopedia of Southern Culture* went to press in 1989, close to 25 percent of the metro Atlanta population was minority; by 2005 that figure was closer to 40 percent. Florida has the highest percentage of foreign-born residents (16.7 percent of its total population) and also has attracted migration from ethnic groups within the country. It is now home to one of every two people of Italian ancestry and to two of every three Jews living in the South. In numbers of foreign-born residents, Florida is followed by Texas (14 percent of its population is foreign born), Georgia, and North Carolina. Howard Odum noted that in 1930 Georgia had only 47 employed persons who were Mexicans, and North Carolina had only 10. The changes in the span of one lifetime are dramatic: the 2000 census records 224,000 (foreign-born) Mexican immigrants in Georgia and 199,000 in North Carolina, with some counties in each state experiencing between 200 to 400 percent increases.

Current demographic changes in the South make discussion of a biracial South outmoded. After the Southwest, the South has the highest proportion of Hispanics/Latinos in the nation. The Census Bureau considers "Hispanic" to mean a person of Latin American descent (including persons of Cuban, Mexican, Puerto Rican, or Central and South American origin) living in the United States who may be of any "race" (which the bureau oddly defines as "White," "Black or African American," "American Indian," "Asian," etc.). The term "Hispanic" refers to the influence of Spanish language and culture. "Latino" arose in the late 1980s and 1990s to emphasize the indigenous cultures and identities of Central and South America independent of Spain (many Latinos have Indian identities in their nations of origin). Across the nation in the 1990s, the Hispanic population increased by 57.9 percent (at a time when the U.S. population on a whole saw an increase of 13.2 percent). Hispanics now compose a larger proportion of the American population than do African Americans. Despite these trends, the general public, the media, and academics remain comfortable discussing the labels "black" and "white" as a kind of default categorization of all things southern. Although such a categorization of the region is intellectually habitual, it is shorter lived than the history of the South and is month by month becoming more passé.

The surge in North Carolina's Latino population over the last decade is in part due to the North Carolina Growers Association and other employers recruiting thousands of workers through the 1989 federal H2A "guest worker" program. Prior to the 1990s the state's farmworkers were predominantly African American. They are now 90 percent Latino—a rapid demographic change apparent in other southern states. As African Americans increasingly leave farmwork for service sector jobs, they are replaced predominantly by Mexicans. They are also displaced in poultry plants, other agricultural processing positions, and light manufacturing and construction by Mexican laborers (these trends are also common in Tennessee, Arkansas, Mississippi, and Alabama). In addition to documented guest worker program recruits, perhaps 50 percent of migrant laborers in North Carolina are working illegally. Their numbers are much more difficult to confirm, as are the percentages of such guest workers who remain and make the South their permanent home. As the labor force has changed, wages have declined. Neither expecting nor demanding benefits, Mexican laborers have accepted such low wages that the average farmworker in North Carolina now earns less than $8,000 a year.

Before the recent surge of Mexican immigrants, Cubans had been one of the largest, and oldest, Latin American groups in the South. In the 2000 census, two-thirds of all Cubans in the United States live in Florida. Old enclaves such as Ybor City remain. Today, Ybor is within the metropolitan area of Tampa and is still home to Cuban social clubs, Catholic churches, grocery stores, bakeries, and Cuban restaurants such as the Columbia. Opened in 1905 by Cuban immigrant Casimiro Hernandez Sr., the restaurant seats 1,700 guests, features flamenco dancing performances, and serves favorite Cuban dishes such as yellow rice and chicken, *boliche*, and flan. Ybor still has a residential area, but the main street shopping area is now an art district and a popular venue for weekend nightlife. A statue of an immigrant family stands in Ybor's Centennial Park, and a museum to cigar factory workers is located near preserved workers' cottages. Many Cuban Social and Mutual Aid Society buildings from the late 19th and early 20th centuries remain (El Pasaje, or the Cherokee Club; El Centro Asturiano, a society for both Italians and Cubans; and the Cuban Club).

Descendants of these early Cuban immigrants to Tampa remain ethnically aware, but they were quickly upwardly mobile and became quite distinct from newer Cuban communities in south Florida. After the Castro revolution of 1959 and until the mid-1970s, approximately 16,000 Cubans risked their lives

Fourth and fifth generations of the Hernandez Gonzmart family who operate the Columbia Restaurant in Tampa, Fla. The original restaurant opened in 1905 as a corner café frequented by Cuban cigar workers (Photograph courtesy of the Columbia Restaurant)

to come to Florida as *balseros* (on homemade rafts) without permission from the Cuban or American governments. Many more came in the famous 1980 Mariel sealift. The last large influx of Cubans came in 1994 when Fidel Castro announced that anyone wanting to leave Cuba was free to do so. Faced with assimilating the over 35,000 Cubans who did, the U.S. government returned rafters collected by the U.S. Coast Guard to Cuba.

South Florida Cubans remain deeply committed to political goals for their homeland and to bringing relatives to the United States, as sadly demonstrated by the 2000 case of Elian Gonzalez, a six-year-old boy who was returned to his father in Cuba after his mother drowned trying to bring him to Florida. Cubans have transformed Miami into a Cuban city in a relatively short time. Once the destination of Yankee developers, Miami is now the center for Caribbean culture in America. Calle Ocho (Eighth Street) features Cuban restaurants, freshly squeezed *guarapo* (sugarcane juice), late-night mambo music, and salsa and merengue dancing. In Hialeah and Little Havana in Dade County, specialty shops and caterers provide dresses and festive Cuban foods for *quinceañera* parties (coming-of-age celebrations for 15-year-old girls). Diverse religious practices from Cuba also characterize Cuban populations in south Florida, including Santeria (the Way of the Saints). Estimates suggest that 90 percent of Cuban Jews came to the United States in the 1960s. Approximately 5,000 to 6,000 Hispanic Jews live in Miami. Members of the Circulo Cubano-Hebreo (the Cuban-Hebrew Social Circle) emphasize themes of homeland and diaspora from Cuba in their ethnic identity.

In 2000 Florida had one of the largest non-Mexican Latino populations in the nation. Although Puerto Ricans have established communities in every southern state since 1980, more live in Florida than in any other state in the region. South Florida has the largest Nicaraguan population outside Managua, and Nicaraguans are perhaps the second-largest Hispanic population in south Florida. Fleeing political upheaval at home, Nicaraguans are ethnically diverse. Those of Miskito identity descend from indigenous Nicaraguans who speak their own language in addition to English and Spanish and mostly come from the Atlantic Coast. Creole/Miskito Nicaraguans speak English and often Spanish, were missionized by Moravians, and their community in south Florida remains organized around the Moravian Prince of Peace Church in Miami. Of Nicaraguan immigrants to Florida, the Creoles came earliest, beginning in the 1950s, and many are now professionals. Mestizos speak Spanish primarily, are Catholic, and come from the Pacific Coast of Nicaragua. Most arrived only after the Sandinistas came to power in 1979, but estimates of their population in the

Miami area reach as high as 400,000. In south Florida the various Nicaraguan ethnic groups mix less with each other than with other Latinos. They often live in neighborhoods with Hondurans and Costa Ricans, but also near Salvadorans and Guatemalans.

New groups of immigrants from the Central and South Americas are shaping new identities in the South with members of other Latino nations, with Jamaicans, Haitians, and other Caribbean new southerners, and through their assimilation with preexisting southern ethnic groups. The next few decades will see the emergence of new Creoles and mestizo cultures in the South's subregions. The 1970s saw some of the first Spanish-speaking Protestant churches in the South, and just 30 years later, Latino evangelicals outnumber Episcopalians and Presbyterians in the South. In North Carolina and other southern states, Roman Catholics outnumber Methodists (one of the three main evangelical denominations in the region). Fiestas are becoming as common on the southern cultural landscape as barbecue cook-offs, peanut festivals, and bluegrass jamborees. Across the South, annual Hispanic festivals—like the Gran Fiesta de Fort Worth, the Fiesta Latina in Asheville, N.C., the Hispanic Festival in Augusta, Ga., and the Festival Hispano in North Charleston, S.C.—are also increasingly appealing to non-Hispanic participants. The character of such festivals demonstrates how immigrant communities assimilate to the southern region and also gauges how our perceptions of what is "southern" continue to evolve.

The U.S. Census reveals that the Asian population of the South grew dramatically in the latter half of the 20th century. The Census Bureau's "Asian" category racializes what are very distinct ethnic identities by subsuming Asian Indians as well as Chinese, Filipinos, Nepalese, Japanese, and Samoans and other Pacific Islanders into the same category, and it is important to note which particular South and East Asian groups have favored the South. While East Asians more commonly settled in California and Hawaii, since the 1970s Filipinos, Koreans, Vietnamese, Hmong, and Asian Indians have been immigrating or migrating to the South so rapidly that close to 20 percent of all Asian Americans now reside in the region. (This figure is almost double the number in the Midwest and about the same as the percentage in the Northeast.) Asian Americans now constitute approximately 4.2 percent of the American population, and this national average was exceeded in one southern state (Virginia has 4.3 percent). However, in only nine states did Asians represent less than 1 percent of the total population, and three of those were in the South (Alabama, Kentucky, and Mississippi).

Nationwide, South Asian Indians are one of the top-five immigrant groups in the early 2000s after Mexicans and along with Filipinos, Chinese, and non-Mexican Latin Americans. Indians also form some of the most highly educated immigrant communities (about 70 percent have a college degree and 40 percent have a master's degree or doctorate). Arriving mostly after immigration reform in 1965, Indians have one of the highest per capita incomes for any ethnic group and have become a significant presence in the medical, engineering, technology, and computing professions as well as the hotel industry. Texas, Georgia, and Florida have developed particularly significant populations, but Hindu temples dot the southern landscape from Baton Rouge to Nashville to Richmond, and celebrations of India's Independence Day are making appearances across the region. Houston is home to multiple Hindu cremation service providers, at least 20 sari boutiques, 15 Indian-owned hair salons, and 20 jewelers in addition to numerous Indian groceries and over a dozen video stores that import the latest Bollywood productions. Known as the Bible Belt or the Sunbelt, the South also has been called the "beauty pageant belt," and first- and second-generation immigrants sponsor an annual Miss India Georgia pageant in Atlanta (the subject of a 1997 documentary). Dallas, Houston, and other southern cities also hold annual Indian and South Asian beauty pageants.

South Asia includes India, Nepal, Pakistan, Sri Lanka, Bangladesh, Bhutan, and Burma (Myanmar), but many immigrants from varied nations and cultures join Indian American communities in the United States. When India alone has over 500 distinct languages and five major religions (Hinduism, Christianity, Islam, Sikhism, and Jainism), diversity is thus reduced by embracing a "South Asian" identity in a new land. In 2005 the University of Florida established the country's first Center for the Study of Hindu Traditions. (The only other center of its kind globally is at Oxford University in England.) Numerous Indian American associations exist across the South from Austin, Tex., to Columbia, S.C., and at many universities.

Until the arrival of Korean war brides and adopted war orphans in the 1950s, the Chinese of Texas and the Mississippi Delta were the earliest and most significant East Asian presence in the South. Most Koreans coming to the South came after the 1965 immigration reform and settled in urban areas, where they own small businesses or work in manufacturing or professional and technical fields. Between the 1990 and 2000 censuses, the Korean population of the South grew nearly 53 percent. Virginia is home to the largest number, followed by Georgia and Florida. While many arrive directly from Korea, others are moving south from the American West. Korean Baptist churches are increasing in numbers, while Korean Presbyterians constitute one of the fastest-growing Protestant denominations in the South.

The Vietnam War, of course, spurred Vietnamese immigration to the United States. After California and Texas, Louisiana, with its Catholic French heritage, was a particularly attractive destination for immigrants from a former French colony. One of the largest Vietnamese enclaves in the United States is the Versailles community in New Orleans, home to multiple Vietnamese churches, Buddhist temples, and Vietnamese groceries. Approximately 12,000 Vietnamese lived in New Orleans in the early 2000s. Many Vietnamese also settled along the Gulf Coast of Mississippi in the early 1980s to work as fishers and in seafood plants. Many of the estimated 10,000 Vietnamese in the area have opened successful restaurants and coffeehouses.

With a population of 135,000, the Vietnamese are the largest East Asian group in Texas, followed by the Chinese and the Filipinos, the latter of whom number to 60,000 in that state. The first significant Filipino immigration to Texas followed the Spanish-American War in 1898, when the United States acquired the Philippines. Many immigrants to the United States at that time chose Texas because of its climate. After World War II, Filipino men who had served in the U.S. armed forces could become citizens, and some of them immigrated to Texas. English had long been one of the Philippines' official languages, and Filipino professionals familiar with the language quickly followed. Filipino Texans have formed their own ethnic associations and continue to teach their children Filipino art, embroidery, dance, and musical forms, but they also have long joined in wider community events — for example, by sponsoring floats in the Fiesta San Antonio. Nationwide, Filipinos are one of the largest immigrant groups, and in two southern states they compose the largest percentages of East Asian populations: in Florida they number just over 54,000 and in Virginia almost 50,000. The next-largest Filipino populations in the South are in Georgia (11,000) and North Carolina (almost 10,000).

The Japanese have come south quite slowly. By 1940 a few hundred Japanese were living as rice farmers in Texas, but no other concentrated communities were noted in the census of that year. Two of the World War II internment camps for Japanese Americans, holding more than 15,000 people, were located in Arkansas, but the vast majority left at the war's conclusion. The 1950 census recorded only 3,000 in the South. Today, North Carolina alone is home to over 5,600 Japanese Americans, almost twice as many Filipinos, 12,600 Koreans, 15,600 Vietnamese, more than 18,000 Chinese, and over 26,000 Asian Indians.

Muslim Arab Americans have also become more visible in the South in the last few decades, although Christian Arab and Middle Eastern Americans have been a part of southern communities since the late 19th century. Florida and Texas are home to Syrian and Lebanese Americans whose ancestors immigrated between the 1880s and the 1940s. During that time period, most immigrants called themselves "Syrian" (Lebanon only achieved independence in 1946) and came to the rural South for farmwork or to establish businesses in Atlanta, Birmingham, New Orleans, and eventually Miami. Now called "Lebanese Americans," the descendants of these original immigrants constitute a significant proportion of Arab Americans living across the country. Ten percent are from a variety of Muslim sects, while the majority are Christian. Their churches include the Chaldean Catholic, Eastern Orthodox, Maronite, and Melkite, and in the South many Arab Americans have joined Roman Catholic as well as Baptist and Methodist congregations. Jacksonville, Miami, Palm Beach, and Tampa have some of the largest communities in Florida, and Dallas, Houston, and San Antonio are home to those in Texas. In Vicksburg, Miss., the focus of the Lebanese community is the St. George Antiochan Orthodox Church. In Mobile, Ala., some of the best-known Lebanese surnames include Kahalley, Kalifeh, Saad, Sudeiha, Naman, and Zoghby.

From 1990 to 2000 the Arab population increased by over 50 percent in North Carolina and Virginia and by almost 60 percent in Florida. In 2000, 26 percent of the Arab population in the United States lived in the South. While Arab Americans have more commonly settled in urban areas of California, New York, and Michigan, three southern states have become home to new, large Arab American populations: Florida foremost, followed by Texas and Virginia. The Arab American populations of Florida and Texas have more than doubled since the 1980 census, in part because of a growing presence of Egyptians, Jordanians, and Palestinians. Having a smaller population than Florida or Texas, Virginia has nonetheless quadrupled its Arab American population since 1980, largely because of the immigration of North Africans. More than 8,000 Kurds live in Nashville (more than any other American city) and affectionately call their new home "Little Kurdistan."

Arab Americans place a strong emphasis on education, and almost 40 percent obtain a bachelor's degree (compared with the national average for Americans of 24 percent). In many cases, new Arab Muslim women immigrants are more likely to assimilate aspects of southern and American culture than are males. Many Muslim women live as professionals in America yet, within their ethnic communities, are expected to succumb to cultural visions of their inequality if they maintain a faith that does not readily syncretize. Rejecting (for women) many of the opportunities that immigrants have intentionally sought, some Muslim men have attempted to erect physical barriers in front of women's prayer space in southern and Appalachian mosques. Young women have instead made attempts to blend their faith with southern traditions. In 2005 the first recognized chapter of the Muslim sorority Gamma Gamma Chi was established in Alexandria, Va. A chapter is also planned for the University of Kentucky in Lexington (a city with a Muslim population of almost 2,500) to blend studying the Koran with sisterhood.

As immigrants do around the world, new immigrants to the South often maintain links with their homeland. They frequently foster the immigration of friends and extended family to join them in their new home. They may also import religious practitioners, educators, and performers of the expressive arts to teach their children their own cultural traditions and to create a focus for a community with other nationals. Many immigrants save money to send to relatives in the homeland and to return there for visits. When people maintain a cultural identity and social, economic, and political links to their homeland but establish a new home abroad, social scientists refer to the processes involved as "transnationalism." Immigrants from the same country may have had different ethnic identities within their home nation states but, finding a newly shared ethnic identity with other nationals in a new land, create social and benevolent associations to foster community and assist recent arrivals. The form and focus of transnational communities entails particular worldviews and shapes the extent to which a new immigrant group assimilates and new syncretized cultural forms develop.

Of the many groups now establishing transnational communities in the South, some have been more surprising to their new neighbors than others. Nationwide, Hmong immigrants from Laos (by way of Thailand) have earned the reputation of the "least assimilatable" immigrants. They have settled in specially chosen communities across the rural South in towns like Mount Airy, N.C., and their animistic traditions (sometimes involving the slaughter of animals in the front yard or the living room of rented apartments) have provoked astonishment. However, many Hmong immigrants have also joined local Christian churches or formed their own congregations. In Mount Airy, Andy Griffith's hometown, they enjoy their new community's annual Mayberry Days festival, which celebrates the *Andy Griffith Show*. Haitians have burgeoning populations in south Florida and the Carolinas. Miami has received the most immigrants of rural peasant backgrounds. To support Vodou rituals in Miami's working-class Little Haiti, goats and poultry are brought from agricultural markets as far away as south Alabama. Yet, many immigrants from Haiti are middle-class and are also successfully integrating into Floridian society at the highest levels. In 2001 Josaphat (Joe) Celestin became the first Haitian-born mayor of a U.S. city, the city of North Miami. In 2000 Phillip Brutus became the first Haitian-born elected representative to the Florida legislature, and Fred Séraphin, a native of Haiti, is now a judge in the Miami-Dade County Courts system.

In addition to new Asian and Latino immigrants, the 21st-century South also attracts newcomers from nations whose immigrants either have not traditionally sought a home in the region or whose predecessors had come before only through slavery (south Florida, for example, now has Icelandic and Igbo cultural associations). In the early 2000s, Eastern Europeans, especially those from Ukraine, Poland, and Russia, have the highest rates of immigration (among Europeans generally) to the United States, and increasing numbers are coming south. Since the terrorist attacks of September 2001, longer Immigration and Naturalization Service processing times for popular destinations such as New York City and Washington, D.C., have led to more immigrants choosing southern cities such as Nashville, Tampa, and Charlotte. Charlotte, a city of slightly more than 600,000, has over 65 ethnic associations engaging, among other groups, French Americans, Arabs, Iranians, Jamaicans, Cambodians, Somalians, Finns, Turks, Ethiopians, Welsh, Armenians, Nubians, Eritreans, and Ecuadorians. Among African immigrants to the United States, Nigerians have had the highest numbers in the early 2000s. After New York, Texas attracts the most Nigerians of any state, and of the 12 top destinations for new arrivals, Georgia ranks sixth, Florida seventh, and North Carolina eleventh. Ethnic identities such as Igbo, Hausa, and Yoruba (just the most prominent of hundreds of ethnic groups in a nation created by colonial administrators rather than from within) remain strong in Nigeria and translate into distinct cultural associations across the Atlantic. However, despite a recent history of ethnic civil war (1967–70) in their native land, even these newcomers sponsor a united and national Miss Nigeria U.S.A. Pageant out of Atlanta.

Current studies of globalization focus on economic and social trends that enhance the mobility of people, the exchange of ideas, and the rapid increase in communication and trade internationally. Anthropologist James Peacock has noted that current trends in globalization are in some ways a return to colonial and post-Revolutionary patterns. Southern ports linked trade routes between North America, the Caribbean, Europe, and Africa, constituting early globalization in the 17th and 18th centuries. During the 19th and 20th centuries, the South was less globally and more regionally focused on an identity and way of life that was in contrast to what was "northern." In the later 20th century, as cultural dualism evolved to pluralism and now multiculturalism, the South reglobalized through commercial exports such as Coca-Cola, CNN, Bank of America, Delta Airlines, and FedEx, through the export of political leaders such as Jimmy Carter, Bill Clinton, and George W. Bush, and through the reception of new southerners from around the world. Global influences are now reshaping the South and southern identity as they once shaped the colonial region. This volume offers a sampling from the four centuries of immigration, creolization, and ethnic life that have forged, and continue to define, the South and its many subregions.

CELESTE RAY
University of the South

Roger Abrahams, *Singing the Master: The Emergence of African American Culture in the Plantation South* (1992); Charles S. Aiken, in *Homelands: A Geography of Culture and Place across America*, ed. Richard Nostrand and Lawrence Estaville (2001); Frederik Barth, *Ethnic Groups and Boundaries: The Social Organization of Cultural Difference* (1969); Mark Bauman, *Dixie Diaspora: An Anthology of Southern Jewish History* (2006); Shane K. Bernard, *The Cajuns: Americanization of a People* (2003); Marilyn Dell Brady, *The Asian Texans* (2004); Carl A. Brasseaux, Keith P. Fontenot, and Claude F. Oubre, *Creoles of Color in the Bayou Country* (1994); Allan Burns, *Maya in Exile: Guatemalans in Florida* (1993); Edward Campbell, ed., *Before Freedom Came: African-American Life in the Antebellum South* (1991); Barbara Carpenter, ed., *Ethnic Heritage in Mississippi* (1992); Robert Chaudenson, *Creolization of Language and Culture* (2001); Lucy Cohen, *Chinese in the Post–Civil War South: A People without a History* (1984); Ceclia Conway, in *Appalachians and Race: The Mountain South from Slavery to Segregation*, ed. John C. Inscoe (2001); Clare Dannenberg, *Southern Anthropologist* (Fall 2004); Virginia Domínguez, *White by Definition: Social Classification in Creole Louisiana* (1986); James H. Dorman, ed., *Creoles of Color of the Gulf South* (1996); Toyin Falola and Matt Childs, eds., *The Yoruba Diaspora in the Atlantic World* (2004); Leon Fink, *The Maya of Morganton: Work and Community in the Nuevo New South* (2003); Andrew K. Frank, *Creeks and Southerners: Biculturalism on the Early American Frontier* (2005); Jack Forbes, *Black Africans and Native Americans: Color, Race, and Caste in the Evolution of Red-Black Peoples* (1988); Jillian E. Galle and Amy L. Young, eds., *Engendering African American Archaeology: A Southern Perspective* (2004); Michael Gomez, *Exchanging Our Country Marks: The Transformation of African Identities in the Colonial and Antebellum South* (1998); Gwendolyn Midlo Hall, *Slavery and African Ethnicities in the Americas: Restoring the Links* (2005), *Africans in Colonial Louisiana: The Development of Afro-Creole Culture in the Eighteenth Century* (1992); Kimberly S. Hanger, *Bounded Lives, Bounded Places: Free Black Society in Colonial New Orleans, 1769–1803* (1997); Arnold Hirsch and Joseph Logsdon, eds., *Creole New Orleans: Race and Americanization* (1992); Joseph Holloway, ed., *Africanisms in American Culture* (1990); Thomas Ingersoll, *Mammon and Manon in Early New Orleans: The First Slave Society in the Deep South, 1718–1819* (1999); Samuel C. Hyde, ed., *Plain Folk of the South Revisited* (1997); Charles Joyner, *Shared Traditions:*

Southern History and Folk Culture (1999); Sybil Kein, ed., *Creole: The History and Legacy of Louisiana's Free People of Color* (2000); David La Vere, *Contrary Neighbors: Southern Plains and Removed Indians in Indian Territory* (2000); Daniel C. Littlefield, in *Bridging Southern Cultures*, ed. John Lowe (2005), *Rice and Slaves: Ethnicity and the Slave Trade in Colonial South Carolina* (1981); Elizabeth Mancke and Carole Shammas, eds., *The Creation of the British Atlantic World* (2005); Jesse McKee, *Ethnicity in Contemporary America: A Geographical Appraisal* (2000); Gary B. Mills, *The Forgotten People: Cane River's Creoles of Color* (1977), *National Genealogical Society Quarterly* (December 1990); J. Kenneth Morland, ed., *The Not So Solid South: Anthropological Studies in a Regional Subculture* (1971); Howard Odum, *Southern Regions of the United States* (1936); Ted Ownby, ed., *Black and White Cultural Interaction in the Antebellum South* (1993); James Peacock, Harry Watson, and Carrie Matthews, eds., *The American South in a Global World* (2005); Theda Perdue, *"Mixed Blood" Indians: Racial Construction in the Early South* (2003); William S. Pollitzer, *The Gullah People and Their African Heritage* (1999); Robert Seto Quan, *Lotus among the Magnolias: The Mississippi Chinese* (1982); Celeste Ray, *Southern Heritage on Display: Public Ritual and Ethnic Diversity within Southern Regionalism* (2003); Ben Sandmel and Rick Olivier, *Zydeco* (1999); Jon F. Sensback, *A Separate Canaan: The Making of an Afro-Moravian World in North Carolina, 1763–1840* (1998); Mechal Sobel, *The World They Made Together: Black and White Values in Eighteenth-Century Virginia* (1987); John Thornton, *Africa and Africans in the Making of the Atlantic World, 1400–1800* (1992); Thomas Tweed, *Southern Cultures* (Summer 2002); Thomas Walls, *The Japanese Texans* (1996); Sheila S. Walker, ed., *African Roots/American Cultures: Africa in the Creation of the Americas* (2001); Martha Ward, *Voodoo Queen: The Spirited Lives of Marie Laveau* (2004); Walter Williams, ed., *Southeastern Indians since the Removal Era* (1979); Peter Wood, *Southern Exposure* (Summer 1988).

American Indians

People first came to the South about 13,000 years ago in the Paleoindian period as nomadic hunters and gatherers who used Clovis stone tools, erected temporary dwellings or camped in rock shelters and caves, and hunted mastodons and ground sloths. With the extinction of such megafauna at the end of the Pleistocene, southerners of the Archaic period (about 8000 B.C. to 1000 B.C.) became less migratory and eventually more sedentary through their use of horticulture. They grew sunflowers (for seeds), squash, and gourds and also left huge middens from shellfish consumption both in coastal areas and along southern rivers. The Woodland period (about 1000 B.C. to 1000 A.D. and until European contact in some areas) saw the introduction of corn, the construction of mortuary mounds, and the beginnings of a hierarchical society that developed into chiefdoms.

When Juan Ponce de León arrived in Florida in 1513, some native southerners were living with Woodland traditions while others had embraced a Mississippian lifestyle, a culture unique to the South and dating from about 1000 to 1600 A.D. Mississippian people lived in square houses, used shell-tempered pottery, made cane basketry, had a symbolic system scholars call the Southeastern Ceremonial Complex, and built flat-topped pyramidal mounds on which they erected religious structures or dwellings for their male and female chiefs (as at Etowah and Ocmulgee in Georgia, Moundville in Alabama, Emerald Mound in Mississippi, and Town Creek in North Carolina). A sedentary lifestyle and growing populations depended on intensive agriculture and a staple diet of corn, beans, and squash. Competition for valley farmlands led to increased warfare. Labor specialization led to the development of religious and artistic classes, and because of such stratification and the possibility that some chiefdoms were paramount over others, many scholars believe the Mississippian societies are more aptly called protostates than chiefdoms.

Native southerners first encountered Europeans through the explorations and colonization attempts of Ponce de León and Lucas Vásquez de Ayllón. Arriving at Bradenton on Florida's west coast in 1539, Hernando de Soto's expedition through the South to the Mississippi River brought bloodshed, enslavement, and disease. Native southerners' susceptibility to introduced European diseases (smallpox, scarlet fever, measles, typhoid, diphtheria, and others) was a prime factor in depopulation rates, which, by some conservative estimates, accounted for well over one-third of the population in the 18th century alone and for perhaps as much as 70 percent in the period from 1500 to 1600. With depopulation came a loss of political and religious leaders, and the Mississippian towns declined. Not all societies had documented epidemics; the chiefdoms of the Calusa and Apalachee of Florida were noted exceptions. Indigenous societies in the Southeast were very culturally diverse; those in the interior were most markedly different from coastal cultures. As chiefdoms collapsed and recombined, social organization became more focused on language-related ethnic or national groupings. The main cultural groupings that survived the colonial era (1600–1776) included Algonkians (probably some of the oldest southerners), speakers of Iroquoian languages (thought to have moved into the Carolinas and southern Appalachian Mountains during the Woodland period), Caddoan speakers (concentrated in western Louisiana, Texas, and Oklahoma), Siouans (scattered across the South from the Gulf Coast to Georgia and the Carolinas), and Muskogean speakers (speakers of the most dominant language group who lived from the Gulf Coast to Kentucky).

While small, coastal native nations were often destroyed through disease, warfare, or enslavement, larger nations in the southern interior endured through their greater population numbers and distance from European settlements. Some prospered through the deerskin trade of the 18th century, and groups such as the Creek, Cherokee, Chickasaw, Choctaw, and Catawba raided other native communities to sell captives to English, French, and Dutch slavers who shipped them to the Caribbean and to coastal plantations in Virginia, South Carolina, and French Louisiana. American Indians' abilities to play European powers against each other ceased with the Treaty of Paris in 1763, through which Spain lost Florida and France lost its North American empire. While the Catawba supported the Patriots in the Revolution, many Native American tribes fought against them, and when the British left the South in 1781, American Indians were faced with the new United States and its zeal for expansion.

American Indians of European American descent, who were not uncommon because of intermarriage with frontier traders, became a new "mixed-blood" class and were expected to mediate between Native American communities and the new Americans. While such persons were considered Indians because of American Indians' use of matrilineal descent, they were sometimes able to avoid losing their homes during the Removal Period by, for example, claiming to be "Black Dutch" or through their Scottish ancestry and kin. They were often enculturated to American ways of thinking, adopted Christianity, established schools, shaped national governments imitative of those of European Americans, and grew cash crops using black slave labor. Those American Indian groups most outwardly assimilated became known as the Five Civilized Tribes (the Cherokee, Choctaw, Chickasaw, Creek, and eventually the Seminole), and their "mixed-blood" members often signed away their lands in disastrous treaties with the U.S. government.

Alfred Boisseau, Louisiana Indians Walking along a Bayou, 1847, oil on canvas
(New Orleans Museum of Art, gift of William E. Groves, 56.34)

With President Andrew Jackson's "Indian wars" and his Indian Removal Act of 1830, native southern nations suffered the loss of ancestral homelands and further depopulation. The first to be removed west of the Mississippi under the 1830 act, the Choctaw, lost perhaps a third of their people, and estimates suggest at least a quarter of the Cherokee died who embarked on the 1838–39 Trail of Tears. Several hundred Seminoles managed to remain in south Florida after resisting Removal through war, but most were marched west. In Indian Territory, removed members of the Five Civilized Tribes reestablished communities and national governments and many attended mission schools. At the beginning of the Civil War, all five tribes signed treaties with the Confederacy, but opinions about the war were greatly divided among the Cherokee, Creek, and Seminole. The Reconstruction government deemed all previous treaties with the tribes—and the rights the tribes had held therein—to be forfeit, and each nation was required to negotiate new treaties, through which they suffered significant land losses. These losses continued after the 1887 Dawes Act reallocated lands of American Indians to non-Indians under the pretense of enabling the Indians "better assimilation." The survival of any Indian Territory outside U.S. government control ended when Oklahoma became the 46th state in 1907.

Those native southerners who had avoided Removal most often retained their identity, language, and community through isolation in an increasingly biracial South. In the Jim Crow period they avoided segregated schools and churches by creating their own. Since the 1960s, ongoing cultural revivals have heightened their profile once again on the southern cultural landscape and re-newed the efforts of many tribes to achieve state and federal recognition. While emphasizing their local traditions and identity, southeastern Indians also share many cultural traditions. Most play stickball or the oldest game in the United States, chunkey, in which players throw long, greased sticks at smooth gran-ite or quartz disks rolled across the ground. Stomp dances, religious dances performed on ceremonial, or stomp, grounds, are also common to southeast-ern tribes with variations. In most stomp dances, men dance and sing while women provide the rhythmic accompaniment to the songs by dancing with "shell-shakers," which are box tortoise shells that are filled with pebbles, laced together, and strapped to the lower legs (although banned on some ceremo-nial grounds, tin cans often replace tortoise shells today).

Many southeastern tribes had clan systems. Most clan systems are exoga-mous and, among the Cherokee and the Seminole, endogamous marriages are still discouraged. Clans are matrilineal; a mother must have clan membership for her children to have a clan. Some tribes have largely forgotten their clans. However, recent cultural revival (related to a general emphasis on identity in America's multicultural age) has inspired efforts to return to clan systems. Many American Indian tribes have adopted the Plains-style powwows fostered by Pan-Indianism, yet blend this tradition with their own southeastern songs, clothing, tribe-specific dances, and other public rituals. Through powwows, tribes of contested status reassert their own local customs and identities to other American Indians and to non-Indians. Both tribe-specific and intertribal pow-wows have become potent means for tribes to regain control of their own rep-resentations and the interpretation of their own heritage.

Today, American Indians constitute just under 1 percent of the U.S. popula-tion, but several of the largest American Indian groups are in the South, includ-ing the Chickasaw, Seminole, Lumbee (not a federally recognized tribe), and Cherokee. The Cherokee is the largest group in the South, according to the U.S. Census (which includes Oklahoma in the southern region). The Eastern Band of Cherokee Indians in western North Carolina, which strictly requires one-sixteenth Cherokee ancestry for membership, has almost 13,000 tribal citizens, with 7,400 living on reservation land. The Eastern Band is far outnumbered by descendants of those removed to Indian Territory who can claim Chero-kee citizenship by simply tracing an ancestor listed as Cherokee on the Dawes rolls (lists compiled between 1898 and 1914 of members of the Cherokee, Choc-taw, Creek, Chickasaw, and Seminole tribes in Indian Territory). The Chero-kee tribal government recognizes close to 260,000 citizens, with approximately 90,000 of these living within the jurisdictional boundaries of the Cherokee

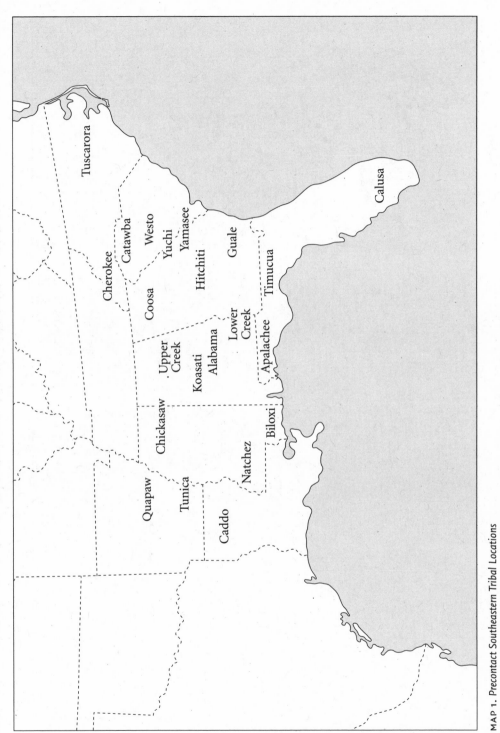

MAP 1. Precontact Southeastern Tribal Locations

(Adapted from Rachel A. Bonney and J. Anthony Paredes, eds., Anthropologists and Indians in the New South [2001])

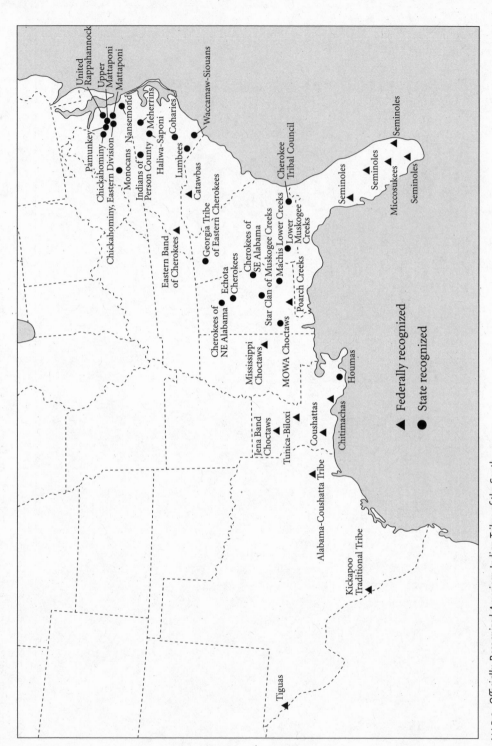

MAP 2. Officially Recognized American Indian Tribes of the South
(Adapted from Theda Perdue and Michael D. Green, The Columbia Guide to American Indians of the Southeast [2001])

Nation of Oklahoma, and the United Keetoowah Band of Cherokee Indians (also in Oklahoma) has approximately 16,000 citizens. However, hundreds of thousands more Americans consider themselves of Cherokee descent or claim a Cherokee ancestor, although most are too far removed to qualify for tribal membership.

Southerners are more likely to assert American Indian ancestry than European or African Americans in other regions. As sociologist John Shelton Reed has noted, the most common genealogical lore entails a mythic "Cherokee Princess in the family tree." In the late 1990s only 2 percent of southerners identified as Indian, but 40 percent claimed some native ancestry, almost double the number (22 percent) who claimed descent from a Confederate soldier. Close to 725,000 southerners claimed American Indian identities on the 2000 U.S. Census, and well over 1 million more claimed to be American Indian *and* another identity, but relatively few of either category are actually enrolled members of a tribe.

Of the 562 federally recognized American Indian nations in the United States, only 13 are in the South (excluding Oklahoma). The southern states are home to about 60 of the almost 230 tribes lacking federal recognition. Despite a history of Jim Crow laws that in effect denied the continued existence of Indian communities, southern states are also home to the majority of the tribes that have state recognition alone. Among these, Alabama has 9 state-only recognized tribes, followed by Virginia with 8 and North Carolina with 6 (and 14 other groups that have petitioned for recognition). Louisiana has at least 5 tribes recognized only by the state and a Biloxi-Chitimacha Confederation of Muskogees that encompasses three communities located in Terrebonne and Lafourche Parishes. In 2005 two tribes became the first to be recognized by the South Carolina Division of Vital Records: the Waccamaw and the Pee Dee Nation of Upper South Carolina.

To force rapid assimilation during the 1940s and 1950s, the federal government pursued a program to terminate relations with Indian nations and end both their self-government and federally sponsored social services. However, by the early 1960s a policy of self-determination had replaced termination, and tribes began regaining their sovereignty and reestablishing government-to-government relations with the United States. Today, federal recognition of tribal status requires demonstration that a tribe has existed as a distinct community since first contact with Europeans. In the case of combined tribes, evidence must confirm that members descend from historic tribes. For example, the Tunica and the Biloxi of Avoyelles Parish, La., merged with remnants of the neighboring Avoyel, Ofo, and Choctaw tribes over the centuries to form a new group with identifiable traditions and gained recognition as the Tunica-Biloxi in 1981.

To receive services from the Bureau of Indian Affairs, a tribe must have federal recognition. Such recognition also signifies status to non-Indian neighbors and to other Indian nations. Federally recognized tribes have sovereignty and form their own governments. They have the power to make and enforce both civil and criminal laws; to tax; to license, zone, and regulate activities; to engage in commercial activity; and to exclude persons (Indian and non-Indian) from tribal territories. The federally recognized tribes in the southern states include the once "terminated" Catawba Indian Nation of South Carolina, the Eastern Band of Cherokee (North Carolina), the Mississippi Band of Choctaw (Mississippi), the Seminole and Miccosukee (Florida), and the Poarch Band of Creeks (Alabama). Of the three tribes recognized in Texas—the Tigua, the Kickapoo Traditional tribe, and the Alabama-Coushatta—only the latter are considered part of the southeastern culture area. Louisiana has four sovereign nations: the Chitimacha, the Coushatta, the Jena Band of Choctaw Indians, and the Tunica-Biloxi.

CELESTE RAY
University of the South

James Axtell, *The Indians' New South: Cultural Change in the Colonial Southeast* (1997); Karen Blu, *The Lumbee Problem: The Making of an American Indian People* (1980); Cecile Elkins Carter, *Caddo Indians: Where We Come From* (1995); Robert Conley, *The Cherokee Nation: A History* (2005); Clyde Ellis, Luke Eric Lassiter, and Gary H. Dunham, *Powwow* (2005); Robbie Ethridge and Charles Hudson, eds., *The Transformation of the Southeastern Indians, 1540–1760* (2002); John Finger, *The Eastern Band of Cherokees, 1819–1900* (1984); Raymond Fogelson, ed., *Handbook of North American Indians, Volume 14: Southeast* (2004); Andrew Frank, *Creeks and Southerners: Biculturalism on the Early American Frontier* (2005); Patricia Galloway, *Choctaw Genesis, 1500–1700* (1995), ed., *The Hernando de Soto Expedition: History, Historiography, and "Discovery" in the Southeast* (1997); Arrell Gibson, ed., *America's Exiles: Indian Colonization in Oklahoma* (1976); James B. Griffin, *Archaeology of the Eastern United States* (1952); Charles Hudson, *The Catawba Nation* (1970), *The Southeastern Indians* (1976), *Knights of Spain, Warriors of the Sun: Hernando de Soto and the South's Ancient Chiefdoms* (1997); Alice Kehoe, *America before the European Invasions* (2002); Patricia Lerch, *Museum Anthropology* (June 1992); Scott Malcolmson, *One Drop of Blood: The American Misadventure of Race* (2000); Bonnie G. McEwan, ed., *Indians of the Greater Southeast: Historical Archaeology and Ethno-*

history (2000); Jerald T. Milanich, *Florida's Indians from Ancient Times to the Present* (1998); Christopher Oakley, *Keeping the Circle: American Indian Identity in Eastern North Carolina, 1885–2004* (2005); Anthony J. Paredes, ed., *Indians of the Southeastern United States in the Late Twentieth Century* (1992); Theda Perdue and Michael D. Green, *The Columbia Guide to American Indians of the Southeast* (2001); Timothy Pertulla, *The Caddo Nation: Archaeological and Ethnohistoric Perspectives* (1992); John Shelton Reed, *Southern Cultures* (Spring 1997); George Roth, in *Anthropologists and Indians in the New South*, ed. Rachel Bonney and Anthony Paredes (2001); Helen Rountree, *The Powhatan Indians of Virginia: Their Traditional Culture* (1989); Nancy Shoemaker, *A Strange Likeness: Becoming Red and White in Eighteenth-Century North America* (2004); Gerald Sider, *Lumbee Indian Histories: Race, Ethnicity, and Indian Identity in the Southern United States* (1993); John R. Swanton, *The Indians of the Southeastern United States* (1946); Brent Weisman, *Unconquered People: Florida's Seminole and Miccosukee Indians* (1999); Walter Williams, ed., *Southeastern Indians since the Removal Era* (1979); Peter Wood, Gregory Waselkov, and Thomas Hatley, eds., *Powhatan's Mantle: Indians in the Colonial Southeast* (1989); J. Leitch Wright, *The Only Land They Knew: The Tragic Story of the American Indians in the Old South* (1981).

Europeans

Spanish explorers were the first Europeans to contact native southerners and initiate settlements that make the South the oldest European-inhabited region of the United States. Juan Ponce de León discovered *La Florida* in 1513. The first European to discover the Chesapeake Bay, Lucas Vázquez de Ayllón, founded the unsuccessful colony of San Miguel de Gaundape in South Carolina (thought by some scholars to perhaps be the first place to have African slaves in North America). He died there in 1526. Hernando de Soto arrived on Florida's west coast in 1539, explored the South from the Carolinas to Texas, and died in present-day Arkansas near the Mississippi River in 1542. Prior to English settlement in Jamestown, Spanish Jesuits tried to establish a mission in the area in 1570. Spaniards established America's first city in 1565 at St. Augustine in Florida and developed a quite ethnically heterogeneous society. After three centuries of colonial endeavors, Spain ceded Florida to the United States in 1821. The largest Spanish American enclave for late 19th-century and 20th-century Spaniards was Tampa, Fla., portions of which the U.S. military occupied during the 1898 Spanish-American War.

Despite Spaniards' significance in shaping subsequent European interactions with American Indians in the region and their enduring contributions to southern culture, the category "Spanish" does not appear in the ancestry sections of southern state-by-state social characteristics profiles. (Between the 1980 and 1990 U.S. Censuses, the "Spanish origin" category was subsumed under "Hispanic origin.") However, several Spanish enclaves endure to the present. During Spanish control of Louisiana (1763–1800) settlers represented various Spanish ethnic groups, including Andalusians, Basques, Catalans, Galicians, and Canary Islanders. The Canary Islanders (Los Isleños), who have lived in St. Bernard's Parish, La., since the 1770s, maintained domestic use of their Spanish dialect well into the 20th century, despite living among Acadians, African Americans, and Anglo-Americans, and despite significant exogamy. Surnames still common in the area include Alleman, Caballero, Falcon, Fernandez, and Molero. The Isleños Heritage and Cultural Society (formed in 1976) encourages bilingualism and Isleños foodways and has organized heritage pilgrimages to the Canary Islands and an annual fiesta with flamenco dancing. The Canary Islanders Heritage Society of Louisiana was formed in 1996 to promote genealogical research, the study of traditional crafts, the construction of monuments commemorating Isleños ancestors, and ongoing cultural links with the people of the Canary Islands. In Florida close to 10,000 descendants of another Spanish ethnic group, the Minorcans from one of the Baleric Islands, retain a sense of identity and community in St. Augustine. The Minorcan Quarter of that city exhibits vernacular architectural styles, and their fishing traditions, religious festivals, and foodways still influence St. Augustine life.

Although some British sailors had been set ashore in Texas in 1567 after defeat by the Spanish, the first successful English colony in the South was established four centuries ago, in 1607, at Jamestown, Va. Of the three main colonizing powers in the South—the Spanish, the French, and the English—the English still have the largest number of descendants who indicate an awareness of their heritage on U.S. Censuses, but nationwide rank only as the fourth most-reported ancestry group. The English were so numerous and influential in southern history that they are sometimes dismissed as "the nonethnic norm," yet in 2000 only 8.7 percent of the U.S. population self-identified as being of English descent (down from 13 percent in 1990). Despite the cavalier image prominent English settlers in Virginia imparted to southern aristocrats in general, census identification with German ancestry marginally overtakes that with English ancestry in the state. While in the 1990 census the South had the highest percentage of any region of respondents claiming English ancestry (35 percent of all those across the country), in 2000 residents of Maine, New Hampshire, and Vermont were twice as likely to claim English ancestry as were residents of any southern state.

In the South identification of English ancestry remains highest in eastern-most states, especially in towns and cities, and on the eastern coast (except Savannah, where more persons identify as being of Irish descent). For example, Fredericksburg and Richmond, Va., New Bern, N.C., and Aiken and Charleston, S.C., all report English as the largest ancestry group. Further west, in Nashville, Tenn., Florence, Ala., and Little Rock, Ark., English is the second-largest group (although English ancestry is only the fourth-largest group indicated for the states of Arkansas, Texas, and Kentucky, in sync with the national average). Georgia, North Carolina, and Alabama report the highest percentage of their state populations as having English roots. Louisiana has the lowest representation, with English being only the fifth-largest ancestry group in the state; Louisianans most commonly report a French identity.

French settlers of the colonial period settled predominantly in Louisiana, where 16 percent of residents still report French descent. In the 2000 census 546,000 residents of Louisiana reported French ancestry, followed by 467,000 in Texas, 445,000 in Florida, 143,000 in Virginia, 128,000 in North Carolina, and 126,000 in Georgia. In 1682 René-Robert Cavelier, Sieur de La Salle, reached the mouth of the Mississippi River, naming the lands he had passed "Louisiane" for King Louis XIV. He founded a failed settlement on the eastern Texas coast, but in 1699 Pierre Le Moyne, Sieur d'Iberville, established the first permanent settlement of Fort Maurepas (now Biloxi) and became the first governor of Louisiana. His brother, Jean-Baptiste Le Moyne, Sieur de Bienville, founded New Orleans in 1718. The French influence on southern foodways, linguistics, architecture, and religion has proved enduring. French members of the Capuchin and Ursuline orders set up some of the oldest school systems in the United States (only Harvard, William and Mary, and Yale are older). French Mardi Gras traditions include the rural *courir* (run), in which costumed men perform songs as they travel by horse from house to house collecting the ingredients for a communal gumbo.

The two main French identities to endure to the present are the Creoles, whose ancestors came directly from either Spain or France, and the Cajuns, who moved south from Acadia in maritime Canada. Cajuns or Creoles compose the majority of Louisiana residents who reported speaking French in the home on the 1990 U.S. Census. To have fostered such an ethnically diverse colony in Louisiana, the French settlers in the South were less ethnically diverse than the Spanish. Walloons (French-speaking Belgians) settled in Louisiana in the 18th century, but the Protestant Huguenots (Calvinists) were one of the largest French groups to settle outside of French territory.

Huguenots arrived in Florida in 1564 and established a settlement called

La Caroline at the mouth of the St. Johns River, but the Spanish massacred these settlers the following year. The Fort Caroline National Memorial (about 45 miles north of St. Augustine) remains a testimony to their quest for religious freedom. The 1598 Edict of Nantes granted rights to French Protestants, but its revocation in 1685 by Louis XIV further spurred emigration. Huguenots had landed in Virginia as early as 1619 and had asked Charles I for refuge in the English Carolinas as early as 1629, but it was his son, Charles II, who made significant settlement possible by granting lands in 1663. The first Huguenots arrived in South Carolina in 1670, but after 1685 Charleston (founded as "Charlestown" or "Charles Towne") became a favored destination. Many settled at Goose Creek (20 miles inland from Charleston) and Santee (about 40 miles north of Charleston), where their plantations produced silk, olive oil, wine, and naval supplies, and still others moved to tideland areas, where they built rice plantations.

Charleston's Huguenot Church is the oldest continuously active Huguenot congregation in America. Congregants hold an annual service commemorating the Edict of Nantes and take pride in wearing the Huguenot cross (a Maltese cross with a dove attached), which is believed to have identified French Protestants to one another in public places as early as the 1600s. Typical surnames of Huguenot descendants in the area include Chastain, Du Val, Gourdine, Fuion, Fuqua, Lemay, LaRue, Martin, and Rambout.

Many other European groups came to the South seeking freedom from religious persecution. Almost 50 percent of arrivals in the first 10 years of Georgia's settlement (1733–42) were non-English Protestants, including Palatines, Scots, Swiss, Moravians, and Salzburgers. About 200 of the 19,000 Protestants expelled from the Austrian archbishopric at Salzburg in 1731 came to settle in the colony of Georgia. The Georgia trustees began the last of Britain's 13 American colonies "to provide a home for impoverished Englishmen and persecuted foreign Protestants." Salzburgers settling northwest of Savannah in 1734 named their community Ebenezer, attempted to convert the Yamacraw and Creek Indians to Christianity through mission work, and built the Jerusalem Evangelical Lutheran Church, which still stands on the banks of the Savannah River. They were later joined by Swiss and Palatine settlers. These German-speaking Georgians engaged in lumber processing and silk production. Surnames of these settlers, such as Arnsdorff, Gnann, Lastinger, Rahn, and Zittrauer, are still common in the area.

Thousands of German Lutherans, Anabaptists (Mennonites), and members of other Protestant sects also immigrated to the South in the early 1700s. Many came from the Palatinate of southern Germany along the Rhine (the modern state of Rhineland-Pfalz) and were called Palatines or Palatinates. German Dunkers from the original congregation, formed in 1708 near the village of Schwarzenau along the Eder River in Germany, came to Virginia and the Carolinas by the late 1700s. Settling near rivers (convenient for full-immersion baptisms), the Dunkers created Dutchman's Creek Settlement near the Yadkin River about 20 miles north of Salisbury, N.C. (the home area of Daniel Boone, who was of Quaker background).

Waldensians (also known as Waldenses) from the Cottian Alps of northern Italy settled Valdese, N.C., in 1893. The Waldensian Church is the oldest evangelical Protestant church in existence, predating the Reformation. Persecuted over several centuries in Italy and France, the Waldensians eventually found haven in Switzerland until their return to the Cottian Alps in 1689. This return from exile is celebrated in Valdese on the second Saturday of August with the annual Waldensian Festival, first held in the American bicentennial year of 1976. The Waldensians were quick to organize bakeries, a mutual assistance society, and a hosiery mill, while continuing to make Waldensian wines and ciders, preserve their architectural traditions and foodways, and speak their language (French, not Italian). Many Waldensians are now Presbyterians and Methodists.

The Protestant Moravians also settled in North Carolina. Persecuted for their faith in Bohemia and Moravia, the Moravians found a sponsor in the Saxon Count Nicholas Ludwig von Zinzendorf. They formed an unsuccessful settlement briefly near Savannah, Ga., in 1733–40. By 1753 they had settled near what is today Winston-Salem, N.C. They called their new home Wachovia—a name adopted by the huge North Carolina banking firm that originated there—in honor of the Zinzendorf family estate in the Austrian Wachau Valley. Their first communities were at Bethabara and Bethania, but the central Moravian town, founded in 1766, was Salem.

As did the Quakers who migrated in significant numbers to North and South Carolina, and to Georgia beginning in the mid-1770s, the Moravians emphasized education and set up a school for the Cherokee in the first decades of the 19th century. The Quakers still maintain Guilford College in Greensboro, N.C. (begun in 1837), and the Moravian settlement at Winston-Salem remains home to a girl's boarding school and a women's college. Old Salem attracts many domestic and international tourists with its living history museum interpreting the 18th- and 19th-century Moravian lifestyle. Several blocks of the settlement preserve the architectural style of their homeland, employing *Fachwerk* (half-timbering, or timber-framed buildings infilled with brick or wattle and daub and often covered with plaster). Moravian spiced cookies and sugar cakes are marketed across the state and beyond. Residents of Winston-Salem decorate for the Christmas holidays with the Moravian multipointed star, which appears on porches and in hallways from the first Sunday of Advent through 7 January (Old Christmas).

Jews also came to the South in significant numbers in the colonial period. The first Jewish immigrants to the South were Sephardic, descendants of Jews expelled from Portugal and Spain in the late 1400s. Two of the oldest Jewish communities in America began in the 1730s in Charleston and Savannah. By the late 18th century nearly one-quarter of America's Jewish population had settled in these cities. By the mid-19th century Ashkenazi, Yiddish-speaking Jews from Eastern and Central Europe, had come to predominate both Charleston and Savannah congregations. The first Jewish governor in America was David Emanuel, elected governor of Georgia in 1801. In 1819 Moses Elias Levy, of Sephardic heritage, purchased 92,000 acres near Gainesville, Fla., and developed an agricultural community for European Jews escaping persecution. Named Pilgrimage Plantation, the colony was destroyed at the outbreak of the Second Seminole War in 1835. Between 1850 and 1880 northern Florida became home to several more enduring Jewish communities. One of the earliest was at Jacksonville, where Democrat Morris A. Dzialynski became mayor in 1881. Jews fought for the Confederacy in the Civil War and occupied political offices such as surgeon general and secretary of state. Judah P. Benjamin filled the latter position, had his image on the Confederate two-dollar bill, and escaped Union troops by hiding in the Gamble Mansion in Florida's Manatee County.

While Jewish women joined southern organizations such as the United Daughters of the Confederacy, exclusion of Jews from country clubs and New Orleans Catholic Mardi Gras krewes persisted into the 20th century. However, the Krewe du Jieux now follows the annual Zulu parade with Jewlu, a marching club with a jazz-infused klezmer band that tosses painted bagels to parade crowds. Jewish communities in southern cities have involved themselves in surprising ways in other civic traditions and hybrid foodways (for example, Creole matzoh balls and Pesach[Passover] fried green tomatoes). German Jews settling in Memphis, Tenn., founded Reform Judaism congregations, and later arrivals from Eastern Europe formed Orthodox congregations. While these congregations continue to maintain different levels of observance, they cooperate in the ASBEE-Kroger Annual Kosher BBQ Contest and Festival—a pork-free event that also involves other Memphis Jewish organizations such as B'nai B'rith Youth, the Jewish Boy Scouts, and Chabad Lubavitch of Tennessee, a Hasidic organization.

Today, Jews constitute about 2.2 percent of the U.S. population. Twenty-one percent live in the South, and about 10 percent of all American Jews reside in

Florida. Some of the largest concentrations of southern Jewish populations are in Fort Lauderdale (215,000), Miami (135,000), South Palm Beach County and West Palm Beach, Fla., and Atlanta (80,000).

The first Germans had come to Virginia in 1608, the year after the founding of Jamestown and 12 years before the Pilgrims landed at Plymouth Rock, but some of these first arrivals left the English settlement to join Chief Powhatan. Along with those seeking religious freedom, Swiss and German speakers from Alsace in France also settled in the piedmont in the first half of the 18th century at places called Germantown, Frankford, and Germania — place names that re-appeared with frequency when Germans later settled west of the Appalachian mountains. With the Scots-Irish, they were the predominant settlers on the Virginia frontier and in the Blue Ridge Mountains. The culture that Scots-Irish, German, and English settlers shaped in the Virginia frontier spread across the Backcountry and into the Midwest.

So many Germans came to 18th-century Louisiana that the area on the Mississippi River in today's parishes of St. John and St. Charles acquired the appellation "German Coast." Most came from the German Rhineland, but some also came from Switzerland. Near places such as Bayou des Allemands (Germans' Bayou) they intermarried with Acadians, which explains why some Germanic surnames (such as Folse, Himel, Toups, and Stelly) are now considered Cajun. Louisiana was home to more German arrivals in the 1850s, but by the 1890s many Germans were once again going to Virginia, where they were the largest immigrant group at that time. These new Germans settled across the state, with significant numbers choosing Richmond. Many were second- and third-generation Americans who moved to Virginia from Maryland, Pennsylvania, or New York but still spoke German. A German-American association formed in 1890 in Richmond and sponsored an annual German Day. President Ronald Reagan officially proclaimed 6 October 1987 German-American Day, as approved by Congress, and Virginia's governor also issues an annual proclamation. Today, German heritage societies are active beyond the Tidewater across the South. German architectural and farming traditions are interpreted at many southern museums, such as the Frontier Culture Museum in Staunton, Va., and the 19th-century German pioneer village at New Braunfels, Tex.

Germans are the largest ethnic group in the United States. Twenty-three percent of the population reported German ancestry in the 1990 census. A smaller number (42.8 million, or 15 percent of the population) reported German or part-German ancestry in 2000. Although now surpassed by Latinos, Americans of German ancestry still count for nearly one out of every six Americans responding to the census. However, only a few of the 29 states in which German was the largest ancestry group (in terms of percentages of state populations) in 2000 were in the South. Virginia had 828,644 residents, or 11.7 percent of its population, self-identify as German, West Virginia (tangentially southern) had 14 percent, Kentucky had 12.7 percent, and Florida had 11.8 percent. However, in Florida, Virginia, and Texas, German was the ancestry reported more frequently than "American," and Texas had the highest number of respondents, with 2,068,981 self-identifying as German (although this figure is only 9.9 percent of the Texas population).

Although German is the nation's largest self-reported ethnic group, few German Americans now exhibit ethnic boundary markers. Exceptions include the Amish and Mennonites (often of Swiss or Dutch origin), who have also settled throughout the South in the last century. Amish and Mennonites moved to Punta Gorda and Sarasota, Fla., originally to grow celery in the 1930s. Their settlement at Pinecraft is now a neighborhood within the Sarasota city limits. In addition to a Saturday farmers market, they operate at least five Amish restaurants in the city (Dutch Oven, Sugar & Spice, Yoder's, Dutch Haus, and Der Dutchman), offering shoofly pie and spaetzle (noodles). Beginning in the 1960s Amish and Mennonites also began settling in the Ozarks and in Tennessee at small rural communities like Belvedere, Tenn., where they still rely on farming and woodcrafting, maintain a distinctive style of religious faith, wear plain clothing, continue traditional foodways, and are endogamous. Yet, other Mennonite communities, such as that associated with College Hill Mennonite Church in Tampa, Fla., or the Iglesia Menonita Encuentro de Renovacion in Miami, are ethnically and occupationally diverse.

The Dutch and the Swiss have also had an impact on southern states in their formative periods. While Dutch merchants had come to Jamestown in the 1640s, Dutch settlers first arrived in Kentucky in the early 1780s from Pennsylvania and built meetinghouses in the tradition of the Dutch Reform Church. In Mercer County, Ky., the Old Mud Meeting House of timber framework with wattle and daub still stands near Harrodsburg. Swiss and German settlers led by Baron Christoph von Graffenried settled the second-oldest town in North Carolina, New Bern, at the confluence of the Trent and Neuse Rivers in 1709–10. Over 12,000 North Carolinians claim Swiss descent today, including members of Charlotte's Swiss Society, which regularly holds Jass (a Swiss card game) tournaments. The Swiss Descendants' Club of London, Ky., commemorates those who settled the Kentucky frontier.

In 1869 the Tennessee Colonization Agency recruited close to 100 Swiss families to the Cumberland Plateau. Finding the proffered land unimproved and remote from railroad access, half of the would-be colonists left. Those who re-

mained settled in the area around Beersheba Springs and formed the community of Gruetli-Lager, where Baggenstoss, Bahnholzer, Bouldin, Segrist, Nuss-
baum, and Zaugg are still common surnames. As elsewhere in the South, their
German language, *Deustch*, caused them to be called "Dutch" by neighbors,
and when these Swiss opened a bakery in Grundy County just over a century
ago, they named it the Dutch Maid. The bakery still offers traditional pastries
and imported Swiss candies. Descendants of these Swiss settlers continued to
produce traditional Swiss cheeses into the 1970s and also founded the Marugg
Company, which produces traditional scythes for haying. The annual Swiss Historical Society Celebration takes place each July at the Stoker-Stampfli Farm
Museum and features tours of the old farm buildings, local musicians, and,
of course, bratwurst and sauerkraut. Other Swiss settled in Hohenwald near
Columbia, Tenn. Just over 10,000 Tennesseans reported Swiss ancestry on the
2000 census.

The experience of the Irish in the South aptly illustrates how ethnic, rather
than racial, politics have been largely ignored in studies of antebellum southern life. A significant escalation of Catholic Irish immigration to America began
in the second decade of the 19th century, prior to the famines. Much has been
written about their negative experiences in the Northeast, but those 10 percent
who settled south of the Mason-Dixon Line have received less attention. Settling largely in urban areas, the Irish helped maintain urban growth rates in the
South, with 65 percent of South Carolina's Irish living in Charleston and 58 percent of the Irish living in Alabama choosing Mobile. In Georgia, Augusta and
Atlanta had sizable Irish populations and Savannah was home to almost 5 percent of the South's antebellum Irish born. Common surnames of Irish settlers
in Georgia included Thompson, O'Neill, Ryan, Griffin, Luckett, and Darden.

Louisiana, the most Catholic of southern states, attracted the most South-
bound Irish, 60 percent of whom lived in New Orleans by 1860. Many Irish
came to New Orleans on ships used to transport cotton to Liverpool (Irish passengers made the return trip more lucrative for shipping merchants) and continued to work in the shipyards or worked digging canals along the Mississippi
River. Although they never had a "Quarter" in New Orleans, their cultural and
occupational solidarity fostered the notion of the city's Irish Channel neighborhood, which still references their unique New Orleans Irish identity.

In the Northeast, social conditions caused Irish immigrants to turn inward
and refuse to assimilate. Irish immigrants to the South, never seriously threat-
ening the status quo or dominating the population of any city, had a greater
opportunity for acceptance and, in some cases, social mobility despite a rigid
class system. They also met with greater acceptance in the antebellum South

because of their contributions to the urban work force (depleted by demands for rural slave labor) and their willingness to take on potentially high-mortality occupations deemed too dangerous for slaves. Hibernian societies and other immigrant-aid organizations formed in Atlanta, Charleston, New Orleans, and Savannah. In each city, Irish Catholic communities also found a focus in church life: New Orleanians erected St. Patrick's Church in 1833, and Savannahans began the Cathedral of St. John the Baptist in 1799.

The Civil War hastened the decline of ethnic distinctiveness for many groups, as regional loyalties reshaped ethnic as southern identities. Seeking parallels between their southern experience and their Irish history, Irish immigrants' ethnic activities in the 19th century (parades, fund-raisers, and other events) placed a celebration of Irishness firmly within a southern context. Likewise, contemporary celebrations of Irishness tend to blend with southern themes. For example, in 2003 the town of Erin, Tenn., celebrated St. Patrick's Day with a fish fry, wildlife display, and parade incorporating Confederate battle flags, beauty pageant queens, Shriners dressed as stereotypical hillbillies, pots of "gold," a regiment of Irish Confederate reenactors, slogans in the Irish language, bagpipe bands, and even a float with a young man posing as the crucified Christ. Since 1854 the town of McEwen, Tenn., has held an annual Irish Picnic (now each July) that features music, Irish dancing, and a flea market, but it is best known for being named in 1988 by the *Guinness Book of World Records* as the world's largest outdoor barbecue. Savannah is home to one of the largest St. Patrick's Day parades in the country. First organized in 1824, the parade now winds through the city's historic squares for over four hours and attracts close to 400,000 visitors. Irish and Celtic festivals featuring Irish folk music and Irish step-dancing competitions take place annually throughout the South, and Gaelic sporting clubs are becoming more prominent on the southern cultural landscape with the arrival of new immigrants in the 1980s and 1990s. In 2000, 10.8 percent of Americans self-identified as Irish on the census and were the second-largest ancestry group nationally. Of southern states, Florida reported the highest percentage (10.3 percent) and Mississippi reported the lowest (6.9 percent).

While the Welsh were not prominent in the settlement of the South (their immigration to Pennsylvania is better known), a number of Welsh heritage societies flourish today, such as the Welsh Society of the Carolinas, the St. David's Welsh Society of Georgia, and the Alabama Welsh Society. Florida is home to two St. David's Societies, and Knoxville, Tenn., and Fredericksburg, Va., also have Welsh societies. The 2000 census reveals that many southern towns with total populations of 30,000–40,000, such as Florence, Ala., and Lynchburg,

Va., report modest populations (100–200) that indicate an active awareness of Welsh ancestry. Cornish heritage societies are also forming in Texas, and Cornish Cousins of the Southeast is an eight-state society designed to unite Cornish descendants living in Florida, North and South Carolina, Georgia, Alabama, Tennessee, Kentucky, and Virginia. In 2005 the Cornish Cousins of the Southeast sponsored a gathering at Mars Hill College in western North Carolina, a location selected because of the Cornish presence in relatively nearby Ducktown, Tenn., Gold Hill, N.C., and Dahlonega, Ga.

Scottish immigrants to the South were members of three distinct ethnic groups: Highland Scots, Lowland Scots, and the Scots-Irish (or Ulster Scots), who had settled in Northern Ireland before immigrating to America. On America's first census in 1790, people of Scottish birth or descent represented 8.3 percent of the population. The South had the highest percentage of residents with Scottish origins, led by Georgia (15.5 percent), South Carolina (15.1 percent), North Carolina (14.8 percent), and Virginia (10.2 percent). Some of the first St. Andrew's Societies, Scottish immigrant aid societies, formed in Charleston (1729, the first in North America), Savannah (ca. 1737), and Alexandria, Va. (ca. 1760). Solicited by the Trustees for Establishing the Colony of Georgia, hundreds of Highlander families immigrated to the pine barrens of the Georgia coast beginning in January 1736 to settle and protect the new British colony under military governor James Oglethorpe.

North Carolina was such a popular destination for Highlanders that it earned the epithet "land of the God-blessed Macs." Highlander immigration, especially from the Western Highlands and Isles, began in the early 1730s and increased through the late 1760s, peaking in the two years before 1776. Induced by bad harvests and the oppressive social and political climate following the failed Jacobite Risings, whole communities immigrated together. Descendants of Cape Fear Valley Highlanders pioneered settlement in Alabama, Tennessee, Mississippi, and Texas. Well over 1,200 had settled Argyle in Florida's Panhandle (near DeFuniak Springs in Walton County) by the mid-19th century.

Close to 100 communities across the South host annual Scottish Highland games, with their accompanying clan society gatherings and dancing, bagpiping, harp, and fiddle competitions. Southern Scottish Americans annually celebrate Tartan Day on 6 April, St. Andrew's Day on 30 November, and the birthday of 18th-century poet Robert Burns on 25 January. All southern states have active Scottish country dance groups and Scottish heritage societies.

The first Lowland Scots were transported to Charleston, S.C., in 1682–83 for being Covenanters (Presbyterians seeking political and religious liberty in Scotland). Many later immigrants (even those among the landed and professional classes) arrived as indentured servants. Lowlanders assimilated most rapidly of the three Scottish ethnicities. They did not as often settle in groups, and while Highlanders retained Gaelic for generations, Lowland Broad Scots tended to give way within one generation to more American, upwardly mobile accents and dialects.

In part because of repressive trade laws, famine, and a decline in the linen industry, more than 100,000 Ulster Scots came to the colonies between the second decade of the 1700s and about 1760. They were considered Irish until the Revolution when, as Patriots, they named themselves Scots-Irish to convey their distinctiveness from Loyalist Scots-Highlanders. Later the name served to distinguish them from Celtic or native Catholic Irish, who came to America in the hundreds of thousands in the 19th century.

The Scots-Irish remained a separate group in America through religion, politics, a tendency to settle on the frontier, and choice, rather than by any continuing affinity with Ulster, where they had always been marginal (even among other Protestants). They famously brought Jack tales, ballads, and fiddle traditions to their new country and, with Germans and Scandinavians who also settled on the frontier, forged a vernacular architectural style.

The Scots-Irish comprised the largest number of non-English Europeans coming to the colonies during the 18th century. More than half of the European settlements in Appalachia and the Ozarks were those of Scots-Irish, with relatively isolated, individual family homesteads employing a mixed economy of animal husbandry and diversified crops. Along with the Germans, the Scots-Irish were the largest ethnic group to enter America in colonial times and remain the largest ethnic group in the South today. Approximately half of all Scots-Irish in the United States (47 percent) live in the southern region.

In the late 19th century, the United States received new immigrants from Southern and Eastern Europe, but the war-devastated South drew comparatively few of them. Those immigrating to the South after the Civil War retain some of the most distinctive traditions and enduring communities but compose significantly lower percentages of the southern population than older, established European and African groups (although their numbers are sometimes larger than American Indians in southern states).

The South had become home to small numbers of Italians before the late 19th century. Italians arrived in Jamestown in 1622, they accompanied French explorers on the Mississippi River in the 1680s, and southern Italians fought in the American Revolution. In 1850 Louisiana had the largest Italian-born population in the United States. Before Italian unification in 1861, New Orleans was one of the primary destinations of Italian immigrants to America, especially immigrants from the Kingdom of Sicily. Southern Italians and Sicilians continued to prefer predominantly Catholic Louisiana; almost 16,000 had taken on farmwork in the state by the beginning of World War I. Italian immigrants came in significant numbers from 1880 to 1920, especially farmers who found employment with southern plantation owners. In Texas they worked in the railroad and mining industries and farmed cotton and rice, and in Louisiana and Mississippi they worked on sugar and cotton plantations—often displacing African American workers there. Children frequently worked in the fields alongside both parents.

The experiences of Italian Americans in the South were not always happy: their dark complexions led them to be subjected to Jim Crow discrimination and, even in New Orleans (where a portion of the French Quarter became Little Sicily and Little Palermo), there were lynchings. Some owned small grocery stores, and many Louisiana Italians eventually bought land in Tangipahoa Parish and grew strawberries for which the area is still famous. The industrial centers of Birmingham, Ala., and Chattanooga, Tenn., also attracted Italian immigrants after the Civil War, as did more rural areas in Arkansas that became home to settlements of northern Italians. Several hundred Genoese settled Tonitown, Ark., where an annual grape festival still honors their main crop and where surnames such as Ardemagni, Bariola, Ceola, Maestri, Morsani, Pianalto, Sbanotto, Taldo, and Zulpo remain common. By the first decade of the 20th century, Italians also lived at Daphne and Lambeth, Ala., and Valdese, N.C. Italians constitute the seventh-largest ethnic group according to the 2000 census (5.6 percent of the U.S. population), yet they compose less than 3 percent of the populations of many southern states. Louisiana still has one of the highest percentages, with Italians numbering 4.4 percent of the state population, outnumbered by Florida with 6.3 percent.

Louisiana Italians often sponsored St. Joseph's Day altars on 19 March (the feast day of the saint); these were also once popular in Tampa, Fla., where Italians (particularly Sicilians) had come to work in the cigar industry. Communities held processions, and families constructed altars with baked goods and other foods in anticipation of Saint Joseph's intervention for a particular need. While this tradition has declined in the last two decades, ethnic organizations such as the Sons of Italy and local branches of the National Italian American Foundation remain popular across the South, as do heritage societies such as the Italian Cultural Association of Greater Austin, Tex., and the Italian-American Club of Venice, Fla., which sponsor annual festivals. Many Italian American men are also involved in Catholic fraternities such as the Knights of Columbus. In Tampa's neighboring Ybor City, historic Italian social clubs, such as the century-old L'Unione Italiana, endure. Ybor had a Latin American Fiesta (of which Elvis Presley was honorary king in 1961) and now has an association of that name that operates as a krewe in Tampa's pre-Lenten, pirate-themed Gasparilla festivities. (When the original fiesta began in 1927, the term "Latin" meant "Spanish, Cuban, or Italian," not "Central or South American," as "Latino" implies today.)

Other southern Europeans who became southerners in America include the Greeks, who first arrived at St. Augustine, Fla., in 1768. Greek merchants and sailors also settled in New Orleans in the 1700s and founded the first Greek Orthodox Church in America there in 1864. While Greeks settled in south Alabama and coastal Mississippi, one of the largest Greek settlements in America began north of Tampa at Tarpon Springs in 1895. The sponge harvesting industry on the Gulf of Mexico had attracted well over 2,000 Greeks by the first decade of the 20th century. Floridian Greek communities also exist in Miami, West Palm Beach, Orlando, and Jacksonville. Today, over 18 percent of Greek Americans live in the South, with population concentrations also in urban areas of Georgia, Alabama, North Carolina, and Virginia. Ethnic identification remains strong. More recent immigrants speak at least some Greek in the home. Traditional music is common both at home and at public events, and Greek musicians are available for hire in southern cities such as Columbia, S.C., Gulf Shores, Ala., Biloxi, Miss., and Little Rock, Ark. Greek restaurants are plentiful from southern Appalachia to the Lowcountry, and Texas Greek communities sponsor food festivals in Houston, Waco, Fort Worth, and Dallas. Many such events occur at local Greek Orthodox churches, which provide a strong community focus for Greeks in the South.

Many Eastern Europeans went to the North or Midwest in the 19th century, but Texas (with its larger, productive farms) attracted more of these newcomers than other southern states. The Slavic Lutheran Wends came to Texas in 1855 from Lusatia in eastern Germany to avoid forced Germanization. The Wends, who called themselves Sorbs, settled in Lee County in a town they named Serbin. Their descendants still hold a Wendish festival, participate in a Wendish heritage society, and create traditional Easter eggs using wax batik and embossing.

In the early 1800s, non-Moravian Czechs began forming small communities in Georgia, Alabama, Mississippi, and, in particular, Texas (home to 250 of them). Today, almost 190,000 Texans claim Czech ancestry. In 2006 Caldwell, Tex., held the 22nd annual Kolache Festival, celebrating Czech heritage and Texans' favorite stuffed pastry. At Caldwell's Czech Heritage Museum, visitors may view displays of "Tex-Czech" heritage, including shepherds' equipment, bagpipes, flutes, and Wallachian beekeeping traditions (Wallachia now being in Romania). The central Texas city of West claims to be the "Czech heritage capital" of Texas and since 1976 has hosted the annual Westfest celebration, which attracts as many as 25,000 attendees. The festival features a Catholic "Polka Mass" with hymns sung to polkas and waltzes, "Miss Westfest" and baking contests, a parade, horseshoe and washer pitching, and demonstrations of 19th-century Czech settlers' crafts. Taroky, a Czech card game, remains popular in West, and tournaments regularly take place in Temple, Victoria, and Fort Worth.

While many southern Czechs and Hungarians have joined Protestant denominations, others in Texas and Louisiana remain Catholic. In Louisiana's twin towns of Libuse and Kolin, annual festivals celebrate Czech dancing, foodways, music, and needlework. Of the more than 5,000 who now claim Czech ancestry in the state, only the elders speak the language. Livingston Parish, La., is home to the largest rural Hungarian settlement in the United States. Socially isolated and largely endogamous through the early 20th century, Hungarians there became assimilated Hungarian Americans by the nation's bicentennial year, and at today's Hungarian heritage events participants are as likely to hear New Orleans jazz as Hungarian folk music.

The most recent Europeans to enter the South have come in significant numbers since the collapse of the Soviet Union (most significantly Russians, Ukrainians, and Poles). A large proportion have chosen Florida (the southern state with the largest percentage of foreign-born residents after Texas; 13.3 percent of Florida's foreign born are from Europe). Bulgarians, Hungarians, Estonians, Romanians, and Poles have multiple cultural associations in Florida. However, many have also settled in Virginia and Texas. Nearly 3 in every 10 European-born immigrants between 1990 and 2000 had a bachelor's degree or higher. Bulgarians had one of the highest labor force participation rates of the total foreign-born population, and 53.9 percent of immigrants had a bachelor's degree or higher (the percentage for Russians was 51.7). These new immigrants are more likely to work in professional and management occupations than the foreign-born population from outside of Europe.

By 2000 almost 500,000 Russians had come to the South, settling mostly in urban areas. Russian Jews readily join local congregations, and Russian Orthodox parishes are growing rapidly in Houston, near Atlanta, and especially in Florida. Even tiny towns such as Dover in central Florida (population 2,800) have Ukrainian congregations, and larger cities, such as Charlotte, also have Ukrainian American cultural societies. Cities such as Atlanta and Orlando now have schools of Russian ballet. Specialty food shops run by new immigrants (and predominantly patronized by new immigrants) abound, and even chain grocery stores in areas with high rates of recent Russian settlement now stock borscht, Kindzmarauli wine, and Ukrainian cookies and candy. Many southern communities are now seeing the growing popularity of Russian and Turkish steam baths, which are also catching on with non-Russian clientele. While some playful creolizations such as deep-fried cabbage rolls might not endure, these new European immigrants are sure to contribute cultural traditions that may one day be deemed southern, or at least be celebrated in a southern style.

CELESTE RAY
University of the South

Valentine Belfiglio, *The Italian Experience in Texas* (1995); Carl A. Brasseaux, ed., *A Refuge for All Ages: Immigration in Louisiana History* (1996); Barbara Carpenter, ed., *Ethnic Heritage in Mississippi* (1992); Gilbert Din, *The Canary Islanders of Louisiana* (1988); Leonard Dinnerstein and Mary Dale Palsson, eds., *Jews in the South* (1973); Walter Edgar, *South Carolina: A History* (1998); Marcie Cohen Ferris, *Matzoh Ball Gumbo: Culinary Tales of the Jewish South* (2005); Peter Steven Gannon, *Huguenot Refugees in the Settling of Colonial America* (1985); Henry Glassie, *Patterns in the Material Folk Culture in the Eastern United States* (1969); David Gleeson, *The Irish in the South, 1815–1877* (2001); Patricia Griffin, *Mullet on the Beach: The Minorcans of Florida, 1768–1788* (1991); David Hackett-Fischer, *Albion's Seed: Four British Folkways in America* (1989); Terry G. Jordan-Bychkov, *The Upland South: The Making of an American Folk Region and Landscape* (2003); James Leyburn, *The Scotch-Irish: A Social History* (1962); Ella Lonn, *Foreigners in the Confederacy* (1940, 2000); Duane Meyer, *The Highland Scots of North Carolina, 1732–1776* (1961); Earl Neihaus, *The Irish in New Orleans* (1965); Maida Owens, in *Swapping Stories: Folktales from Louisiana*, ed. Carl Lindahl, Maida Owens, and C. Renne Harvison (1997); Anthony Parker, *Scottish Highlanders in Colonial Georgia* (1997); Celeste Ray, *Highland Heritage: Scottish Americans in the American South* (2001), *Transatlantic Scots* (2005); John Shelton Reed, *One South: An Ethnic Approach to Regional Culture* (1982); Robert Rosen, *The Jewish Confederates* (2000); Claus Wust, *The Virginia Germans* (1969); Joseph Zierden and Martha Zierden, eds., *Another's Country: Archaeological and Historical Perspectives on Cultural Interactions in the Southern Colonies* (2002).

Historic African Ethnicities

During the past few decades, scholars have made great progress in pinpointing patterns of introduction of African ethnicities into four major regions of the American South: the Chesapeake, the Carolinas, lower Louisiana, and the Gulf South. This progress has been mainly the result of the creation and use of relational databases as innovative tools in history. The two major relevant databases are the Trans-Atlantic Slave Trade Database and the Louisiana Slave Database, 1719–1820. The Trans-Atlantic Slave Trade Database gives very substantial information about Atlantic slave-trade voyages, which brought enslaved Africans directly from African regions and ports to colonies, states, and ports in the United States. However, this database contains little information on ethnicity, nor does it take into account the transshipment of slaves to other ports and regions after they arrived at their initial port of sale in North America. Its use therefore involves considerable speculation about which ethnicities were exported from particular African ports and regions during particular times, as well as about their final destinations. This drawback can be overcome to a significant extent by studying the African ethnicities of slaves listed in documents elsewhere in the Americas (the British West Indies, Brazil, and Spanish America) during particular time periods. The Louisiana Slave Database gives more precise information about African ethnicities. It was constructed from documents recording self-reported ethnicities of African slaves located in particular times and places in lower Louisiana. These largely self-identified African ethnicities were found in documents written primarily in French, secondarily in Spanish, and the remainder in English.

Documents generated in English colonies contain comparatively little information about African ethnicities. Neither English colonies nor the United States required notaries to record and keep documents involving slaves as public records. Therefore many sales of slaves, inventories of slaves after the death of masters, wills, marriage contracts, and other types of documents were private papers of individuals. Many of these documents have not been preserved. Few of these English-language documents recorded the African ethnicities of the slaves. Newspaper advertisements for runaway slaves are the major source of information about African ethnicities. Daniel Littlefield pioneered the study of such advertisements for South Carolina, and Michael A. Gomez effectively used them for runaway slaves in his study of African ethnicities in the United States. Margaret Washington Creel pioneered a predatabase study of the origins of slaves in the Sea Islands off the coast of South Carolina and Georgia. However, slaves who ran away were not necessarily representative of the slaves who were present in any particular colony or state.

Studies of the African Diaspora in the Americas began mainly during the early 20th century among anthropologists, most notably Nina Rodriguez in Brazil, Fernando Ortiz in Cuba, and, a generation later, Frances and Melville Herskovits in the United States. Fieldwork was a primary methodology. They often studied communities of African descent in the Americas, linking them with particular regions or ethnicities in Africa by seeking out shared cultural traits. Their work is useful, informative, and fascinating and their methodologies more sophisticated than some recent critics have credited. Nevertheless, their approach poses problems for the study of the African Diaspora in the Americas. Religion, worldview, and aesthetic principles—including the styles and social role of the plastic arts, music, musical instruments, and dance—are among the most enduring and resilient cultural heritages. But they are also the most generalized. There are many common cultural features in Africa. It is not always easy to disaggregate which features are characteristic of any particular ethnicity or region. Very few scholars are familiar with a substantial number of African languages. Some seize upon a word or name they recognize and extrapolate it widely to prove the presence and influence of a particular African ethnicity in America. But the same or similar names and words exist in several African languages and can have the same, a similar, or a different meaning.

The result is sometimes romanticized and inaccurate views of the influence of particular African ethnicities and languages. In the United States, Swahili becomes the African language, but few speakers of Swahili were brought to the United States. Yoruba becomes the African ethnicity, although Yoruba (written "Nago" or "Lucumí" in American documents) presence was not very substantial anywhere in the Americas before the late 18th century. Except for Louisiana, where Nago (Yoruba) were 4 percent of identified African ethnicities, Yoruba presence in the United States was insignificant. The numbers and proportions of African slaves brought from the Gold Coast/Ghana to the United States have been exaggerated. Thus, the mythology about the African ethnicities of slaves brought to the United States endures.

African ethnicities from Greater Senegambia/Upper Guinea played a major role in populating the South. Greater Senegambia extends from Senegal through Sierra Leone. Bamana, Fulbe, Mandingo, and Wolof were prominent among Africans shipped from Senegal. Kanga, Temne, and some Gola were shipped from Sierra Leone. The skills of these Africans were especially needed in rice and indigo production and in the cattle industries of Carolina, Georgia, the Florida Panhandle, and lower Louisiana. During the 18th century, Greater Senegambians were more clustered in colonies and states that became part of the United States than anywhere else in the Americas. These states include Carolina, Georgia, Louisiana, the Lower Mississippi Valley, and the northern coast of the Gulf of Mexico extending across Texas, Louisiana, Mississippi, Alabama, and the Florida Panhandle. Senegambians also appear in large numbers in the early Chesapeake (Maryland and Virginia).

From the study of transatlantic slave-trade voyages, it appears that the

United States was the chief 18th-century destination of Greater Senegambians after the Northern European powers legally entered the Atlantic slave trade. Studies of transatlantic slave-trade voyages to the United States are reasonably revealing about trends in ethnic composition because there was no large-scale, maritime transshipment trade to other countries. This conclusion must be qualified because of the unknown (and probably unknowable) number and ethnic composition of new Africans transshipped from the Caribbean to the East Coast ports of the United States. But it is likely that Greater Senegambians were quite significant in this traffic because of selectivity in the transshipment trade from the Caribbean. Regarding African ethnicities arriving in Carolina, the artificial separation between Senegambia and Sierra Leone obscures the picture. Thus, the role of Greater Senegambians was very important in Carolina and probably elsewhere as well, including the Sea Islands off the coast of Carolina and Georgia and other rice-growing areas of Carolina, Georgia, and Florida.

The patterns for Louisiana are clear and not at all speculative. In the French slave trade to Louisiana (1719–43), 64.3 percent of the Africans arriving on clearly documented French Atlantic slave-trade voyages came from Senegambia. Using the Trans-Atlantic Slave Trade Database for English voyages to the entire northern coast of the Gulf of Mexico—as well as additional Atlantic slave-trade voyages found in Louisiana documents that were included in the Louisiana Slave Database—reveals that slave-trade voyages coming from Senegambia composed 59.7 percent of all voyages coming directly from Africa to Louisiana and the northern coast of the Gulf of Mexico between 1770 and 1803. Nevertheless, the African coastal origin of Louisiana slaves during the Spanish period was much more varied than what is reflected in Atlantic slave-trade voyages. The vast majority of new Africans arriving in Spanish Louisiana had been transshipped from the Caribbean, especially from Jamaica, where Gold Coast Africans were preferred and retained. Very few Gold Coast/Ghana Africans were found in Louisiana documents. Under Spanish rule (1770–1803), 30.3 percent of Louisiana Africans were from Senegambia and 20.8 percent were from Sierra Leone, totaling 51.1 percent from Greater Senegambia (see Table 1). If we exclude slaves described as "Guinea" or "From the Coast of Guinea" from the Sierra Leone category, Africans from Sierra Leone drop to 6.7 percent. The result is a minimum of 37 percent of Africans of identified ethnicities from Greater Senegambia in Spanish Louisiana. Africans listed as Guinea were likely to be from Sierra Leone.

The large numbers of Greater Senegambians brought to Carolina, Florida, and lower Louisiana involves technology transfer from Africa to the Ameri-

TABLE 1. *Eighteen Most-Frequent African Ethnicities by Gender in Louisiana, 1719–1820*

Ethnicity		Male	Female	Total
Bamana	Individuals	413	53	466
	Percentage	88.6	11.4	100
	Percentage of total Africans	4.9	.6	5.5
Mandingo	Individuals	617	305	922
	Percentage	66.9	33.1	100
	Percentage of total Africans	7.3	3.6	10.9
Nar/Moor	Individuals	101	35	922
	Percentage	74.3	25.7	100
	Percentage of total Africans	1.2	.4	1.6
Poulard/Fulbe	Individuals	160	50	210
	Percentage	76.2	23.8	100
	Percentage of total Africans	1.9	.6	2.5
Senegal/Wolof	Individuals	363	234	597
	Percentage	60.8	39.2	100
	Percentage of total Africans	4.3	2.8	7.1
Kisi	Individuals	51	35	86
	Percentage	59.3	40.7	100
	Percentage of total Africans	.6	.4	1.0
Kanga	Individuals	210	129	339
	Percentage	61.9	38.1	100
	Percentage of total Africans	2.5	1.5	4.0
Aja/Fon/Arada	Individuals	126	117	243
	Percentage	51.9	48.1	100
	Percentage of total Africans	1.5	1.4	2.9
Chamba	Individuals	276	139	415
	Percentage	66.5	33.5	100
	Percentage of total Africans	3.3	1.6	4.9
Hausa	Individuals	122	11	133
	Percentage	91.7	8.3	100
	Percentage of total Africans	1.4	.1	1.6
Mina	Individuals	430	198	628
	Percentage	68.5	31.5	100
	Percentage of total Africans	5.1	2.3	7.4
Nago/Yoruba	Individuals	247	111	358
	Percentage	69.0	31.0	100
	Percentage of total Africans	2.9	1.3	4.2

TABLE 1. *Continued*

Ethnicity		Male	Female	Total
Edo	Individuals	38	28	66
	Percentage	57.6	42.4	100
	Percentage of total Africans	.5	.3	.8
Igbo	Individuals	287	237	524
	Percentage	54.8	45.2	100
	Percentage of total Africans	3.4	2.8	6.2
Ibibio/Moko	Individuals	61	21	82
	Percentage	74.4	25.6	100
	Percentage of total Africans	.7	.2	1.0
Calabar	Individuals	88	59	147
	Percentage	59.9	40.1	100
	Percentage of total Africans	1.0	.7	1.7
Kongo	Individuals	2,064	924	2,988
	Percentage	69.1	30.9	100
	Percentage of total Africans	24.4	10.9	35.4
Makwa	Individuals	67	35	102
	Percentage	65.7	34.3	100
	Percentage of total Africans	.8	.4	1.2
Total	Individuals	5,721	2,721	8,442
	Percentage	67.8	32.2	100

Source: Gwendolyn Midlo Hall, Slavery and African Ethnicities in the Americas: Restoring the Links *(2005); calculated from Hall, Louisiana Slave Database, 1719–1820.*

cas. In the two major rice-growing states of Anglo-United States, 44.4 percent of Atlantic slave-trade voyages arriving in Carolina and 62.0 percent arriving in Georgia listed in the Trans-Atlantic Slave Trade Database brought Africans from Greater Senegambia. But the number of slaves on voyages arriving from Greater Senegambia was substantially smaller than on voyages arriving from other African regions.

These gross, static figures are impressive enough. But when we break down calculations for Anglo-United States colonies and states over time and place, we see a wave pattern clustering Africans from Greater Senegambia. In Carolina, 50.4 percent of all Atlantic slave-trade voyages to that colony entered into the Trans-Atlantic Slave Trade Database arrived between 1751 and 1775, with 100 (35.2 percent) coming from Senegambia and 58 (20.4 percent) from Sierra Leone—a total of 55.6 percent coming from Greater Senegambia. Mandingo

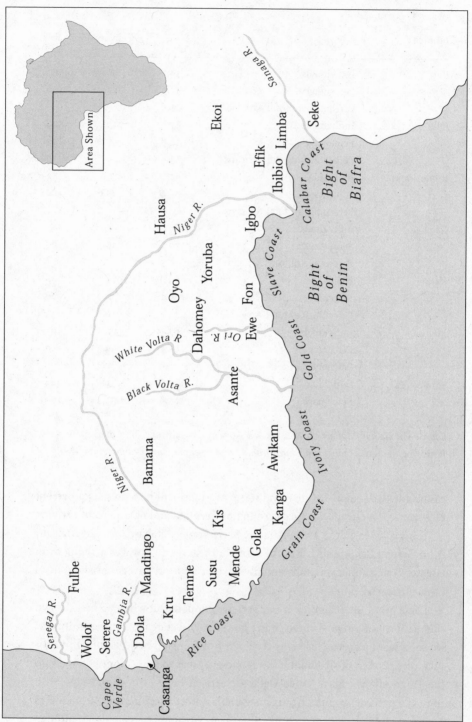

MAP 3: Select Ethnic Groups of Greater Senegambia/Upper Guinea (from Senegal to Sierra Leone) and Lower Guinea East (from the Ivory Coast to Cameroon)

and Fulbe were being exported from both of these regions. During this time period, Britain had occupied the French slave trading posts along the coast of Senegambia. Close to half (44.7 percent) of the English Atlantic slave-trade voyages from Senegambia (narrowly defined as excluding Sierra Leone) went to Britain's North American mainland colonies. Five out of six Atlantic slave-trade voyages to British West Florida ports along the northern coast of the Gulf of Mexico came from Senegambia. It is safe to say that between 1751 and 1775, the majority of slaves loaded aboard English ships leaving from Senegambia were sent to regions that would become part of the United States. As northern traders and Euro-African suppliers took over the Atlantic slave trade on these coasts during the Age of Revolutions (1750–1800), voyages bringing Africans to the United States from Greater Senegambia originated mainly in various ports on the American side, were heavily involved in smuggling and piracy, were never documented in European archives, and were unlikely to be included in the Trans-Atlantic Slave Trade Database. There is little doubt that most of these voyages brought Greater Senegambians to the United States as well as to the British Caribbean and Saint-Domingue/Haiti.

There was a clustering of Atlantic slave-trade voyages from the same African coasts to regional ports in the Chesapeake. The Igbo from the Bight of Biafra had a significant presence in the Chesapeake, but slaves from Greater Senegambia contributed a formative culture for some areas of the Chesapeake, as well. Nearly half of the voyages bringing about 5,000 Africans to Virginia between 1683 and 1721 came from Senegambia (as narrowly defined). The Igbo were valued there for several reasons. Like the Wolof and the Fon, but in contrast to most other African ethnicities, there were as many women as men among them. Igbo women mated freely with men of other ethnicities and they generally had more surviving children than women of other ethnicities. Thus, they were valued in regions that placed a high premium on natural reproduction of the slave population, but Igbo men and women did not adjust well to gang labor. Rice and sugar planters generally refused to buy them. In the Chesapeake, however, tobacco was the major crop and it was grown on small estates.

West Central Africa was at times a significant source of slaves brought to South Carolina. In English-speaking regions they were generally called "Angolans." (In French and Spanish regions they were generally called "Congo.") The Stono Rebellion of 1739 (the largest slave rebellion in the colonies prior to the Revolution) has focused attention on West Central Africans. But a majority of Atlantic slave-trade voyages arrived in Carolina from West Central Africa only between 1730 and 1739. The Stono Rebellion, well described as a Congo revolt, evidently discouraged Carolina planters from bringing in more West

Central Africans. For the rest of the 18th century, Greater Senegambia became the major source of Atlantic slave-trade voyages to South Carolina. West Central Africa did not become a significant source of Africans for Carolina again until 1801, only six years before the foreign slave trade to the United States was outlawed on 1 January 1808. Many of these late-arriving West Central Africans were transshipped to Louisiana to work its burgeoning sugarcane plantations. Throughout the 18th century, some Congo could be found in Louisiana, and Africans from Mozambique (almost entirely Makua) were transshipped to Louisiana from St. Domingue/Haiti. During the Spanish period, the Congo were clustered in New Orleans, but in the early United States period, more Congo were brought to Louisiana's new sugar-producing areas — rural Orleans and St. Charles Parishes. Increasing numbers of the Igbo from the Bight of Biafra were brought to Louisiana, especially after the Atlantic slave trade was outlawed in 1808. The Atlantic slave trade remained legal below the equator, and enslaved Africans smuggled into the United States generally came from slave-trade ships heading for Cuba captured by pirates. The ethnicities of these Africans were heavily Igbo and Congo.

There is clearly a generalized, and sometimes more specific, African influence on religion, music, and culture of the South. Senegambian cultural influences in Louisiana are clear. These include the Louisiana Creole language and the style, social role, and forms of Creole music and cooking (especially gumbo). Evidence of African-influenced religious practices include reverence for ancestors, spirit possession, herbal medicine, and, especially, Bamana names (from Mali) for amulets. Voodoo practices in Louisiana came from two main sources. First, the early and persistent presence of African ethnicities from the Bight of Benin clustered upriver from New Orleans, mainly Fon, Mina, and Nago/Yoruba; and second, from the massive immigration of French Haitians with their slaves, which took place during 1809–10 following the Haitian Revolution of 1807. In both Senegal and Louisiana, there is a large and growing consciousness of common demographic, historic, and cultural ties, and cultural tourism now moves in both directions.

New research continues to refine our perceptions of African origins. In the South Carolina and Georgia Sea Islands, the myth of Yoruba ancestry is being challenged. The Gullah language derives from Sierra Leone, and the word "Gullah" comes from the Gola ethnicity of that land. In religion, reverence for ancestors, the ring shout (a song employing West African dance patterns in which participants shuffle in a single file and clap out a complex counterrhythm), and spirit possession are clearly African in origin, but they are difficult to trace to any particular African ethnicity. Research, especially that by Douglas B. Chambers, continues to trace the Igbo influence on the culture of Virginia. There is an escalating fascination among African-descended peoples to find the ethnicities of their ancestors.

GWENDOLYN MIDLO HALL
New Orleans, Louisiana

Douglas B. Chambers, *Slavery and Abolition* (April, 1997); Margaret Washington Creel, *"A Peculiar People": Slave Religion and Community-Culture among the Gullahs* (1988); David Eltis, David Richardson, Stephen D. Behrendt, and Herbert S. Klein, eds., *The Atlantic Slave Trade: A Database on CD-ROM Set and Guidebook* (1999); Michael A. Gomez, *Exchanging Our Country Marks: The Transformation of African Identities in the Colonial and Antebellum South* (1998); Gwendolyn Midlo Hall, *Africans in Colonial Louisiana: The Development of Afro-Creole Culture in the Eighteenth Century* (1992), *Slavery and African Ethnicities in the Americas: Restoring the Links* (2005); Daniel C. Littlefield, *Rice and Slaves: Ethnicity and the Slave Trade in Colonial South Carolina* (1981); John K. Thornton, *American Historical Review* (October 1991); Lorena Walsh, *From Calabar to Carter's Grove: The History of a Virginia Slave Community* (1997).

Latinos

The term "Latino," often used interchangeably with "Hispanic," refers to people who identify with a Latin American origin or ancestry. The South currently has the fastest-growing Latino population in the United States. Between 1990 and 2000 the Latino population in the South doubled from over 6.5 million to more than 11.5 million, with states like Texas, North Carolina, and Georgia experiencing the most growth. Latinos represent a great diversity of national, socioeconomic, regional, and ethnic differences. While most Latinos in the region are from Mexico or are of Mexican descent, other groups, such as Puerto Ricans, Cubans, Guatemalans, Hondurans, El Salvadorans, Colombians, Peruvians, and Ecuadorians, also have a strong presence in urban and rural areas. Latinos' citizenship status in the United States varies: they are U.S. citizens; immigrants with student, tourist, and work visas; agricultural guest workers; and undocumented individuals. They all share the common bond of the Spanish language, although a significant number of Latin American immigrants also speak an indigenous American language.

While some southern states such as Texas and Florida have had a Latino presence for over a century, most Latinos today—especially in southeastern states like Georgia, North Carolina, Arkansas, Alabama, South Carolina, and Tennessee—have immigrated within the last 20 years or are the children of immigrants. States with the highest national rates of increase of the Latino population between 1990 and 2000 include North Carolina (394 percent), Arkansas (337 percent), Georgia (300 percent), Tennessee (278 percent), South Carolina (211 percent), and Alabama (208 percent). In some counties—like Mecklenburg County, N.C., which encompasses Charlotte—the Latino population has increased by 500 percent since 1990. A majority of the newcomers were young, foreign-born males seeking job opportunities in cities, towns, and rural areas previously unsettled by Latin Americans. In this regard, southern Latino communities differ from those in other regions of the country.

Of all the southern states, Texas has the longest history of Latino settlement and migration. More than one-third of contemporary Texans have Latin American (predominantly Mexican) ancestry. Texas was a territory of Mexico before its annexation by the United States through the Treaty of Guadalupe Hidalgo in 1848. Many Tejanos, or people whose forebears lived in Texas when it was still part of Mexico, are proud of this heritage. As a state bordering Mexico, Texas, predictably, has experienced the recent immigration of many Latinos, especially in its southern and western parts and in large cities like Houston, Dallas, and San Antonio. In these cities, Latino festivals are common and the local cuisine reveals a heavy Mexican influence. Texas's Latino population is the largest in the South, with over 6.5 million people.

Florida also has a history of longtime Latino settlement by Cubans, Puerto Ricans, and Mexicans. As early as the 1940s and 1950s, Mexicans migrated seasonally to Florida to work in orange and other citrus fruit orchards. While Cubans had come to Florida for over a century, the majority living there today are part of the refugee movement that began in the 1960s, when many Cubans started migrating to Miami and other cities to escape the dictatorial regime of Fidel Castro. Throughout Florida, almost 1 million Cubans have built communities and gained political representation as the largest Latino group, making the state attractive to other Latino immigrants. Nearly 100,000 Dominicans live in Florida, which is also home to the second-largest concentration of Puerto Ricans (half a million) in the United States. Jacksonville has a particularly large community of Puerto Ricans. Florida's fast-growing Latino populations are located in Orlando, Miami, and along the Gulf Coast.

In other southeastern states, Latino migration is more recent. States like Georgia, North Carolina, and South Carolina have experienced an unprecedented influx of Latino immigrants in the past 20 years. While some are highly skilled workers with employment and student visas for working in academic institutions and corporations, the majority of Latinos work in the low-skilled sector, and many are undocumented. Their United States–born children form

Bus depot in the city of Celaya, Guanajuato, Mexico, with all destinations listed being in the American South (Niklaus Steiner, photographer)

a rapidly growing subgroup of Latinos in the South. Other Latino populations include refugees from El Salvador, Guatemala, Honduras, and Cuba that the federal government has relocated to cities in the South. A rising number of Latinos have also relocated from other parts of the United States, as in the case of Mexicans who lived in California before moving to the Southeast or Dominicans who have moved to the Charlotte area from New York and Massachusetts. In the South, where there are fewer urban areas than in other parts of the country, Latinos often concentrate in communities by nationality, region, or even by the towns in which they were born. In North Carolina, for example, Costa Ricans have settled in Lincolnton, Guatemalans in Morganton, and Mexicans from the town of Celaya in Orange County.

A number of factors have contributed to this recent demographic change. Economic instability in origin countries is the root of many migrants' desires to seek a better life in the United States. In Mexico, for example, the 1994 devaluation of the peso under President Ernesto Zedillo and the ensuing economic crisis exacerbated widespread poverty in the country and incited a wave of migration to the United States. Today, the U.S. minimum wage is seven times higher than Mexico's minimum wage. Political conflict and environmental disaster are also factors behind the presence of Latino refugee communities in the South. In countries like El Salvador, a bloody civil war between 1980 and 1992 claimed the lives of approximately 75,000 people and caused thousands of refugees to seek asylum in the United States. Armed conflict in Colombia has also displaced thousands, many of whom moved north. In 1998 Hurricane Mitch devastated Honduras, and many of those left homeless have chosen to emigrate.

Perhaps the most important reason why the South has become a new Latino migrant destination is the economic boom of the 1990s and subsequent growth in the region. The South has become an increasingly popular recipient of foreign investment and corporate relocation because of the development of technological, communication, and transportation infrastructures. Notable growth has occurred in North Carolina, where the Charlotte area intensified its banking and finance infrastructure and the Raleigh-Durham area became home to a number of high-tech companies. In Georgia, Atlanta's suburbs have swiftly expanded into the rural areas of counties to the north.

Southern economic prosperity of the 1990s created job opportunities that attracted Latinos living in other regions of the United States as well as Latin American countries. The construction industry relies heavily on Latino labor; in North Carolina, for example, Latinos make up 29 percent of the labor force. The 1996 Olympic Games in Atlanta created a demand for construction workers that attracted thousands of Latino workers and their families. In addition to construction, a number of other industries and agricultural sectors recruit primarily undocumented immigrant labor. As urban areas grow and salaries increase in areas like Atlanta, Memphis, Birmingham, Nashville, and the suburbs of Washington, D.C., the service industry has also expanded, creating jobs for Latinos in restaurants, hotels, elder care, cleaning, and landscape companies.

A visible minority own or manage businesses, restaurants, landscaping companies, or small *tiendas* (stores).

In the South, as in other regions of the United States, agricultural production is reliant upon Latino labor. Meat-processing plants in Virginia, North Carolina, Tennessee, and Georgia employ thousands of Latinos to slaughter and clean chickens and hogs. In Florida, Latinos form the base labor for the seasonal citrus fruit industry, where most oranges are picked by hand by undocumented immigrants for wages that average less than half of what private, nonfarmworkers earn. Other crops harvested include tobacco, Christmas trees, apples, sweet potatoes, and cucumbers. Not all farm labor is undocumented; the federal H2A program, created in 1986, is a temporary guest worker program that allows farmers to hire foreign laborers after documenting a shortage of American workers. One-third of the nation's 30,000 guest workers, primarily Mexican in origin, work on North Carolina farms. A common misconception about undocumented Latino immigrants is that they deplete public resources and do not pay taxes. To the contrary, studies increasingly show that underpaid Latino labor significantly boosts local and state economies. In North Carolina, for example, Latinos have contributed more that $9 billion to the state's economy through their purchases, taxes, and labor.

Strong connections persist between Latino communities in the South and their home countries. Innovations such as the Internet and cheap international phone cards make regular communication possible between family members and friends. The globalized media industry allows the same *telenovela* (soap opera) to be broadcast by the Univision channel in Knoxville, Tenn., and Celaya, Mexico. In cities like Durham, N.C., Latinos are filming soap operas that chronicle life in America. The proliferation of money-sending businesses like Vigo and Western Union also allows migrants to send their paychecks back home electronically, the funds arriving in Mexico within hours.

Physical travel between Latin America and the South has become easier, as bus companies have created routes from anywhere in Mexico to dozens of small-town and large-city destinations in the South. Many Latinos travel seasonally to follow agricultural cycles or to visit family members scattered across North and Central America. A bus trip from the Mexican state of Michoacán to Richmond, Va., takes 24 hours and may stop in Fort Worth, Jacksonville, Athens, and Charlotte before heading north to Virginia. (Such a trip typically costs between $300 and $500.) Another popular mode of travel to and from Latin America involves an extensive network of "coyotes," or guides who illegally transport migrants across the Mexican border to destinations in U.S. cities. Because the U.S. Bureau of Citizenship and Immigration Services has increased fortification of the United States–Mexican border in recent years, the job of a coyote has become increasingly dangerous but more lucrative. Coyote fees for border crossings have increased from $500 in the late 1990s to $1,500 by some accounts in 2004. Travel routes also facilitate the transport of Mexican food products (fruits and vegetables as well as nonperishable goods) by truck to markets in the southern United States.

The strength of migrant communication networks and daily arrival of new immigrants in communities throughout the South constantly reinforce Latino identity and its essential component of Spanish-language use. Spanish radio stations are easily accessible, and Spanish-language newspapers have wide dissemination in cities and rural areas. In cities like Miami, Spanish is spoken everywhere. Some cities have even introduced bilingual education programs in which instructional languages in schools are divided evenly between Spanish and English.

With these transnational connections, Latinos are able to import Latin American products to the United States. Latino-owned *tiendas* sell goods from Mexico and Central America, such as avocados and *nopales* (prickly pear cactus); candles with images of Our Lady of Guadalupe, the patron saint of Mexico and the Americas; and Goya brand canned products. Restaurants buy imported foods and are able to feature national cuisine. El Salvadorian eateries serve *pupusas* (corn flour and cheese tacos), Mexican *taquerias* (taco stands) offer the cinnamon rice drink *horchata*, and Cuban cafés have meat-filled sandwiches cubanos. While some Latino foods share commonalities with traditional southern cuisine (for example, the Mexican version of hominy is called *pozole*), migrants have also brought new foods to the South that vary from traditional "Tex-Mex" cuisine found in fast-food restaurants like Taco Bell. In addition to cheesy beans, fajitas, and nachos, Latinos have introduced handmade corn tortillas, fresh green chile sauces, and plantains (a relative of the banana eaten in the Caribbean), which are quickly becoming a part of southern menus.

While Latino identity is reinforced by transnational connections and frequent arrivals, immigrants also integrate into U.S. society. Latin Americans and their United States–born children learn English, identify themselves as "American," and permanently settle in the United States. Their presence also creates changes in "native" southern communities. Latinos challenge traditional measures of diversity and the always-inadequate oppositions of "white" and "black." Schools and civic organizations are increasingly celebrating Latino Heritage Month in October, and enrollment in Spanish courses is at an all-time high for community colleges in the South.

A number of Latin American religious holidays and traditions are celebrated in the South with variations. Catholicism is the official religion of many Latin American countries, and 70 percent of Latinos in the United States are Catholic. Twenty-three percent of Latinos are Protestant, the majority of which are Pentecostal Evangelical Christian. In the United States, worship services are an important way for Latinos to meet and reconnect with people from home, and areas with high Latino populations have multiple churches offering Spanish-language Masses or church services.

Popular traditions celebrated include the *quinceañera*, in which girls celebrate their fifteenth birthday with a religious ceremony and party. In the United States, as in Latin America, many Latina girls wear elaborate dresses and hire bands to celebrate the event. *El Día de los Reyes* (Three Kings Day), also known as Epiphany, is a Christian holiday celebrated in Mexico and in Mexican American communities in the South on 6 January. Children receive gifts of candy and toys, and families eat a traditional bread roll called *rosca de reyes* with tamales (a cornmeal snack wrapped in corn husks) and hot chocolate.

El Día de los Muertos (the Day of the Dead) is a Mexican holiday honoring deceased loved ones, celebrated on the first day of November. *Cinco de Mayo* (the Fifth of May, often confused with the Mexican Independence Day) commemorates the defeat of the invading French army at Puebla, Mexico, in 1862 and is celebrated in many American cities with Mexican populations. *El Día de la Raza* is celebrated on Columbus Day by many Latinos in recognition of the injustices of European conquest of the New World.

Notable Latino festivals celebrated in the South include the world-famous Calle Ocho (Eighth Street) Festival in Miami, the grand finale to Mardi Gras, which is known as *carnaval* in Latin America. Many southern cities have Latino festivals such as the Gran Fiesta de Fort Worth (15–17 July), the Festival Peachtree Latino in Atlanta (August), the Fiesta del Pueblo in Raleigh (October), Fiesta Latina in Asheville (April), and the Puerto Rican Cultural Parade of Tampa (April).

Music is an important part of Latino identity that is reproduced, improvised, and blended with American southern musical genres. A number of regional and national genres are popular with Latino groups in the South. Tejano music is the folk-derived music of Mexican-descended Texans. Now internationally popular, Tejano music (of which there are a number of subgenres, including polka-influenced *norteño* music) represents the blending of rock and roll, blues, and Mexican accordion music. After breakout Tejano performer Selena Quintanilla Perez and her band Los Dinos added *cumbia* music (a Colombian four-beat rhythm) to Tejano music, the genre began to attract Latino audiences outside of Mexico and southern Texas. Today, Tejano bands routinely tour southern U.S. cities.

Other musical genres popular among Latinos in the South and throughout the world are reggaeton, a music influenced by Caribbean drumming rhythms of Puerto Rico and Jamaica, and hip-hop. Latinos also enjoy salsa, a dance music popular among Cubans and Puerto Ricans; merengue, a two-beat, hip-swaying dance from the Dominican Republic; and the slower *bachata* music, also of Dominican origin, with a *cumbia* beat and electric guitar instrumentation in its contemporary form. Many Latinos consider dancing to be an important part of their culture and identity, and it is nearly always present at festivals, social events, nightclubs, and family gatherings.

HANNAH GILL
University of North Carolina at Chapel Hill

Gastón Espinosa, Virgilio Elizondo, and Jesse Miranda, *Hispanic Churches in American Public Life* (2003); Leon Fink, *The Maya of Morganton: Work and Community in the Nuevo New South* (2003); Ramona Hernández and Francisco L. Rivera-Batiz, *Dominicans in the United States: A Socioeconomic Profile, 2000*, in Dominican Research Monographs (2003); John Kasarda and James H. Johnson, *The Economic Impact of the Hispanic Population on the State of North Carolina* (2006); Rakesh Kochhar, Roberto Suro, and Sonya Tafoya, *The New Latino South: The Context and Consequences of Rapid Population Growth* (2005); Paul A. Levengood, in *The American South in a Global World*, ed. James Peacock, Harry Watson, and Carrie Matthews (2005); Raymond Mohl, in *Globalization and the American South*, ed. James C. Cobb and William Stueck (2005); Arthur D. Murphy, Colleen Blanchard, and Jennifer A. Hill, eds., *Latino Workers in the Contemporary South* (2001).

South Asian and East Asian Ethnicities

In 1989, when the first edition of the *Encyclopedia of Southern Culture* appeared, Asians in the South were largely an underappreciated group. In 1965 Congress passed the Immigration and Nationality Act that removed barriers for Asian immigrants, thus enabling the staggering growth of Asian groups in America. Over the next two decades, the South would lag behind West Coast states, the Midwest industrial centers, and the port cities of the Northeast in attracting Asian immigrants, but the 1990s became a watershed period for the emergence of Asian groups in the region. In that period, for example, the growth rate of Asian Indians in Dixie became second only to Latinos.

The 2000 U.S. Census showed that the total Asian population in the South had grown from 1.3 million in 1990 to 2.3 million. By 2000 Texas, Florida, and Virginia were among the top 10 states in Asian population, and during the 1990s the number of Asians in Georgia, Tennessee, North Carolina, and South Carolina had doubled. Among southern states in 2000, Virginia showed the largest percentage of Asians (4.5 percent), followed by Texas (3.2 percent) and Georgia (2.8 percent). The Chinese, whose history in the South goes back to the first half of the 19th century, represented the largest group, with Indians the second largest. The 1990s also saw the near doubling of the South's Vietnamese, Cambodian, and Korean populations. Only the Japanese failed to experience these tremendous growth rates (see Table 2).

The growth of Asian communities coincided with the recent population boom in many parts of the South, including the major metropolitan areas, like Atlanta and Houston, and the burgeoning suburbs, like Northern Virginia. An unavoidable trope, the term "Asian" encompasses lands and nations that may have little connection to one another except for their eastern location. The label erases the voluminous distinctions between them and works to racialize what are different ethnic groups. National labels such as "Korean" and "Indian" also ignore the tremendously diverse ethnic backgrounds of immigrants from those countries. The term "Indian" indicates a national identity more than an ethnicity, encompassing groups such as Gujaratis, Bengals, Telegus, Tamils, or Rajasthanis. In the South alone, there may be more Gujaratis than Laotians or Japanese. Similarly, the term "Chinese" lumps together families from mainland China, Hong Kong, Taiwan, and Malaysia. Names like "Asian" or "Indian" express a panethnicity that enables assimilation into American culture.

One could explain the Asian presence in the South prior to 1965 as a by-product of two forces: Christian missions and military campaigns and bases. With the possible exception of dislocated Vietnamese and Cambodians who came to the South in the 1970s, these factors hardly account for the recent dramatic increase of Asians; nor do they explain why individuals choose Dixie over California or New England. Among new arrivals, one observes a variety of social, economic, and educational backgrounds. Indians, Chinese, Japanese, and Koreans generally occupy the top end of the economic scale, with many involved in white-collar businesses, engineering, medical professions, computer science, and hotel management. The involvement of Indians in hotel management is well known and is depicted in the 1991 film *Mississippi Masala*, set in Greenwood, Miss. By one estimate they manage about 20 percent of the hotels in South Carolina. In Atlanta, Ga., the Korean population has more than doubled in the last decade, with over 500 Korean-owned businesses and 40 churches. A seven-mile stretch of the Buford Highway that runs through At-

TABLE 2. *State Populations of Asian Southerners, 2000*

State	Total	Indian	Cambodian	Chinese	Filipino	Hmong	Japanese	Korean	Vietnamese
Alabama	30,868	6,900	552	6,039	2,727	3	1,966	4,116	4,628
Arkansas	19,869	3,104	23	2,971	2,489	27	1,036	1,550	3,974
Florida	261,672	70,740	2,447	44,546	54,310	118	10,897	19,139	33,190
Georgia	170,469	46,132	2,905	25,749	11,036	1,468	7,242	28,745	29,016
Kentucky	29,400	6,771	314	5,171	3,106	10	3,683	3,818	3,596
Louisiana	54,022	8,280	310	6,936	4,504	14	1,519	2,876	24,358
Mississippi	18,396	3,827	59	3,022	2,608	9	766	1,334	5,387
North Carolina	111,817	26,197	2,232	18,017	9,592	7,093	5,664	12,600	15,596
South Carolina	35,521	8,356	538	5,723	6,423	519	2,448	3,665	4,248
Tennessee	55,890	12,835	1,139	8,939	5,426	146	4,304	7,395	7,007
Texas	552,580	129,365	6,852	98,898	58,340	347	17,120	45,571	134,961
Virginia	256,673	48,815	4,423	35,403	47,609	45	9,080	45,279	37,309

Source: 2000 U.S. Census.

lanta's Doraville suburb has become known as Koreatown, with a Korean shopping center called Seoul Plaza, the largest in the South. In the Carolina Piedmont, Vietnamese and Cambodians generally arrived in the South with fewer immediate financial resources, taking on jobs in the textile, poultry, and furniture industries. They have also been innovative in starting small-scale businesses, restaurants, and convenience shops.

The expansion of interstate highways throughout the South has been critical for networking among Asian groups. The majority of Hindu and Sikh temples, mosques, Buddhist centers, and Asian churches scattered throughout the South are located in cities or near interstate highways, which enables greater accessibility. Even families in more remote places make the occasional journey to religious centers, which have become social centers as well, reflecting a traditional southern pattern. Such religious centers, along with the multiple Asian-related associations sprouting up throughout the South, have effectively sponsored national, ethnic, and religious holidays, bazaars, concerts, and workshops. The Indian Association of Charlotte states that its mission is "to share Indian culture with the people of the Carolinas and to foster a better understanding of the cultural diversity of India in its local community." Indians sponsor a variety of festivals, including *Diwali* (Indian New Year) and Indian Independence Day; Chinese celebrate the Harvest Moon festival and the Chinese New Year; and, in the spring, devout Buddhists of many backgrounds observe a special Buddha Day.

One can identify many reasons why Asians in large numbers recently came to the South and, having once arrived, why they choose to stay: warm climate, hospitality, family values, a preference for smaller cities and towns, abundant rural areas, the availability of cheaper land, job relocation, escape from the stress of big city life, the slower pace, and the appreciation of religion. One can argue that the Confucian value of filial piety, which many East Asians embrace, finds a more receptive home in the South. The South Carolina folk saying that both natives and Chinese love rice and worship their ancestors has new relevance. In general, Asian traditions place a premium on family obligations, such as taking care of aging parents. Among Indian and Southeast Asian families, three generations also often make up a household—a practical, economic consideration, but also expressive of the close ties encouraged between children and grandparents. A generation ago, such domestic patterns were hardly uncommon among native southerners, who have found them increasingly difficult to maintain.

The history of Asian groups in the South reaches much farther back than normally assumed. During the antebellum period, the port cities of New Orleans, Savannah, and Charleston received Indian, Filipino, and Chinese seamen. The first significant interface with Asia began in the early 19th century through the work of Baptist and Episcopal missionaries. This endeavor reflected a major trait of southern cultural experience—the impact of evangelical Christianity. Southern churches contributed greatly to missions in China, which would continue until the dawn of the communist revolution. During the antebellum period, some of the first Chinese individuals visiting the South came through missionary sponsors, who believed that biblical and theological studies in America would benefit their work among Chinese churches.

After the Civil War, planters and businesspeople interested in replacing slave labor entreated Chinese workers in California to move to the South. This endeavor, they believed, would bring about "the elevating and saving influence of our holy religion" to Chinese people. Though some Chinese, mostly male, did take up the offer, the plan was largely unsuccessful. In general, Chinese labor came at a higher price. Chinese males came to Texas to work on railroads and cotton plantations. Many stayed and married into white and black families. The Chinese families arrived in postbellum Mississippi Delta towns and started grocery and supply stores, often within African American communities. They were effective in adhering to traditional customs and to their identity as Chinese. They founded separate schools and churches; but, in the Jim Crow South, they were often identified as "colored." In 1943, when Congress repealed the Chinese exclusion laws of 1882, there were only about 5,000 Chinese living in the South. By 1950 the number had doubled.

One of the most fascinating stories about Asian individuals who settled in the South in the 19th century is that of Chang and Eng Bunker, the original "Siamese twins." After many years touring America and Europe, Chang and Eng made their homes in North Carolina, married local women, had 21 children between them, and operated a plantation with about 30 slaves. The Bunker twins also embraced the Baptist faith and contributed land for the White Plains Baptist Church, which they helped build. During the Civil War, two of their sons would serve in the Confederate army. Today, their descendants in North Carolina commemorate Chang and Eng with an annual reunion.

From 1990 to 2000 the growth rate among Indians has exceeded any other Asian group, nationwide increasing from 815,447 to 1,899,899. Today, Texas ranks fourth among all states, with 142,689 Indian citizens; the heaviest concentration live in the Houston area. After the 1965 Immigration Act, Indians took advantage of the growing Texas economy. Punjabi Sikhs are well represented in San Antonio, Dallas, and Houston. They were among the most active groups in sponsoring peace workshops in the wake of the terrorist attacks of September 2001. In Texas, Gujuratis are perhaps the largest Indian ethnicity. Many embrace the Swaminarayan form of Vaishnava devotion, one of the most global

Dennis Bunker, last surviving grandson of Chang and Eng Bunker, and his wife Hero stand in front of an image of the famous twins, 1992 (Celeste Ray, photographer)

forms of Hinduism. Houston is also home to many South Indians, who have built the largest temple in Texas. The temple is eponymous for the presiding deity, the goddess Meenakshi, and is located in Pearland, outside of Houston.

Significant interface between Asians and southerners involves food and music. Unlike 10 or 20 years ago, small southern towns now often host Indian or Chinese restaurants. At local festivals and fairs, Chinese dishes may appear along with barbecue, assorted fried foods, and boiled peanuts. Chinese and Vietnamese favor pork and chicken; their restaurants may feature barbe-cue dishes "Vietnamese style." In a recent food issue of the *Oxford American*, chef Wally Joe, owner of a fine-dining Chinese restaurant in Memphis, speaks of "pig's feet brazened Chinese style" as among his favorite southern dishes. Spiced iced tea now frequently appears on menus in Indian restaurants. By and large, the southern proclivity for deep-fried foods, sauces, and rice has received a boost from Asian additions. For generations, South Carolinians and Louisi-anans have led the country in rice consumption, a rate that has increased with the introduction of other rice-centered cultures.

The exchange between Asian and southern music holds creative promise. Indian musical ensembles have formed throughout the South, making appear-ances at numerous venues, including weddings, religious festivals, community fairs, and college campuses. In Greenville, S.C., the Indian Association spon-sors an annual bazaar that features both classical and contemporary music and dance in order to raise money for Meals on Wheels. Indian dance associations have sprung up throughout the South and increasingly attract non-Indians. Musical festivals such as the Leaf Festival in Black Mountain, N.C., MerleFest in Wilkesboro, N.C., and South by Southwest in Austin, Tex., have showcased world music, including Asian forms. Some researchers in southern colleges have produced settings that juxtapose varied musical genres and instruments: pairing the Appalachian fiddle with a Tibetan folk song, the banjo with Indian tabla. The Asian presence, then, may yet stimulate another musical genre in the long list of southern hybrid forms. Of course, in the South religion and music have gone hand in hand. An innovative example of this is the work of John Herrmann, a Zen roshi and "old-time" banjoist living near Asheville, N.C., who integrates meditation with the clawhammer technique of playing banjo.

Among recent Asian immigrants, Vietnamese, Cambodians, and Laotians relate the strongest to themes of loss, cultural alienation, and a haunted past, which historically have reverberated in southern culture. The Vietnamese Mon-tagnards ("mountain people") served with American forces and came to Amer-ica after the fall of Saigon in 1975. Today, North Carolina has the highest con-centration of Montagnards (about 5,000) living anywhere outside of Vietnam. Former U.S. Special Forces officers in North Carolina often helped in the re-settlement of Montagnard families. In their novels and stories, writers Wayne Karlin and Robert Olen Butler intertwine the experiences of Vietnam veter-ans from the American South with those of Vietnamese relocated to south-ern places. In an interview, Butler stressed that the landscape and ambience of southern Louisiana is critical to his stories of the Vietnamese in a way that California — although home to the largest number of Vietnamese in the United

States—could never be. Of the 60,000 Asians who live in Louisiana, almost half are Vietnamese. In the coastal and Delta areas, many are involved with the fishing industry. They have formed tight-knit communities in which Vietnamese remains the household language. On the Gulf Coast, Vietnamese have been active participants in the shrimp industry, which, in the late 1970s, created conflict with Euro-American fishers (becoming the subject of Louie Malle's 1985 film *Alamo Bay*). At the fishing town of Seadrift, Tex., the conflict resulted in the death of a white shrimper and galvanized threats from hooded Ku Klux Klan members, who were targeted by a successful lawsuit from the Southern Poverty Law Center. In recent years, Vietnamese and Euro-American fishers formed an alliance to protest the importing of low-priced shrimp from other countries, including Vietnam and China.

In the post–World War II period, many Japanese immigrants also arrived in America with a "war-haunted past," but the South received few of these. Among the approximately 17,000 Japanese who were interned in two Arkansas camps during the war, almost all chose to locate elsewhere afterward. One family settled in North Little Rock and started a nursery, and their descendants have recently raised money for the restoration of camp cemeteries. During the American occupation, and later when stationed at military bases in Japan, some southern soldiers married Japanese women and returned home with "war brides." Asian wives groups (Korean, Filipino, and Vietnamese, as well as Japanese) are not uncommon at military bases, like Fort Bragg in North Carolina. In recent years, perhaps the most significant Japanese contribution has come through the business sector. The interface between Japanese and southern business ventures has been the subject of a work by Choong Soon Kim, a Korean anthropologist living in Tennessee, who finds some common social values between Japanese and southern society. In Greenville, S.C., the Tsuzuki family, which owned a company supplying patented technology to local textile mills, generously donated to the Greenville Symphony and the building of a performing arts center that has helped revitalize downtown Greenville. More recently, the Tsuzuki family donated a family Buddhist temple to Furman University. The temple was dismantled and shipped from Japan, secured in storage, and is scheduled to be reassembled on a lot near the campus's Japanese gardens. With a chapel on one side of campus and a Buddhist temple on the other, this former Baptist school now experiments with landscaping religious pluralism.

In the first half of the 20th century, the Southern Baptist Convention (SBC), the Protestant group most actively involved with missions, sent more missionaries to China than to any other country. With the end of China missions, the SBC in Asia directed its energies to Korea, Taiwan, Hong Kong, Philippines, and

Japan. Their history with SBC missions explains, at least in part, why more Chinese Christian Churches in America are affiliated with the SBC than any other denomination. Various factors play into the attraction that the Baptist denomination has for the Chinese, including its conservative theology, the autonomy of the local congregation, and the accenting of ethnicity. Chinese, as well as Korean and Vietnamese, churches in the South tend to promote ethnic identity and are more likely than mainstream groups in California to maintain ethnic names for churches.

In the last two decades Asian groups in the South — especially Chinese, Koreans, and Laotian Hmong — have done their share of church planting. Perhaps the Koreans provide the best example of this development. Most Koreans who arrived in large numbers in the 1970s and 1980s were already Christians, the majority of them Presbyterians. They became active in creating distinctive Korean church communities, as in the growing district of Koreatown in Doraville, Ga. Korean Presbyterians are among the fastest-growing Christian communities in the South. Baptists have also had important gains among Koreans. Second-generation Koreans have become more Americanized and less concerned about Korean identity, but they remain highly evangelical. Korean Christians and southern evangelicals share critical cultural features, such as patriarchy, focus on family, discomfort with gay marriage, the conversion experience, and a general critique of secular values.

Southerners have not discouraged the establishment of non-Protestant Asian communities, be they Catholic, Buddhist, Muslim, or Hindu. Most Laotians, Cambodians, and Vietnamese are Buddhists, though of different schools. Laotians and Cambodians are Theravadan Buddhists, while Vietnamese belong to Pure Land or Chan schools. Cambodians value filial piety and express this through annual rites, such as *Chol Chnam* (New Year in mid-April), when children give gifts to their parents; and *Pchum Ben*, a festival for ancestors observed in mid-September. The few Buddhist monks and nuns living in temples scattered throughout the South dedicate themselves to a life of contemplation, but they also assume pastoral duties among the laity, including teaching Sunday school classes and performing house and business consecrations and rites for ancestors.

For some Buddhist arrivals, however, evangelical Christianity has become a viable option. Its message rings with a sense of assurance and finality that many undoubtedly find comforting. Such churches provide a framework for selecting what is good and useful from the host culture. Embracing a Christian identity can be seen as a step toward becoming more American, yet it does not entail rejecting all that is Asian or Buddhist. Indeed, one may remain in some sense a Buddhist while worshipping as a Christian. Vietnamese Catholics have also made the South their home. Undoubtedly, the Catholic sensibility contributed to the attraction that southern Louisiana holds for this group. Interestingly, the Vietnamese, who respect both Buddhist and Christian models of renunciation of the world, now supply a disproportionate number of American seminarians studying for the Catholic priesthood.

The relation between religious identity and southern culture appears to be the most problematic among Indian religious groups. The majority of Indians are Hindu. Throughout the South, one finds the vast range of Hindu devotional and philosophical perspectives represented. Probably the most challenging aspect of Hindu practice for native southerners is the role of *murti* (meaning "form" or "statue") in devotion, which may appear to evangelical Christians to be a form of idolatry—an impression unfortunately reinforced by the Hindu proclivity to call the image an "idol." But Hindus and Christians differ strongly in how they interpret that word. In the Protestant South, Hindus make special efforts to highlight their monotheist perspective and to interpret the *murti* as symbols of divinity. Still, the visual component of worship, strongly expressed by the word *darsan* (to see the sacred), stands out in a culture that in matters of worship has often privileged "word" over "image."

Among Asian groups, Indian Hindus have been least likely to convert to Christianity. However, Hindus have creatively drawn from other aspects of church life, such as tithing, fund-raising campaigns, Sunday schools, teenage camps, reunion dinners, and building recreational and educational facilities. Rather than undermine Hindu practice, southern religiosity actually reinforces its seriousness through the adaptation of new patterns. Many temples are found in the suburbs, even on blocks adjacent to Christian churches. As Christians have done in the past, Hindus now are claiming the landscape through names. In the newsletter of a temple community in Cary, N.C., board members suggested naming their neighborhood Balaji Colony ("Balaji" being a form of the God Vishnu). Balaji devotees, in particular, are active in creating Sanskrit hymns that praise southern states and cities (such as Atlanta and Houston) with temples dedicated to Venkatasevara (another name for Balaji). A hymn titled "Appearances of Venkatesavara" praises Texas as "the majestic state garlanded by the Rio Grande River, a land where Venkatesavara sports with the Goddess Lakshmi." Along with such hymns, Hindus consecrate their homes, fields, and communities with sacred water from India. In new subdivisions of Houston, Atlanta, Greenville, and Charlotte, house consecrations help meaningfully commingle tradition and living in a new place.

If Asian ethnicities challenge the traditional white/black paradigm, they also remind us of what has always been the creole character of southern life. Undoubtedly, matters of ethnicity, race, and religion will continue to affect the region's character. Despite the persistence of ethnocentric attitudes and Asian groups' ambiguous position in a stereotypically biracial society, these new southerners are increasingly laying claims to the southern landscape. This happens less through any deliberate attempts to refashion self-identity than through an evolving ethos that unites place and family. For instance, this can be expressed through the respect given to the dead through funerary rites and care for gravesites. The Cambodian Buddhist who buries (rather than cremates) a loved one in the town cemetery, or the Hindu who cremates but chooses to scatter grandmother's ashes in a Carolina river rather than take them back to India, has staked some lasting claim on southern places.

SAM BRITT
Furman University

Rudiger V. Busto, in *Revealing the Sacred in Asian and Pacific America*, ed. Jane Naomi Iwamura and Paul Spickard (2003); Christina Chia and Hong-an Truong, *Southern Exposure* (Summer 2005); Lucy M. Cohen, *Chinese in the Post–Civil War South* (1984); Roger Daniels, *Asian America: Chinese and Japanese in the United States since 1850* (1988); John Y. Fenton, *Transplanting Religious Traditions: Asian Indians in America* (1988); Bill Ong Hing, *Making and Remaking Asian America through Immigration Policy, 1850–1990* (1994); Choong Soon Kim, *Japanese Industry in the American South* (1995); Stephen L. Klineberg, in *Asian American Religions*, ed. Tony Carnes and Fenggang Yang (2004); Ho-Youn Kwon, Kwang Chung Kim, and Stephen Warner, eds., *Korean Americans and Their Religions* (2001); Randall M. Miller and George E. Pozzetta, eds., *Shades of the Sunbelt: Essays on Ethnicity, Race, and the Urban South* (1988); Maureen Ryan, in *South to a New Place*, ed. Suzanne Jones and Sharon Monteith (2002); Savita Nair, *SAGAR: South Asia Graduate Research Journal* (Fall 1995); George Brown Tindall, *Natives and Newcomers: Ethnic Southerner and Southern Ethics* (1995); Raymond Brady Williams, *Religions of Immigrants from India and Pakistan: New Threads in the American Tapestry* (1988); Joanne Waghorne, in *The Expanding Landscape: South Asian and the Diaspora*, ed. Carla Petievich (1999); Fenggang Yang, *Chinese Christians in America* (1999).

Southern Appalachia and Mountain People

As a subregion of the South, the Appalachian South has forged its own unique identities. Mountain inhabitants historically have been ethnically diverse and are increasingly so today. The three bands of southern Appalachia—the Allegheny-Cumberland (parts of West Virginia, Kentucky, Tennessee, and Alabama), the Blue Ridge (parts of Maryland, Virginia, North Carolina, and Georgia), and the Great Appalachian Valley (parts of Maryland, Virginia, Tennessee, Georgia, and Alabama) — have been the subject of their own extensive mythology disconnected from that of the Old South. Novelist Lee Smith expressed the cultural dissimilarities between the Lowland South and southern Appalachia when she described her mountain home as "far from the white columns and marble generals." In terms of outsiders' perceptions, she noted: "Appalachia is to the South what the South is to the rest of the country. That is: lesser than, backward, marginal, Other."

Beginning with the introduction of outside interests cutting timber, mining coal, and establishing manufacturing industries in the 1880s, local color writers and missionaries have popularized images of southern Appalachia that still shape stereotypes of the region and the ways in which "mountain people" see themselves. From "uplift literature" portraying the region as a social problem, to romantic and fanciful theses about residents' feuding, supposed Elizabethan dialects, and fallacious status as the most "Anglo-Saxon" of all American populations, outsiders have represented distorted images of Appalachia to serve their own purposes. The fiction of Mary Noialles Murfree (1850–1922) and the local color writings of Emma Bell Miles (1879–1919) and Horace Sowers Kephart (1862–1931) were sympathetic to mountain people, but they still helped formalize myths about Appalachian people as static anachronisms. John Charles Campbell's *The Southern Highlander and His Homeland* (1921) was one of the first works of systematic scholarship that to some extent documented diversity within the region, but it was nevertheless shaped by a missionary agenda. Journalists, tourists, and educators wrote accounts of their forays among people they deemed "the last frontiersmen" who entertained them with folktales, "ancient" ballads, and the use of "archaic" language. By the turn of the 20th century, the charming frontier people image had been replaced by the more lasting and harmful stereotype of superstitious, incestuous, lazy, whiskey-distilling hillbillies. The efforts by both CBS and NBC television networks to produce hillbilly "reality shows" in the first few years of the 21st century demonstrate how such degrading perspectives still appeal to the public imagination outside the region and still foster a particular self-consciousness among mountain people.

Mountain people are known for their egalitarianism and individualism, their firm connections to place and extended family, and their dedicated church attendance. The Mountain South is home to a proliferation of evangelical denominations with Methodists, heterogeneous Baptists, and Holiness-Pentecostal churches being the most common. Although the region is named for the Appalachee Indians, today the Cherokee and other Native Americans now com-

Mountaineer with his two grandsons, Breathitt County, Ky., 1940 (Marion Post Wolcott, Library of Congress [LC-USF34-055706-D], Washington, D.C.)

prise only 0.3 percent of the Appalachian population. The majority of southern Appalachian people (about 85 percent) are descendants of the two most predominant ethnic groups to displace American Indians late in the colonial period: the Scots-Irish and the Germans. These settlers came down the Great Wagon Road from Philadelphia to what was then called the Backcountry. In some states, Scots-Irish constituted half or more of the European settlers in Appalachia, which remains an area where some of the largest numbers of people self-identify as such on the U.S. Census. It is these immigrants who created bluegrass music with acoustic stringed instruments (British and Irish fiddle traditions, combined with acoustic guitar, mandolin, upright bass, resonator, or Dobro, guitar, and African-derived banjo), who left the region the legacy of the Hatfields and McCoys, who preserved the rich tradition of British ballads and Jack tales (the latter made famous in recent years by the Hicks family), and who maintained weaving traditions (taught in Appalachian "settlement schools" a century ago and today at Berea College in Kentucky and Crossnore School in North Carolina). Southern Appalachian foodways are a blend of American Indian, British, and German traditions, and vernacular architecture styles merge Scots-Irish, English, German, and Scandinavian adaptations to the backwoods frontier.

Scholars once considered mountain folk the cultural descendants of what historian Frank Lawrence Owsley called "the plain folks of the Old South" — predominantly yeoman farmers with few or no slaves. However, hierarchy and slave ownership were a part of southern Appalachian society, and the "father of Appalachian Studies," Cratis Williams, observed that internal socioeconomic diversity undermines generalizations about the region. He noted that while southern Appalachia was home to the town dweller, the valley farmer, and the branch water mountaineers ("hollow folk"), stereotyping targeted the latter and was extended to everyone living within the geographic area. The Mountain South had a mixed farming economy with small farms and reliance on hunting and open-range livestock grazing, but as timber and mining companies acquired land and mineral rights, profits left the region, taxes soared, and many farmers could no longer make a living from, or retain, their land (a process that continues today with wealthy outsiders building extravagant summer homes and resort communities). If some antebellum mountaineers could be considered middle-class "plain folk," their standard of living actually declined in the postbellum economy and with "modernization." Many farmers took mill work or went to the coal mines, which provided a slim livelihood, dangerous working conditions, and black lung disease. The mechanization of coal mining and the closure of many mines led to high unemployment and entrenched poverty, so that Appalachia remains one of the poorest regions in America. As part of President Lyndon Johnson's War on Poverty, Congress created the Appalachian Regional Commission (ARC) in 1965 to further social and economic development in the region and create or expand highways to decrease isolation. Today, southern Appalachia is still predominantly rural, with few cities and many government forests and parks. It still has some of the highest rates of working poor in the nation. Residents usually take on wage labor while also keeping subsistence gardens, Christmas tree farms, or fruit orchards. Many mountain folk work in tourism-related occupations. Southern Appalachia's population is growing at a higher rate than that of northern Appalachia, in part because of immigration and in-migration.

Southern Appalachia and its people have been the subject of speculation, romance, prejudice, and scholarship since the late 19th century, but in 1977 a group of teachers, scholars, and regional activists began the Appalachian Studies Association to encourage research and improve communication between Appalachian people, their communities, and governmental and educational institutions. Many association scholars are natives and have taken the ongoing national biases against Appalachian people to task. Redressing the negative representation of mountain people, they also have found that even when positive ethnographic and historical accounts of southern Appalachian life have appeared, these have still rendered all but the "Anglo-Saxon frontiersmen" invisible. In the last two decades, scholars have begun to address the ethnic diversity of the mountain population and document the ways in which new immigrants from Latin America and Southeast Asia continue to add to mountain culture.

While African Americans arrived in the mountains first as slaves, free blacks had also settled in the region by 1790. Historian Richard Drake has noted that, although the majority of antislavery societies in the United States prior to 1830 were in southern Appalachia and Unionist sentiment was strong there during the Civil War, a slave-owning elite did exist in many counties. Generally, the Mountain South had smaller populations of slaves, with many areas having black populations of under 1 percent. The only Appalachian county to have a 50 percent black population at the beginning of the Civil War was Madison County, Ala. At the end of the 19th century, newly freed slaves came in search of work in the coal mines. Today, African Americans comprise about the same proportion of the population of southern Appalachia as they do the total U.S. population (12 percent), but they comprise only 2 percent and 3 percent, respectively, of the populations of central and northern Appalachia. According to the ARC, most African Americans in southern Appalachian counties live in towns rather than rural areas, with the largest concentration being in Jefferson County, Ala., which encompasses the city of Birmingham.

A group of Kentucky performance poets have coined a new ethnonym, "Affrilachian," to describe African American mountain people. The Beck Cultural Center in Knoxville, Tenn., features displays on African American history in eastern Tennessee. Berea College in Kentucky, the first interracial college in the South, established a Black Cultural Center in 1983. The Highlander Folk School founded by Miles Horton in 1932 in Monteagle, Tenn. (now the Highlander Research and Education Center in New Market, Tenn.) was engaged in activism during the southern labor movements of the 1930s, the civil rights movement from the 1940s to the 1960s, and the Appalachian people's movements of the 1970s and 1980s and was visited by Rosa Parks and Martin Luther King Jr. In *Colored People: A Memoir* (1994), Harvard scholar Henry Louis Gates has written of experiencing desegregation where he grew up in the company town of Piedmont, W.Va. African American recording artists playing traditional Appalachian music include Etta Baker, "Sparky" Rucker, and the old-time string band Martin, Bogan, and Armstrong. The first "Black Banjo: Then and Now Gathering" took place at Appalachian State University in Boone, N.C., in 2005.

Appalachia attracted ethnic Protestants such as French Huguenots, Welsh

Baptists, and French-speaking, Italian Waldensians (Waldenses) from the Cottian Alps of northern Italy. In 1893 over 200 Waldensians settled Valdese, N.C. Their unique Protestant religious heritage predates the Reformation and caused their forebears centuries of persecution, but after a century in the Mountain South many have now become Presbyterians and Methodists. Nineteenth-century settlers brought with them distinctive Alpine architectural traditions, and many of their structures are now of historic interest for visitors to Valdese. Traditional ciders, wines, and foods, in addition to particular stories, French hymns, and games such as bocce, also feature in the annual Waldensian Festival held each August.

Although Eastern and Southern European immigrants came to work in the coal mines between 1890 and 1910, southern Appalachia did not attract significant new immigrants until the latter 20th century. Buncombe County, N.C., has now become home to close to 100 resettled Ukrainians. Since 2000, nearly half of the region's new residents are from minority groups. Thousands of Hmong (tribal people from the mountains of Laos who fought with the U.S. military in the Vietnam War) have been resettled in western North Carolina since the 1980s, adding a new dimension to life in small towns such as Mount Airy (population 8,000 and famed as Andy Griffith's hometown and the home of "Siamese twins" Eng and Chang Bunker). Hmong were attracted to Mount Airy to work in its hosiery mill, and when the mill closed, many have moved again. As with many Hmong resettlements, the Hmong at Mount Airy rapidly became U.S. citizens but kept to themselves. They are reluctant to acculturate and, although they sometimes attend local churches, they have caused consternation by sacrificing chickens to the spirits within the living rooms of their public housing projects. Marrying young and producing large families, they maintain ties with Hmong in other towns, with many gathering at a large settlement in Hickory, N.C., for their major holiday, Hmong New Year.

Hispanic immigration has been rising rapidly across the South, and the Mountain South is no exception. Construction work, apple and cherry orchards, vineyards, poultry plants, and nurseries have all offered employment opportunities. Throughout the region, the number of classes offering English as a second language has grown tenfold since 2000. Many Hispanic immigrants are living in the United States illegally and, not being classed as refugees like the Hmong, find obtaining citizenship a long process. However, Hispanics are more likely to get involved in the local community and to also establish their own Catholic churches, businesses, and stores.

Leaving their homeland during the civil war of the 1980s and 1990s, Guatemalan Maya have immigrated to Morganton, N.C., and to Appalachian communities in Georgia and Alabama, where they settle together with others from their home villages. After an initial immigration period, spouses and relatives, schoolteachers, and practitioners of traditional arts soon follow. Many younger male Mayans are engaged in farmwork, the nursery or poultry industries, or work for resort communities. With other Latino immigrants, Guatemalan Mayans are renting and buying houses in small towns that had previously experienced depopulation and changing the face of the Mountain South and what it means to be "of" southern Appalachia.

CELESTE RAY
University of the South

Allen W. Batteau, *The Invention of Appalachia* (1990); Patricia Beaver, *Rural Community in the Appalachian South* (1986); Patricia Beaver and Helen Lewis, in *Cultural Diversity in the U.S. South*, ed. Carole Hill and Patricia Beaver (1998); Dwight Billings, Gurney Norman, and Katherine Ledford, eds., *Confronting Appalachian Stereotypes: Back Talk from an American Region* (1999); Harry M. Caudill, *Night Comes to the Cumberlands* (1963); Wilma Dunaway, *Slavery in the American Mountain South* (2003), *The First American Frontier: Transition to Capitalism in Southern Appalachia, 1700–1860* (1996); Ron Eller, *Miners, Millhands, and Mountaineers: Industrialization of the Appalachian South, 1880–1930* (1982); Elizabeth Englehardt, *The Tangled Roots of Feminism, Environmentalism, and Appalachian Literature* (2003); Leon Fink and Alvis E. Dunn, *The Maya of Morganton: Work and Community in the Nuevo New South* (2003); Wilburn Hayden, *Journal of Appalachian Studies Special Issue: Appalachia Counts: The Region in the 2000 Census* (2004); Kirk Hazen and Ellen Fluharty, in *Linguistic Diversity in the South: Changing Codes, Practices, and Ideology*, ed. Margaret Bender (2004); Anthony Harkins, *Hillbilly: A Cultural History of an American Icon* (2004); Elvin Hatch, *Appalachian Journal: A Regional Studies Review* (Fall 2004); Benita Howell, ed., *Culture, Environment, and Conservation in the Appalachian South* (2002); C. David Hsiung, *Two Worlds in the Tennessee Mountains: Exploring the Origins of Appalachian Stereotypes* (1997); John C. Inscoe, *Mountain Masters, Slavery, and the Sectional Crisis in Western North Carolina* (1989); ed., *Appalachians and Race: The Mountain South from Slavery to Segregation* (2001); Terry Jordan and Matt Kaups, *The American Backwoods Frontier: An Ethnic and Ecological Interpretation* (1989); Mary LaLone, in *Signifying Serpents and Mardi Gras Runners: Representing Identity in Selected Souths*, ed. Celeste Ray and Eric Lassiter (2003); Deborah McCauley, *Appalachian Mountain Religion: A History* (1995); W. K. McNeil, ed., *Appalachian Images in Folk and Popular Culture* (1989); Frank L. Owsley, in *The South: Old and New Frontiers*, ed. H. C. Owsley (1969); Mary Beth Pudup, Dwight B. Billings, and Altina L. Waller, eds., *Appalachia in the Making: The Mountain South in the Nineteenth Century* (1995); Henry D. Shapiro, *Appalachia on Our Mind: The Southern Mountains and Mountaineers in the American Consciousness, 1870–1920* (1978); Nina Silber, in *Appalachians and Race*, ed. John C. Inscoe (2001); Robert P. Stuckeret, *Journal of Black Studies* (March 1993); William H. Turner and Edward J. Cabbell, eds., *Blacks in Appalachia* (1985); David Whisnant, *All That Is Native and Fine: The Politics of Culture in an American Region* (1983), *Modernizing the Mountaineer: People, Power, and Planning in Appalachia*, revised ed. (1994); Jerry Wayne Williamson, *Hillbillyland: What the Movies Did to the Mountains and What the Mountains Did to the Movies* (1995).

Southerners

The 21st-century South is home to many ethnic groups, but since at least the 19th century some in the region have tried, with little success, to establish white southerners as having a particular ethnic heritage, first as cavaliers and more recently as Celts. Beginning in the late 1960s and early 1970s, sociologists (most importantly John Shelton Reed) and historians (most prominently George Brown Tindall) took a new approach. Influenced by an increasing national interest in ethnicity, aware that the region's distinctive social system based on a rural one-crop economy and rigid system of white supremacy was rapidly passing, yet convinced that despite such changes a "South" would persist, Reed, Tindall, and other scholars proposed that southerners be looked upon as an ethnic group. Proponents of "southerners as ethnics" realized that the concept of "ethnicity" did not fully fit the southern experience and so sometimes labeled southerners as "quasi-ethnics" or wrote of employing an "ethnic analogy." The analogy proved inexact because the South had never been a nation, although Reed pointed out it had at least been a failed one. Nevertheless, the concept of southerners as ethnics took hold as a useful way to describe the amorphous yet persistent notions of southern identity and distinctiveness. By 1980 southerners even commanded an entry in an encyclopedia of American ethnic groups.

Tindall and others who employed the concept of ethnicity saw its potential to define "southernness" in a way that would acknowledge that African Americans had played a central role in the creation of the region's culture and that could provide an identity that embraced both blacks and whites. More recently, other scholars have endorsed the idea of southerners as ethnics as a means to include not only whites and African Americans, but also other groups. The new proponents build from the idea of the South as a persistent folk culture and stress the creole nature of that culture. They celebrate diversity within the region, where the early proponents of southerners as ethnics often sought to identify southerners' shared distinctiveness.

In both cases, the idea of southerners as ethnics rested in southerners' sense of their own identity; most thought of and identified themselves as "southerners," albeit with varying degrees of intensity, and perceived that people outside the region did as well. Beyond the sense of a distinctive identity, Reed, Tindall, and other early proponents of southerners as ethnics built their case on two different but obviously interrelated bases: history and culture. In the first, southern ethnicity was rooted in a distinctive past: slavery, the Confederacy, a rural post–Civil War social order built on a one-crop economy, a one-party political system and disfranchisement, and rigid segregation. The region's historical experience did not so much live on in memories of specific events (even southerners' knowledge of the Civil War proved surprisingly shallow) as it did in a generalized sense of grievance. The region, southerners maintained, had long been mistreated and looked down upon by the North. Basing southern ethnicity in history, though, undermined the idea of an identity shared by blacks and whites. Although proponents pointed to a common, if tragic, racial past, the attitudes of white and black southerners toward the region's racial history and the persistent division along the color line led Tindall and others to argue that the region held not one but two ethnic groups: black and white.

The second basis offered for southern ethnicity — culture or a core of shared beliefs and practices — could more often unite black and white. In addition to their sense of grievance, southerners widely shared three beliefs that distinguished them from other Americans: a strong sense of and pride in place, deeply held conservative religious beliefs, and a ready acceptance of personal violence rooted in a traditional sense of personal honor. Proponents of a southern ethnicity also pointed to a strong attachment to family and various other forms of behavior. Language — not just a pronounced accent but different dialects and a proclivity for certain usages ("y'all" and "mama," among others) — marked southerners as an ethnic group. So, too, did distinctive tastes in foods, among them grits, okra, fried green tomatoes, and MoonPies. A few observers even included such phenomena as country music and stock car racing, both of which had their roots in the region. The rise of both to national popularity at the beginning of the 21st century, however, raises questions about the persistence of southerners' distinctive ways, as does the discovery that by that time only about a quarter of southern adults claimed to use "mama" and even fewer regularly ate grits. Perhaps the pervasive power of modern American popular culture will eventually overcome many aspects of southern ethnicity. Proponents of the idea of southerners as persistent ethnics would counter that the South is always changing but never disappearing.

GAINES FOSTER
Louisiana State University

James C. Cobb, *Redefining Southern Culture: Mind and Identity in the Modern South* (1999); Lewis M. Killian, *White Southerners*, revised ed. (1985); Celeste Ray, ed., *Southern Heritage on Display: Public Ritual and Ethnic Diversity within Southern Regionalism* (2003); John Shelton Reed, *The Enduring South: Subcultural Persistence in Mass Society* (1972), *Southerners: The Social Psychology of Sectionalism* (1983); George Brown Tindall, *Journal of Southern History* (February 1974), *Natives and Newcomers: Ethnic Southerners and Southern Ethnics* (1995).

Afro-Cubans

"Afro-Cuban" (*afrocubano*) is a term that was invented by Cuban anthropologist Fernando Ortiz in the early 20th century. Those whom the term designates often suggest it fails to capture the nuances of Cuban history and seems to qualify citizenship in the nation that Cubans of African descent were instrumental in creating. Historically, the African population was proportionately much larger in Cuba than in the United States. Expanded sugar production in 19th-century Cuba rested on the labor of African slaves. Yet there were many more free people of color in Cuba than in the South under slavery. Afro-Cuban mutual aid societies (*los cabildos de naciones*) enabled retention of African languages and fostered syncretic Afro-Catholic religions (e.g., Santeria). African-derived music and folklore have strongly influenced Cuban popular culture. Afro-Cuban music has enjoyed sustained popularity in the United States. Dizzy Gillespie's mid-20th-century collaboration with Cuban musicians Tito Puente, Mario Bauza, and Celia Cruz helped establish a strong audience for salsa. Drums and metaphors from African religious traditions flavor this musical genre, which continues to draw broad interest. One example is the Buena Vista Social Club, a Cuban ensemble reviving a classic era of Cuban popular music and composed partially of the musicians who played in a prerevolution dance club of the same name.

More than half of the soldiers in the Cuban revolt against Spain in 1895 were black or mulatto. It was during this revolution (and the earlier revolt of 1868) that Afro-Cubans first migrated to Florida and Louisiana. Cigar production in Key West and Tampa attracted Cuban settlers. Afro-Cubans accounted for about 15 percent of these 19th-century Cuban migrants. Smaller settlements of cigar workers located in Jacksonville and New Orleans. In addition to cigar workers, these early communities included a large number of Cuban intellectuals and political figures prominent in exile political organizations.

The end of the war against Spain in 1898 coincided with the rise of Jim Crow laws in the United States. Afro-Cubans were adversely affected by these laws. Segregated social clubs formed. Sociedad La Unión Martí-Maceo (the Martí-Maceo Society, founded in Tampa in 1900 in honor of José Martí and Antonio Maceo, important leaders in the Cuban fight for independence) still remains in existence, as does El Círculo Cubano, the white Cuban club founded in 1899. The leading centers of Cuban settlement in the United States during the early 20th century, Ybor City and West Tampa, were enclaves with elaborate social, recreational, and political organizations. Afro-Cubans were integrated into these enclaves, but with growing distance from white compatriots.

Cigar-worker migration to Florida slowed during the Depression of the 1930s and ended completely with the 1961 embargo against Cuban tobacco imports. The very large influx of anti-Castro Cuban exiles, beginning in 1959, targeted Miami far more than

Tampa; the Cuban histories of Key West and Jacksonville were by then nearly forgotten. Fewer than 10 percent of the immediate post-1959 immigrants were Afro-Cuban. Second- and third-generation Afro-Cubans in Tampa became more isolated, cut off from contact with Cuba and increasingly involved with African Americans.

The 1980 "Mariel boatlift" (a mass exodus of Cubans prompted by a downturn in the Cuban economy and having the sanction of Cuban president Fidel Castro) included a much larger proportion of Afro-Cubans, many of whom remained in Miami. More recent waves of immigrants and refugees on rafts have continued to include Afro-Cubans. Despite an increase in numbers, however, black Cubans of Miami have remained spatially and socially separate from white Cubans. Jim Crow and southern patterns of residential segregation explain only part of this phenomenon. The issue of racial diversity among Cubans has a long history of ambivalence. José Martí, who sought national unity and an end to Spanish rule in the 1890s, urged Cubans to ignore racial differences and forget past injustices. However, this sanction discourages discourse about racial problems and has made Afro-Cubans relatively invisible.

Average incomes of Cuban immigrants exceed those of all other Latino ethnic groups in the United States. Black Cubans, however, have been shown to earn significantly less than their white counterparts. In Miami, especially, segregation between black and white Cubans is greater than for the population as a whole. Neverthe-less, among recent immigrants and their children, there remains a strong identification with Cuba, and cultural elements such as food and music continue to favor the homeland. In Tampa, descendants of immigrants are more varied in identification and cultural preferences. Fewer speak Spanish or regularly eat Cuban food. Many still attend the St. Peter Claver Catholic Church, and a smaller number continue to belong to the Martí-Maceo Society. The majority of descendants, however, more strongly identify as African American.

SUSAN D. GREENBAUM
University of South Florida

Alejandro de la Fuente, *A Nation for All: Race, Inequality, and Politics in Twentieth-Century Cuba* (2001); Susan Greenbaum, *More than Black: Afro-Cubans in Tampa* (2002); Guillermo Grenier and Alex Stepick, eds., *Miami Now! Immigration, Ethnicity, and Social Change* (1992); Pedro Perez Sarduy and Jean Stubbs, eds., *Afro-Cuba: An Anthology of Cuban Writing on Race, Politics, and Culture* (1993).

Alabama-Coushattas

The Alabama-Coushatta Tribe includes over 1,000 members, about 500 of whom live on a reservation of approximately 4,600 acres in east Texas. As a Southeastern Woodlands group, the Alabama-Coushatta trace their ancestry back to the Mississippian moundbuilders and belong to the Muskogean linguistic family, which also includes the Creek, Choctaw, Seminole, and Chickasaw. They encountered Hernando de Soto during his 1539–41 expedition, when he visited Alabama and Coushatta towns in northeastern Mississippi, northern Alabama, and southern Tennessee. By the late 1600s, the two groups had moved to the area of present-day Montgomery, Ala. There they participated in the Upper Creek Confederacy. By the mid-1700s autonomous yet interconnected Alabama and Coushatta towns began migrating independently from Alabama. Some groups settled in parts of Louisiana and Florida before crossing into Texas in the 1780s. The contemporary Alabama-Quassarte town in Oklahoma represents groups who were removed from Alabama in the 1830s. The Texas tribe maintains some contact with the Oklahoma group and closer ties with the Coushatta tribe of Louisiana.

The Alabama and Coushatta peoples negotiated relationships with the colonizing French, Spanish, and English and, later, with Americans, Texans, and Mexicans who vied for political and economic alliances with both tribes. Non-Indians such as Stephen F. Austin and Sam Houston cited the tribes' reputations as "civilized," friendly, and peaceful to prevent their removal from east Texas in the 19th century. In 1840 the Republic of Texas first tried, unsuccessfully, to find reservation land for the Alabama and Coushatta. The state of Texas designated reservation land for the Alabama in 1853, and the Coushatta joined them there.

After the Civil War the Alabama and Coushatta experienced poverty and disease, without federal or state government aid. In 1881 Presbyterian missionaries came to the reservation and pressured the tribe to give up many native practices, but they also provided the education and medical care that the state and federal governments neglected. In the 1880s the railroad brought the lumber industry to east Texas and engaged Alabama and Coushatta individuals in a wage-labor economy. While alleviating poverty, the wage-labor system exacted a cultural toll. However, anthropologist M. R. Harrington documented the significant retention of cultural practices into the 20th century despite assimilative pressures.

During the 1910s and 1920s both the state and federal governments began to give aid to the tribes. In 1928, to increase the size of the reservation, the federal government purchased more land and deeded it collectively to the Alabama-Coushatta. The name has remained hyphenated ever since. After the Indian Reorganization Act of 1934, the Alabama-Coushatta organized as a tribe and created a constitution that prescribed, among other things, strict membership and residence rules.

In 1955 the federal government terminated its trusteeship relationship with the Alabama-Coushatta, thereby transferring the responsibility to the state of Texas. However, in response to a dispute over hunting rights and an adverse ruling by the state attorney general, the Alabama-Coushatta Tribe sought and regained federal recognition in 1987.

In the 1960s the tribe began a tourist enterprise with funding from the state of Texas. Today, the Alabama-Coushatta Tribe promotes economic development on its own initiative. In 2001 the Alabama-Coushatta began limited gaming with the opening of an entertainment center. However, the state opposed and closed the operation in spite of the drastic increase in jobs and economic improvements that it brought not only to the reservation but to the entire area. The tribe continues to pursue negotiations on gaming with the state.

In the 21st century the Alabama-Coushatta Tribe conducts instruction in native language, pine-needle and river-cane basket making, and traditional dance. Individuals work and attend school in the surrounding area and participate in local Presbyterian, Baptist, and Assembly of God churches. In addition, people maintain the observance of matrilineal clans and traditional medicinal techniques and foodways. Individuals have also revived inter-tribal networks across the United States through participation in political and business activities, powwows, and athletic events.

STEPHANIE MAY DE MONTIGNY
University of Wisconsin–Oshkosh

Daniel Jacobson, *Ethnohistory* (Spring 1960); Geoffrey D. Kimball, *Koasati Grammar* (1991); Howard Martin, *Myths and Folktales of the Alabama-Coushatta Indians of Texas* (1977); Stephanie A. May, "Performances of Identity: Alabama-Coushatta Tourism, Powwows, and Everyday Life" (Ph.D. dissertation, University of Texas at Austin, 2001), "Alabama and Koasati," in *Handbook of North American Indians, Volume 14: Southeast,* ed. Raymond Fogelson (2004); Harriet Smither, *Southwestern Historical Quarterly* (October 1932); John R. Swanton, *Bureau of American Ethnology Bulletin 137* (1946).

Appalachian African Americans

African Americans have a long history in Appalachia. Arriving first in the 18th and 19th centuries as slaves, their numbers remained relatively small until the opening of the coal fields in the late 19th century. The need for miners encouraged a dramatic in-migration of free African Americans from the Deep South.

In West Virginia, the heart of central Appalachian coal country, the number of African American miners increased from just under 5,000 in 1900 to over 11,000 a decade later. By 1930 West Virginia had 22,000 African American miners. In Kentucky, African American miners numbered 2,200 in 1900 and 7,300 in 1930. These miners either followed family members to the central Appalachian region or were directly recruited by coal companies. While dispersed throughout the region, significant numbers of African Americans found their way to Kanawha and McDowell Counties in West Virginia and Harlan County in Kentucky. In the region's coal towns, African Americans stood on a comparatively equal footing with European Americans, as coal companies strove to maximize profits by keeping racial antagonism low and placing the most skilled workers in the appropriate jobs, regardless of race. As Appalachians, African Americans presently experience the myriad effects of poverty, including the dilapidated housing, low

Joe Thompson at the Black Banjo Gathering, Appalachian State University, Boone, N.C., 2005
(John Maeder, photographer, Appalachian Wanderings)

educational attainment, and limited access to health and social services that typify this marginalized subregion. As a minority among mountain people, African Americans additionally suffer the historical consequences of racism.

Any discussion of African Americans in Appalachia relates to a demographic understanding of Appalachia itself. The region, as delineated by the Appalachian Regional Commission in the 1960s, includes counties in 12 states stretching from Mississippi to New York. In the southern, central, and northern subregions, African Americans comprise 13, 2.2, and 3.6 percent of the population, respectively. Of the 1.7 million African Americans living in Appalachia, approximately 76 percent are in the southern subregion, 22 percent are in the northern subregion, and

2.8 percent are in the central subregion. The 10 Appalachian counties with the highest percentages of African Americans are in Mississippi and Alabama. Additionally, those counties with the highest numbers are urban or adjacent to urban areas.

Implicit in any discussion of blacks in Appalachia is their distinctiveness in relation to other African Americans in the South based on their mountain experience and heritage. Practicing religious and musical traditions of their Deep South kinfolk, rural Appalachian African Americans also had ties to industrializing America. These African Americans, however, have largely been ignored in the media and in scholarship. In their "discovery" of Appalachian culture in the late 19th and early 20th centuries, outsiders stereotyped Appalachian residents as isolated, backward, violent, and, not least of all, Anglo-Saxon. Over the past 20 years the people of Appalachia, including African Americans, have become increasingly critical of their pejorative representation in mainstream America.

Accompanying the rise of "place-based" studies and identity politics in the 1990s, African Americans began actively claiming an Appalachian identity. William H. Turner and Edward J. Cabbell's *Blacks in Appalachia* (1985) considered specific African American communities in the mountains and black coal miners. In the early 1990s a Kentucky-based performance group, the Affrilachian Poets, began to give voice to the frustrations of African Americans in Appalachia who feel excluded from historical and contemporary understandings of what it means to be of Kentucky and/or Appalachia. In Pennington Gap, Va., the county's first school for blacks, Lee County Colored Elementary School, has become the Appalachian African American Cultural Center. The center collects oral histories, photographs, copies of slave documents, and material culture pertaining to the African Americans' historical experience in the region.

MICHAEL CRUTCHER
University of Kentucky

Dwight B. Billings, Gurney Norman, and Katherine Ledford, eds., *Back Talk from Appalachia: Confronting Stereotypes* (1999); William H. Turner and Edward J. Cabbell, eds., *Blacks in Appalachia* (1985); Frank X. Walker, *Affrilachia* (2000).

Barbadians

In an influential article, historian Jack Greene called Barbados a "cultural hearth" for the southeastern slave states. The Barbadian influence has probably been exaggerated, but English colonists from that island undoubtedly had an important role in causing early South Carolina to resemble the West Indies in several ways. South Carolina's slavery-dominated plantation economy was later exported through South Carolinians, both black and white, to other southeastern states.

Another historian, Peter Wood, called South Carolina a "colony of a colony." By 1670, when the first permanent English settlement was made near Charleston, Barbados was already a mature and exceedingly wealthy sugar-producing colony. Land was scarce on the 166-square-mile island, as large sugar "factories" squeezed out opportunities for small farmers and their families. Barbadians played a key role in establishing the newer English colony. Sir John Colleton, who had gone out to Barbados after the defeat of King Charles I's forces in the Puritan Revolution, apparently took the lead in obtaining the Carolina charter for eight English noblemen. The most important of the eight Proprietors in the settling of South Carolina, Anthony Ashley Cooper, first earl of Shaftesbury, had also owned a Barbados plantation and had other Caribbean interests. Although a Barbadian attempt to settle Carolina in the 1660s failed, some Barbadians joined the successful 1669–70 settling expedition from England.

In South Carolina's early years as

a colony, much of the shipping from England came by way of Barbados. In the beginning, significant numbers of Barbadian free blacks, indentured servants, and slaves moved to the new colony, but the numbers have been inflated by counting people who only passed through Barbados on their way from England to South Carolina. After the 1690s, rice became the staple crop of South Carolina. Slave populations of more than 80 percent and dreadful mortality developed in Lowcountry parishes that shared the names of parishes in Barbados. The slave code, the harshest on the continent, was also modeled on that of Barbados, but the parallels should not be overstated. South Carolina also came to have a very wealthy white elite, but it never became a monocultural economy like Barbados and its plantation owners were never absentee to the same degree.

Three Barbadians became South Carolina governors in its Proprietary era, and emigrants from that island formed part of the powerful Goose Creek faction that troubled the colony's owners by refusing to stop selling Native Americans into slavery and by trading with pirates. While serving as the third governor in 1672–74, Sir John Yeamans—who earlier had arranged the murder of a man so that he could marry the man's wife—infuriated the earl of Shaftesbury by selling to Barbados for a profit provisions that were urgently needed in Carolina. The third Barbadian governor, Robert Gibbes, obtained the office of governor by bribery in 1710. London merchants demonstrated that they could also be rapacious colonists in South Carolina's early years. Given that astonishingly little is now known of the origins of the colony's early leaders, too much may have been made of the role of the aggressive Barbadians in the formation of South Carolina.

CHARLES H. LESSER
South Carolina Department of Archives and History

Peter F. Campbell, *Some Early Barbadian History* (1993); Jack P. Greene, *South Carolina Historical Magazine* (October 1987); Charles H. Lesser, *South Carolina Begins: The Records of a Proprietary Colony, 1663–1721* (1995).

Black Seminoles

From the late 17th century through the mid-19th century, slaves who escaped to Florida from the South Carolina and Georgia Lowcountry found homes and allies among the Seminole. The name "Seminole," in fact, meant "runaway" and had been adopted after the group detached themselves from the Creek Confederacy. The Seminole called the runaway slaves *estelusti* and considered them free. Black Seminoles lived in separate villages near at least a dozen Seminole towns, the earliest being in the current Alachua, Leon, Levy, and Hernando Counties. While the Seminole held African-born slaves and had enslaved Yamasee Indians who were prisoners of war, they protected these escapees from slave catchers. When *estelusti* had resided with the Seminole for long periods they became known as maroons, as did the free blacks who had also chosen to settle with the Seminole. Eventually they became Black

Seminoles with a blended cultural heritage and a unique history tied to both slavery and Removal.

Black Seminoles (or Seminole Maroons) spoke Gullah and the Muskogee or Mikasuki languages of the Seminole, and they sometimes served as interpreters between the Seminole and English speakers. Some scholars suggest they developed an Afro-Seminole Creole (a blend of Gullah, Spanish, English, and Muskogee). They adopted the brightly colored clothing and the moccasins of the Seminole, often lived in thatched palmetto plank houses of the Seminole architectural tradition, and danced at Green Corn ceremonies; but they also continued their own cultural traditions, such as "jumping the broom" at marriage celebrations and giving their children African-derived names (for example, names based on the day of the week on which the child was born, such as "Cudjo" for Monday and "Cuffy" for Friday) or "slave names" (such as Abraham and Caesar). Originally from Africa's Rice Coast, Black Seminoles or their ancestors had grown rice on plantations in South Carolina and Georgia and grew rice crops in Florida in addition to raising corn (about one-third of which they paid annually to their Seminole defenders).

During the Revolutionary War the Black Seminoles allied with the Seminole and the British against the colonists, and when Florida was once again under Spanish control (1784–1821) the Spanish employed Black Seminoles to trade with Indians. When Spanish rule ended, some Black Seminoles moved to Andros Island in the Bahamas (where their descendants live today). Others, resisting the U.S. government's repeated attempts to reenslave them, fought against Andrew Jackson during the First Seminole War (1817–18) and under their own captains with Osceola's warriors in the Second Seminole War (1835–42).

Juan Caballo, a Black Seminole leader in the Second Seminole War, was known as a "Black Seminole chief" and a freeman of African, Spanish, and Native American ancestry. The majority of Seminoles and at least 500 Black Seminoles were removed to Oklahoma, where they became known as Freedmen. Caballo founded the Black Seminole town of Wewoka there. By 1849 Creek slave traders in Indian Territory had managed to limit the rights of free blacks and Caballo led his people to Mexico, which had abolished slavery in 1829. There, Black Seminoles were known as cowboys and lauded for their military successes against the Comanche and Apache. In 1870 Black Seminoles in Mexico were invited to settle in Texas and serve as scouts for the U.S. Cavalry. Several won the Medal of Honor (the highest military decoration awarded by the United States) and many served as Buffalo Soldiers. Today, Brackettville, Tex., is home to the Seminole Indian Scout Cemetery Association.

In 2000 the Seminole Nation in Oklahoma changed its membership criteria, and most Seminole Freedmen are no longer eligible for enrollment. However, the different descendant populations in Nacimiento in the Mexican state of Coahuila, in Texas, and in

Fourteen-year-old Matthew Griffin of Groveland, Fla., dresses in traditional Black Seminole Indian clothing when giving public presentations on his ancestors (Sherry Boas, photographer, originally appeared in the Orlando Sentinel, August 2005)

Oklahoma retain a sense of identity through oral tradition and through ongoing social and marital links between their communities. Called *Mascogos* in Mexico, Black Seminoles have blended Mexican, Indian, and African traditions. Those on both sides of the border claim Indian fry bread, enchiladas, hot tamales, *sufkee* (a cinnamon-flavored hominy dish), and *tetta poon* (a sweet potato desert) as Black Seminole food-ways. Historically, the populations living in the United States have been more endogamous, while groups in Coahuila have intermarried with Mexicans. For festival occasions, traditional costumes can include calico skirts and bodices for women and feathered turbans and brightly colored hunting shirts for men. One of the largest Seminole Maroon gatherings takes place each September in Brackettville, where English and Spanish speakers mix to the sounds of African spirituals and Tex-Mex music in commemoration of a hybrid cultural inheritance and shared history.

CELESTE RAY
University of the South

LILLIAN AZEVEDO-GROUT
University of Southampton

Rebecca Bateman, *Ethnohistory* (Spring 2002); Jeff Guinn, *Our Land before We Die: The Proud Story of the Seminole Negro* (2002); Ian F. Hancock, *The Texas Seminoles and Their Language* (1980); Rosalyn Howard, *Black Seminoles in the Bahamas* (2002); Kevin Mulroy, *Freedom on the Border: The Seminole Maroons in Florida, the Indian Territory, Coahuila, and Texas* (1993); Kenneth Wiggins Porter, *The Black Seminoles: History of a Freedom Seeking People* (1996); Richard Price, ed., *Maroon Societies: Rebel Slave Communities in the Americas*, 3rd ed. (1997); Scott Thybony, *Smithsonian* (August 1991); Bruce Twyman, *The Black Seminole Legacy and North American Politics, 1693–1845* (1999).

Brass Ankles/Redbones

Prior to the late 1960s, when they fell into disuse, the terms "Brass Ankles" and "Redbones" were the pejorative nicknames of presumably "mixed-race" communities in South Carolina's Lowcountry and Louisiana's western hills and plains. The origin of the terms is not known. Generally, the people to whom the terms were applied resented the designations, usually defining themselves as "Indian," "white," or sometimes both.

In South Carolina, individual Brass Ankles and a few families passed as "mulatto" or "colored." But these represented only a minority of the larger Brass Ankle population. During the mid-20th century, anthropologists and sociologists characterized or defined all of the Brass Ankle communities as "tri-racial isolates" (enclaves of multiethnic and interracial culture and descent) and also predicted the demise of such communities. Only South Carolina had populations labeled as Brass Ankles. Today, their primary communities are located near Pineville and Moncks Corner in Berkeley County, around Holly Hill in Orangeburg County, in Ridgeville and Summerville in Dorchester County, and in Jacksonboro, Walterboro, and Smoaks in Colleton County. Starting in the late 19th century, most of these communities developed separate social institutions, especially churches. The state also supported several "Indian" schools in various Brass Ankle locales. Although African ancestry is certainly a component of several Brass Ankle communities, Native American ancestry is well documented for some of the families in Berkeley County, and those living just north of Holly Hill in Orangeburg refer

Brass Ankle family at home near Summerville, S.C., January 1939
(Mary Post Wolcott, Library of Congress [LC-USF34-050605-D], Washington, D.C.)

to themselves as "Santees" and maintain an Indian ethnic identity. Those living between Ridgeville and Walterboro claim descent from a refugee band of Natchez, exiled from Louisiana by the French colonists, who asked for and received Settlement Indian status from South Carolina in 1747. Beginning in the 1960s and 1970s, several communities organized themselves into Indian associations. Largely through the efforts of these associations to educate the public, the term "Brass Ankle" was virtually abandoned and is seldom heard in contemporary times.

"Redbone" is a more generic term, widely utilized historically across much of the South. Its precise meaning and application varies in time and place, but it always denotes an implication of "racial" mixture. The term has documented usage, particularly in African American speech, in Virginia, Tennessee, and South Carolina, and in Louisiana it came to designate mixed and geographically and socially isolated communities found in nearly every western parish—from Sabine Parish in the north, through Rapides Parish (near Alexandria), and down to Calcasieu Parish in the southwest.

There are perhaps more than 20,000 Louisiana Redbones. Most descend from South Carolinians who were defined as mulattos or "other free persons." While South Carolinians use the term "Redbone," its use there generally indicates "mixed-race" persons within the African American community. The westward migration of Brass Ankles and Redbones commenced shortly after the United States acquired Louisiana in 1803. In the new territory, they married into Creole, French, and Indian families, resulting in a unique cultural heritage—at once Anglo, African, Spanish, French, and Indian of several regional tribes. Despite their numbers and dispersal, Louisiana Redbones are largely unstudied. Documentary evidence indicates that at least some Redbone families are primarily of Native American heritage.

The Brass Ankles and Redbones are prominent examples of the many "little races" that dotted much of the South. Some of these mixed communities have dispersed or disintegrated, their members passing categorically into white and black urban and suburban worlds. Discriminatory forces often fostered a sense of separateness, tighter community ties, and distinct identity. Where effective accommodative leadership emerged, Brass Ankles and Redbones successfully resisted categorization as "Negro" and established their own stores, churches, and schools. Their persistence reveals the variegated ethnic tapestry of the South.

C. S. EVERETT
Vanderbilt University

Virginia DeMarçe, *National Genealogical Society Quarterly* (March 1992); Wes Taukchiray, Alice Bee Kasikoff, and Gene Crediford, in *Indians of the Southeastern United States in the Late Twentieth Century*, ed. J. Anthony Paredes (1992).

Caddos

Archaeological investigations reveal that Caddo groups were settled throughout valleys of Oklahoma, Louisiana, Texas, and Arkansas by 800 A.D. A distinctive culture emerged as Caddos developed a successful horticultural economy, a highly effective political structure, a viable interregional trade network, and well-planned civic-ceremonial centers that were also the scene of elaborate mortuary rituals.

Civic-ceremonial centers employed earthen mounds as platforms for temples and for the burial of social and political elites. Objects unearthed from Caddo sites are rich in symbolism—pottery vessels with distinctive shapes and unique decorative designs, carved stone pipes, sheet copper masks, marine shell gorgets, cups, and dippers. The spiritual leader of all Caddos was the *Xinesi*, the keeper of an ever-burning fire whose prayers beseeched *Caddi Ayo*, "Leader Above," to forgive Caddo misdeeds and provide for their needs.

Caddo families built large, sturdy homes constructed of vertical timbers, lashed by saplings and cane, daubed with clay, and covered with thatch. An outdoor workspace and elevated corn crib commonly stood near a dwelling. Gardens planted with beans, pumpkins, and sunflowers, fields of corn, and wooded areas separated households.

The earliest written descriptions of Caddo people appear in the chronicles of Spanish and French explorations (after the death of Hernando de Soto, Luis de Moscoso led his expedition and entered Caddo territory in 1542; the French explorer René-Robert Cavelier, Sieur de La Salle, arrived in Texas in the late 1600s). They describe Caddo

Young Caddos learning traditional Turkey Dance songs at the drum (Rhonda Fair, photographer)

farmsteads grouped in dispersed communities with names usually prefixed by "na," meaning "place of" (e.g., Nadaco).

The chief civil authority for each Caddo community was the caddi, an inherited position. A prestigious caddi might have preeminence over others. Communities were grouped geographically into three separate branches of the Caddo nation. The Natchitoches lived in the area of the present Louisiana city named for them; the Hasinai, meaning "Our People," lived in east Texas; and the Kadohadacho centered on the great bend in the Red River. "Caddo" derives from the French abbreviation of Kadohadacho, and before the middle of the 19th century only the Kadohadocho were called Caddo.

The Caddo were historically and politically significant during the 18th and 19th centuries, when their homeland became disputed borderland between the Louisiana Territory and the province of Texas. Spanish missionaries, military leaders and government officials, French traders and governors, Mexican presidents, and American Indian agents recognized the powerful influence and political astuteness of prestigious Caddo caddis and vied for the favor of Tinhiouen (caddi ca. 1760 to 1789) and Dehahuit (ca. 1800 to 1833). The Caddos declared neutrality, maintained authority over neighboring tribes in the region, and boasted that no white man's blood was spilled on their soil.

Strong and gifted leadership could not offset population loss from epidemics or control land grabs by immigrants who advanced the western frontier of the United States. Diminished by disease and plagued by Osage raids, the Caddo moved from the Red

River in the 1790s and resettled between the Sabine River and Caddo Lake. The Natchitoches, greatly reduced in number and surrounded by Anglo-Americans, eventually merged with the Caddo and Hasinai. Epidemics subsequently devastated the Hasinai. Survivors in eight formerly populous communities came together in two, Anadarko [Nadaco] and Hainai.

The Caddo were coerced into ceding their Louisiana homelands to the United States in 1835. Treaty terms bound them to move outside the borders of the United States and "never more return to live, settle, or establish themselves as a nation, tribe, or community of people." Most moved to Texas within a year. Prevented from establishing permanent villages by Texas militia and frontier people, they were essentially homeless until a Brazos River reserve was opened for them in 1855. Four years later, anti-Indian agitators ignited hostilities that forced them to abandon the Brazos Reserve for Indian Territory (now Oklahoma).

In 2004 approximately 4,800 Kadohadacho, Hasinai, and Natchitoches descendants were enrolled members of the federally recognized Caddo Nation in Oklahoma. Their seat of government is in Caddo County, Okla. An elected chairperson and council replaced the traditional role of the caddi in 1938, but new generations continue to learn ancient Caddo culture embedded in stories, songs, dances, and ceremony.

CECILE ELKINS CARTER
Mead, Oklahoma

Cecile Elkins Carter, *Caddo Indians: Where We Come From* (2001); Wallace Chafe, "A Note on the Caddo Language," in *Caddo Indians: Where We Come From* (2001); Vynola Beaver Neukumet and Howard L. Meredith, *Hasinai: A Traditional History of the Caddo Confederacy* (1988); Timothy K. Perttula, *"The Caddo Nation": Archaeological and Ethnohistoric Perspectives* (1992); Clarence Webb and Hiram Gregory, *The Caddo Indians of Louisiana* (1978).

Cajuns

Louisiana became a French colony in 1682. The largest concentration of French settlement was in the southernmost part of Louisiana, where French language and culture endure into the 21st century.

South Louisiana is culturally, historically, and linguistically connected to the French-speaking world, but it is hardly homogeneous. The great variety of subregional dialects of French derive from three main currents: the colonial French that developed among the descendants of the French who first began to settle Louisiana in 1699, the Creole that developed among the descendants of the African slaves brought to work on the French colonial plantations, and the Cajun French that evolved among the descendants of Acadians who began to arrive in Louisiana in 1765 after they were exiled by the British from their homeland in what is now Nova Scotia. Yet there is little pure linguistic or cultural stock today. The basic sources influenced each other in areas where the groups came into frequent contact. Many move effortlessly and even unconsciously between dialects according

Cajun family eating crawfish (Greg Guirard, photographer, courtesy of the Center for Louisiana Studies)

to the context. All three basic sources were also modernized by steady trickles of immigration—especially in the 19th century by the so-called *petits Créoles*, economic immigrants from France, and by refugees from the Haitian revolution—as well as by contemporary academic influences.

French was the language of everyday life and government in Louisiana into the 19th century. But the Louisiana Purchase in 1803 and statehood in 1812 placed serious pressure on French Louisiana to conform to the language and culture of the United States. By the time of the Civil War, there were Acadian generals, governors, bankers, and business leaders. For less upwardly mobile Acadians, the war was simply not their affair. These did not join the effort willingly, and once drafted into the service of the South, they strained to get out of it. Yeoman farmers had

no one else to run their farms in their absence, so many simply deserted and walked home from nearby battlefields.

With the end of the Civil War, French Creoles understood that their future was necessarily going to be American; they immediately began to send their children to English-language schools. By the turn of the 20th century, their transition to English was virtually complete. Ordinary Cajuns did not similarly change until much later, beginning with the arrival of Anglo-American farmers from the Midwest in the 1880s and reinforced by the arrival of Anglo-American oil workers and developers from Texas, Oklahoma, and Pennsylvania in the early 1900s. This process was intensified by the nationalistic fervor that preceded and accompanied World War I, the relief efforts that accompanied the great flood of 1927, and the agricultural and economic depressions of the 1920s and 1930s — all of which brought national-level relief efforts exclusively in English.

Beginning in 1916, mandatory English-language education was imposed in the southern part of the state in a well-meaning effort to haul the French-speaking Cajuns into the American mainstream. As a result, Cajun children were punished for speaking the language of their parents in school, often by teachers with the same surnames as the students. After World War II, GIs returning from service in France spurred a Cajun cultural revival that was fanned by local political leaders who used the 1955 bicentennial of the Acadian exile from Nova Scotia as a rallying point for the revitalization of ethnic pride. In 1968 the state of Louisiana officially fostered the movement with the creation of the Council for the Development of French in Louisiana, which attempted to establish French as a second language in elementary schools.

Today's Cajuns are friendly, yet suspicious of strangers; easygoing, yet guarded with their opinions and emotions; deeply religious, yet amusingly anticlerical; proud, yet quick to laugh at their own foibles; and unfailingly loyal, yet possessed of a frontier independence. Cajuns are immediately recognizable as a people, but they defy simplistic definitions.

While the French language struggles to maintain its role in the cultural survival of south Louisiana, the sounds of rock, country, and jazz music are incorporated by young Cajun musicians today as naturally as were the blues and French *contredanses* of old. New cultural blends continue to emerge in connection with recent Hispanic and Southeast Asian arrivals, including crawfish-filled tamales and egg rolls.

BARRY JEAN ANCELET
University of Louisiana at Lafayette

Barry Jean Ancelet, *Cajun and Creole Music Makers*, revised ed. (1999), *Cajun and Creole Folktales* (1994); Barry Jean Ancelet, Jay Edwards, and Glen Pitre, *Cajun Country* (1991); Shane K. Bernard, *The Cajuns: Americanization of a People* (2003); Carl A. Brasseaux, *Acadian to Cajun: Transformation of a People* (1992), *The Founding of New Acadia* (1987); Glenn R. Conrad, ed., *The Cajuns: Essays on Their History and Culture*, revised ed. (1983); James H. Dormon, *The People Called Cajuns: An Ethnohistory* (1983); Marcia Gaudet and James C. McDonald, *Mardi Gras, Gumbo, and Zydeco* (2003); C. Paige Gutierrez, *Cajun Foodways* (1992).

Cambodians

Cambodian immigrants in the South are almost exclusively Khmer, the primary ethnic group of their Southeast Asian homeland. The Khmer empire and culture, tracing its origins back more than 2,000 years, experienced an era of greatness during the Angkor period (800 to 1400 A.D.), from which much of contemporary Khmer culture — dance, music, mythology, and Buddhism — derives. Subsequently dominated by a series of foreign powers, Cambodia gained independence in 1954 only to become embroiled in the Vietnam War. The nationalist Khmer Rouge (communist Khmer) seized power in Cambodia in

Cambodian classical dancers performing Tepmamorom, *a dance about harmony, Greensboro, N.C. (Cedric N. Chatterley, photographer)*

1975 after the U.S. military withdrew. During the Khmer Rouge's four-year reign of terror, more than 2 million citizens were executed or starved to death.

In the early 1980s, 150,000 Cambodian refugees were resettled in the United States. Data from the 2000 cen-sus records a Cambodian population reaching 300,000 and indicates the growth of Cambodian communities in several southern states, including North Carolina (2,681), Georgia (2,905), Texas (6,852), Virginia (4,423), and Florida (2,447). Many Cambodian refugees have been drawn to the South for economic and climatic reasons. Although raised as farmers and fishers, many Cambodians have come to work in furniture factories and textile mills across the South.

For 20 years these new southerners have focused on building new lives, forming Buddhist temples, and reestablishing their annual calendar of ceremonies. Asian markets now nestle within small southern strip malls and stock not only the dried fish, spices, jasmine rice, and cooking utensils used in Cambodian kitchens, but also the incense, candles, and golden statues central to Buddhist religious practice. In communities across the region, language, foodways, storytelling, dance, music, and wedding traditions have also been carefully preserved and passed on to the next Cambodian American generation. Many communities have nurtured traditional Khmer dance groups; Cambodian high school students in traditional silk costumes and gold jewelry perform these classical and folk dances for their friends and teachers during annual International Day celebrations on campus, citywide multicultural festivals, and other public events.

Southern Cambodian communities have reestablished an annual calendar of Buddhist ceremonies that includes major events such as the May celebration of Visakha Puja Day, the day of the birth, enlightenment, and death of the Buddha; the summer celebration of Buddhist Lent and its series of sermons about the life of the Buddha; and the fall *Kathin* ceremony, in which the congregation presents new robes and personal supplies to the monks. *Chol Chhnam*, the Cambodian New Year's celebration, increasingly draws hundreds, even thousands, of participants to temples across the region to recommit themselves to their Buddhist beliefs, offer significant support to the Buddhist temples (*wats*) they have founded, and to bolster their relationships with other Cambodian families. A national holiday held in the dry season prior to the annual rice plantings in Cambodia, the celebration also includes social games and playful water fights meant to invoke the rains and guarantee good harvests.

While their communities prosper, the current struggle for both first- and second-generation Cambodian Americans living across the South is to craft a new identity that honors both their memories of their ancestral land and their experiences in their new home.

BARBARA LAU
Duke University

May M. Ebihara, Carol A. Mortland, and Judy Ledgerwood, eds., *Cambodian Culture since 1975: Homeland and Exile* (1994); David W. Haines, ed., *Refugees as Immigrants: Cambodians, Laotians, and Vietnamese in America* (1989); Barbara Lau, "The Temple Provides the Way: Cambodian Identity and Festival in Greensboro, North Carolina" (M.A. thesis, University of North Carolina at Chapel Hill, 2000).

Canary Islanders (Isleños)

Canary Islanders—long known as "Isleños," or "Islanders"—came from a cluster of 13 Spanish islands off the African coast and entered the colony of Louisiana (then under Spanish rule) between the years 1778 and 1783. They arrived as recruits for the Louisiana Infantry Regiment and to bolster the Spanish presence in the colony. However, Governor Bernardo de Gálvez instead employed the married recruits and their often large families as settlers. Consequently, nearly 2,000 Isleños established themselves in lower Louisiana in St. Bernard Parish virtually adjacent to New Orleans, at Barataria across the Mississippi River from the city, upriver at Galveztown at the junction of the Amite River and Bayou Manchac, and on Bayou Lafourche. Mostly poor and illiterate farmers, they struggled long and hard against adversities such as floods, hurricanes, disease, and poorly allocated settlement sites. By the close of the colonial period, only their St. Bernard and Lafourche settlements survived.

After the 1803 Louisiana Purchase, the Isleños, who became the first Hispanic community incorporated into the United States, mostly disappeared. Through the 19th century, they lived in small and isolated enclaves composed principally of Spaniards who preserved their culture and speech, but they were surrounded by larger populations of Acadians, Anglo-Americans, African Americans, and other ethnicities, who rarely acknowledged their culture. Few Isleños improved their economic status and acquired lands and slaves in the antebellum era, and the Civil War destroyed the holdings of most of those who had. In the "Bourbon Age" that followed Reconstruction in Louisiana—when vested interests such as railroad, mining, lumber, cotton, and

sugar companies and corrupt planters and politicians in the notorious New Orleans ring dominated political life—a few more Isleños gradually assimilated into Louisiana's cultural mainstream, acquired an education, and left behind their traditional occupations as farmers, fishers, and hunters.

In the 20th century, modernization brought further change and broke down the isolated enclaves that had retained distinct traditions and the Canarian dialect. Improved means of transportation and communication—railroads, automobiles, paved roads, newspapers, radio, movies, and television—facilitated Isleño assimilation. Twentieth-century wars, especially World War II, spurred mobility and heightened awareness of life beyond the Islanders' secluded communities. Use of Spanish declined as schools insisted that Isleño children speak only English, and dissatisfied youth often abandoned their "bumpkin" niches to meld into Louisiana's cultural milieu. Moreover, the Isleños had never practiced endogamy, and with growing assimilation greater numbers married outside their community. Today, few Canary Islanders claim Isleño descent on both sides of their families. The Spanish monoglots typical of the 19th century have disappeared, and their 20th-century bilingual and bicultural descendants who grew up in households where the Isleño language and culture predominated are now elderly and few in number.

Nevertheless, since the 1970s in St. Bernard Parish, where ethnic identity has retained its most enthusiastic followers, members of Los Isleños Heritage and Cultural Society have sought to preserve their cultural past and reacquaint their children with the Spanish language. Leaders in the community established the Isleño Museum and Village, with artifacts and vernacular architecture that recall St. Bernard's history (another museum has recently opened in Donaldsonville on Bayou Lafourche). In 1996 the Canary Islanders Heritage Society of Louisiana was founded in Baton Rouge. Each spring a festival in St. Bernard focuses attention on Canary Islander heritage, with traditional costumes, typical Isleño foods (based on rice and seafood locally obtained and with a distinctive Louisiana flavor), and the Spanish *décima* tradition of folk poetry, which relates stories about Isleño life. A few hardy Isleños retain vestiges of the folk medicine, prayers, and related customs brought from the Canary Islands and practiced before the quality of medicine improved and spread to their isolated communities. While Isleños (who are predominantly Catholic) observe Christmas, Easter, and Lent, All Souls' Day, when tombstones are whitewashed and graves tended, is particularly well celebrated. Finally, in recognition of their singular experience, Louisiana's Isleños have recently been recognized by the U.S. government as a distinct Hispanic group.

GILBERT C. DIN
Fort Lewis College

Gilbert C. Din, *The Canary Islanders of Louisiana* (1988); Los Isleños Heritage and Cultural Society, *Los Isleños: A Louisiana Local Legacy* (2000); Raymond R. Mac-

Curdy, *The Spanish Dialect of St. Bernard Parish, Louisiana* (1950); Dorothy L. (Molero) Benge and Laura M. (Gonzales) Sullivan, *Los Isleños Cookbook: Recipes from Spanish Louisiana* (2000); Cecile Jones Robin, *Remedies and Lost Secrets of St. Bernard's Isleños* (2000).

Catawbas

Members of the Catawba Nation of American Indians numbered 2,423 in the 2000 U.S. Census. While Catawbas live in communities across the country, 500 continue to make their homes on the Catawba Indian Reservation, a 630-acre tract located eight miles east of the city of Rock Hill, S.C., along the banks of the Catawba River. The Catawba reservation sits within the tribe's ancestral land. It serves not only as the center of tribal political and business affairs, but also as the focal point for preservation of Catawba culture.

When the ancestors of today's Catawba Indians signed the Treaty of Augusta in 1763, they could not have foreseen the succession of frustrating legal battles that would influence virtually all of their affairs and much of their history. For 230 years, the Catawba filed land claims against the state of South Carolina; eventually, the claims were resolved in the courts and through federal legislation.

Although linguistically related to Siouan peoples, the Catawba of the pre-European contact period shared many of the cultural characteristics of the ancestors of today's Cherokee tribe. Scholars attribute their blended culture to the tribe's geographic location in a transitional zone between "hill tribes" (like the Cherokee) and "southern chiefdoms" (like the Waxhaw). Early Catawba cultural characteristics included sociopolitical organization into small tribal groups located in villages situated near rivers; hunting patterns based on seasonal cycles; cultivation of corn, beans, squash, and gourds; pottery making; and spiritual practices associated with the building of burial mounds. The Catawba forged relationships with some neighboring tribes but fought against the Cherokee, who allied with British colonial governments. (The Catawba allied themselves with the Patriots in the American Revolution.)

The Catawba story is one of survival. After contact with Europeans, which began as early as the 1560s and intensified in the early 1700s, members of the tribe sought to maintain their way of life while recognizing that encroaching Europeans had to be accommodated. In the mid-1700s, notable Catawba leader King Hagler skillfully forged alliances with prominent South Carolina citizens and politicians from whom he secured various, albeit insufficient, forms of support. A tragic result of contact with non-Indians was a devastating smallpox epidemic among the Catawba in 1759, which reduced the tribe's population by 60 percent to a total of 400 members living in a single village. In 1763 the Catawba and South Carolina signed the aforementioned Treaty of Augusta, setting aside the tribe's 15-square-mile reservation.

In 1840 the state of South Carolina and the Catawba Nation signed yet another treaty, this time at Nation's Ford, in which the tribe relinquished lands in exchange for promised financial support and a new reservation. The state never made good on these promises and, significantly, the agreement was signed in violation of the Nonintercourse Act of 1790, a law requiring the consent of the U.S. Congress in land transactions involving American Indians.

During the mid-1800s, a time when the federal government forcibly moved eastern tribes westward to Oklahoma Indian Territory, the Catawbas adamantly remained in South Carolina. As early as the 1880s the tribe sought legal redress for the loss of their land in 1840. The late 1800s also saw the arrival of Mormon missionaries in Catawba country, leading to the conversion of many tribal members (most modern-day Catawbas remain Mormon).

On 14 June 1993 Gilbert Blue, the elected chief of the Catawba Nation, and South Carolina governor Carroll Campbell signed an agreement that led to the passage of the federal Catawba Land Claims Settlement Act (signed by President Bill Clinton on 27 October 1993). The terms of the act included restoration of the Catawba Nation's federal recognition (terminated in 1959) as well as payment of $50 million to the tribe. The act stipulated that the funds be used for land acquisition, economic and social development, education, and per capita payments to tribal members. The settlement has led to cultural preservation initiatives focused on Catawba language, storytelling, and pottery making. Catawbas sponsor reservation-based educational programs for Indians and non-Indians as well as a website that details cultural preservation initiatives. Continued sponsorship of the annual *Yap Ye Iswa* (Day of the Catawba) festival, as well as some members' participation in pan-Indian powwows, are additional means Catawbas take to assure their survival as American Indian people and the preservation of their culture for future generations.

JIM CHARLES
University of South Carolina at Spartanburg

Douglas Summers Brown, *The Catawba Indians: The People of the River* (1966); Charles M. Hudson, *The Catawba Indians* (1970); James H. Merrell, *The Catawbas* (1989), *Indians' New World: Catawbas and Their Neighbors from European Contact through the Era of Removal* (1989).

Cherokees, Eastern Band

As a consequence of their ancestors' 19th-century Removal by the U.S. government, the majority of contemporary Cherokees are part of the Cherokee Nation of Oklahoma. However, the Eastern Band of Cherokee Indians—a federally recognized tribe of about 12,500 members—occupies a reservation of some 57,000 acres in traditional homelands in the mountains of western North Carolina. Its origins date to treaties of 1817 and 1819 that permitted certain members of the Cherokee Nation to separate and reside on private reservations outside the tribal domain. About 50 individuals and their families did so and claimed to be U.S. citizens, though their precise legal status was uncertain. They maintained a traditional Cherokee cultural outlook and continued their association with relatives and friends on the nearby tribal reservation. The 1835 Treaty of New Echota obligated the Cherokee Nation to cede its lands and migrate to present-day Oklahoma, but William Holland Thomas, an Anglo merchant and adopted Cherokee, staunchly defended the right of those holding private reservations to remain, and he helped them acquire additional lands. Neither the United States nor the state of North Carolina attempted to evict these Indians. A few members of the Cherokee Nation hid out in the mountains or otherwise avoided Removal, and they soon joined the Cherokee who legally remained in North Carolina. By 1839 about 1,100 Cherokees lived in the state, with perhaps 300 more in Georgia, Tennessee, and Alabama.

Between 1839 and the outbreak of the Civil War, North Carolina Cherokees lived quietly on marginal mountain lands and endured periodic attempts to enroll them for Removal to the West. Had their lands been more attractive to whites, they probably would have been forced to leave. Their way of life blended Cherokee culture with that of their poor white neighbors. They lived as nuclear families in log cabins and raised corn on tiny individual farms, mixed Christianity with Cherokee beliefs and practices, sought consensus in periodic councils, and fiercely competed in the Indian game of stickball. Few of these Cherokees spoke English, and most relied on Thomas to protect their interests. With the coming of the war, Thomas incorporated Cherokee and European

Cherokee woman making pottery in North Carolina (Hugh Morton, photographer)

American mountaineers into his own Confederate military force, the Thomas Legion. A much smaller number of Cherokee served on the Union side.

At the war's end, the Indians were impoverished, starving, disease-ridden, and divided into factions. Thomas was suffering the onset of mental illness and could no longer provide effective leadership nor protect Cherokee lands. To remedy the situation, the United States in 1868 recognized the Indians as the Eastern Band of Cherokee and placed the tribe under the supervision of the Bureau of Indian Affairs. By 1880 the federal government had established a tribal reservation consisting of a number of scattered units in southwestern North Carolina and was also providing educational opportunities for Cherokee children. In 1889 the Eastern Band incorporated under North Carolina law, and with later amendments this charter provided a political and economic framework under which the Indians continue to operate.

From the 1890s through the 1920s, the Eastern Band's economy centered on commercial exploitation of tribal forests by outside corporations. By 1930, however, the new Great Smoky Mountains National Park, adjoining the Qualla Boundary (the official name of the reservation), promised to make tourism the economic mainstay. Park visitors, it was believed, would also want to see "real" Indians. The Great Depression and World War II delayed development, but since 1945 a growing Indian-based tourist infrastructure, especially in the town of Cherokee, has accommodated millions of reservation visitors. In 1982 the Eastern Band opened a high-stakes bingo hall that attracted visitors from all over the eastern United States, and in 1995, under the terms of the 1988 Indian Gaming Regulatory Act, it set up a small casino. Two years later a much larger casino opened under outside management; by 2003 it featured a 15-story hotel, had about 900 employees, and brought the Eastern Band $139 million a year — enough to support major tribal improvements and annual payments of about $6,000 to every enrolled member. Gaming income and a tribal sales tax also support the preservation and enhancement of tribal culture, partly through the Cherokee Preservation Foundation. This economic growth and the increasing per capita payments have exacerbated old disputes over who deserves to be included on the tribal roll.

Since 1975 federal Indian policy has encouraged self-determination for all tribes, and by the early 21st century the Eastern Band was originating and supervising most of its own programs while the Bureau of Indian Affairs operated in an advisory capacity.

JOHN FINGER
University of Tennessee

John R. Finger, *Cherokee Americans: The Eastern Band of Cherokees in the Twentieth Century* (1991), *The Eastern Band of Cherokee Indians, 1819–1900* (1984); Sharlotte Neely, *Snowbird Cherokees: People of Persistence* (1991).

Cherokees, Prior to Removal

According to both native and nonnative accounts, Cherokee history has been characterized by the interplay of centripetal forces (such as pressure from encroaching Indian and European American groups) and centrifugal ones (such as the diaspora-spawning Removal of 1838–39). Among the most important themes characterizing Cherokee life before 1838 were the importance of individual and town-level autonomy, complementarity based on gender and generation, and social organization based on exogamous matrilineal clans. But in the generations prior to the forced Removal to Indian Territory, the Cherokee political structure gradually became more centralized and hierarchical, gender complementarity shifted to give some priority to the power and resources controlled by men, and matrilineal descent was challenged by European American models of kinship and property transmission. A society that had been internally balanced and reinforced by its traditional subdivisions grew divided by new ones based on descent, religion, traditionalism, and attitudes toward Removal.

Elohi, a Cherokee migration account, tells of Cherokees migrating to their historic location from a flood-plagued land and fighting off sequential waves of invading enemies, of whom Europeans are merely the latest manifestation. By 1835 a series of land cessions would leave the Cherokees centered in northwestern Georgia and with only a fraction of their lands, which had once extended from northern Alabama and South Carolina to the Ohio River and from the Tennessee River on the west to the Catawba River on the east.

Archaeological evidence suggests that Appalachian Summit communities showing cultural continuity with the historic Cherokee may date back to 1000 A.D. One source estimates the precontact Cherokee population at 28,000 to 30,000. Speaking an Iroquoian language (thought to have split from related languages at least 3,500 years ago), the Cherokee were linguistically isolated in a region where Muskogean languages predominated. European accounts of the historic Cherokee begin through 16th-century encounters with Spanish explorers in the southern Appalachians. Towns of this period and region, which were perhaps associated with Cherokees, featured communal structures built on mounds and had populations subsisting on a combination of maize horticulture and hunting.

In the late 17th century, Cherokees began establishing trade relations with the British, and the deerskin trade came to dominate Cherokee economic life. The objective of men's hunting shifted from subsistence to individual wealth accumulation (or the payment of debts). New dependencies developed on commodities such as metal tools, firearms, cloth, and alcohol. Some scholars argue that their mountain location made the Cherokee better able to withstand some of the devastating consequences of early European contact, particularly the epidemics and slave trade that decimated other southeastern tribes. They remained relatively strong and well organized compared to neighboring groups. Some also argue that early 18th-century Cherokee communities were ethnically and linguistically diverse, reflecting the coalescence of various local remnant populations. In 1800 the Cherokee had an estimated population of 16,000.

Ethnohistory and archaeology provide a more complete picture of Cherokee cultural life during the 18th century. Cherokees lived in five regional groupings of autonomous towns clustered along river valleys in northern Georgia, South Carolina, southwestern North Carolina, and western Tennessee. These town clusters, consisting of 10 to 12 villages with populations of 100 to 600 people each, corresponded to dialects in the Cherokee language and represented different ecological adaptations. Towns were organized around a council house, a more open summer townhouse, and a plaza or square ground. Individual households contained extended matrilineal kin and consisted of a summer house and a winter or hot house for medicinal and other uses.

The social, economic, and ceremonial life of towns was organized by a system of seven exogamous, matrilineal clans, whose names are represented as follows by contemporary Eastern Band Cherokees: *Aniwahya* (Wolf); *Anikawi* (Deer); *Anitsiskwa* (Bird); *Aniwodi* (Paint); *Anisahoni* (Blue); *Anigatagewi* (Wild Potato); and *Anigilohi* (Long Hair). Clans regulated marriage, provided hospitality to traveling clan members, exacted retribution for the killing of their members, and had specific ceremonial obligations. Women held considerable power as clan leaders. Towns were also divided into two complementary men's organizations: the white or peace organization, dominated by the older men, and the red or war organization, controlled by the younger men. The red organization led military, trading, and hunting expeditions; the white organization dominated town politics unless the town was under attack.

Women controlled the local horticultural economy, based on corn, beans, squash, and other crops. They also gathered vegetable foods, especially wild greens, and medicinal herbs. Though women were responsible for cultivation, men assisted with clearing the fields and with the harvest. Men hunted game, most commonly deer.

Spiritual and medicinal activity focused on taboo observation and the respectful treatment of spiritual beings. Medicine men treated patients with a combination of formulaic prayer designed to summon curative spirits and remove malevolent ones, give herbal treatments, and provide other ac-

tions such as immersion in water or scratching. The focus of the ceremonial year was the Green Corn ceremony. Some accounts suggest that spiritual leadership was hereditary at one time through the existence of a priestly clan, since destroyed or expelled. In historic times, however, spiritual and medicinal power seems to have been linked to individuals.

The Cherokee fought unsuccessfully against the colonists during the American Revolution, and the new American government engaged in widespread retaliatory raids on Cherokee towns. As they were emerging from the disastrous consequences of that war, the Cherokee encountered a new challenge at the turn of the 19th century—the "civilization" program. A combination of federal entities, missionaries, and some members of their own communities sought to introduce new cultural elements, such as European American agricultural modes of production (including the use of African slave labor), Christianity, formal education, and centralized government. These new practices and institutions were not adopted equally or at all by every member of Cherokee society and produced some lasting divisions, sometimes pitting those of mixed European American and Cherokee ancestry ("mixed bloods") against those of Cherokee descent only ("full bloods"). This new, nonmatrilineal way of thinking about kinship and descent further undermined traditional culture. Some argue, though, that the Cherokee were highly adaptable in their response to these pressures, and that they therefore enjoyed a kind of renaissance in this period. One of their most triumphant achievements—the invention of an indigenous writing system for the Cherokee language (the Cherokee syllabary) by the monolingual traditionalist Sequoyah—occurred in the 1820s.

MARGARET BENDER
Wake Forest University

Fred O. Gearing, *Priests and Warriors: Social Structures for Cherokee Politics in the 18th Century* (1962); William G. McLoughlin, *Cherokee Renascence in the New Republic* (1986); Howard Meredith and Virginia Sobral, eds., *Cherokee Vision of Elohi* (1997); James Mooney, *Myths of the Cherokee and Sacred Formulas of the Cherokees* (1982); Theda Perdue, *Cherokee Women: Gender and Culture Change, 1700–1835* (1998); Christopher B. Rodning, in *Between Contacts and Colonies: Archaeological Perspectives on the Protohistoric Southeast*, ed. Cameron B. Wesson and Mark A. Reese (2002); Gerald F. Schroedl, in *Indians of the Greater Southeast*, ed. Bonnie G. McEwan (2000), in *Archaeology of the Appalachian Highlands*, ed. Lynne P. Sullivan and Susan C. Prezzano (2001); Circe Sturm, *Blood Politics: Race, Culture, and Identity in the Cherokee Nation of Oklahoma* (2002); Russell Thornton, *The Cherokees: A Population History* (1900).

Chickasaws

The Chickasaw in late pre-Columbian times numbered an estimated 4,000 and claimed a territory astride western Kentucky, Tennessee, northern Alabama, and Mississippi. Most Chickasaw lifeways resembled those of their neighbors—Choctaw, Creek, Cherokee, and Natchez. The Chickasaw are related to the Choctaw; the tribes' Muskogean language, except for mild dialectal differences, is the same. Early European observers described these Indians as "tall, well-built people, with reddish skin, raven black hair, and large, dark eyes." They had a strong warrior tradition, and their incessant wars with neighboring tribes led them to replace losses in combat by adoption of captives and absorption of tribal remnants. Chickasaw men were hunters and warriors first and farmers only on occasion. Chickasaw women and Indian slaves cleared land, cared for crops, and gathered firewood.

During the 18th century, the Spanish, French, and British vied for Chickasaw support in their drive for control of the Lower Mississippi Valley. British traders from Charleston eventually succeeded in building an alliance with the Chickasaw. Between 1720 and 1752, French armies from New Orleans invaded Chickasaw territory to force the tribe to abandon its allegiance to the British, but each invasion ended in French defeat. Chickasaws served with British armies in the Lower Mississippi Valley during the Seven Years' War (1756–63). Chickasaws also supported the British during the American Revolution, fighting in Tory armies in the west against American insurgents.

Soon after 1800 the Chickasaw came under the influence of missionaries and white neighbors settling on the margins of their territory. Indian youth attended mission schools, became literate, and eventually ascended to positions of tribal leadership. Several became slaveholders and developed productive plantations on tribal lands.

Through successive treaties with federal officials, Chickasaw leaders ceded tribal territory in western Tennessee and Kentucky, so that by 1830 all that remained of their once vast domain was a residual area in northern Mississippi and a fragment in northern Alabama. By the Treaty of Pontotoc in 1832, and an amendatory treaty in 1834, the Chickasaws agreed to sell their eastern lands and remove to Indian Territory. In 1837 Chickasaw and Choctaw leaders signed the Treaty of Doaksville, whereby the Chickasaw accepted a home in the Choctaw Nation. In 1855 a treaty with the Choctaw permitted the Chickasaw to establish a separate union in south-central Indian Territory. They adopted a constitution that provided for an elective council, a chief executive (governor) of the Chickasaw Nation, a judiciary, and a public school system. In the antebellum period the Chickasaws sustained themselves by farming, raising livestock, and frontier trade.

During 1861 the Chickasaw Nation joined the Confederate States of America, and Chickasaw companies fought in several campaigns against Union troops in the Indian Territory. The Chickasaw were required to follow the provisions of Reconstruction, which included freeing their slaves and altering their constitution to provide equal civil and social status for freedpeople.

Pressed by the federal Dawes Commission during the late 19th century to adopt allotment in severalty (meaning the parceling of land separately and to individuals rather than communally), Chickasaw and Choctaw leaders finally submitted by signing the Atoka Agreement in 1897. The following year the Curtis Act set forth the process for dissolving the Chickasaw Nation, and in 1907 the Chickasaw were absorbed into the new state of Oklahoma.

ARRELL MORGAN GIBSON
University of Oklahoma

James R. Atkinson, *Splendid Land, Splendid People: The Chickasaw Indians to Removal* (2003); Robbie Ethridge and Charles Hudson, eds., *The Transformation of the Southeastern Indians, 1540–1760* (2001); Arrell Morgan Gibson, *The Chickasaws* (1971); John I. Griffen, ed., *The Chickasaw People* (1974); Daniel F. Littlefield, *The Chickasaw Freedmen: A People without a Country* (1980); Theda Perdue and Michael D. Green, *The Columbia Guide to American Indians of the Southeast* (2001).

Chickasaws in the 20th Century

The motto most associated with the Chickasaw is "Unconquered and Unconquerable," a legacy imparted to them as the only tribe in the Southeast never to have lost a battle. Their national seal depicts a warrior holding onto the long bow that made them such fierce adversaries. One of the last holdouts among southeastern tribes, the Chickasaw reluctantly signed the Treaty of Doaksville in 1837, which secured them new land in Indian Territory (Oklahoma). By the close of the 19th century, the federal Dawes Commission had decided to assimilate American Indians by dispersing their lands through mandated allotments, allowing all residual acreage to be acquired by increasingly abundant European Americans. Despite this legacy of Removal and assimilation, the Chickasaw remain a vibrant, sovereign nation.

Through many years of legal negotiations and economic endeavors, the Chickasaw Nation has resiliently organized as a political unit. Governor Bill Anoatubby has held the highest Chickasaw Nation political office since the early 1990s, providing a consistency and stability rare for most Indian populations. Occupying almost 8,000 square miles in all or part of 12 counties in south-central Oklahoma, they continue to purchase available lands nearby. Current tribal enrollment stands at about 39,000, with more than half the members living on tribal territory. Blood quantum requirements for enrollment are much like their tribal neighbors who require that an enrolled ancestor on the Dawes Commission rolls be documented.

The Chickasaw belong to the Muskogean linguistic family. Their oral and written language is similar to that of the Choctaw Nation, although some dialect differences emerge in Chickasaw speech. During the 17th and 18th centuries, the Chickasaw language served as the principal language of commercial and tribal communication for all the tribes along the lower Mississippi River. The word "Chickasaw" is the anglicized version of the tribe's name for itself, *Chikasha*, which roughly translates to "he who walked ahead." Today, elders assist in the teaching and learning of the language. A Chickasaw "talking" dictionary is available on CD-Rom to encourage younger speakers. According to a recent estimate, only about 300 speakers remain, not all of whom are fluent.

Unfortunately, historians and anthropologists have recorded relatively little about the Chickasaw compared to other Oklahoma and southeastern tribes. A traditionally matrilineal, agricultural society, much of Chickasaw culture was lost or went underground as they were forced into federally sponsored "Indian programs" and mission boarding schools.

A tribute to their heritage is the revitalization of stomp dances, all-night ceremonial dances that the Chickasaw believe their ancestors performed at the beginning of time. What locals call the Kullihoma Reservation, a small community east of Ada, Okla. (the governmental seat of the Chickasaw Nation), is the preferred site for stomp dances and is also home to reconstructions of traditional Chickasaw homes. Visitors can tour a rectangular summer house, circular winter house, and stilted corn cribs. Gatherings and special events continue to take place at Kullihoma.

Today, considered a highly "progressive" tribe, the Chickasaw have developed state-of-the-art services to meet most needs of a growing nation. In the area of health care, the Chickasaw began what would be a major movement among Indian nations, by successfully "compacting" or taking control of their own health services in 1994. Comprehensive health care is now available through four facilities located throughout Chickasaw country.

Tribal administrators also have developed a wide variety of youth and family services, programs for the elderly and disabled, cultural programs, innovative mapping services for planning, development, and maintenance, and a highly advanced technical department that constructs multimedia websites about the Chickasaw Nation's history and heritage.

LISA J. LEFLER
Western Carolina University

SAMANTHA HURST
University of California, San Diego

Duane Champagne, *Social Order and Political Change: Constitutional Governments among the Cherokee, the Choctaw, the Chickasaw, and the Creek* (1992); H. B. Cushman, *History of the Choctaw, Chickasaw, and Natchez Indians*, ed. Angie Debo (1999); Anne K. Hoyt, *Bibliography of the Chickasaw* (1987); Arrell M. Gibson, *The Chickasaw* (1971); John R. Swanton, *The Indians of the Southeastern United States* (1988); Muriel H. Wright, *A Guide to the Indian Tribes of Oklahoma* (1986).

Chinese

Chinese first came to the South to work in cotton and sugarcane fields and in construction of Texas railroads. Young men from the artisan and peasant classes also traveled as sojourners to Texas, Mississippi, and Louisiana. These first arrivals were especially from the Sze Yap (or Four Counties) district of the Guangdong Province in southern China. In 1867 the first Chinese workers, called the derogatory name "coolies," arrived in Natchitoches, La., at the encouragement of local cotton and sugar planters. These first Louisiana arrivals were Spanish speakers, as they came not from the western United States or directly from China but from Havana and Matanzas, Cuba, where they had been fulfilling contract agricultural labor. Much like other Chinese who came to the United States in the 1800s, the Chinese in the South sent most of their money home to their families and originally planned to retire to their homeland. Their prosperity encouraged the immigration of family members and friends.

During Reconstruction, planters and business owners began recruiting Asians as a new source of labor to replace freed slaves. Most found employment in agricultural work, although some took railroad construction jobs. They soon realized their new role in the plantation system would not foster the wealth with which they had hoped to return to China, and many left farmwork in the late 19th century to work in laundries and restaurants in urban areas. In the rural Mississippi Delta, many Chinese opened small grocery and agricultural supply stores. There they found their economic niche by supplying African Americans, who were often turned away or refused credit by white grocers, with new cash purchasing power. Chinese men replaced slave labor at the sugar plantations in Jefferson Parish, La., where they often intermarried with African Americans or American Indians. Fewer than 1,000 Chinese had come to the South before the federal Chinese Exclusion Act of 1882.

Once the Exclusion Act was repealed by the 1943 Magnuson Act, the Chinese communities in Mississippi attracted new arrivals and communities also began forming in Houston and San Antonio. By 1900 El Paso had a small Chinatown. In Texas, cultural distinctions separated the "Old" and "New" Chinese immigrants and continue to do so. The Cantonese-speaking, 19th-century immigrants were mostly from southern China, while 20th-century arrivals were from various other locations in China and predominantly spoke Mandarin. The older immigrants came mostly from peasant backgrounds, were upwardly mobile, and often succeeded in business. The newer immigrants were of China's elite and focused on the professions. Descendants of the older immigrants long maintained a focus on clan or family association (defined by surname). Today, Chinese New Year may still be celebrated, and a Confucian emphasis on family obligations remains strong. Many Chinese in the South are now Baptists.

Considered "colored," Chinese children attended African American schools. The Chinese established a few private schools in Texas and Mississippi with the assistance of Baptist missions, whose members sought to convert Chinese immigrants and provide a vehicle for acculturation. Not until the 1950s and 1960s, when approximately 10,000 Chinese called the South home, did Chinese children begin attending white public schools.

Many southerners came to see the Chinese as having a social identity "between black and white" in a biracial hierarchy. Chinese grocery stores were almost always established in mixed African American and Chinese neighborhoods. Neighborhood residents, both black and Chinese, were the regular clientele for these "mom and pop" establishments, although whites also patronized them on occasion.

The lack of a Chinatown such as those in more urban areas has not prevented the Delta Chinese from forming a distinct community. Although there has been some competition between family-owned businesses, extended families form support networks. Store labor is shared, with both young and old taking their turns stocking shelves and bagging groceries. Meals are in a traditional family style, usually with Chinese dishes, but those sitting at the table rotate in shifts while the store is open.

Regular mahjong nights (a gambling game for four players) often characterize evenings with families and neighbors, and tournaments even take place at Chinese Baptist church halls. Birthday and wedding celebrations have a distinctly Chinese style, with traditional decorations (such as wall hangings of calligraphic characters), speeches given in Cantonese, and Chinese food. Holidays such as Chinese New Year and the New Moon Festival are recognized, typically with smaller, extended family gatherings. Cantonese, the dialect of the Guangdong Province and most of the Delta Chinese, is passed on to children in varying degrees in the home.

The number of Chinese families in the Mississippi Delta continuing to live a "grocery store" lifestyle is shrinking, as many of the younger generation are moving away for other opportunities

Chinese grocery, Vicksburg, Miss., 1975 (William R. Ferris Collection, Southern Folklife Collection, Wilson Library, University of North Carolina at Chapel Hill)

and going into the professions. Delta retirees are frequently replaced not by their children, but rather by Chinese families looking to immigrate into the area. New immigrants are increasingly coming from large urban areas within the United States to escape the higher cost of living in cities like New York, Los Angeles, and Chicago. This is true across the South, as small towns from Arkansas to southern Appalachia are now home to Chinese restaurants and fast-food takeouts. Additionally, Chinese herbal shops and Chinese medical practitioners are becoming easier to locate even in the rural South. Chi gong (Qigong) and Tai chi groups—practicing breathing and moving exercises related to the martial arts but focused on health and the mind/body/soul relationship—are now more common in urban areas and on southern university campuses. China's historical relations with the South are also beginning to receive more attention from scholars. For example, the first Chinese women to be educated in the United States were May-ling Soong and her sisters, who studied at Wesleyan College in Macon, Ga. May-ling was later to become Madame Chiang Kai-shek, one of China's most significant political and military leaders in the first half of the 20th century.

MELINDA CHOW
University of Memphis

Lucy Cohen, *Chinese in the Post–Civil War South: A People without a History* (1984); James W. Loewen, *The Mississippi Chinese: Between Black and White* (1988); Robert Seto Quan, *Lotus among the Magnolias: The Mississippi Chinese* (1982); Ronald Takaki,

Strangers from a Different Shore: A History of Asian Americans (1998).

Chitimachas

The Chitimacha tribe of Louisiana maintains a reservation adjacent to the town of Charenton in St. Mary Parish in south Louisiana. According to their oral history, the Chitimacha "have always been here." They are the only tribe in Louisiana to occupy a portion of their aboriginal homeland. Today, the Chitimacha tribe operates its own school (constructed in 1978 to replace the small and outdated schoolhouse then in use), provides social and emergency services to tribal members in the Charenton vicinity, and operates the Cypress Bayou Casino. Current tribal membership is just under 1,075 individuals.

Current Chitimacha culture is an amalgam of Chitimacha and Cajun influences. Generally, the Chitimacha are Christians, predominantly Catholics and Baptists. Historically, the Chitimacha once participated in stomp dances at dance grounds along lakeshores of south Louisiana to mark social and religious occasions, but these dances are no longer held. The Chitimacha language is all but lost, with the last fluent speaker, Benjamin Paul, having died in 1934. Fortunately, ethnographers such as Morris Swadesh and John Swanton recorded enough of the language in writing and on wax cylinders for there to be a renewal. Since 1996 the Chitimacha language has been taught to the youth at the Chitimacha Tribal School and at Yamahana, the early-learning center on the reservation.

Documentary evidence and information from tribal interviewees has increased knowledge of the Chitimacha tribe prior to European contact. The Chitimacha's hereditary class system did not allow for upward movement and required commoners to employ different forms of address for the elite. Swanton's early 20th-century research revealed that totemic clans based on matrilineal descent also existed, but the Chitimacha recalled only the wolf, bear, dog, and lion clan by that time.

The Chitimacha subsisted on maize, potatoes, and wild game, especially deer, alligator, and aquatic species. As hunters they employed bone, stone, or garfish scale–pointed arrows, or they used blow guns and wooden darts and nets for fishing. Prolific ceramic producers until about two centuries ago, the Chitimacha continue to make baskets that imitate ceramic design. The Chitimacha are especially proud of their double-woven baskets. According to tribal tradition, a deity taught the Chitimacha basketry techniques that included 51 different design elements, which are now combined to create hundreds of different basket designs in various shapes and sizes.

At the time of European contact, the Chitimacha were one of the most powerful tribes between Florida and Texas. Pierre Le Moyne, Sieur d'Iberville, an early French explorer, encountered the Chitimacha and one of their subtribes, the Washa, along the Mississippi River in 1699. In 1706, as a response to slave raids and French aggression, a group of Chitimacha killed Jean Francois St. Cosme and several members of his party, who were missionaries to the Natchez. Another French explorer, Jean-Baptiste Le Moyne, Sieur de Bienville, bribed other tribes to make war on the Chitimacha until 1718, when a Chitimacha chief met Bienville in the fledgling city of New Orleans. Many Chitimacha were enslaved during the 12 years of conflict. Villages located along Bayou Lafouche, then called the River of the Chitimacha, and those farther to the east were pushed to the south and to the west. Many Chitimacha retreated across the Atchafalaya Basin to villages of their nation located along Grand Lake and the Bayou Teche, where the tribe remains today.

When peace came the French, and later the Spanish and American governments, officially recognized the integrity of the Chitimacha tribe and its land ownership rights. After the Jefferson administration purchased the Louisiana Territory, the Chitimacha lands received protection through the Indian Nonintercourse Act. In 1826 the Chitimacha claimed 20 arpents front and 40 deep on either side of the Bayou Teche, totaling approximately 5,440 acres. However, the U.S. government injudiciously processed land claims from the preceding French and Spanish governments to distribute "unclaimed" lands to new settlers.

Forced to sue the federal government to confirm title to their lands in 1846, the Chitimacha retained only 1,093 acres, about one-fifth of what they possessed 20 years earlier. This land base withered further through sales by Eugenia Soulier Rouge, "chieftess," and

because of judgments against the tribe for state taxes. Sara McIlhenny, a friend of the tribe and collector of their baskets, intervened to protect 261.54 acres of tribal lands, which were put in trust for the tribe in 1919. In recent years, the tribe purchased 693 acres in the vicinity of tribal trust lands and now owns a total of 955 acres, approximately 443 of which are trust lands.

In 1916 the Chitimacha tribe was federally recognized by the U.S. government. Having had a traditional government with a chief, the General Council of the Chitimacha People voted to adopt a constitutional form of government on 7 November 1970. The constitution gives membership criteria, provides for residence on trust lands, and, most importantly, regulates governance of tribal affairs through a five-member tribal council. The chief executive of the Chitimacha tribe is the tribal chairperson.

JASON EMERY
Chitimacha Tribe of Louisiana

Dayna Bowker Lee, *The Chitimacha Land Base from the Colonial Period to the Present* (1991); Herbert Hoover, *The Chitimacha People* (1975); John R. Swanton, *Indian Tribes of the Lower Mississippi Valley and Adjacent Coast of the Gulf of Mexico* (1911); Gertrude C. Taylor, *Attakapas Gazette* (1981).

Choctaws

Approximately 8,900 enrolled members of the Mississippi Band of Choctaw Indians live in eight recognized communities across east-central Mississippi and in smaller communities in southern Tennessee and southern Mississippi.

Choctaw children in traditional dress (Photograph courtesy of Mississippi Band of Choctaw Indians)

Oral traditions provide two explanations for the Choctaw presence in the South. According to the migration legend, the Choctaw once lived west of the Mississippi River until scarce game and divine guidance led them to their present home in Mississippi. In the emergence legend, the Choctaw were created along with the other major tribes of the Southeast—the Chickasaw, Creek, Cherokee, and Seminole—from an earthen mound. The Choctaw, the last to be created, were chosen to stay at this point of creation. In both stories, the sacred Nanih Waiya mound figures centrally as the exact location of the Choctaw homeland.

Written records first identify the Choctaw by name at the end of the 17th century, although Chief Tuscaloosa, who thwarted Hernando de Soto in 1540, is frequently identified as Choc-taw. By the 18th century the Choctaw were mired in colonial wars, allying first with the French against the British and Chickasaw, and then later with the new Americans against the Spanish and the Creek. Allegiance to the United States, however, did not protect the Choctaw from the harsh colonial policies of the new nation. Pressured into a series of treaties during the early 19th century, the Choctaw ceded over 28 million acres of land to the U.S. government. The Treaty of Dancing Rabbit Creek in 1830 marked the beginning of the Indian Removal from the Southeast, with the Choctaw being the first to go.

According to the treaty, the Choctaw could remain in Mississippi and assimilate or remove to Oklahoma and retain federal recognition as Choctaw. Those who left formed the Choctaw Nation of Oklahoma, which today numbers over 20,000. Those who stayed in Mississippi were forced to eke out a living as squatters and then sharecroppers on land they once owned. They remained isolated in a biracial South, where they could not be white and to be black was to be disempowered by segregation. One benefit of this isolation, however, was the continued development of a unique ethnic identity, allowing the community to maintain their language and social customs.

Throughout most of the 20th century, the majority of Choctaw worked as farmers. Stickball and dancing were the dominant forms of entertainment, particularly during long weekends when communities would gather. This tradition developed into the annual Choctaw Fair, a combination of reunion, festival, stickball tournament, country and indigenous music concert, and cultural display. The fair is a useful symbol of Choctaw daily life, with its combination of traditional and mainstream culture. Basketball is as common today as swamp-cane basket weaving. With little existing information about traditional Choctaw religion, the majority of the Choctaw today are Christian, although most also maintain some degree of belief in the old stories and practices of the elders.

In 1934 the U.S. Congress passed the Indian Reorganization Act, which allowed tribes once again to govern themselves independently. By 1945 the Choctaw had ratified a constitution and elected Joe Chitto as their first tribal chairperson. In 1979 Phillip Martin became tribal chief and began a series of economic ventures on the reservation that now include an 80-acre industrial park, a construction company, two casinos, and a resort area, helping make the tribe one of the largest employers in the state. Only a decade ago, over 90 percent of the population was fluent in the Choctaw language. The statistics are beginning to invert, with over 90 percent of Choctaw children under the age of five not able to speak the language. To combat this language loss, the tribe is engaged in a series of programs to teach, maintain, and reinvigorate the language and customs of the tribe.

While tribal members maintain a specific tribal identity, they are also making efforts to connect to American Indians across the country. The Choctaw are active members of a number of national Indian organizations, such as the Native American Sports Association and the United South and Eastern Tribes. Further, tribal groups such as the Chahta Alla Youth Council meet with American Indian youth groups across the country. More recently, the tribe has begun hosting intertribal powwows that bring American Indians of all tribes together.

TOM MOULD
Elon University

Patricia Galloway, *Choctaw Genesis* (1995); Tom Mould, *Choctaw Prophecy: A Legacy of the Future* (2003); John. H. Peterson Jr., *The Mississippi Band of Choctaw Indians: Their Recent History and Current Social Relations* (1971); John R. Swanton, *Source Material for the Social and Ceremonial Life of the Choctaw Indians* (1931).

Coharies

The Coharie Indian tribe is primarily located in Sampson and Harnett Counties in southeast North Carolina. The tribe consists of approximately 2,600 members, living in the New Bethel Indian community north of Clinton, the Holly Grove Indian community in south Clinton, the Shiloh Indian community in rural Sampson County, and the Dunn Indian community in rural Harnett County. By tradition, the Coharie Indian tribe descends from the Neusiok Indians, who were forced from their homelands in northeastern North Carolina in the 18th century.

The Coharie tribe had a small presence in Sampson County by the late 18th and early 19th centuries. In 1859, for example, tribal members established subscription schools for Indian children at a time when the state provided no public support for the education of Indians. This began a tradition in the Coharie community by which schools and churches became the two most important institutions of membership inside the tribe. In 1910 the tribe was successful in lobbying the Sampson County government for a school especially for tribal members. The county established Shiloh Indian School, which operated until 1940. In 1911 tribal members petitioned the state for an additional school in Sampson County, upon which New Bethel Indian School was established in the New Bethel community. Other schools for the exclusive use of tribal members were later opened in North Carolina, including one in the Holly Grove community (ca. 1923)

and one in Dunn (1942). Established in 1943, the East Carolina Indian Training School in Sampson County enrolled only Indian children in grades 1–12 until 1966.

With the creation of the Shiloh Pentecostal Holiness Church in 1907, members of the Coharie tribe began establishing exclusively Indian churches within the tribal territory, a practice continued until 1965. These institutions served political purposes as well as religious purposes. Tribal leaders would use the churches as a forum to discuss and address tribal issues.

In the early 20th century, Coharie tribal members created a formal system of government with the establishment of the Sampson County Indian Clan. From the 1910 record documenting the election of the tribe's first chief, the purpose of the clan was to govern tribal affairs. The state of North Carolina officially recognized the tribe in 1911; however, because of complaints from the non-Indian local community, the law was rescinded in 1913. It was not until four years later, in 1917, that the state again recognized the Coharie Indian tribe.

The tribe's headquarters are in Clinton, N.C. The Coharie Intra-Tribal Council, Inc., an organization consisting of elected representatives from each of the Coharie tribal communities, administers its programs and governs tribal affairs. Goals of the organization include promoting health, education, and the social and economic well-being of the Coharie tribal membership. The Coharie Intra-Tribal Council operates two daycare centers, a fish farm, a tribal federal housing program under the Native American Housing and Self Determination Act, job training assistance programs, and several programs dedicated to the needs of tribal elders.

The Coharie sponsor a number of cultural programs, including the annual Coharie Powwow held every September on the original grounds of the East Carolina Indian Training School. This event is the successor of the original Indian Day started in 1969 by tribal leaders to celebrate Coharie history. Today, the annual powwow remains one of the region's most popular celebrations, attended by both tribal members and the local non-Indian community.

Currently the tribe is working toward obtaining federal recognition. Their efforts began in the early 1980s by submitting a letter of intent to petition for federal recognition to the Bureau of Indian Affairs. The tribe continues research to complete a documented petition.

CLYDE ELLIS
Elon College

John Lawson, *A New Voyage To Carolina*, ed. Hugh T. Lefler (1984); James Mooney, *Siouan Tribes of the East* (1894); Theda Perdue, *Native Carolinians: The Indians of North Carolina* (1985); Theda Perdue and Michael Green, *The Columbia Guide to American Indians of the Southeast* (2001); Thomas E. Ross, *American Indians in North Carolina: Geographic Interpretations* (1999); Ruth Wetmore, *First on the Land: The North Carolina Indians* (1975); Clyde Ellis, *Our State* (November 2000).

Conchs

A Conch today is regarded as any native of the Florida Keys. Identity requires no other imperative commonly associated with ethnicity, not even the distinction of being a descendant of the first Conchs of the Florida Keys.

Origins, vocation, and association with the conch (an edible gastropod mollusk of tropical waters) were the primary defining characteristics of the original Conchs. They were British subjects of the Bahamas who came to the Florida Keys in the early 19th century. Hailing from British, Irish, and African stock, they were white, black, and of mixed lineage. Many had been slaves or were a generation removed from slavery in the British West Indies and probably British Florida. Some were descendants of separatists known as Eleutheran Adventurers, who left England for the Bahamas in 1649 seeking freedom from the English church and government. According to one source, most among the Adventurers had been fisherfolk of Cockney origin, and in the Bahamas they dwelled mainly on the island of Abaco. Their number expanded significantly when British Loyalists fled the North American mainland for the Bahamas during the American Revolution. Eventually, the opportunities in fishing, sponging, turtling, and wrecking drew Conchs to the Florida Keys. As late as the 1930s, workers for the Federal Writers' Project reported that an English lilt was noticeable in the speech of Florida Conchs.

As in the origins of the name "cracker," competing theories explain the Conch derivation. The term almost certainly originated in the Bahamas and derives from the conch and its place in the culture of the island dwellers. According to one theory, Conchs got their name when at some point they informed British authorities that they would rather eat conchs than pay taxes to the Crown. Given that the conch was a principal source of protein in the diet of Bahamians, the story seems apocryphal. Sources also say that when Bahamians recaptured Nassau from the Spanish in 1783, they raised a flag with a conch shell emblazoned on its canvas. In yet another story, inhabitants of a small island, uncertain of which national flag to honor during the British and Spanish struggle over the Bahamas, returned a salute from a passing American ship by raising a conch shell attached to the end of a pole. Although politics may have been a factor, ethnonym derivation likely has more to do with diet and the conch shell's use as a horn. When blown, it allowed for communicating across and between islands.

Through the early 20th century, Florida Conchs remained a distinguishable people who, with one notable exception, generally confined themselves to the Keys. Following World War I, black Bahamians began migrating to the south Florida mainland for seasonal jobs in farming and at resort hotels. A permanent colony that established itself on Singer's Island in Lake Worth and later at Riviera acquired the name Conch. The men tended to work as fishers, and the women wove palm-thatch baskets, hats, purses, and other items for sale to tourists.

With Key West as the nominal capital, the Florida Keys are now known as the Conch Republic, made popular by the music and culture of Jimmy Buffett. A symbolic designation rather than a legally constituted entity, the Conch Republic arose in 1982 when residents staged an act of secession from the Union in protest of a U.S. Border Patrol blockade set up north of the Keys on U.S. 1.

Much like Cajun culture, Conch heritage has been co-opted by distorted symbolism, popular culture, and tourism. Whether built by Conchs or not, the historic houses of 19th-century wood-frame construction in Key West are commonly referred to as examples of classical Conch architecture. The original Conch houses, however, were constructed from mortar made from a mixture of water, sand, and lime (obtained from burning conch shells), with conch shells serving in place of bricks and stones. The Conch diet is preserved in the nouveau cuisine of Florida conch chowder, conch fritters, conch salads, and conch stew found on restaurant menus and in popular cookbooks. At retail outlets throughout the Keys, tourists can buy conch shells as keepsakes, which the original Conchs believed brought bad luck. Finally, newcomers with no ancestral link to the original Conchs are given the appellation "Freshwater Conchs" when they establish permanent residence in the Keys.

JACK E. DAVIS
University of Florida

Abbie M. Brooks, *Petals Plucked from Sunny Climes* (1880); Mark Derr, *Some Kind of Paradise: A Chronicle of Man and the Land in Florida* (1989); Federal Writers' Project, *Florida: A Guide to the Southernmost State* (1949); Stetson Kennedy, *Palmetto Country* (1989); Raymond A. Mohl, *Florida Historical Quarterly* (January 1987); Maureen Ogle, *Key West: History of an Island of Dreams* (2003); Chris Sherrill and Roger Aiello, *Key West: The Last Resort* (1978).

Coonasses

"Coonass" commonly refers to Cajuns in Louisiana and Texas. However, the origin and precise meaning of the term and its suitability in regional discourse are matters of debate among Cajuns and scholars who study Cajun culture.

An often-cited explanation for the origin of coonass suggests the ethnonym derived from the standard French word *conasse*, meaning a stupid person, a bungling prostitute, or an unhealthy prostitute. It was allegedly used by continental French soldiers during World War II to describe Cajuns serving in France, whom they viewed as francophone bumpkins. *Conasse* was then supposedly anglicized into "coonass," and it gained widespread currency as a negative label for Cajuns. However, this hypothesis has never been substantiated. Other interpretations offer coonass as a play on the epithet "coon" that alludes to the alleged "racial impurity" of Cajuns or portrays them as lower in status than African Americans. What is known is that coonass was frequently used in reference to Cajuns by the 1950s and was also applied to elements of Cajun culture—

"coonass food" and "coonass music," for example. Despite its original negative connotations, Cajuns appropriated coonass within the context of ethnic revival of the 1960s and 1970s as an exotic self-ascriptive ethnic label. This rehabilitation of the word was evident in the proliferation of coonass bumper stickers, T-shirts, and even tattoos.

Not all Cajuns accept coonass as a suitable appellation. In 1977, for example, a Cajun filed a lawsuit against his employer after he was terminated for protesting a supervisor's repeated use of the label. Various organizations devoted to the preservation of Cajun culture—and often led by socioeconomic and intellectual elites—began to oppose the use of coonass, denouncing it as a vulgar term. They treat it as an ethnic slur parallel to those used for African Americans and Hispanics. Spurred by these sentiments, in 1981 the Louisiana State Senate passed a resolution to "condemn the use of the term 'coonass' and to condemn the sale or promotion of any items containing that term."

Some writers associate coonass with a particular component of the Cajun population. Some scholarship, for example, suggests that it is used primarily by young working-class Cajun males with a vague sort of identification with the traditions and symbols of Cajun culture and who use coonass as a macho assertion of their "earthy pungent masculinity." This interpretation also proposes that their use of coonass is a critical reaction to the elitism in some factions of the Cajun ethnic movement. Other scholars follow a related theme by proposing that coonass is overwhelmingly part of male speech and that some young men prefer it to Cajun as a means of resisting the increasing commodification of the label "Cajun" for cultural tourism.

Despite opposition to the term, many Cajuns commonly use coonass and its "polite" variant, "coonie." Men more frequently make reference to coonasses, but Cajuns of both sexes and all ages frequently self-ascribe the term and employ it in reference to elements of local culture, especially in conversations with outsiders.

"Coonass" interchanges with "Cajun" in ethnic jokes, but it also evokes positive traits linked to Cajun identity. Whether male or female, a person who demonstrates proficiency in French, speaks English with a pronounced Cajun accent, cooks Cajun food well, or is an outdoors enthusiast may be called a "real" or "pure" coonass.

While commonly self-ascribed by Cajuns, the use of coonass by non-Cajuns can spark a wide variety of responses, ranging from indifference to hostility when insulting modifiers like "dumb" or "damn" accompany the term. Thus, the term "coonass" and/or the specific contexts where it is used serves to articulate ethnic group boundaries. At the same time, controversy over the label indicates diversity within a population often perceived as a homogeneous entity. As identities have gradually creolized from disparate traditions in the American South, the involution and division within this ethnic group (itself shaped in the southern context) offers an interesting

view of identity politics and contestation and reveals the continuing importance of regional ethnic identities in a globalizing age.

ROCKY SEXTON
Augustana College

Shane K. Bernard, *The Cajuns: Americanization of a People* (2003); James Dormon, *The People Called Cajuns* (1983); C. Paige Gutierrez, *Cajun Foodways* (1992); Rocky Sexton, *Cajuns, Germans, and Les Americains* (1996); Nicholas Spitzer, *Zydeco and Mardi Gras* (1986); Shana Walton, *Flat Speech and Cajun Ethnic Identity in Terrebonne Parish, Louisiana* (1994), "Louisiana's Coonasses: Choosing Race and Class over Ethnicity," in *Signifying Serpents and Mardi Gras Runners: Representing Identity in Selected Souths*, ed. Celeste Ray and Eric Lassiter (2003).

Coushattas

From the 1800s to today, the Coushatta Tribe of Louisiana has centered its community three miles north of the town of Elton. Referring to themselves in their own Muskogean language as the Koasati, the Coushatta originally lived in the area of the Upper Tennessee River Valley. The tribe first entered the historic record after encountering Hernando de Soto in 1540; by the mid-1700s, the Coushatta had migrated to the present-day region of Alabama and were affiliated with the Creek Confederacy. Over the next 500 years, the Coushatta relocated several times in order to remain neutral in conflicts between the Spanish, French, British, and American governments.

The Coushatta tribe was officially terminated from the rolls of the federal government in 1953, despite protests from tribal members; they petitioned for and again received recognition as a federal Indian tribe in 1973. In the subsequent 30 years, the tribe has expanded its reservation land base, created an administrative complex that provides a multitude of services to the community, and, in 1995, opened a land-based casino that has made a significant economic impact on the region. Despite centuries of hardship, the Coushatta people have a vital, thriving community and receive wide recognition for their well-preserved cultural traditions.

Many of the Coushatta tribal members still speak Koasati as their first language, although the tribe is considering the necessity of developing language preservation programs for its young people. The Indian church has consistently played a major role in community cohesion. In addition to religious services and social events, the church serves an educational function. Until the 1960s Coushatta children went to elementary school in a small two-room schoolhouse located behind the Indian church building. Portions of the church services are still conducted in the Koasati language, as are other major community events.

The Coushatta are particularly known for the high quality of their traditional handcrafts, most notably their baskets woven from swamp cane or longleaf pine needles. Coushatta baskets are displayed in museums throughout the world. Older Coushatta basket makers recall the days when longleaf pine needle trees were plentiful in the area. Today, however, most of the land surrounding the tribal community has been clear-cut by timber companies, who reforest with shortleaf pine trees. Coushatta basket makers now experience difficulty obtaining sufficient quantity and quality of longleaf pine needles.

Another popular practice in the Coushatta community is traditional and contemporary Indian dancing. Tribal members have performed dances throughout the surrounding area, most notably at events such as the annual tribal powwow held in Kinder, La., every October, and traveled to compete in powwows throughout the United States and Canada. With its contemporary dance styles and customs, the powwow provides an avenue for community members and visitors to gather together and share Indian culture.

The Coushatta Tribe of Louisiana is governed by a four-member elected tribal council and an elected tribal chairperson, functioning as the tribe's CEO. The five-member tribal council oversees all of the tribe's programs and services, including the Departments of Health, Education, Housing, Social Services, Maintenance, and Law Enforcement—all of which provide comprehensive services to the tribal community. The tribal council also directs all economic development activities of the tribe, one aspect of which, Grand Casino Coushatta, has made the tribe a major economic force in Louisiana. As a federally recognized Indian tribe, the Coushatta Tribe of Louisiana is a sovereign nation within the United States, with all of the legal, judicial, and economic rights associated with that status.

LINDA PARKER LANGLEY
Louisiana State University at Eunice

David H. Corkran, *The Creek Frontier, 1540–1783* (1967); Bobby H. Johnson, *The Coushatta People* (1976); David Jurney, "Diaspora of the Alabama-Koasati Indians across Southeastern North America" (Ph.D. dissertation, Southern Methodist University, 2001); Geoffrey D. Kimball, *Koasati Grammar* (1991); John R. Swanton, *Early History of the Creek Indians and Their Neighbors* (1988).

Creoles

Always a confusing and controversial term, the word "Creole" means many things to many people. According to etymologists, the term derives from the Latin *creare*, meaning "to beget" or "to create." After the European discovery of America, Portuguese colonists used *crioulo* to denote an American-born slave of African descent. The word eventually came to be applied to all American-born colonists living along the Gulf Coast, regardless of ethnic origin, including those living as far eastward as Mobile and Pensacola. The latter groups were eventually called Gulf Coast Creoles in order to distinguish them from Creoles residing in present-day Louisiana—the state that has been most commonly associated with all things Creole. There, in the 18th century, the Spanish introduced the word *criollo*, which evolved into "Creole," meaning persons of African or European heritage born in America.

By the 19th century, black, white, and mixed-ancestry Louisianians used the term to distinguish themselves from the foreign-born and from Anglo-American settlers. During the antebellum period, mixed-ancestry Creoles of Color (*gens de couleur libre*, or "free persons of color") became a distinct ethnic group with many of the legal rights and privileges of whites. They often possessed property, received formal education, and occupied a middle social ground between whites and enslaved blacks. After the Civil War, however, with the development of an increasingly biracial social hierarchy, most Creoles of Color lost their privileged status and joined the ranks of impoverished former black slaves.

All the while, however, the word "Creole" persisted as a term also referring to white Louisianians, usually of upper-class, non-Cajun origin—although, confusingly, even Cajuns sometimes were called Creoles, primarily by non-Cajuns. Like the Creoles of Color, these white Creoles (also called French Creoles) suffered socioeconomic decline after the Civil War. In rural south Louisiana, newly impoverished white Creoles often intermarried with the predominantly lower-class Cajuns and thus were assimilated into Cajun culture. Many names of French Creole origin, like Soileau, Fontenot, and François, are now widely considered Cajun in rural south Louisiana.

In cosmopolitan New Orleans, "Creole" is still invoked to describe upper-class white society. Along with enslaved blacks and Creoles of Color, French-Catholic white Creoles dominated early New Orleans society. After the Louisiana Purchase (1803), how-

Creole girls, Plaquemines Parish, La., 1935
(Ben Shahn, Library of Congress [LC-USF33-006159-M1], Washington, D.C.)

ever, they increasingly shared the
city, albeit begrudgingly, with Anglo-
Protestants who inhabited the city's
aptly named "American Sector." By
the mid-19th century, French Creoles,
Anglo-Protestants, and other ethnic
groups of European descent were inter-
marrying in New Orleans and thus
blurring distinctions between their previously distinct populations. "Creole"
also describes New Orleans cuisine,
which, although clearly influenced by
European foodways, focuses on spicy
dishes abundant with local seafood.
Staples include dishes like shrimp
remoulade, bouillabaisse, and crawfish
bisque.

Elsewhere in present-day Louisiana, the term "Creole" refers most
commonly to persons of full or mixed
African ancestry, their French dialect,

and their Roman Catholic traditions.
Creoles of African heritage generally
employed the term "Creole of Color" in
reference to Creoles of mixed-ancestry
and used the term "black Creole" to
refer to Creoles solely or largely of
African descent.

In recent decades both of these
African-derived groups have down-
played distinctions based on skin color
and social standing in order to work
for cultural preservation. More often
describing themselves as simply Creole,
they founded a preservation group in
1982 named C.R.E.O.L.E., Inc. (Cultural
Resourceful Educational Opportunities
toward Linguistic Enrichment). Zydeco,
an accordion-based music that draws
heavily on Afro-Caribbean and rhythm
and blues influences, is their most well-
known form of expressive culture. The

rural community of Plaisance hosts the annual celebration of the genre at the Southwest Louisiana Zydeco Festival.

Ultimately, the meaning of the word "Creole" remains elusive, with some black, white, and mixed-ancestry individuals futilely claiming exclusivity to the ethnic label.

SHANE K. BERNARD
Avery Island, Louisiana

Carl A Brasseaux, Keith P. Fontenot, and Claude F. Oubre, *Creoles of Color in the Bayou Country* (1994); James H. Dormon, ed., *Creoles of Color of the Gulf South* (1996); Nicholas Spitzer, ed., *Louisiana Folklife: A Guide to the State* (1985), in *Creoles of Color of the Gulf South*, ed. James H. Dormon (1996); Sybil Kein, *Creole: The History and Legacy of Louisiana's Free People of Color* (2000); Joseph G. Tregle, in *Creole New Orleans: Race and Americanization*, ed. Arnold R. Hirsch and Joseph Logsdon (1992), *Louisiana History* (Spring 1982).

Cubans

The Cuban communities in Miami and south Florida represent the largest concentration of Cubans in the United States. According to the 2000 U.S. Census, 700,000 (60 percent) of the 1.2 million Cubans in the United States reside in metropolitan Miami, making it the largest ethnic group in the city. The community traces its origins to 1959, when political and social changes implemented by the Cuban Revolution led by Fidel Castro triggered a mass migration of political exiles to south Florida. Since then, Miami has served as the main point of entry for Cuban immigrants, and the city has

experienced four periods of increased Cuban migration: 1959–62, 1965–73, 1980, and 1994–95. Miami is today the city with the third-largest concentration of Cubans in the world.

Florida has welcomed Cuban migrants since the 1830s, when high tariffs and labor strife in Cuba led to the relocation of the cigar industry to Key West and the creation of the first Cuban community in the state. In the 1860s the cigar industry expanded into Tampa, attracting thousands of Cuban cigar workers and their families, who helped found Ybor City. The two communities grew rapidly in the next 30 years until Cuba won its independence from Spain in 1898. In the 20th century Florida became a favorite and convenient haven for Cuban political leaders and activists. From the 1920s to the 1950s, political opponents of every Cuban government sought asylum in Miami. Members of those exile communities were usually small in number, ranging from a few hundred to a few thousand. When Fidel Castro overthrew dictator Fulgencio Batista in 1959, there were 35,000 Cuban exiles living in the United States. Most returned after the revolutionary triumph and were soon replaced by those disaffected with the revolutionary government.

The current Cuban communities in Miami and south Florida were founded by political exiles hoping to return to Cuba as soon as its political climate changed. However, the longevity of Castro's regime, the failure of U.S. measures to incite political change in the country (e.g., the Bay of Pigs invasion and the economic embargo), and the passing of the first generation of exiles—coupled with the coming of age of a second and third generation of Cuban Americans—transformed the community from one of temporary political exiles to permanent residents and citizens with an active interest in government. Miami, Hialeah, Coral Gables, and Sweetwater all had Cuban American mayors by 1985. Cuban Americans also made impressive gains in the Florida legislature, and in 1989 Ileana Ros-Lehtinen, a Republican Florida state legislator, became the first Cuban American woman elected to the U.S. House of Representatives. In 2004 Republican Mel Martínez became the nation's first Cuban American U.S. senator.

The Cuban community's success in American politics has been surpassed only by its economic and educational success. Cubans have the highest income and educational rates of all Latino groups in the United States, and their entrepreneurship has helped make Miami a financial center for Latin America. Today, the city boasts more than 50 international banks (many of them owned or managed by Cuban Americans), two major Latin American television networks (Univision and Telemundo) that transmit exclusively in Spanish, dozens of Spanish-language newspapers, and more than 40,000 Cuban-owned businesses.

Cubans have also had a deep cultural impact on the region, from religion to culinary practices, music, art, and popular festivals. Cuban sandwiches and Cuban restaurants such as the Columbia are famously associated with Tampa. Ybor City (now within Tampa's metropolitan boundaries) remains home to Cuban social clubs, grocery stores, bakeries, and Spanish-speaking Catholic churches. Afro-Cuban religions like Santeria also migrated to the South, and botanicas (Santeria stores) can be found throughout south Florida. Cuban music—led by "Miami sound" creators Gloria and Emilio Estefan and popularized by superstars like Celia Cruz, Albita Rodriguez, and John Secada—is almost synonymous with Miami. Every year since 1980, the Miami Cuban community hosts the Calle Ocho Open House to celebrate Cuban culture with music, food, and art. The event, usually attended by more than 1 million people, has become the largest Latino festival in the United States.

FÉLIX MASUD-PILOTO
DePaul University

María Cristina García, *Havana USA: Cuban Exiles and Cuban Americans in South Florida, 1959–1994* (1996); Miguel González-Pando, *The Cuban Americans* (1998); Guillermo Grenier and Lisandro Pérez, *The Legacy of Exile: Cubans in the United States* (2003); Félix Masud-Piloto, *From Welcomed Exiles to Illegal Immigrants: Cuban Migration to the United States, 1959–1995* (1996); Alejandro Portes and Alex Stepick, *City on the Edge: The Transformation of Miami* (1993).

Czechs

Since the mid-1800s Czechs have formed an important, though relatively small, ethnic group in the South. Czechs created settlements in Georgia, Alabama, Mississippi, Louisiana, Florida, Arkansas, Texas, and Oklahoma. By the beginning of the 20th century, over 250 Czech communities had developed in Texas in places such as Flatonia, Dubina, Caldwell, Richmond-Rosenburg, and Houston. These communities have long shared a commitment to keeping their land and maintaining strong family units. Particularly in rural areas, families often live on inherited or shared land that places them in close proximity to extended family members. Such strongly interwoven communities perpetuate transgenerational traditions.

From the late 1800s to the early 1900s, Czechs in the South often established presses and published newspapers and bulletins in their language. Additionally, they formed lodges and *sokols* (social groups) in many communities. Lodges generally maintained support of widows and orphans, assisted the poor, and provided socialization for the men of the community. No longer extant, southern *sokols* were dedicated to creating "sound minds and bodies." They were focused on gymnastics and provided entertainment in the forms of contests and educational games until the mid-20th century.

Czech communities throughout the South celebrate their heritage and culture at yearly festivals dedicated to the sharing of genealogical information, history, foodways, material culture, music, and dance. The well-known kolache, a Czech fruit-filled pastry, has become a Texas favorite. In other parts of the South, kolaches have become a commercialized food sold at dough-

nut shops and bakeries. Sometimes, kolaches are filled with sausage and look more like the commonly known pig in a blanket. Many Czech cooks make poppyseed cakes, braided holiday breads, and a wide array of traditional cookies. Czech gatherings also feature roast goose, duck, and pork and an array of sausages. Dumplings often accompany these dishes. At one time, Czechs were noted beer brewers and winemakers.

Many Czechs continue to be devoted to needleworking, carving, whittling, and quilting. Needle artists often crochet pieces derived from older Czech patterns, producing table scarves, doilies, and other crocheted items. Many Czech communities have maintained a strong commitment to dance traditions, and they continue to produce Czech dancing costumes. These entail a white, lace-trimmed blouse, a black or red vest embroidered with flowers or other traditional motifs, with a red skirt for women and black pants for men. Some community members make jewelry from Czech glass beads. The *kraslice*, an egg-decorating tradition using a wax-and-dye method, has survived in many Czech communities. These eggs are elaborately decorated with intricate traditional designs, and Czechs often give them as Easter presents.

Czechs continue to play traditional music at dances and gatherings. Among the many native dances popular at gatherings is the polka. The accordion, clarinet, and tuba form the backbone of most Czech musical groups, and Czech music regularly features in the

Czech descendants in Texas and the Louisiana Red River Valley annually gather to commemorate their heritage and enjoy traditional dancing, music, and Czech cuisine. Here a young woman prepares traditional Czech pastries called kolaches (Photograph courtesy of Lisa Abney)

programming of some central Texas radio stations. Singing and instrumental music remain important aspects of Czech culture.

Initially, when Czechs first came to the United States from the Czech portions of Silesia and from Bohemia and Moravia (three of the regions that later became Czechoslovakia), most immigrants practiced Catholicism. However, in the South many have become Methodists, Episcopalians, Lutherans, or Baptists. Most Czech settlers farmed (predominantly growing tobacco and cotton) or were craftspersons (especially woodcarvers, stonemasons, and leatherworkers). Others owned businesses ranging from saloons to clothing stores. Their industriousness and tightly

knit communities, coupled with their use of Czech languages, did not allow for extensive relationships beyond the Czech community. Over time, and with their growing use of the English language, Czech communities have become less endogamous. While they maintain strong family ties and friendships, they embrace visitors to their community festivals and celebrations. Czechs now proudly celebrate both their American and Czech heritage and demonstrate a deeply rooted sense of patriotism for both countries. Many Czechs entered the military during both world wars and subsequent conflicts, and current military members receive strong support from their communities.

In the contemporary South, Czech

folk traditions survive in varying ways, although Czech-language speakers are dwindling in number. Unlike some immigrant groups to the United States whose traditions have been overshadowed by mainstream American culture, Czechs continue to document, transmit, and preserve their culture.

LISA ABNEY
Northwestern State University

Karel Bicha, *The Czechs in Oklahoma* (1980); Sean N. Gallup, *Journeys into Czech-Moravian Texas* (1998); Clinton Machann and James W. Mendl, *Czech Voices: Stories from Texas in the Amerikán Národní Kalendár* (1991); Rosie Ann Locker Walker, *A History of the Rural Schools of the Czech Communities of Kolin and Libuse* (1986).

English

In 1994 Bill C. Malone, the leading historian of country music, was asked to address a Shakespeare festival in New Orleans. The organizers were convinced, he recalls, that "Appalachian folk culture was Elizabethan and that the old mountain ballads and love songs were survivals from the days of Shakespeare." A local paper publicized the lecture with a feature article titled "The Bard with a Gun Rack?" Malone was compelled to inform his hopeful audience that neither country music nor any other aspect of the modern South was a pure survival of English culture, but it is doubtful that he did much damage to their faith in the theory. They were expressing one version of a remarkably persistent idea of southern identity: that the South or some part of it represents the miraculous survival of antique English ways

in an otherwise modern America. We can recognize this idea in legends about remote Appalachian coves whose residents still address one another in Elizabethan idiom, but also — at nearly the opposite end of the socioeconomic spectrum — in the determined Anglophilia of wealthy southerners from the 18th century onward. Amid the Victorian Gothic buildings of the University of the South, one may even now glimpse students and professors hurrying to class in black, Oxford-style academic gowns, an explicit bow to the idea of English origins for southern culture.

The idea, of course, is not altogether fanciful. Though the French and Spanish arrived in the region first and many ethnic groups followed, the European settlers who most strongly shaped the culture of the American South were English, beginning in 1607 at Jamestown. By 1660 some 50,000 of them had arrived in Virginia and neighboring Maryland. Though initially their numbers were thinned by disease, Indian attacks, and the inability of the mostly male population to reproduce itself, eventually a stable and recognizably English culture was established in the Chesapeake. Indeed by 1660 that culture was becoming determinedly English, and English in a particular way. From 1641 to 1676 — the term of Sir William Berkeley's long governorship of Virginia — the colony became a haven for emigrating cavaliers, for Royalist refugees during the Cromwell interregnum, and for the younger sons of Royalist families after the Stuart Restoration of 1660. Berkeley went out of his way to recruit such colonists, and he found most of them, as David Hackett Fischer has shown, in the same place: a cluster of 16 counties in the south and west of England that Fischer, borrowing from the novelist Thomas Hardy, calls "Wessex." (The nearly simultaneous settling of New England drew overwhelmingly from the culturally different counties of East Anglia). From Wessex came the families — Byrd, Randolph, Carter, Washington, Lee, and others — who for generations formed the economic and political elite of Virginia and whose mode of life created a pattern for would-be aristocrats throughout the South. When these aristocrats felt the need for a theoretical justification of their lives, they could look, as the proslavery writer George Fitzhugh did in the 1850s, to the work of Robert Filmer, the 17th-century Royalist philosopher from Kent whose own relatives had joined the migration to Virginia and helped form that transplanted Wessex elite. The same region, as Fischer also shows, supplied not only the aristocracy of the new colony but also most of its indentured servants — many of whom eventually became landowners themselves. To a remarkable degree these settlers preserved cultural usages — architectural, culinary, religious, erotic, and many others — of the English region from which they came.

Through most of the 17th century one could speak of Virginia, Maryland, and eventually the other southern colonies as ethnically as well as culturally English. Afterwards, however, the immigration of many other groups — French Huguenots fleeing oppression, Scots-Irish and Germans seeking land and opportunity, and of course African slaves in ever-increasing numbers — enlarged and considerably complicated the ethnic picture of the South. And though English folkways did not disappear any more than did the aristocratic families who had helped transplant them (a Byrd continued to represent Virginia in the U.S. Senate until 1983), increasingly "Englishness" became a mythic and chosen hallmark of southern identity, rather than a literal and unavoidable matter of fact. During the Civil War, for instance, Confederate partisans found it useful to characterize the conflict in ethnic and cultural terms, identifying southerners as literal descendants of English cavaliers, hard-wired with inherited affinities for chivalry and aristocracy, and Yankees as latter-day Roundheads, a democratic mob contemptuous of order and tradition. This information might have surprised the typical unruly, anarchic, and very likely Scots-Irish volunteer in General Robert E. Lee's army — just as a rhinestone-clad denizen of Nashville's Music Row might be astonished to be identified as a living avatar of Shakespeare's England. But many southerners, both past and present, would take great pleasure in the idea that, by carefully burnishing whatever English ancestry they could boast, they were simultaneously perfecting their "southernness."

JOHN GRAMMER
University of the South

David Hackett Fischer, *Albion's Seed: Four British Folkways in America* (1989); T. H.

Breen, ed., *Shaping Southern Society* (1976); Jack P. Greene, *Pursuits of Happiness: The Social Development of Early Modern British Colonies and the Formation of American Culture* (1988).

French

French settlers have come to the South for over four centuries. Their influences are most clearly discernible in specific areas, especially Charleston, S.C., and the southern parishes of Louisiana.

In May 1562 French Huguenot Jean Ribault founded the short-lived settlement of Fort Charles (named for his king, Charles IX) in present-day South Carolina. Huguenots arrived in Virginia between 1619 and 1621, financed by the English Crown, to produce silk and wine (although they grew tobacco instead). More French Huguenots came to the shores of South Carolina and southern Virginia in the wake of Louis XIV's 1685 Revocation of the Edict of Nantes. By the early 1700s Huguenot merchants occupied entire streets in Charleston, and the current Church and Market Streets became the French Quarter. Other Huguenots emulated English planters in growing cotton, indigo, and rice further up the Santee River and became so populous that the river was called the "French Santee."

The first French Huguenot church organized in Charleston as early as 1681 and still operates as the only independent Huguenot congregation in America and celebrates a commemorative liturgical service in French every spring. Huguenots also left their imprint on Carolinian architecture and city planning and through individuals' contributions to colonial history. The paternal grandparents of Revolutionary War hero Francis "Swamp Fox" Marion were both industrious Huguenots from New Rochelle. Henry Laurens served as a president of the Continental Congress and was a signer of the Treaty of Paris. His son John was an aide-de-camp of George Washington, a special envoy to Paris (securing French aid during the American Revolution), and a chief negotiator after General Charles Cornwallis's Yorktown surrender.

In 1682 René-Robert Cavelier, Sieur de La Salle, descended the Mississippi from Canada claiming the vast territory he traversed for Louis XIV and calling it "Louisiane." Two years later, La Salle returned with 400 colonists and began the ill-fated Fort St. Louis settlement on the Texan eastern coast. In 1699 Pierre Le Moyne, Sieur d'Iberville, established Fort Maurepas at present-day Biloxi, Miss. He became first governor of Louisiana and was later succeeded by his brother Jean-Baptiste Le Moyne, Sieur de Bienville, who, in 1718, established a settlement he named *La Nouvelle-Orléans* (New Orleans) in honor of Philippe, Duc d'Orléans, then the regent of France. New Orleans soon became the capital of Louisiana, with early settlers living on the river in a fortified square referred to as the Vieux Carré (Old Quarter, at the heart of New Orleans's now-renowned French Quarter). After British acquisition of maritime Canada, Acadians began arriving in the 1760s. They became the "Cajuns," in distinction from the "Creoles" whose families had come directly from France or Spain or by way of the Caribbean. Creoles tended to settle in New Orleans and along the Mississippi up to Baton Rouge (the state capital since 1849), whereas many Cajuns moved to the south-central region of Lafayette and toward the southwestern bayous.

Fleeing the French Revolution, a sizable influx of noble refugees settled in the New Orleans area and began a theater and other refinements, so that the city soon became the "Paris of America." French Creoles built the finest homes between Levee and Bourbon Streets, with *porte cochère* entrances (then popular in France), interior courtyards, gardens, and iron stairways leading to upper apartments with iron balconies. During the Haitian Revolution (1791–1803), more than 15,000 immigrants settled in Louisiana, including French planters, francophone free people of color, and slaves who served both of those groups. All became part of the Creole population.

After the Americans' 1803 purchase of the Louisiana Territory, French customs continued. Creoles still wielded power in southern Louisiana and encouraged the adoption of a civil law code based on the Latin-inspired model of Napoleonic France. Louisianian civil law remains quite different from the British-inspired common law of the other 49 states. Throughout the 19th century, French political refugees continued to seek shelter in New Orleans as various revolutionary moments played out in France. They established opera and debutante evenings at The-

atre d'Orleans, Catholic services at the Saint-Louis Cathedral, periodic *soirées dansantes* (evening dancing parties), the King's Ball opening Carnival Season with *gâteau des rois* (king cake), French-language newspapers, a library with contemporary books in French, and a general *joie de douceur* reminiscent of their homeland.

Elsewhere, an abortive experimental settlement for grape and olive production brought French to Demopolis, Ala., in 1816. No more successful would be Victor Considérant's 1850s utopian settlement in Texas, although some of the French settlers would play prominent roles in the early life of Dallas. Recruited by enterprising Frenchman Henri Castro, Alsatians came to Castroville, Tex., in 1844, and annual St. Louis Day festivals celebrate ancestral origins with both Texas barbecue and Alsatian sausage.

French traditions endure in Louisiana. In New Orleans, French foodways blended with the spicy seasonings of Spanish and Caribbean cooking. To the west, Cajuns developed hearty and peppery dishes with African and Antillean influences such as "dirty rice" and gumbos. Cajuns also preserved French folktales and continued a circle dance, perhaps of Breton origin, now known as the *fais-do-dos*. The use of French, however, has waned through the 20th century. By the 2000 U.S. Census, more Floridians and New Yorkers spoke French in the home than Louisianans. With the influx of Haitians during the 1990s and with more Québécois choosing the Sunbelt for retirement, Florida boasts the largest number of French speakers in the South and in the United States, being second only to the province of Quebec for the North American continent.

GEORGE POE
University of the South

Mathé Allain and Glenn Conrad, eds., *France and North America: Over 300 Years of Dialogue* (1973); Ronald Creagh, *Nos Cousins d'Amérique: Histoire des Français aux Etats-Unis* (1988); Jerah Johnson, *Contemporary French Civilization* (Summer/Fall 1994); Virginia Brainard Kunz, *The French in America* (1966); Bertrand Van Ruymbeke and Randy Sparks, eds., *Memory and Identity: The Huguenots in France and the Atlantic Diaspora* (2003).

Germans

One of the largest ethnic components of the American population, Germans settled in the southern region from the early colonial period through the 19th century. Where they formed concentrated settlements, they built and maintained German subcultures that thrived, at least in attenuated forms, into the contemporary era.

In the 18th century, thousands of Germans traveled the Great Wagon Road from Pennsylvania into the Virginia Backcountry, the Carolinas, and as far south as Georgia. Several hundred Germans settled along the Mississippi River between Baton Rouge and New Orleans in the 1720s. German groups, often religious in character and organized by colonizers seeking refuge and prosperity in America, continued to venture to the South through the 19th century. Transnational links and the good reports on agricultural land from promoters and travelers encouraged the formation of German emigration societies after 1830. The Auswanderungs Gesellschaft planned a settlement in Arkansas, and the Rhein-Bayerische Gesellschaft and the Mainzer Adelsverein established German colonies along the Brazos River in Texas and elsewhere. However, with the opening of western lands and the economic and social dislocations caused by the Civil War, the South no longer appeared as inviting for agricultural colonies. Planters had wanted to replace black workers with German and other immigrants after the Civil War, but few Germans responded to their appeals, and those who did remained only briefly in the South. John G. Cullman successfully recruited Germans to Cullman County, Ala., and in the last three decades of the 19th century German colonies were established in southwest Louisiana, which helped develop the large-scale rice farming that now characterizes that area.

Germans continued to contribute to southern urban life, adding cultural diversity, ethnic politics, Old World arts and crafts, and an infrastructure of social and cultural organizations. By the 1840s many Germans had come South through the port of New Orleans, often arriving on the cotton ships trading between New Orleans and Bremen. Especially after the enforcement of Otto von Bismarck's May Laws that limited the rights of Catholics in Germany, Catholic New Orleans served as a primary southern port of entry in the second half of the 19th century. Some immigrants moved up the Mississippi

Schmidt Brothers saloon, Fredericksburg, Tex., date unknown
(University of Texas Institute of Texan Cultures, San Antonio, No. 068-0720, courtesy of the Kilman Studio)

River in search of jobs or land, but many remained in New Orleans or the river towns to work on the levees, on railroads, on the docks, or as laborers and artisans. In cities such as Memphis and Louisville the German population swelled to more than 10 or 15 percent in the 1850s. Other Germans left northern ports to seek work in Richmond's iron industry or went to other industrializing towns in the Upper South.

The urban Germans developed a rich associational life throughout the South. In Richmond, for example, a German rifle club, *turnverein* (athletic club), Schiller society, benevolent society, drama club, choral group, and freethinkers' congregation brought German culture to the city. In Memphis as late as the 1870s, the German population of no more than 4,000 persons supported 18 benevolent and fraternal societies, a fire company, eight lodges, five militia companies, several theater groups, and a host of religious and social associations. Even a small German population, as in Mobile in the 1880s, could boast at least a German school, a charity organization, a choral society, a gymnasium, and a Lutheran church. German newspapers (mostly in *Hochdeutsch* rather than native dialects) sprang up in every southern city, and German heroes and festivals were celebrated in print and parades as recently as the early 20th century in some places. Educated, affluent urban Germans supported German-language theater and high culture in Richmond, Charleston, Memphis, Nashville, and New Orleans, but the bulk of the German population gravitated toward American entertainments and speech as the natural concomitant of their work and dispersed residence patterns in southern cities.

By World War I, German cultural traditions in the South perhaps remained strongest in rural areas. In subtle ways the intensive agriculture of German farmers created a specific cultural landscape, particularly in the German enclaves of the Shenandoah Valley of Virginia, in scattered communities in the Carolina piedmont, in Cullman County, Ala., in south-central Tennessee, in the Arkansas Ozarks, along the Missouri River in Missouri, and in several pockets in eastern Texas. Because Germans view their farms as permanent homes rather than speculative investments, they have tended to farm them more intensively than non-Germans, with greater per-unit productivity and locational stability. In addition, they traditionally have exhibited relatively higher rates of land ownership wherever they have clustered in numbers. In rural architecture, Missouri German, Texas German, or Shenandoah German vernacular styles evolved, and in the Shenandoah Valley rural isolation and German population density kept alive Fraktur writing, basket weaving, and pottery making for several generations after immigration.

German ethnic subcultures, with their high religiosity, family centeredness, and conservative values, grew in rural areas, nurtured by German agricultural societies, social clubs, fraternal and benefit associations, churches, and, as late as the 1950s in a few instances, a German-language press. Rural isolation and German churches served as the twin pillars of German ethnicity for over a century, but since World War II mass communications, improved roads, changed market conditions, and consolidated school systems have combined to erode rural German distinctiveness. Today, "German" restaurants, festivals, folk art, architecture, and, especially, Lutheran and Reformed churches survive as reminders of southerners' colonial and more recent German origins. Almost every large southern city is home to a German heritage association. Texas, Virginia, and Florida have the most German American organizations, followed by North Carolina, Georgia, and Alabama, but even D'Iberville, Miss., has a Germania Club.

RANDALL M. MILLER
St. Joseph's University

Aaron Spencer Fogleman, *Hopeful Journeys: German Immigration, Settlement, and Political Culture in Colonial America* (1996); Russell L. Gerlach, *Immigrants in the Ozarks: A Study in Ethnic Geography* (1976); Terry G. Jordan, *German Seed in Texas Soil: Immigrant Farmers in Nineteenth-Century Texas* (1966); Terry G. Jordan-Bychkov, *The Upland South: The Making of an American Folk Region and Landscape* (2003); John Nau, *The German People of New Orleans, 1850–1900* (1958); A. G. Roeber, *Palatines, Liberty, and Property: German Lutherans in Colonial British America* (1993); Charles van Ravenswaay, *The Arts and Architecture of German Settlements in Missouri* (1977); Klaus Wust, *The Virginia Germans* (1969).

Greeks

St. Augustine, Fla., is home to descendants of the first concentration of New World Greek settlers (1768).

Greek sailors and merchants also settled in New Orleans beginning in the latter 18th century and founded the first Greek Orthodox church in the Americas there in 1864. One of the largest Greek settlements was at Tarpon Springs, Fla., which grew from 562 Greeks in 1895 to 2,212 in 1910 because of the rapid development of the sponge-harvesting industry in the Gulf of Mexico. Contemporary Tarpon sponge fishers continue to produce some of the finest quality sponges in the world, while a few boats offer tourists a glimpse of the harvesting process. National Heritage Award recipient Nick Toth maintains a family tradition of creating diving helmets for local sponge fishers.

Today, Florida leads the region in both the number and percentage of Greek Americans, who are concentrated in the Tarpon Springs/Clearwater area, Jacksonville, Orlando, and the corridor from Miami to West Palm Beach. There are sizable Greek American communities in Atlanta, Birmingham, Charlotte, Houston, Richmond, and Norfolk. Recent Greek American migration to the Sunbelt, combined with a stream of immigration from Greece, has almost doubled the number of Greek Americans in the South since 1990. According to the 2000 U.S. Census, Greek Americans number 1,153,307, with 18.7 percent residing in the states that had been part of the Confederacy.

Despite extensive intermarriage and assimilation, southern Greek Americans maintain their cultural heritage through strong familial ties, social organizations, and the Greek Orthodox Church.

Domestic arts, such as home decoration and food preparation, express aesthetics while fulfilling basic needs. Older women use needlework skills to create beautiful tablecloths, bedspreads, pillowcases, towels, coverlets, and rag rugs or intricate regional costumes required for dancing groups or religious parades. Families also express ethnic identity through the display of Greek artifacts representing historic village life, ancestral regions, religious beliefs, and national identity.

Commercial establishments sell Greek foods, but many regional, sacred, and community foodways remain relatively unknown to outsiders. In some communities the *kafeneion* (coffeehouse) still provides a place for men to share coffee and spirits, play cards, smoke, and discuss politics or sports. Women still make *Prosforo*, the bread used in Greek Orthodox services, by combining flour, yeast, water, and salt and then stamping loaves with the *sfragida* (a wooden seal carved with religious symbols). Along with wine, oil, and prayer lists of loved ones, they present *Prosforo* to the priest, who places it on the altar to be consecrated by the Holy Spirit. The congregation consumes the bread during Holy Communion.

Greek Orthodox icons serve as vehicles of divine power and grace. Churches display icons on walls, ceilings, stands, and screens, while families usually hang them along with other religious artifacts in private areas of the home. The recent resurgence of Orthodoxy and resulting expansion of churches provide steady work for several excellent Greek iconographers residing in the South, such as Elias Katsaros in Alabama and Ioannis Filippakis in Florida.

Greek American music and dance are integral to community events. Musicians regularly perform popular and rural, old and new music. Unfortunately, traditional instruments are increasingly rare, and electric amplification, rhythm machines, and synthesized backup sound loops often prevail. In large communities, some musicians continue to play regional styles. For instance, in Florida the late National Heritage Fellowship recipient Nikitas Tsimouris played the Kalymnian *tsabouna* (bagpipe), while Nick Mastras and Florida Folk Heritage Award winner Kostas Maris continue to perform Cretan music on the *lyra* and *laouto*.

Greek Americans celebrate many festive occasions, from life-cycle events to religious holidays and secular observances such as Greek Independence Day. Church groups organize most large heritage events, which function primarily as fund-raisers but offer the public a chance to sample Greek popular music, dance, and food or to buy Greek products. Festivals typically represent a narrow range of Greek American culture rather than the extensive traditions shared within the community. Nonetheless, they provide opportunities for elders to teach vital traditions to young people.

The most famous Greek regional event in the South is Epiphany in Tarpon Springs in early January, which preserves a strong Greek character and maritime heritage. Orthodox priests

Nikitas Tsimouris playing a Kalymnian tsabouna, 1995 (Robert L. Stone, photographer, courtesy of Florida Division of Historical Resources, Florida State Archives)

have blessed local waters on Epiphany for centuries, and boats do not sail in the "unhallowed" sea between Christmas and Epiphany. In Tarpon Springs, schools and businesses close so that residents can join the thousands of visitors for the festivities. Epiphany opens with a divine liturgy celebrated by the visiting archbishop in St. Nicholas Cathedral. Afterward, altar boys swinging censers streaming fragrant incense lead a procession of church officials bearing banners, jeweled crosses, and gold medallions, young people in costumes, dance troupes, and city officials to Spring Bayou. The archbishop blesses the waters then casts a white cross into the bayou. About 50 youths dive for the cross from a semicircle of boats. The lucky young man who finds it is greeted with cheers of delight and carried to the cathedral to be blessed. The divers then parade to the *glendi*, a celebration with food, dancing, and music. At night, the city celebrates at the Epiphany Ball.

TINA BUCUVALAS
Florida Folklife Program

Tina Bucuvalas, *Florida Heritage Magazine* (Fall 1999); Tina Bucuvalas and Steve Frangos, *Techne: Greek Traditional Arts in the Calumet Region* (1985); Melvin Hecker and Heike Fenton, eds., *The Greeks in America, 1528–1977: A Chronology and Fact Book* (1978); Charles C. Moskos, *Greek Americans: Struggle and Success* (1980).

Guatemalan Mayans

Fleeing a particularly bloody civil war in Guatemala during the 1980s and 1990s, thousands of Maya came to the South and are among the newest groups to add to the region's ethnic diversity. The new Mayan culture of the southeastern United States is a complex tapestry of different migration histories, languages (over 31 different Mayan dialects are spoken in Mexico and Guatemala), and degrees of assimilation. South Florida, one of the major destinations for the first wave of Guatemalan Maya, was home to 20,000 refugees by 1990. Indiantown, Fla., near West Palm Beach, became known as a "Maya town." These pioneer Mayan immigrants and many others after them have moved into the Carolinas, Georgia, and Alabama. Initially living in enclave neighborhoods and communities like Indiantown, they later moved to follow the crops and work opportunities in almost every county

in the Southeast. Southern states have experienced something of an "instant migration," with entire Mayan communities appearing in just a few years and the region's Mayan population growing to approximately 200,000 by the end of 2003. A true census is all but impossible to conduct because of farmworkers' mobility, the fear that many Maya have of being deported because their immigration papers are not in order, and the lack of any accurate way of identifying Maya in school documents or other official records.

There have been three waves of migration of Mayan people to the southeastern United States: an initial refugee wave, a family unification wave, and an economic adventurer wave. The first of these was the most dramatic. Beginning in 1982, hundreds of Mayan people arrived in the United States with horrific stories of torture, burned villages, and the destruction of their way of life at the hands of a Guatemalan government engaged in civil war since 1960. The violence in Guatemala continued into the 1990s, allowing first-wave Guatemalan Maya to meet new immigrants with experiences that reawakened their own social memories of exodus. The first-wave immigrants tended to come from small towns and villages and speak primarily, and sometimes exclusively, Maya. They often came with children and other family members.

Beginning in the late 1980s, the second wave of Maya consisted mostly of spouses, parents, and especially single male relatives of those who earlier had gained a foothold in the United States. This second wave of Maya came from

Kanjobal Mayan woman in traditional dress at a festival in Indiantown, Fla. (Photograph courtesy of Joan Flocks)

and resort communities (like Jupiter, Fla., or Morganton, N.C.), where they have found an economic niche in landscape services or the poultry industry. Others follow vegetable harvests as migrant farmworkers have for decades. The first and second wave of pioneers have now settled into life in the Southeast, sending their children to school and purchasing homes, and in the process arresting the decline of many small southern towns. Many Maya go back and forth to Guatemala and build schools and homes there with the profits of their work in the United States. Some of the children of the first wave have gone through college and have returned to Guatemala as teachers, social workers, and lawyers to help their friends and families. For many of the young Maya, farmwork remains a common job choice. Young Mayan men often live in rooms with eight to ten others and find entertainment in drinking beer and hanging out. Their lives characterize another kind of assimilation of the Maya in the South. Still others, especially the pioneers who came to escape oppression and fear, have tried to create a new hybrid culture, marrying the advantages of their new homeland with the traditions of their old. While most remain Catholic, some have learned English and joined Protestant churches, and yet they still hold festivals dedicated to their hometowns. Once ashamed of being Maya, they now take pride in their heritage.

ALLAN BURNS
University of Florida

larger cities like Totonicapan or Jacaltenango in the Northwestern Highlands of Guatemala. This group included many schoolteachers and others with skilled trades; they were quick to organize clubs and soccer matches, and they often saved funds for trips back to Guatemala and for financing cultural festivals featuring traditional Mayan dance companies from their hometowns. They began living a transnational life, simultaneously participating in the cultures of the U.S. Southeast and Guatemala.

The third wave of Guatemalan Maya consists predominantly of young Mayan males, including teenagers, and a few families. Some third-wave immigrants live in enclave communities at the outskirts of golf course

Allan F. Burns, *Maya in Exile: Guatemalans in Florida* (1993); Leon Fink, *The Maya of Morganton: Work and Community in the Nuevo New South* (2003); Nora Hamilton and Norma Stoltz Chinchilla, *Seeking a Community in a Global City: Guatemalans and Salvadoranians in Los Angeles* (2001).

Gullahs

The Gullah culture and language, referred to as "Geechee" in parts of Georgia, is widely considered the strongest link African Americans have with their African roots. Known primarily as the Creole language of blacks living on the islands and mainland coast of South Carolina and Georgia, the term "Gullah" also encompasses other aspects of island and coastal culture with direct links to Africa.

Speculations on the etymology of the term "Gullah" include the suggestion that Gullah derives from *Angola*, or *N'gulla*, as it would have been pronounced. The Gullah language is the only surviving creolized form of English created in the South that remains spoken there. Gullah retains linguistic features that African slaves of various backgrounds brought to the Georgia and South Carolina Lowcountry in the 18th century and first half of the 19th century. Gullah exhibits striking parallels with African languages such as Krio in syntax, intonation, and phonology. The most noted characteristics include the use of singular nouns and the use of the present verb tense when referring to the past. Gullah was once a spoken language only, but now books contain recipes, stories, and biblical texts with translations into Gullah.

Slaves familiar with rice production on the western coast of Africa were especially sought after for southern rice plantations on the barrier islands (the Sea Islands) and up to 30 miles inland. After 1807 an illegal trade kept the rice plantations supplied with West African slaves until the mid-1850s. By 1850 the Lowcountry slave-to-white ratio reached as high as 20 to 1. The isolation of the islands and coastal area, the numerous African-born slaves, and the limited presence of European Americans resulted in the continuation of African ways of life.

After emancipation, most former slaves remained in the area and, once the rice economy failed, found work in the seafood industry, fishing, producing cast nets, and canning. Gullahs also earned income through basket weaving and took jobs in factories and trucking. Over the last century many have migrated to Atlanta, New York, and other cities with large African American populations.

Because of their geographic isolation, Gullah/Geechee people were able to maintain arts, crafts, religious beliefs, rituals, foodways, and linguistic traditions that are born directly of their West African roots and that have shaped a unique culture within the South since colonial times. The Gullah are famous for the art of sweetgrass basketry and for producing walking sticks, fishing nets, strip quilts, and decorated calabashes. Rice remains the center of the Gullah diet. Onion, tomato, salt, and pepper pervade many dishes. African foods such as okra and peanuts as well as peas, corn, turnips, collard greens,

Sweetgrass baskets are an important Gullah traditional craft still practiced in the Lowcountry
(Richard Pillsbury, photographer)

and sweet potatoes are other staples of the Gullah diet. Gullahs claim hoppin' John as their own as well as gumbo with shrimp and rice, the Lowcountry boil, and red rice.

Gullah folktales, like tales from Africa, are populated with trickster rabbits, lazy elephants, smart monkeys, cruel masters, and God. In native island communities, storytellers say their craft is experiencing resurgence. While folklore often focuses on the ominous conjuring of Gullah "root doctors," such people were and are knowledgeable about both the curative and toxic effects of herbs and roots. African traditions also endure in practices relating to death and burial. Broken bottles, broken pottery, clocks, mirrors, and

other symbolic articles are placed at grave sites.

Gullah language and culture survives today on the coast of Georgia and South Carolina, but in ever decreasing homogeny. Many of the isolated islands are now accessible by road. The advent of radio, television, and mass culture has taken its toll on the communities, as has resort development and real estate speculation. Small pockets of black communities with strong Gullah roots can still be found on places like St. Johns Island, S.C., and Sapelo Island, Ga.

A resurgence of interest in promoting and retaining the old ways relies on charismatic individuals such as the "Chieftess Queen Quet" Marquetta L.

Goodwine. Beaufort, S.C., annually hosts a Gullah Festival on Memorial Day. Nearby St. Helena Island has a festival in early November, and a third festival is held in early September on Sapelo Island, Ga.

WILLIAM S. BURDELL III
St. Simons Island, Georgia

Marquetta L. Goodwine, *Legacy of Ibo Landing: Gullah Roots of African American Culture* (2002); Joseph Holloway and Winifred Kellersberger Vass, *The African Heritage of American English* (1993); Patricia Jones-Jackson, *When Roots Die: Endangered Traditions on the Sea Islands* (1987); Charles Joyner, *Down by the Riverside: A South Carolina Slave Community* (1984); William S. Pollitzer, *The Gullah People and Their African Heritage* (1999); Lorenzo Dow Turner, *Africanisms in the Gullah Dialect* (1949).

Haitians

Haitian immigrants and their descendants constitute one of the largest minority populations in the southeastern United States. Haitian communities abound in Georgia, Louisiana, North Carolina, and South Carolina, but the greatest concentration resides in Florida. Because of difficulties inherent in contacting immigrant populations, no exact census count exists of Haitian immigrants and their children. However, the 2000 U.S. Census estimates the current Haitian population in the state of Florida at over 230,000.

Haitian presence in the southeastern United States dates back to the colonial period. During this time large numbers of colonial masters and free people of color (including their slaves who were forced to immigrate) fled a war-torn Saint-Domingue (later renamed Haiti) to establish themselves in the United States in cities such as Charleston and New Orleans. Perhaps as many as tens of thousands of Haitians left their island home for the Southeast. Slaves in Saint-Domingue were enlisted to fight against the British during the American Revolution, and many lost their lives in the famous Battle of Savannah.

After the Haitian Revolution (1791–1804), Haiti emerged as the first country to abolish slavery and the colonial system. The United States pursued a policy of marginalization with post-revolutionary Haiti, and Thomas Jefferson, in an effort to expatriate Africans from the United States, chose Haiti as the destination country (although Africa's Liberia later became the primary destination). This began a brief but significant migration of Africans from the South to Haiti.

Following the Haitian Revolution, mass numbers of Haitian immigrants, who had temporarily fled to Cuba, Jamaica, and other nearby islands, migrated to the southeastern United States. Another large migration came with the political tyranny of the Duvalier regimes (1950s–80s), which led hundreds of thousands of severely impoverished Haitians to seek refuge along the coast of Florida. This wave of immigrants came to be referred to as "boat people."

Assimilation for the Haitian boat people—the majority of whom possessed minimal formal education, little material wealth, and no English literacy—was difficult. Racism and linguistic differences served to solidify a wholly unique identity in the South. Today, cross-ethnic relationships with Hispanics, African Americans, or other Caribbean groups are still difficult to establish. However, the second generation of Haitian Americans is finding common expressive language through new cultural forms. These include music (the new rap and hip-hop), forms of sociability (gangs and cliques), and language (Zo), which are strengthened through community radio and local networks with Haitian Creole broadcasts and a focus on Haiti and Haitian communities abroad. Haitians also find community through Haitian businesses, markets, churches, discrete Vodou temples, and botanicas (spiritual healing houses that also sell medicinal herbs, oils, and candles for the performance of Vodou rituals).

Haitian immigrants make a significant contribution to the U.S. economy, mainly in the agricultural industry and service sector. A growing segment of this population is entering white-collar and technological professions, and Haitian Americans hold public office in several Florida counties. Haitian immigration has also reshaped the cultural and religious practices of the communities in which these immigrants established themselves. New Orleans is the most well-known example, with its Haitian-influenced cuisine and Vodou religious traditions. The mainstream South, however, is also beginning to embrace vibrant elements of Haitian cultural tradition. Popular celebrations in many cities are officially promoted and publicly supported. For example,

the Haitian Carnival, Haitian arts festivals, and Haitian Flag Day celebrations are no longer confined to Haitian ethnic enclaves, but are increasingly a component of public festivity in larger cities such as Miami, Fort Lauderdale, Tampa, and West Palm Beach.

LOUIS H. MARCELIN
University of Miami

Arnold R. Hirch and Joseph Longsdon, eds., *Creole New Orleans: Race and Americanization* (1992); Whittington B. Johnson, *Black Savannah, 1788–1864* (1996); Paul Lachance, *Louisiana History* (Spring 1988); Michel S. Laguerre, *Diasporic Citizenship: Haitian Americans in Transnational America* (1998); Louis H. Marcelin, in *Neither Enemies nor Friends: Latinos, Blacks, Afro-Latinos*, ed. Anani Dzidzienyo and Suzanne Oboler (2005); Louis H. Marcelin and Louise M. Marcelin, *Census 2000 Ethnographic Evaluation Report 6: Ethnographic Social Network Tracing among Haitian Migrant Farm Workers in South Florida* (2001); Gary B. Nash, *Forging Freedom: The Formation of Philadelphia's Black Community, 1720–1840* (1988); Leon D. Pamphile, *Haitians and African Americans: A Heritage of Tragedy and Hope* (2001); Brenda Gayle Plummer, *Haiti and the United States: The Psychological Moment* (1992); Ira Reid, *The Negro Immigrant: His Background Characteristics and Social Adjustment, 1899–1937* (1939); Michel-Rolph Trouillot, *Haiti, State against Nation: The Origins and Legacy of Duvalierism* (1990).

Haliwa-Saponis

With 3,800 members, the Haliwa-Saponi Indian tribe is the third-largest tribal community in North Carolina. The tribe derives its name from the northeastern counties of their residence, Halifax and Warren, and from the ancestral Saponi people. Oral tradition and historical documentation also indicate ancestry from the Nansemond of Virginia and the Tuscarora of North Carolina. Depopulation and reduced tribal territories followed European colonization of the 18th century.

During the mid-1700s and early 1800s, the ancestors of the Haliwa-Saponi gradually migrated into an unsettled land called the "Meadows" in northeastern North Carolina. Haliwa-Saponi families practiced endogamy and subsisted, much like their ancestors, on farming, gathering, and hunting wild game. Many escaped Removal in the 1830s by keeping their identity secret. More fortunate Haliwa-Saponis farmed their own land, while others labored on the farms of local white planters for low wages. The Haliwa-Saponi participated in local government through voting and serving on juries before being disfranchised in 1835.

The Haliwa-Saponi stayed virtually unto themselves until the late 1800s, when a relatively large contingent of non-Indians (European Americans and African Americans) migrated to the Meadows to occupy the lands and exploit its natural resources. Local and state governmental policies of classifying all nonwhite individuals — Indians as well as blacks — as "colored" led to friction with the new settlers. Labels such as "free persons of color" and mulatto — classifications that often included persons of Indian descent — obscured the Indian identity of the Haliwa-Saponi. To combat such labeling, Indian traditionalists held secret meetings during the late 1800s to push for a separate Indian classification and a tribal organization and to build Indian churches and an Indian school. Leaders such as Tilman Lynch urged the Indians to be counted as such on official documents, while Alfred Richardson sought tribal recognition from the federal government. Both families and their supporters lobbied successfully for all-Indian educational institutions, such as Secret Hill School in Halifax County and Bethlehem School in Warren County.

But the social and racial tensions of the Jim Crow era, combined with the community's physical isolation, precluded successful and persistent Indian leadership and tribal recognition. However, John C. Hedgepeth, known as a "radical" for Indian people, emerged as the community's new leader in the 1930s. Hedgepeth, Lonnie Richardson, James Mills, Jerry Richardson, and others helped the Indians register and be listed as "Indian" on official documents such as voter registration cards and World War II draft registration cards. Some of these leaders traveled south to Pembroke, N.C., to meet with successful Lumbee educators. In the early 1950s local Indian leaders received enough community support to organize the Haliwarnash Indian Club, predecessor of the modern Haliwa-Saponi tribal government. W. R. Richardson quickly became the first officially elected chief for the Haliwa Indian tribe, holding that office for more than 40 years.

By 1953 the tribe established Mount Bethel Indian Baptist Church, originally called the Saponi Indian Baptist

Church. Within four more years, the tribe was operating the Haliwa Indian School, the only fully tribally supported nonreservation school in the United States. Tribal elders relate that some traditional language persisted into the 20th century. With assistance from the Chickahominy tribe of Virginia and other tribes from throughout the eastern United States, the Haliwa-Saponi adopted the powwow, holding their first in 1965 in celebration of official state recognition. Not only did the powwow serve as both a personal and public symbol of Indian identity, it also sparked cultural revitalization, including pottery and renewed use of the Saponi and Powhatan languages.

The Haliwa-Saponi tribe is governed by an 11-member tribal council and employs approximately 75 employees. Tribal government programs include housing, daycare, an elder-care program, a cultural program, an after-school program, disaster assistance, and job training. Another step toward self-determination is the recently established Haliwa-Saponi Tribal School. The tribe owns approximately 300 acres in Halifax and Warren Counties and has plans to develop that acreage for the benefit of tribal members and the community at large. Economic development and the tribe's 100-year bid to be federally recognized remain top priorities.

MARVIN RICHARDSON
Haliwa-Saponi Tribe

Marvin Richardson and C. S. Everett, in *Signifying Serpents and Mardi Gras Runners: Representing Identity in Selected Souths*, ed. Celeste Ray and Luke Eric Lassister (2003); Thomas Ross, *American Indians of North Carolina: Geographical Interpretations* (1999).

Hmong

An ethnic group from the highlands of Laos in Southeast Asia, the Hmong first came to the United States in 1975 at the close of the Vietnam War. Loyal to the Laotian monarchy and its U.S. ally, tens of thousands of Hmong fled persecution from the Vietnamese-backed regime—first to refugee camps in Thailand and then as refugees to the United States. Large Hmong communities formed in the Upper Midwest, the Northeast, the Mid-Atlantic states, and California. The 2000 U.S. Census reported that over 200,000 Hmong resided in the United States.

While few Hmong resettled directly in the South, Hmong families have been moving to the South in great numbers since the 1980s. Many southern states offer employment opportunities for non-English speakers in textile mills, factories, and poultry processing. The climate and landscape in many southern areas resemble conditions in the Asian Southeast. After experiencing the stresses of urban inner-city life, many Hmong prefer the smaller communities, opportunities to purchase land in rural areas, better schools, and family-oriented values they have found in the South.

Hmong live in every southern state, but the largest communities are in North Carolina, Georgia, and South Carolina, followed by Texas and Tennessee. There are an estimated 7,100–

Hmong choir in an Alliance church in Stone Mountain, Ga.
(Lee Wilson, photographer, Teaching Museum South, Hapeville, Ga.)

12,000 Hmong in North Carolina, with the largest groups in Hickory and Morganton. Georgia has between 2,500 and 4,000 Hmong, and South Carolina has between 1,500 and 3,500. The U.S. Census reports numbers at the lower ends of these ranges, but it is likely that refugees were undercounted.

The Hmong religion combines aspects of animism and ancestor worship, and some traditional religious practices endure in southern communities, particularly with reference to healing ceremonies. However, many of those who have chosen to live in the South have converted to Christianity, generally preferring fundamentalist churches like the Christian and Missionary Alliance or the Southern Baptists, although a notable number are Lutheran, Methodist, and Catholic.

Southern Hmong are as self-sufficient as possible, purchasing farmland for extended family to inhabit and cultivate. Isolated farmland enables cultural maintenance, the use of the home language, and large social gatherings not possible in crowded urban environments. Hmong raise livestock and grow traditional foods and herbs as well as cash crops.

Many Hmong have jobs outside of the home, preferring employers that offer generous benefits to those that pay higher wages but do not provide benefits. Even at work, Hmong prefer to be with other Hmong, and many employers accommodate them by hiring all-Hmong work crews who work under the supervision of a Hmong manager.

The Hmong in the United States retain their traditional social organization of exogamous clan and family lineages. Clan and lineage membership influences marriage choices, settlement plans, and political power within Hmong communities. Although Hmong families experience the stresses of assimilation and acculturation that confront most refugees and immigrants, their history provides them with an identity that is independent of national borders. Despite radical changes in gender roles, mobility, occupation, language, media, and other influences of the dominant society, many youthful Hmong maintain strong allegiances to their Hmong identity, history, and culture.

Even after conversion to Christianity, Hmong still celebrate many of their traditions, including Hmong New Year. In Laos this holiday extended over the full harvest season and provided a chance to visit friends and relatives in other villages, conduct business, consume traditional rice dishes, and arrange auspicious marriages. In the United States, Hmong groups in different locations often celebrate Hmong New Year on American holidays. (For example, the Georgia Hmong celebrate Hmong New Year over the Thanksgiving holiday.) Traditional genres of music, narrative, and art continue to dominate Hmong expressive culture in the United States. Although many Hmong traditions have adapted to changing lifestyles and new expressive forms have emerged, a surprising number of cultural traditions remain essentially unchanged.

DEBORAH DUCHON
Atlanta, Georgia

D. A. Duchon, *Urban Anthropology* (Spring 1997); Joanne Cubbs, *Hmong Art: Tradition and Change* (1986); Julie Keown-Bomar, *Kinship Networks among Hmong-American Refugees* (2004); Nicholas Tapp, Jean Michaud, Christian Culas, and Gary Yia Lee, *Hmong-Miao in Asia* (2004); Donald A. Wilcox, *Hmong Folklife* (1986).

Houmas

"Houma" is a contracted ethnonym from the Muskogean term *chakchiuma*, meaning "red crawfish" or "people of the red crawfish." In 1907 anthropologist John R. Swanton applied "Houma" to several related "mixed-blood" or "triracial" communities scattered around the bayou country of southern Louisiana, primarily in Terrebonne and Lafourche Parishes. Today, members of these related communities live in seven southern Louisiana parishes and may number up to 20,000 people.

Historical and genealogical research confirms the community descends in part from American Indian ancestors. Most contemporary Houmas descend from a man called Houma Courteau, alias "Iacalobe." Courteau was identified on the federal census of 1810 as "Courto, a Savage" and in a deed of 1822 as "Iough-la-bay alias Courteau of the Beloxy Nation," along with his Indian wife "Marianne Mingoloi," sister of "Louis Le Sauvage," and at least two other Indian women who married French men. Tribal ancestry also includes native Chitimacha and possibly Apalachee as well as some German and African heritage. The most common Houma family names are Billiot, Verdin, Dardar, Naquin, Parfait, Verret,

Creppell, Fitch, Dion, Chaisson, Foret, Solet, and Gregoire.

In many respects, the Houma differ little from the more conservative of their Cajun neighbors. Most people in both groups are Catholic, and crawfishing and shrimping have been the economic mainstays of the Houma, just as for many Cajuns. Houma cuisine and dialect is generally reminiscent of what most Americans might recognize as "Cajun." The similarities highlight the cultural fusion characteristic of Louisiana, pointing to the influence of many cultures in the region—Native American as well as French, African, and "American." Still, anthropological and sociological studies conducted over the past century show that the Houma have maintained an "Indian" ethnic identity at least since the late 19th century. This ethnicity may have developed in response to, or as a component of, the legal racial segregation following Reconstruction. By the time of the First World War, most Houma men self-identified as "Indian," although draft board registrars remarked variously that Houmas were "born of white and Indian parents," were of "Indian and Caucasian" heritage, or that they "registered as Indian but [are] mixed breed."

One of the major problems faced by the Houma and all other Indian communities in the state was the lack of good public education facilities. For several generations, tribal members who did not fish were limited to other blue-collar careers, such as working on offshore oil rigs. In the early 1960s the Houma began formal reorganization as a tribe under the name Houma Indians of Louisiana, Inc. They demanded civil rights, improved educational opportunities, and the means to communicate with other Indian communities. Feeling underrepresented by organizational leadership, a faction broke away in 1974 under the name Houma Alliance. Reconciliation through mediation led to the merger of the two groups in 1979 as the United Houma Nation, which subsequently filed a petition with the federal Bureau of Indian Affairs (BIA) for formal acknowledgement and recognition as a historic Indian tribe. When the petition was deemed insufficient by the BIA in 1994, a faction of the United Houma Nation again broke away and formed the Biloxi-Chitimacha Confederacy. Though recognized as Indian tribes by the state of Louisiana and its Office of Indian Affairs, formal recognition of both groups by the federal government is pending.

Irrespective of their modern political differences, the Houma and the Biloxi-Chitimacha represent the rich cultural fabric and heritage of Louisiana and stand as living proof of the depth and persistence of Louisiana's many Native American Indian communities.

C. S. EVERETT
Vanderbilt University

Sarah Sue Goldsmith, *Advocate Magazine* (23 June 1996); Hiram F. Gregory, in *Indians of the Southeastern United States in the Late 20th Century*, ed. J. Anthony Paredes (1992); Max E. Stanton, in *The Not So Solid South: Anthropological Studies in a Regional Subculture*, ed. J. Kenneth Morland (1971).

Huguenots

In the late 17th and early 18th centuries, South Carolina received more Huguenot immigrants than any other British colony in North America. Their story illustrates the complicated matrix of religious, national, and commercial dynamics that shaped European settlement patterns in the Americas. As a distinct group, the Huguenots initially made a large impact on colonial South Carolina but were comfortably assimilated by the late 1700s.

The Huguenots were French Protestants who adhered to John Calvin's Puritanism. Gaspar Coligny, the French Navy's celebrated Huguenot admiral, attempted to establish the first Huguenot settlement at Charlesfort on Port Royal in 1562. The Spanish eradicated the settlement in 1564 as a perceived threat to their possessions in Florida. In an age in which religious dissent equated with political subversion, the French state's persecution of Huguenots culminated in the St. Bartholomew's Day Massacre of 1572. Henry IV gave them protected status with the Edict of Nantes in 1598, but his successors failed to consistently honor that policy.

As the protections of the edict eroded in the 17th century, Huguenots began to leave France. Large-scale emigration followed Louis XIV's revocation of the Edict of Nantes in 1685. Many went to England, expecting the Protestant nation to welcome them. They found, however, that the English expected them to conform to the Church of England, that London artisans resented potential competition from Huguenots, that the English regarded a French-speaking population with suspicion, and that Huguenots were expected to augment the white population of England's North American colonies.

Beginning in 1680, significant numbers of Huguenots came to Charleston, S.C., directly from England. The white population was only about 3,000 at the time, so a group of several hundred represented a sizable minority. For several decades, three qualities preserved the Huguenots' distinctive identity: they were Puritan, francophone, and endogamous. At first their English neighbors attempted to suppress their political rights, but the South Carolina Naturalization Act of 1697 secured a climate of political tolerance.

Some Huguenot families settled in Charleston, where they became prominent merchants, while others became planters in the rural areas of South Carolina. Historian Jon Butler has emphasized that the political economy of the planters' world, especially the practice of owning slaves, created a shared experience with their English neighbors that transcended the Huguenots' ethnicity. R. C. Nash and others point to the situation in Charleston, where Huguenot identity was undermined by exogamy, the small social universe of the merchant class, and the 1706 Church Act, which made the Church of England the established church in South Carolina.

Although Huguenots still organized along ethnic lines and Huguenot business leaders founded a benevolent association called the "South Carolina Society" in 1737, some scholars argue that the Huguenots of South Carolina were effectively absorbed into English Protestant society by the middle of the 18th century. Historians tend to contrast Butler's explanation of the rural planters with the Charleston account, and then champion one narrative or the other, but it is entirely plausible that both are correct. Two different social classes could have arrived at assimilation by different means.

Huguenot societies have been established in every state in the South. The Huguenot Society of South Carolina came into being in 1885, on the 200th anniversary of the Revocation of the Edict of Nantes. Currently it has about 2,000 members. The society publishes the *Transactions of the Huguenot Society of South Carolina* and holds an annual meeting in Charleston. Some Huguenot descendants belong to the Huguenot Church in Charleston (the only such church in the United States), which has an annual service in French. A distinctive Huguenot cross is worn by some descendants, especially at commemorative events.

Southerners today are accustomed to witnessing vibrant celebrations of the social origins of distinctive groups, each using their ethnicity to enrich the present and perhaps also inflect the future. Awareness of Huguenot heritage takes the form of genealogical research, articles in academic journals, occasional reenactments, and eulogies extolling the Huguenot ancestry of the deceased. It is primarily a nostalgic retrospec-

tive appreciation of one's Huguenot connections from long ago.

CHRISTOPHER P. TOUMEY
University of South Carolina

Richard M. Golden, ed., *The Huguenot Connection: The Edict of Nantes, Its Revocation, and Early French Migration to South Carolina* (1988); Raymond Mentzer and Andrew Spicer, eds., *Society and Culture in the Huguenot World, 1559–1685* (2002); Bertrand Van Ruymbeke and Randy J. Sparks, eds., *Memory and Identity: The Huguenots in France and the Atlantic Diaspora* (2003).

Hungarians of Livingston Parish, Louisiana

The largest rural Hungarian settlement in the United States is in eastern Livingston Parish, La. Most of the 600,000 Hungarians immigrating to the United States between 1870 and World War I were in search of better economic opportunities and settled in industrial centers in the Northeast. A few, however, ventured to the pine forests of southeastern Louisiana and found work at the Brackenridge Lumber Mill. The first three Hungarian settlers, Julius Bruskay, Adam Mocsary, and Theodore Zboray, arrived in 1896 and encouraged friends and relations to join them by writing of the warm climate, the ready mill work, and their ability to purchase land on credit as mill workers—an opportunity they would never have had in their native land. A small community called Maxwell grew around the mill, which increasing numbers of Hungarian settlers renamed "Arpadhon," meaning "the home of Arpad" (the name of the legendary unifier of the

The Hungarian harvest dance is a continuing tradition in Hungarian Settlement, La. (Jim King, photographer, courtesy of the Arpadhon Hungarian Settlement Association)

Magyar tribes who founded Hungary in 896).

By 1908 a train depot called Albany, about a mile north of Arpadhon, became the center of local commerce, and when the Lumber Mill closed in 1916, Arpadhon became primarily a farming community. The name "Arpadhon" faded from use as many began to refer to the area as "Hungarian Settlement," and it continued to attract more Hungarians over the next 20 years. By 1935 Hungarian Settlement was home to approximately 200 Hungarian families (1,500 people). Most lived and worked on small family farms of 20 acres each.

During the early years, the Magyars of Hungarian Settlement kept their ethnic identity primarily through isolation. At first, they married only within their ethnic group, and the Hungarian language dominated the community. Many did not attempt to learn any more English than was absolutely necessary. The Hungarians stayed mainly to themselves, making every effort to preserve their identity and teach their language and customs to their children.

By 1975 the Hungarians of Livingston Parish had assimilated into southern society, and few spoke the language of their ancestors. In an effort to preserve and promote the local Hungarian culture, a group of residents formed the Arpadhon Hungarian Settlement Cultural Association (AHSCA), which continues as an active force in the community. The AHSCA compiled a cookbook that includes many traditional ethnic family recipes and currently sponsors the Annual Hungarian Harvest Dance, which is held on the first Saturday of October. In traditional costumes decorated in red, white, and green (the colors of the Hungarian flag) and accompanied by authentic Hungarian folk music, participants perform a series of dances that have been passed down for several generations. Some of these include the *Az a Szep* ("That's the Pretty One"), *Meg erett a Fekete Szolo* ("The Grapes Are Ripe"), and variations of the *csardas*, the national dance of Hungary. The AHSCA also organizes Hungarian Heritage Day in May or June of each year. On this occasion, citizens of Hungarian descent age 75 and older are honored with Hungarian music, dancing, and food.

Reminders of Hungarian origins continue to shape Livingston Parish, La. Large green highway signs with the words "HUNGARIAN SETTLEMENT" proudly mark the entrances to this rural ethnic community. Two businesses in the community, Olde World Bakery and Louis Bartus Hungarian Sausages and Pastries, offer a taste of Hungarian delicacies, such as *kiflik* (small, nut-filled pastries), *kalacs* (sweet nut rolls), and *kolbasz* (Hungarian sausage). Less than a quarter-mile south of Albany stands the former Erdey-Kiss Amvets building, which now houses the very active Arpadhon Hungarian Settlement Cultural Association. Though much has changed over the past 100 years, the Hungarians of Albany continue to take pride in their ethnic roots. On occasion, some senior citizens of Hungarian descent in the community still speak the language of their parents and grandparents. With the hard work and determination of the AHSCA and others, many aspects of the Hungarian culture in Livingston Parish will survive for years to come.

VICTORIA MOCSARY
Southeastern Louisiana University

Vonnie Brown, *Viltis: A Folklore Magazine* (December 1973); Ruth C. Carter, "Problems of Adult Education Classes among the Hungarians and Italians in Tangipahoa and Livingston Parishes" (M.A. thesis, Louisiana State University, 1935); Victoria Mocsary, *Arpadhon: The Largest Rural Hungarian Settlement in the United States* (1990); Ginger Romero, *Hungarian Folklife: The Sweet Taste of Yesterday in the Florida Parishes of Louisiana* (1987).

Igbos

Igbo-speaking peoples were the major ethnic group in the densely populated hinterland of what Europeans called the Calabar Coast in the Bight of Biafra, now present-day southeastern Nigeria. Of the estimated 1.7 million slaves taken from Biafra in the transatlantic trade, about 75 percent (1.2 million) were Igbo. Those arriving in the South went predominantly to the Chesapeake (ca. 1715–55).

Before their international diaspora, Igbo-speaking people thought of themselves in strictly local terms, but across the Atlantic they learned to identify themselves collectively as "Eboe." Throughout the Americas, the Igbo gained a reputation as "bad" slaves. They specialized in passive-aggressive forms of resistance, such as running away, slow work, sullenness, and suicide. Among fellow slaves they also were reputed to be great poisoners, conjurers, and "obeah-men," and they allegedly had the secret ability to fly. Traditional Igbo *obia* (doctoring) included wide use of poisons as well as healing charms, and these continued to be used by conjurers in the Chesapeake. In historical Igboland, one of the greatest kings of the ancient Nri civilization (fl. ca. 1500–1700 A.D.) was Ézè Nri Fenenu, who reputedly gained the power to fly and who reigned so long (1575–1625) that "he refused to die."

White men apparently found Igbo women to be particularly beautiful. Some enslaved Igbo women used their beauty to negotiate their way through chattel slavery. This strategy could bring special privileges to their mixed-race children. In an extreme case, John Carruthers Stanly (1774–1846?), the son of an enslaved Igbo woman in North Carolina, was manumitted in 1808. He became a barber in coastal New Bern, Craven County, and invested in town lots, farmland, and slaves. In the 1820s, Stanly owned some 2,600 acres and about 125 slaves and worked them in a variety of enterprises from barbering to the production of turpentine. The vast majority of Igbo slaves, including John C. Stanly's mother, remain largely anonymous. However, one of the most famous Africans in the South was Olaudah Equiano, an Igbo born about 1745 in southeastern Nigeria who was enslaved and taken to Virginia. After an odyssey he details in his autobiography, *The Interesting Narrative of the Life of Olaudah Equiano, or Gustavus Vassa, the African, Written by Himself* (1789), he purchased his freedom in 1766, entered commerce, converted to Methodism, and married an English woman.

In the key decades of the second and third quarters of the 18th century in the Chesapeake, when the slave trade fueled the great expansion of settlement from the Tidewater to the piedmont, the largest group of Africans were from Biafra. In Virginia, Bristol merchants pioneered the Biafran trade, and between 1715 and 1755 some 57 percent of the 53,500 Africans brought to the colony came from "Calabar." In the same period, Biafrans counted for two-thirds of the 35,000 Africans brought by Bristol merchants. There was a Bristol-Biafra-Virginia axis in the pre-1750 British slave trade; after 1750 the market

shifted to the West Indies, especially Jamaica, and was increasingly financed by Liverpool merchants. But in the first half of the century in Virginia, some 60 percent of the Africans spoke one dialect or another of Igbo.

In the American South, one may hear echoes of the historical presence of Igbo slaves. That most southern of foods, *hibiscus esculentus*, is known by its Igbo name, *okra* (which is also common to the Bantu language family). In the old North Carolina plantation district along the Meherrin River (Hertford County) across from Southampton County, Va., there is an Ebo Road. In the Upper South there used to be a type of satirical rhyme called a "Guinea" or "Ebo" rhyme, and slaves generally dug pits, or "hidey-holes," in the earthen floors of their cabins that may have been used as Igboesque ancestor shrines. Eighteenth-century slave sites in Virginia often yield cowrie shells, and one includes pewter spoon handles incised with designs evocative of Igbo divination tools. Throughout colonial North America and today in the anglophone Caribbean, the pejorative term blacks wielded against whites, *bukra* (the cross equivalent of "nigger") derives from an Efik-Ibibio word probably brought into English by Igbo slaves. In coastal North Carolina, slaves used to perform a Christmastime masquerade called *jonkonnu* ("John Canoe" or "John Kuners"), which was strikingly similar to male masquerades throughout Igboland. Wherever Igbo were taken, names like Anika (*Nneka*, "Big Mama") and Juba (*Jiuba*, "Fortune") resurfaced, as did tales of the Igbo animal trickster-hero Tortoise, refashioned as Brer Terrapin in the briar patch of slavery. Eighteenth-century diasporic Igbo music, which a contemporary Jamaican observer described as "soft and languishing," may also have been one of the sources of American blues, especially the dulcet piedmont blues of the Upper South.

Through foodways (*okra*), power-ways (*bukra*), religionways (conjure/obeah), and folkways, Igbo slaves struggled against the "soul death" of slavery and left their historical ethnic imprint in southern culture.

DOUGLAS B. CHAMBERS
University of Southern Mississippi

Douglas B. Chambers, *Murder at Montpelier: Igbo Africans in Virginia* (2005), *Slavery and Abolition* (April 2002); Michael A. Gomez, *Exchanging Our Country Marks: The Transformation of African Identities in the Colonial and Antebellum South* (1998); Gwendolyn Midlo Hall, *Slavery and African Ethnicities in the Americas: Restoring the Links* (2005); Elizabeth Isichei, *A History of the Igbo People* (1976); Lorena S. Walsh, *From Calabar to Carter's Grove: The History of a Virginia Slave Community* (1997); John Thornton, *Africa and Africans in the Making of the Atlantic World, 1400–1800* (1998).

Indians (East)

Indian immigration to the United States began as early as 1820 but increased dramatically after India gained independence in 1947. In 1965 amendments to the Immigration and Nationality Act attracted many Indians to the United States. While previous Indian immigrants had been mostly laborers, the amendments gave priority to highly trained and educated professionals. The new immigrants primarily consisted of urban, educated, and English-speaking people. The twin forces of globalization and liberalization in India opened up new avenues for both jobs and educational pursuits for Indians in the United States, leading to renewed migrations beginning in the 1990s.

According to the most recent data provided by the U.S. Immigration and Naturalization Service, India is the second-largest source of legal migrants to the United States. Today, the Indian diaspora in the United States stands at 1.7 million. The size of Indian American communities increased in every U.S. state between 1990 and 2000, with the southern states of Texas, Florida, Virginia, and Georgia among those with the highest number of Indian immigrants. The Indian American population in Florida and Georgia stands at 70,740 and 46,132, respectively. Texas is home to the nation's fourth-largest number of Indians, with a population of well over 130,000 — representing a startling 130 percent growth rate since 1990. With burgeoning high-tech industries, growing universities, and relocation of many corporate headquarters to Texas, an increasing number of Indians are settling in metropolitan areas such as Austin, Dallas–Fort Worth, and Houston. Houston and Dallas are now competing to become the American hub for Air India. First- and second-generation Indian Americans form an important part of the entrepreneurial, investment, and business community in Texas and offer new and innovative ways to handle global sourcing. With India emerging as one of America's global partners, the growing relationship between Texas and India may be expected to thrive.

To serve the cultural and educational needs of the Indian community over the last 50 years, Indians in the South have created a number of organizations. For example, the India Association of North Texas is a nonprofit organization formed in 1962 to promote social, cultural, educational, and charitable activities among Indian Americans. The group involves corporate sponsors, local officials, the consulate general of India, and members of Congress. The Indus Entrepreneurs Houston Chapter unites new Texans from India with other Texans in business and social partnerships and generally promotes Indian professionals.

Indians are prominent in the hotel industry across the South, and Indian restaurants are an increasing presence on the southern cultural landscape. Indian grocery stores provide new immigrants with a direct link to their home country and provide not only *masalas* (spices), basmati rice (now grown in Arkansas and Texas), and Assam tea, but also *agarbattis* (incense sticks), Ganesha and Nataraja bronze statues, and religious calendars—a combination that underscores the twin importance of food and religion among Indians. Hindu congregations have constructed temples across the South, such as the Balaji Temple of Atlanta, the Greater Atlanta Vedic Temple, the Hindu Worship Society of Houston, Tex., and the India Cultural Center

and Temple in Memphis, Tenn. These temples also serve as important centers of cultural exchange and host cultural festivals such as Holi (a "festival of color" honoring Krishna and creation), Diwali (the festival of lights), and Garba (for the goddess of power Shakti-Amba, or Durga), which bring together people from different regions in India. Hindu temples also sponsor music and dance recitals. Some of the most popular classical dance includes Bharatanatyam (classical dance of South India), Odissi (from the state of Orissa), Kathak (classical dance of North India), and Kuchipudi (from the state of Andhra Pradesh).

While there is increasing exogamy, many Indians continue to practice arranged marriages. Indian communities in the South continue to hold traditional wedding ceremonies in which women wear the *sari* (silk drapery), men wear *kurtas* (embroidered robes), and both wear copious gold jewelry. Receptions following the ceremony feature Indian popular music and dance in styles heavily influenced by Bollywood (the Indian film industry). Across the South, Indian American associations celebrate Indian Independence Day on 15 August to remember and honor their home country and to familiarize younger generations with the importance of the day. While many second- and third-generation Indian Americans now consider themselves southerners, an awareness of ethnic origins remains a powerful focus for identity.

ANJALI SAHAY
Old Dominion University

Robert W. Gardner, *Asia and Pacific Migration Journal* (1992); Ajantha Subramanian, in *The American South in a Global World*, ed. James Peacock, Harry L. Watson, and Carrie Matthews (2005).

Irish, Contemporary

Participants in New Orleans's St. Patrick's Day Parade toss cabbages, carrots, onions, and MoonPies to the crowds; the day's event in Jackson, Miss., features a float bearing "Sweet Potato Queens"; and Savannahnans consume green grits on St. Patrick's Day morning. These consciously whimsical fusions of southern and Irish symbols intimate more complex interrelationships between the Irish and the South. Irish communities developed in those southern cities where Irish settled, primarily for work opportunities, from the early 1800s to 1860. They formed Irish associations, established Catholic dioceses and schools, provided mutual aid, and organized events such as St. Patrick's Day parades. Maintaining Irish identity while adapting to the wider society, many of these early Irish immigrants and their descendants also became southerners.

Hibernian societies founded in Savannah, Charleston, and Atlanta in the early to mid-1800s are still in existence. Membership in these fraternal organizations included both Catholics and non-Catholics. In Savannah the Hibernians organized the city's first official St. Patrick's Day Parade in 1824 and welcomed the participation of other Irish societies formed in the mid-to-late 19th-century. Today, the four-hour-long procession through two miles of live oak–shaded streets and squares in the city's historic district is one of the largest St. Patrick's Day parades in the United States. Approximately 400,000 visitors bring about $40 million to the city's coffers during the week of the parade.

In the 1980s and 1990s, five more annual Irish events began in Savannah, and ten new Irish organizations have emerged since 1970. These developments exemplify the remarkable growth of interest in Irish identity in southern cities with historic Irish American communities as well as in rural southern places without deep Irish connections. The economic prosperity of the region in recent decades has attracted many Irish Americans from other parts of the country, as well as immigrants from Ireland. The U.S. Census Bureau reports that of nearly 5 million people who moved to the South from other regions of the country since 1995, close to 640,000 claimed at least some Irish ancestry. Developments in historic preservation and cultural tourism, accessible air travel and information technology, and the international popularity of Irish musical and dance groups also contribute to the burgeoning interest in Irish culture and heritage.

At least 12 new St. Patrick's Day parades have developed in various southern cities since the late 1970s. Irish festivals and "Celtic" festivals (which combine Irish and Scottish themes) and numerous Irish dance competitions take place annually throughout the South. Irish radio programs, specialty shops, and pubs exist in many areas, and Irish fraternal organizations are

Fenian Society members displaying their banner at the 2004 Celtic Cross Ceremony in Savannah, Ga.
(Photograph courtesy of Barbara Henry)

flourishing. The 1990s saw the establishment of Police and Firefighters' Emerald Societies in eight metropolitan areas in the South and at least 12 Ancient Order of Hibernians divisions. Many Irish cultural groups have formed to promote awareness and appreciation of Irish traditions, and courses of Irish interest are now available in dozens of southern colleges and universities. Young Irish immigrants and Irish Americans compete nationally in Gaelic football and hurling as members of the North American division of the Gaelic Athletic Association, with clubs in Atlanta, Charlotte, and Fort Lauderdale.

The proliferation of Irish-themed groups and activities indicates that southern Irish Americans, Irish Americans from other parts of the country, and Irish immigrants to the region are shaping a greatly expanded and more multifaceted Irish presence in the 21st-century South.

BARBARA HENDRY
Georgia Southern University

Dennis Clark, *Hibernia America* (1986); William L. Fogarty, *The Days We've Celebrated: St. Patrick's Day in Savannah* (1980); David T. Gleeson, *The Irish in the South, 1815–1877* (2001); Ray O'Hanlon, *The New Irish Americans* (1998); Celeste Ray, ed., *Southern Heritage on Display: Public Ritual*

and *Ethnic Diversity within Southern Re-*
gionalism (2003); Edward M. Shoemaker,
in *The Encyclopedia of the Irish in America*,
ed. Michael Glazier (1999).

Irish, Historic

Many Roman Catholic Irish came to the
colonial South as indentured servants,
but this migration of mostly single
males was not conducive to forming
ethnic communities. Outside of Maryland, these poor, Gaelic-speaking, often
illiterate immigrants disappeared into
the majority population. They learned
English, became Protestant, and lost
contact with their Irish homes. There
were exceptions, such as the Carrolls of
Carrollton, Md., but the main legacy
of the colonial Irish in the South is the
large number of Protestant Murphys,
Kellys, and Conners scattered throughout the region.

Irish Protestants and Catholics fleeing political persecution in the 1790s
(as a result of the "United Irishmen"
independence movement) shaped the
first Irish communities in the South.
Relatively prosperous, these migrants
built friendships with established Scots-
Irish communities to form Hibernian
societies. Thus, when in the 1820s
poor Irish again began to come to the
South to work on various public works
projects, there were elements of ethnic
support already in place. This migration of laborers continued into the
1840s and exploded with the onset of
the Great Famine in Ireland in 1845. In
reaction to that disaster, families fled
the country, and those who came to the
South predominantly went to urban
areas (although some did form rural

farming communities). The numbers
of native Irish in the South reached its
height in 1860, when over 84,000 lived
in the 11 states that became the Confederacy. However, even with thousands of
Irish also living in Maryland, Kentucky,
and Missouri, the number of Irish in
the South was still only around 10 percent of the total Irish population in the
nation as a whole.

Nevertheless, by concentrating in
towns the Irish had a very visible presence in the 19th-century South. For
example, 22 percent of Savannah's white
population in 1860 was Irish born.
Often doing work that was too dangerous for slaves, most of the urban Irish
lived in desperate housing conditions
and situations exacerbated by alcohol
abuse, crime, and epidemics. However,
Irish communities helped newcomers
find employment and accommodation
and also provided comfort through social activities. Not every Irish person
in the South was a laborer or a domestic. Many worked as police officers,
artisans, and merchants.

The growth in Irish migration
boosted Catholic numbers in the region, and the church formed new dioceses and appointed Irish bishops to
cater to the new flock. One of the most
important Irish clerics in the South was
John England, originally from County
Cork. The bishop of Charleston from
1820 until 1842, England founded the
first Catholic newspaper in the United
States in 1822 and spoke to both houses
of Congress in 1826. Irish clerics and
nuns continued to come to the South
throughout the 19th and 20th centuries.
Their good work in education and

health care helped gain acceptance for the Catholic Irish.

The Irish in the South took a keen interest in politics, both Irish and American. They supported Irish nationalist movements of the 19th century and also supported the Irish struggle for freedom in the 20th century by welcoming the likes of future prime minister Eamon De Valera to the region. As American voters, they were predominantly Democrats. Reluctant secessionists (most voted for Stephen Douglas in 1860), the Irish nevertheless fought for the Confederacy and opposed Radical Reconstruction. This loyalty to the Lost Cause sealed Irish integration within the region. They were thus able to create political machines that dominated southern cities such as Savannah, Charleston, and New Orleans.

After the Civil War, Irish immigration to the South dropped off precipitously as the rapidly industrializing North and Midwest provided far greater economic opportunities than a South dominated by sharecropping and postwar poverty. Irish communities in southern towns became increasingly Irish American. During the 1980s and 1990s, the rise of the Sunbelt South attracted new Irish migrants to the region's major metropolitan areas. This new migration, allied with the movement of large numbers of Irish Americans from the rest of the country, has created a renaissance of Irish culture in the South, resulting in Irish festivals in virtually every southern state, Gaelic games in Atlanta, and a reorganization of the Ancient Order of Hibernians in the region. This combination of new immigrants, northern transplants, and descendants of earlier Irish immigrants has made Irishness more visible in the South than at any time since the 19th century.

DAVID T. GLEESON
College of Charleston

David N. Doyle, *Ireland, Irishmen, and Revolutionary America, 1760–1820* (1981); David T. Gleeson, *The Irish in the South, 1815–1877* (2001); Ronald Hoffman, *Princes of Ireland, Planters of Maryland* (2001); Randall Miller and Jon Wakelyn, eds., *Catholics in the Old South: Essays on Church and Culture* (1985); Kerby Miller, *Emigrants and Exiles: Ireland and the Irish Migration to the United States* (1985); David A. Wilson, *United Irishmen, United States: Immigrant Radicals in the United States* (1998).

Italians

From the importation of Venetian glassblowers to Jamestown in 1622 to the Spoleto Festival in Charleston (a 17-day celebration of opera, music, and drama), Italians have added to the diversity and vitality of the South. Italians migrated to southern states in four distinct phases, reflecting American demands for labor, international labor patterns, and peninsular politics.

Between the age of exploration and the Civil War, Italians appeared prominently in southern history, but their notoriety derived principally from individual exploits rather than group endeavors. The nation state of Italy did not emerge until the late 19th century; thus, the earliest "Italians" represented rival powers, city states, or simply their own interests. Giovanni da Verrazzano charted the Atlantic Coast, and Henry di Tonti explored the southern interior. Italians helped explore and settle St. Augustine, San Antonio, and Savannah. William Paca of Maryland signed the Declaration of Independence, and Thomas Jefferson counted the intellectual Phillip Mazzei as a friend and teacher. Jefferson also persuaded a number of Italian sculptors and architects to help with the building of the U.S. Capitol.

In 1763 English physician Andrew Turnbull imported 1,500 Italians, Greeks, and Minorcans to labor at New Smyrna, his east Florida plantation. The inhumane conditions and brutal treatment took a terrible toll on the indentured servants, who rebelled and fled to St. Augustine, where many of their descendants remain. The New Smyrna debacle marked a dramatic chapter in Italian American history and New World cruelty.

On the eve of the Civil War, few southern states boasted many Italian residents; Louisiana was home to 915 and Mississippi 121, but all other states counted fewer than 100 Italians. During the second phase of Italian migration to the South, between the Civil War and 1920, relatively few Italians came to the region in comparison to the massive numbers concentrated in northern cities. A handful of Italian agricultural communities in the South, however, attracted much attention. The most noteworthy and successful of those rural experiments was in Arkansas. Between 1895 and 1897, about 1,200 Italians from northern Italy were recruited to replace black laborers in Sunnyside, Ark. The experiment failed almost immediately, but a faction led by Father Bandini resettled in what is today Tontitown. Other agricultural colonies claiming varying successes included Bryan and Dickinson, Tex., and Valdese, N.C.

Louisiana attracted more Italians than any other southern state in the early 20th century. Between 1880 and 1914 as many as 16,000 Sicilians migrated to the parish fields and farms. In Hammond, Amite City, and Independence, Italians helped pioneer the strawberry business. In Kenner, Italians achieved success as truck farmers. Vast numbers of Sicilians cut and burned sugarcane fields in places like Napoleonville. Census figures never reflected the fluidity of this floating proletariat. New Orleans alone counted 5,866 Italians in the 1900 census. Sicilians there quickly dominated the fruit and vegetable markets—as they would in many cities—but they encountered a virulent nativism that was especially evident in Louisiana.

Industrial enterprise characterized the third phase of Italian migration. Italians from Bisacquino, Sicily, sought their fortunes in the steel mills of Alabama. In 1890 Jefferson County included 130 Italians, a figure that increased to 2,160 by 1920. Italians constituted the largest ethnic group in Alabama, as in Louisiana. In Birmingham they labored as unskilled steelworkers, and, in typical fashion, they organized 13 mutual aid societies and branched into truck farming and small family enterprises.

Tampa, Fla., offered a unique setting for Italian immigrants: Ybor City. Founded in 1886 by the Spanish manufacturer Vicente Martínez Ybor, Ybor City had evolved as the cigar capital of America by 1900, boasting over 100 cigar factories offering employment to 10,000 Cubans, Spaniards, and Italians. By 1920 almost 3,000 Italian immigrants had settled in Tampa. In Ybor City they learned Spanish, rolled cigars, flirted with and embraced radical ideologies, organized unions, participated in a series of strikes, and eventually achieved an impressive amount of economic mobility as grocers, dairy farmers, and fruit vendors.

Second- and third-generation Italian Americans' migration to the Sunbelt, especially Florida, constitutes the fourth (and still continuing) phase. A number of salient trends appear in this developmental stage. Cities without historic Italian immigrant communities, such as Atlanta, Charlotte, Nashville, and Fort Lauderdale, have attracted thousands of Italian Americans in recent years. The 2000 U.S. Census documents this Sunbelt presence. From a low of 40,400 self-identified Italian Americans in Mississippi to North Carolina (181,982), Louisiana (195,218), Virginia (257,129), Texas (363,354), and Florida (1,003,977), the South has become a favorite destination of Italian Americans. Midwestern and northeastern migrants have imported their social and cultural institutions, and today organizations such as the Sons of Italy and the National Italian American Foundation can be found throughout the South.

GARY R. MORMINO
University of South Florida

Valentine Belfiglio, *The Italian Experience in Texas*, 2nd ed. (1995); Carl Patrick Burkart, "A White Man's Country: Italians in Birmingham, Alabama" (M.A. thesis, University of Georgia, 1998); Richard Gambino, *Vendetta* (1977); Jerre Mangione and Ben Morreale, *La Storia: Five Centuries of the Italian American Experience* (1992); Gary Mormino and George Pozzetta, *The Immigrant World of Ybor City* (1987); Jean Scarpaci, *Italian Immigrants in Louisiana's Sugar Parishes* (1981).

Jena Band Choctaws

Choctaw immigrants began to cross the Mississippi River in large numbers after Spain acquired Louisiana from France in 1763. Prompted by Indian Removal, the Civil War, and poor economic conditions in Mississippi, westward migration continued into the 20th century. Choctaw people established so many communities by the end of the 19th century that, in Louisiana, the term "Choctaw" became synonymous with "Indian." One small band stopped in Jena, Louisiana, along the way to Indian Territory sometime between Removal and the Civil War, settling on Trout Creek in what would become LaSalle Parish. These five families, which became known as the Jena Band of Choctaw Indians, appeared on the 1880 federal census and were visited in 1886 by linguist Albert Gatschet, who traced their origins to Scott and Newton Counties in Mississippi. Gatschet found them settled in log huts in a small clearing on the land of Thomas Whatley, who also owned the store where the Choctaw traded their goods.

Anderson Lewis, Jena Band Choctaw, with tanned deerskin, 1981 (Don Sepulvado, photographer)

The Dawes Act of 1887, designed to break up communal tribal territories into individual land allotments, resulted in the second Indian Removal for the Choctaw. Agents sought out Louisiana Indians eligible for allotment in Indian Territory (Oklahoma), and part of the Jena band made the difficult, nine-month journey there to enroll as full-blood Choctaw. Why the small, disheartened band returned to Louisiana before they were enrolled is not known. Notified by mail that they were still eligible for enrollment and allotment, they were unable to travel back to Indian Territory in the time allowed. About half the tribe returned to Oklahoma in 1915 to find the rolls permanently closed. Several chose to remain there,

however, reducing an already small Jena Choctaw population. The community revitalized around 1919 when a large, extended family from another Louisiana Choctaw community joined with the Jena band. Intermarriage with this family band helped preserve the community and allow the conservation of tribal traditions.

With neither communal nor individual property, Jena Choctaw people did what they could to make a living. Men worked as sharecroppers or in the timber industry, while women served as domestics for the local European American community. As they had for generations, the Choctaw also sold and bartered produce, medicines, hides, and cane baskets at the Whatley store. Public education was not available to community members, and attempts to establish a school for Choctaw children had only short-term success. Not until young tribal servicemen returned from World War II were Choctaw children allowed to attend public schools in LaSalle Parish.

Although social isolation limited opportunities for the Jena band, these same factors helped the small, conservative community preserve traditional social institutions. The chief/council form of government endured until the 1970s, when it was replaced by a constitutional government preparatory to seeking federal recognition as a sovereign nation. In 1995 the Jena band became the fourth sovereign tribal nation in Louisiana. With new sources of funding available, the tribe was able to secure a land base, build a tribal community center, and support housing, social services, and cultural programs, including language and traditional arts. In partnership with the U.S. Department of Agriculture Forest Service and the Louisiana Regional Folklife Program, the Jena band sponsored a two-day, split-cane basketry workshop conducted by weaver Rose Fisher Blassingame. The complete process was videotaped, and each step was narrated in Choctaw by elder Mary Jackson Jones.

No longer isolated along the banks of Trout Creek, tribal members now interact on both a local and national level. Pan-tribalism has introduced powwow culture and material traditions into the social repertoire, and outside marriages bring new ideas and values into the community. Still, the Jena Choctaw work to find a balance between traditional and contemporary life. Community members often participate in dances and other cultural activities with their relatives in Oklahoma and Mississippi, and artistic traditions like split-cane basketry and deer hide tanning remain viable in the community. Choctaw language is still spoken among elders, and language classes allow younger tribal members to learn or relearn their native tongue. While they look to the future and to new opportunities, the Jena Band of Choctaw Indians finds strength and reinforces social identity through the practice and preservation of time-honored traditions.

DAYNA BOWKER LEE
Louisiana Regional Folklife Program

Sarah Sue Goldsmith, Tim Mueller, and Risa Mueller, *Nations Within: The Four Sovereign Tribes of Louisiana* (2003); Fred B. Kniffen, George A. Stokes, and H. F. Gregory, *The Historic Tribes of Louisiana: From 1542 to the Present* (1987); Dayna Bowker Lee, *Uski Taposhik: Cane Basketry Traditions of the Jena Band of Choctaw Indians* (video documentary, 2002).

Jews

Jews do not immediately come to mind when most people think of the South. Yet in the early 21st century, 1 million Jews live in the region, with more than half of them residing in Florida. In south Florida, Jews form 13 percent of the population—the single-largest concentration of Jewish people outside the state of Israel. These Jews are mostly northern transplants, and south Florida certainly does not define the entire southern Jewish experience. Recent Jewish arrivals there—and in larger metropolitan areas of the South, such as Atlanta—have begun to reshape the demographics of the region. In most southern locales, however, Jews continue to form only a small percentage of the population, as they have from their earliest days on the continent.

Three hundred years ago, Charleston, S.C., had one of the largest Jewish populations in America. Five hundred of the city's residents were Jews, representing one-fifth of the 2,500 Jews living in the colonies. Since that time, Jews have established themselves in cities, towns, and villages throughout the region, some of which, like Kaplan, La., or Rosenberg, Tex., they helped found. Before the Civil War, the centers of American Jewish life—and the sources of many social, cultural, and religious institutional changes shaping the character of all American Jewry—were found in Charleston and Savannah, Ga., which had attracted a Jewish community as early as 1733. Not only did Jews in the South take the lead in establishing American Reform Judaism, they also helped mold distinctly southern traditions. They saw themselves as "Jewish southerners" as much as "southern Jews."

Though Jews in the region still comprise less than 1 percent of the South's population, few phases of the southern experience and few places in the South escaped their influence. Individuals such as Mordecai Sheftall of Savannah and Francis Salvador of Charleston served as leaders during the American Revolution. After the Revolution, Jews such as Abraham Mordecai, credited with founding Montgomery, Ala., moved westward, occasionally joining other Jews who had been living along the Mississippi River since the early 18th century. David Yulee of Florida and Judah P. Benjamin of Louisiana were instrumental in gaining status for their states within the Union and later were no less influential in leading their states out of it. Jews became involved in all branches of government at all levels. South Carolinians elected the country's first Jewish governor, and Florida elected the country's first Jewish senator. Jews adopted not only southern folkways, but also the full range of political opinions and passions of their gentile neigh-

Judah P. Benjamin, *secretary of state of the Confederacy (Photographer unknown, Library of Congress [LC-USZC4-12291], Washington, D.C.)*

bors. Jews fought in Confederate regiments and assumed positions within the Confederate military and political leadership, including the offices of surgeon general, judge advocate, quartermaster general, and secretary of state.

During Reconstruction and afterward, Jews contributed significantly to the recovery of the South. Many—such as the Rich brothers in Georgia, the Maas brothers in Florida, and Neiman and Marcus in Texas—rose from peddlers and dry goods dealers to founders of the region's largest and best-known department stores. Others, such as the Lemann and Godchaux families in Louisiana and the Kempners in Texas, expanded beyond their mercantile holdings to become planters. Many southern Jews also used their wealth and/or prominence in public service. Judah Touro of New Orleans became one of the most notable philanthropists of the early 19th century, and Rabbi Henry Cohen is memorialized in Galveston for the role he played in helping the city recover from the devastating flood of 1900.

Jews did not entirely escape the darker side of southern history. While some could be counted among the defenders of all southern institutions—including slavery—courageous southern rabbis and other brave individuals (including many women) risked the fury of their coreligionists and communities by championing civil rights. Violent anti-Semitism occurred only rarely, most notably in the Leo Frank murder case in Georgia in the early 20th century and later when temples were bombed and northern Jews Michael Schwerner and Andrew Goodman killed during the civil rights era. These occasions made Jews throughout the region more aware of their precarious position as a white minority. They were also the victims of other troubling, though nonviolent, affronts: for example, Jews experienced quotas, social restrictions, and exclusion from elite organizations and country clubs. Nevertheless, the Jewish presence demonstrates that the South, throughout its history, has been more than a biracial Christian society. Jews in the South have reflected, as well as contributed to, the region's rich multidimensional milieu.

BOBBIE MALONE
Wisconsin Historical Society

LOUIS E. SCHMIER
Valdosta State College

Mark Bauman and Berkley Kalin, eds., *The Quiet Voices: Southern Rabbis and Black Civil Rights, 1880s to 1990s* (1997); Emily Simms Bingham, *Mordecai: An Early American Family* (2003); Eli Evans, *Judah P. Benjamin: The Jewish Confederate* (1988), *The Provincials: A Personal History of the Jews in the South* (2005); Marcie Ferris, *Matzoh Ball Gumbo: Culinary Tales of the Jewish South* (2005); Melissa Fay Greene, *The Temple Bombing* (1996); Bobbie Malone, *Rabbi Max Heller: Reformer, Zionist, Southerner, 1860–1929* (1997); Leonard Rogoff, *Homelands: Southern Jewish Identity in Durham and Chapel Hill, North Carolina* (2001); Theodore Rosengarten and Dale Rosengarten, *A Portion of the People: Three Hundred Years of Southern Jewish Life* (2002); Louis E. Schmier, ed., *Reflections of Southern Jewry: The Letters of Charles Wessolowsky, 1878–1879* (1982); Clive Webb, *Fight against Fear: Southern Jews and Black Civil Rights* (2001).

Jews, Sephardic

Jewish immigrants began arriving in colonial America in the 17th century. Sephardic Jews—descendants of Jews expelled from Spain and Portugal late in the 15th century—were the first Jews to settle in the South, locating predominantly in Savannah and Charleston. In 1695 a Jew living in Charleston served Governor Archdale as interpreter to the indigenous Creek people, and by 1702 many Jews voted in a general election there. A substantial Jewish community in the South, however, was not established until 1762. Dr. Samuel Nunez led a group from London to Savannah in 1733, founding the Mikve

Israel Congregation there in July 1735. Other early Sephardic settlers included Nunez's son Moses, who was a trader and an interpreter for local Indians, and his son-in-law Abraham de Lyon, who tried, unsuccessfully, to introduce viticulture to the region.

A quarter of America's Jewish population resided in Savannah and Charleston in 1770. The former was predominantly Ashkenazi Jews (Yiddish speakers from Central, Northern, and Eastern Europe) by 1786, but the spiritual leadership remained Sephardic, under the guidance of David Nunez Cardozo and Emmanuel de la Motta. Charleston, home to the largest Jewish community in the United States in 1800, retained only a few vestiges of Sephardic ritual by the mid-19th century.

After its incorporation by the United States in 1803, Louisiana attracted Sephardic settlers. Prayers in their first synagogue followed the Portuguese Jewish tradition. An early 19th-century influx of Sephardim from the Caribbean strengthened their community. Ties with Caribbean communities remained strong in the 20th century.

Evidence exists that *conversos* (Jews or their descendants who converted to Catholicism yet secretly practiced Judaism) were among the members of Juan Ponce de Leon's expeditions and the ill-fated Andrew Turnbull venture in New Smyrna, Florida. The first documented Jews there arrived in 1763; three Sephardic traders from New Orleans established businesses in English-controlled Mobile and Pensacola. They left for more populous Charleston shortly afterward. Moses Levy, a trader whose ancestors were from Morocco, was the next notable Sephardic Jew in early Florida. He purchased property to establish a colony for European Jewish refugees early in the 19th century. Levy's son, David Levy Yulee, was one of the visionaries who led Florida to statehood and served as the state's first U.S. senator. He also helped guide the state into the Confederacy. Yulee married a non-Jewish woman, following a pattern established by many colonial Sephardim.

In the 20th century, Sephardic immigrants from the former Ottoman Empire established new communities in the South. Individual Sephardic pioneers paved the way in Montgomery, Ala. Ralph Cohen migrated there from the island of Rhodes. The close-knit community founded Congregation Etz Achayim (1912) and the Benevolent Society, an organization that collected money for the ill and needy. At its peak, 200 families belonged to the synagogue. They established an economic niche with small clothing stores.

The first Sephardic settlers in Atlanta migrated from Montgomery. Their religious center, Congregation Or Ve Shalom, was founded in 1916, a merger of two earlier congregations. Colonial Sephardic families in Georgia, such as the Alexanders, made a mark in the 20th century. Henry Alexander, one of the attorneys for accused murderer and lynching victim Leo Frank, was the only Jew in the 1909–10 Georgia Legislature session. By the early 1980s, 350 families of Rhodian and Turkish descent prospered in Atlanta.

Twentieth-century Floridian Sephardim were primarily immigrants who retired in the late 1950s and moved south to Miami Beach. In 1957 they created the Sephardic Jewish Center of Greater Miami, which prospered until the 1980s. South Florida's Sephardim also include Turkish and Syrian families who had settled in small towns in Cuba early in the 20th century but fled the country with the Ashkenazi Jews in the late 1950s and early 1960s.

In the 21st century, immigrants from North Africa, the Middle East, and Israel are also part of the southern Sephardic community, even though they might not trace their origins to Spain and Portugal. From their unique order of prayers and distinctive religious tunes in the synagogues to holiday and life-cycle celebrations in the home, Sephardic Jews continue to pass on a sense of history that relates to the centuries-old Spanish origins of most Sephardim. Understanding Jewish diversity is significant to understanding Jewish history in the South from colonial times to the present day.

ANNETTE B. FROMM
Florida International University

James William Hagy, *This Happy Land: The Jews of Colonial and Antebellum Charleston* (1993); Yitzchak Kerem, *American Jewish History* (December 1997); Bertram Wallace Korn, *The Early Jews of New Orleans* (1969); Seymour B. Liebman, in *A Coat of Many Colors: Jewish Subcommunities in the United States*, ed. Abraham D. Lavender (1977); Chris Monaco, *Southern Jewish History* (2002).

Kickapoos

Texas legislators voted in 1977 to recognize the southern "Traditional Kickapoo" as an official tribe in Texas. Also known as the "Kikaapoa" or "Kiwikapawa," they established a reservation in 1983 that replaced a more traditional village built along the Rio Grande near the International Bridge between Eagle Pass, Tex., and Piedras Negras, Mexico. The move to their reservation marked the end of a long journey for people whose name means "roamers" or "moves about." The federal government approved their status as a sovereign American Indian nation in 1989. The Kickapoo Traditional Tribe of Texas is one of the three federally recognized Kickapoo tribes; the other two are the Kickapoo Tribe of Indians of the Kickapoo Reservation of Kansas and the Kickapoo Tribe of Oklahoma.

In 1649 Europeans recorded their first contact with the Kickapoo in what is today Wisconsin. Over the next three centuries, various bands of Kickapoo established villages and encampments in Ohio, Michigan, New York, Pennsylvania, throughout Louisiana Purchase Territory including Kansas, and Indian Territory (later Oklahoma). By 1835 their presence was reported as far east as the Mexican state of Texas. The Republic of Texas was founded in 1836 and its president, Sam Houston, supported land grants for the Traditional Kickapoo. Their diaspora resulted from both military pressures and the Kickapoos' isolationist efforts to avoid contact with Europeans, Americans, and Texans to the point of having representatives from other tribes discuss issues on their behalf.

The Texas Kickapoo evoked contradictory opinions. Many settlers described them as unreceptive to Christianity and aloof, while others found them to be "fearsome warriors," "unconquerable," "homicidal," and the cause of "economic ruin." Yet, explorers Meriwether Lewis and William Clark described the Kickapoo as living peacefully alongside French settlers and being bonded with them by trade. Most southern Kickapoos were known for resisting acculturation.

Until recently, knowledge of Kickapoo lifestyle and culture remained vague. Seminomadic, they hunted bison yet returned to permanent villages in the summers. A tonal component differentiated their speech from other Algonkian dialects. They also had a unique linguistic code called "whistle speech." Unlike most Algonkians, the Kickapoo did not have a completely matrilineal social structure. Although they practiced some matrilocalism (for example, women owned the homes), they were organized into 11 clans based on the male line, with each clan linked by specific totems.

Outsiders rarely witnessed Kickapoo religious ceremonies. They seem to have believed in a cosmic substance that prevailed throughout nature and to have generally sought harmony between the spirit, mind, and body. Some things they thought to be endowed with mystic qualities received special reverence, including dogs.

With Texas statehood in 1845, officials in the United States decided to assist Texans against Mexican and Indian raids by building a line of forts. Most of the violent encounters between U.S. troops and Kickapoo warriors erupted along the Rio Grande near today's Amistad Reservoir, where the Kickapoos had an encampment. By 1881 all Texas Indians, including the Traditional Kickapoo, had been subdued.

Remarkably, the Kickapoo have managed to maintain many traditional ways. Resistance to mainstream Christianity continues. The traditional Drum (or Dream) religion has the most adherents, followed by Kanakuk and the Native American Church. Many Kickapoos still speak the Kickapoo language, and they have one of the highest percentages of "full-bloods" of any tribe in the United States. At the same time, the Kickapoo have suffered the social problems shared by many American Indian nations, such as dealing with epidemic substance abuse. With federal recognition, some innovations, such as a day care center and Head Start program, have contributed to improving reservation conditions. Still, poverty has been the most pressing issue for the tribe. Many Traditional and Mexican Kickapoo work as migrant farmworkers, and — although they are respected by farmers and ranchers as hardworking people — low wages dominate these industries. The recently reopened Lucky Eagle Casino may change the economic realities of the Kickapoo.

Today, the 650 members of the Kickapoo Traditional Tribe of Texas continue their independent, nonconformist ways, but within the American system. Suspicious of fraud, the tribe ousted its entire council by public vote in 2002, and the new council supported an Internal Revenue Service examination of casino records and other funds. While their name has been misused for patent medicines, by Civil War border raiders, and by Al Capp, author of *Li'l Abner,* the real Kickapoo have proved resilient and enduring.

WANDA DOWNING JONES
El Centro College

A. M. Gibson, *The Kickapoos: Lords of the Middle Border* (1963); Felipe A. Latorre and Dolores Latorre, *The Mexican Kickapoo Indians* (1976); Bill Wright and E. John Gesick Jr., *Texas Kickapoo: Keepers of Tradition* (1996).

Koreans

Most Korean immigrants to the South came after the passage of the Civil Rights Act of 1964 and the 1965 Immigration Act. They arrived at a time when the region was developing industrially and commercially and had become a magnet for migration and investment from other parts of the nation and abroad, including Korea.

Although Koreans are relative newcomers to the South, they are a rapidly growing group with a widely dispersed settlement pattern. Their population grew nearly 53 percent between 1990 and 2000. In 1990 Koreans in the South composed 14.4 percent (115,303) of the total Koreans in the United States, but by 2000 they represented 16.35 percent (176,088) of the nation's total Korean population. The South's Korean community is growing at a faster rate than the overall U.S. and southern populations (13 percent and 14 percent, respectively).

According to the 2000 U.S. Census, the largest number of southern Koreans are in Virginia (45,571, or almost 26 percent of the South's Korean population), Georgia (28,745, or 16 percent), and Florida (19,139, or almost 11 percent). From 1990 to 2000 the largest proportional growth of Koreans in the South took place in Georgia (88 percent), North Carolina (73 percent), and Tennessee (64 percent). By 2000 the fewest Koreans were in Mississippi (1,334, or .75 percent of Koreans in the South), Arkansas (1,550, or .88 percent), and Louisiana (2,876, or 1.6 percent).

The small representation of Koreans in the latter states is largely due to the occupational preferences. Most are either small business owners (30 percent), professional and technical workers (26 percent), operators and fabricators (17 percent), or in sales, administration, or support work (13 percent) and are therefore more likely to be located in big cities than in rural areas and small towns. In Virginia, many Koreans have settled near Washington, D.C., but also in Norfolk, Richmond, and Roanoke. The Georgia cities of Atlanta, Augusta, Columbus, Athens, and Macon are now home to significant communities of Koreans. Koreans settling in Florida have tended to cluster in Miami, Orlando, Tampa, and West Palm Beach.

Although Koreans find their niches in major cities, the size of the Korean population in the South is not large enough to form a "Koreantown" comparable to those in Los Angeles, Chicago, and New York. However, a sizable Koreantown is forming along Buford Highway in Atlanta, and most large cities have Korean associations that often sponsor celebrations of *Chusok* (Korean Thanksgiving). The Korean population in the South is growing more rapidly than in the West, where the Korean population had traditionally concentrated. Many Koreans have moved from the West to the South in the wake of racial violence against the Korean community in south-central Los Angeles in April 1992. Many relocated Koreans are learning and experiencing "southern hospitality" as well as the "scarcity values" of fellow Koreans, whose presence had been almost invisible in the South until very recent times. The growth and success of Korean communities in the South will continue to parallel the prosperity of the region as a whole.

CHOONG SOON KIM
University of Tennessee at Martin,
Korea Digital University

Choong Soon Kim, *Urban Anthropology in Tennessee* (1979), *An Asian Anthropologist in the South* (1977).

Lumbees

The Lumbee tribe has approximately 53,000 enrolled members. Over 90 percent live in the southeastern North Carolina county of Robeson or the adjacent counties of Cumberland, Hoke, and Scotland. North Carolina has recognized the tribe since 1885. The federal Lumbee Act (1956) recognized their name and existence but contained "termination language," making them ineligible for most federal services normally afforded Indians. Consequently, a central feature of Lumbee history has been their insistence that they are Indian and their appeals for full federal recognition. The Lumbee are by far the nation's most populous tribe that lacks full federal recognition, yet they have one of the most extensively documented administrative and legislative records of any tribe.

Although the Lumbee lacked schools from 1835 until 1885, when the state recognition statute provided for separate public schools, today they point to education as one of their major accomplishments. In 1887 another state law appropriated funds to establish a normal school to train teachers for the Lumbee, and this school became the University of North Carolina at Pembroke (UNC-P). UNC-P remains an integral part of the Lumbee community, and its Lumbee heritage remains evident in its Department of American Indian Studies, through Lumbee faculty and staff, and through the on-campus Museum of the Native American Resource Center.

In 2004 Robeson County had over 130 Indian churches; many are unaffiliated, but others are Baptist or Methodist. The Lumbee actively attend Sunday services, choir practices, gospel sings, Bible study, youth programs, potluck meals, and annual homecomings. Churches are a hub of social life and a training ground for Lumbee leaders. Many gospel groups perform beyond

Robeson County and have recorded their music. Many of these acts are family groups and include the Oxendines, the Pierces, Charles Bell, the Bullards, and D&L Gospel Singers. Lumbee healers (especially Vernon Cooper and Mary Sue Locklear) use a wide range of plants (including bloodroot, calamus, sassafras, and lobelia) to treat illnesses. The healer's personal faith is an essential part of this work.

The Lumbee are proud of their tradition of activism in the face of discrimination. From 1865–74 Henry Berry Lowry and his band avenged the wartime execution of Lowry's father and brother, and Lowry became the most celebrated folk hero of the Lumbee. An armed crowd of Lumbees dispelled a Ku Klux Klan rally in Maxton in 1958, leading to stories in *Life* magazine and other national media. Thousands of Lumbees campaigned in 1972 to stop the planned demolition of Old Main, the last remaining building from UNC-P's Indian-only days.

Lumbee people focus on the extended family, having frequent (even daily) contact with siblings, parents, and grandparents. Knowing someone's family background is the necessary beginning of a relationship. Therefore, when two Lumbees meet, the first question asked is, "Who are your people?" It is partly the draw of family that leads many Lumbees to consider Robeson County their permanent and authentic home.

Lumbee Vernacular English has received much attention, particularly from linguists working with the North Carolina Language and Life Project,

begun in 1993. This dialect sets Lumbees apart from others both within and outside Robeson County, and they use it in ways that reflect their Indian identity.

Many Lumbees participate in powwows (both in North Carolina and throughout the Southeast) and attend classes in dancing, singing, and drumming. Powwows have been held as part of Lumbee Homecoming for many years and annually by the Guilford Native American Association (Greensboro) since 1976.

Lumbee artists integrate Lumbee history and folk heroes (such as Henry Berry Lowry), Lumbee spirituality, and aspects of their natural environment within their work. Artists include painters Gene Locklear, Gloria Tara Lowery, and Karen Coronado; stone- and wood-carver Michael Wilkins; basket maker Loretta Oxendine; and tobacco twine crocheter Lela Hammond Brooks.

Lumbee history and culture have been celebrated in drama several times. In 1941–42, the pageant *Life Story of a People*, written by Sioux ethnologist Ella C. Deloria, was performed by 150 Lumbees. The outdoor drama *Strike at the Wind!*, telling the story of Henry Berry Lowry, was performed nearly every year from 1976 to 2003. Published Lumbee creative writers whose work reflects their Indian identity include poet Lew Barton, poet and storyteller Barbara Braveboy-Locklear, and poet and short story writer Julia Lowry Russell.

GLENN ELLEN STARR STILLING
Appalachian State University

Karen I. Blu, *The Lumbee Problem: The Making of an American Indian People* (2001); Clare Dannenberg, *Southern Anthropologist* (Fall 2004); Arvis Locklear Boughman and Loretta O. Oxendine, *Herbal Remedies of the Lumbee Indians* (2003); Stanley Knick, ed., *River Spirits: A Collection of Lumbee Writings* (2003); *Lumbee by Grace: Landmarks in Lumbee Identity* (videotape, 2002); Gerald M. Sider, *Living Indian Histories: Lumbee and Tuscarora People in North Carolina* (2003); Glenn Ellen Starr Stilling, *The Lumbee Indians: An Annotated Bibliography Supplement* (<http://www.lumbeebibliography.net>); Walt Wolfram, Clare Dannenberg, Stanley Knick, and Linda Oxendine, *Fine in the World: Lumbee Language in Time and Place* (2002).

Meherrins

The contemporary Meherrin Nation includes about 800 enrolled members. Concentrated in the North Carolina counties of Hertford, Bertie, Gates, and Northampton, the major Meherrin communities developed at the junction of the Meherrin and Chowan Rivers.

The present-day Meherrin tribe has long battled an identity problem. Even within the tribe there appears to be a schism based to a large extent upon perceived differences in racial background. Some "multiracial" members have European and/or African as well as Indian ancestries. Nevertheless, the Meherrins have a unified belief in an Indian heritage. After an arduous struggle, they received recognition from the state of North Carolina in 1986, even though they could not produce "anthropological or historical accounts tied to the tribe's Indian

ancestry" that are generally a criterion for state recognition. A primary goal of the Meherrin is to achieve federal recognition. However, some historians believe the present-day Meherrin tribe possesses only a tenuous link to the historic Meherrin of precolonial and colonial periods. A treaty with the colonial government in 1726 granted land to the Meherrin for a tribal reservation near Winton and Parker's Ferry, at the mouth of the Meherrin River. The Meherrin lost this reservation long ago, but most contemporary Meherrins live within 15 miles of the historic Meherrin reservation.

The tribal name "Meherrin" first appeared in the form "Maharineck" in the account of an expedition by Edward Blade to North Carolina in 1650 and next in an Indian census taken in 1669. The Meherrin were living on Roanoke River in 1761 with the southern bands of Tuscarora, Saponi, and Machapunga and probably went north in the last Tuscarora removal in 1802. The historic Meherrin belonged to the Iroquoian linguistic family.

The Meherrin population was estimated to be 700 in 1600, but by 1669 the tribe had declined to approximately 180. In 1755 their numbers were said to include only seven or eight fighting men, but in 1761 they were reported to have had 21. The population in the 18th and 19th centuries fluctuated considerably, but a rapid increase occurred during the 20th century, approaching 800 members. About one-half of the Meherrins were married to non-Indians in 1980. The Meherrin face a major task of using their existing natural and human resource base to create jobs and to provide higher standards of living and improve social welfare for tribal members. Economic development efforts fall into the areas of agriculture and livestock raising, forestry, tourism and hotels, arts and crafts, and manufacturing and assembly. With a long tradition as farmers, the Meherrin produce large quantities of cotton, peanuts, and corn on their holdings. But because their total numbers are small, they grow only a small percentage of the crops raised in Hertford and Northampton Counties.

Factories in Hertford and Northampton Counties produce such products as farm machinery parts, paper and household products, and clothing. A majority of the Meherrin workforce is employed at these factories, while others are employed at a chicken processing plant. Some Meherrins work in the shipyards of Virginia. A few professionals, including a physician and a dentist, are enrolled in the tribe.

While some Catholics are enrolled members of the tribe, most Meherrins are Baptists. Wearing colorful buckskin regalia, Meherrins participate in intertribal powwows and hold their own annual event, usually in mid-October.

THOMAS E. ROSS
University of North Carolina at Pembroke

Douglas L. Rights, *The American Indian in North Carolina* (1947); Thomas E. Ross, *American Indians in North Carolina: Geographic Interpretations* (1999); John R. Swanton, *The Indians of the Southeastern United States* (1946), *The Indian Tribes of North America* (1968); Ruth Y. Wetmore,

First on the Land: The North Carolina Indians (1975).

Melungeons

The etymology of the term "Melungeon"—as well as the origins, cultures, histories, and linguistic heritage of the people it references—remains contested. Originally a derogatory term, "Melungeon" appears to have referred to mixed-heritage or "mixed-race" families and communities located mostly in east and southeast Tennessee, southwest Virginia, and southeastern Kentucky. Early accounts identified Melungeons as possessing American Indian or African-like features, including copper or dark skin color; straight, dark hair; small stature; and varying eye colors, including blue. Contemporary data do not support an isomorphic mapping of biological features to define Melungeonness. Instead, current public and academic practices identify Melungeons on the basis of locale or family or personal origin, surnames, and probable American Indian or African American intermarriage with Northern Europeans that may include visible phenotypic features attributed to these populations. Some investigators assert possible Portuguese, Spanish, or Turkish (or other Middle Eastern) origins. Recent DNA testing of 100 self-defined Melungeons to establish specific origins was inconclusive.

The first documented usage of "Melungeon" is from the 1813 minutes of a Scott County, Va., Primitive Baptist Church in which several were excommunicated or censured. This document and subsequent early to mid-19th century ethnohistorical materials reveal such strong ostracism of Melungeons that many migrated to isolated upland regions, particularly Stone Mountain (Lee and Wise Counties, Va.) and Newman's Ridge (Hancock County, Tenn.). Communities founded in these upland areas, such as the Newman's Ridge community at Vardy, Tenn., have become labeled as "homeland" Melungeon locales. Melungeons were commonly reported to be poor, rural farmers or tradespeople, although recent studies refute the universality of this claim.

The relative isolation of these communities encouraged romanticized literary treatments beginning in the early 20th century. Receiving especially wide recognition were Jesse Stuart's *Daughter of the Legend* (1965) and Kermit Hunter's outdoor drama, *Walk toward the Sunset* (1969–76, Sneedville, Tenn.). These treatments established exotic, mysterious, but fictionalized cultural narratives in popular culture that have, in turn, resulted in widespread misinterpretations. What was originally a derogatory term denoting anyone of mixed ancestry in a particular southern Appalachian region became an ethnic identifier, denoting a mythologized "other" displaced from mainstream American history.

In contrast, residents of Melungeon locales during this same time period consciously erased "Melungeon" from local vocabularies in order to ease the social, political, and economic stigmas that labeling caused. In Virginia, racial purity policies imposed by Walter Plecker, director of the Virginia Bureau of Vital Statistics (1916–46), reclassi-

fied Melungeons from "mulatto" to "colored." These changes further disenfranchised Melungeons by inclusion in Virginia's eugenics and Jim Crow policies and practices. These practices meant that Melungeons were denied many white educational, economic, and political privileges and were subject to the aggressive sterilization practices endorsed by that state. Tennessee, on the other hand, was less vigorous in its eugenics enforcement and did not adopt a two-race-only policy. Nevertheless, by the 1980s, few residents in historically Melungeon locales publicly identified anyone as Melungeon except in a historical or folkloric context.

The rise of a Melungeon identity movement in the mid-1990s in Wise County, Va., however, redefined the meaning of Melungeon from only that of an exonym (an ethnic designator used by nonmembers) to an autonym (a term used by self-proclaimed members to designate themselves). Supported by the Melungeon Heritage Association (MHA), this movement exists primarily as a virtual phenomenon, with members exchanging genealogies, testimonies, prayers, recipes, and other information through Listservs, websites, personal e-mails, and threaded discussions. Membership is international in range and was purportedly over 75,000 in 2000. Most MHA leaders participate fully in American white society and have relied on genealogical research and other ways of researching family heritage to affirm a Melungeon ancestry. Some also claim African American or American Indian identities. Unresolved tensions exist between those from Melungeon communities and the MHA, in large part because of the attempted shift from a hidden, shunned identity to a public, embraced one.

Movement momentum is sustained by annual gatherings usually in far southwest Virginia or east Tennessee. The mission of the MHA is to "document and preserve the heritage and cultural legacy of mixed-ancestry peoples in or associated with the southern Appalachians." Recent publications endorsed by the MHA support inclusion of other exonyms for mixed ancestry groups of the eastern U.S. uplands (for example, Carmel Indians and West Virginia Guineas) under the Melungeon rubric. Melungeon supporters in central Tennessee have also advocated for recognition as American Indians.

ANITA PUCKETT
Virginia Polytechnic Institute and State University

Chris Everett, *Appalachian Journal* (Summer 1999); Jack Forbes, *Black Africans and Native Americans: Color, Race, and Caste in the Evolution of Red-Black Peoples* (1988); Brent Kennedy, *The Melungeons: The Resurrection of a Proud People: An Untold Story of Ethnic Cleansing in America* (1999); Anita Puckett, *Journal of Linguistic Anthropology* (June 2001).

Mestizos

"Mestizo," from the Spanish *mestizaje*, refers to persons with mixed indigenous, African, and/or European ancestry. In the historical context of eugenics and racial purity movements, the concept of *mestizaje* suggested that Latin American cultural and racial hybridity was a source of creative vitality rather than a regional defect. Today, southern writers of Latin American descent use "Mestizo" to acknowledge their bicultural inheritance and to refuse demands that they choose between either mainstream Anglo or alternative Latino cultural identities.

The South is an important site for the discussion of these issues. In fact, it is home to some of the oldest, as well as some of the newest, Latin American immigrant communities. Latino southerners of Mexican heritage (often called "Chicanos" or "Tejanos") may be the descendants of Mexicans who lived in Texas long before it became part of U.S. territory in 1845. Cuban Americans may be descended from cigar makers who immigrated to Tampa and New Orleans at the turn of the 20th century or from later Cubans who immigrated to Miami following the 1959 Cuban Revolution and after. Since the 1980s, economic crises and political unrest have encouraged immigrants from Mexico and Central and South America to come to work in the chicken processing plants and carpet mills of the Deep South. In the 1990s the trend strengthened as the percentages of Latin American–born populations in Georgia, North Carolina, and Arkansas increased 200 percent. By 2000 southern cities had an increasingly Latino character: Miami's population was almost 50 percent Latino, and the Latino community in Atlanta had reached over 8 percent of the total population.

The children of these immigrants have been exposed to several ethnic traditions as their communities both retain aspects of Latin American cultural practices and simultaneously adapt to dominant Anglo cultures. Increasingly, these children are bilingual or even trilingual, with proficiencies in English, Spanish, and Spanglish (a mixture of English and Spanish that has developed over the past 150 years). They produce hybrid cultural creations such as Latin rock music (exemplified by bands such as Los Lonely Boys). In fact, they draw upon a long history of cultural *mestizaje* in the South through which Mexican Americans and Cuban Americans in particular have crafted hybrid cultural practices in the face of anti-Latino discrimination.

Such hybrid practices are not always appreciated, however, and the resurging interest in Mestizos is an attempt to combat pressures to either fully assimilate to dominant U.S. culture or retain "pure" Latin American cultural forms. Gloria Anzaldúa, a Chicana writer from Texas, writes about Mestizos in order to validate the mixing of Mexican and Anglo cultural traditions in Chicano practice. For instance, she argues that *conjunto* (a Mexican American folk music style borrowing heavily from polka sounds brought by German immigrants to Texas) and Spanglish are not inferior bastardizations of pure forms. Instead, these creative hybrids are increasingly valuable adaptations to globalizing processes that bring people of different cultural backgrounds to the American South. Anzaldúa suggests that adopting a mestizo consciousness will allow Latinos and others to overcome barriers to crosscultural understanding.

In many cases, children of biethnic heritage must struggle at the familial level with these issues. For instance, Marcos McPeek Villatoro, an Appalachian/Salvadoran Latino scholar living in Alabama, uses the term "Mestizo" to indicate his mixed heritage and his refusal to fully assimilate to southern cultural traditions when this means denying aspects of his Latino heritage. He suggests a mestizo identity as a way of acknowledging the importance and value of a biethnic inheritance, especially where the children of such mixture can be denigrated as "mongrels" belonging to neither of their parents' cultural traditions.

While writers have only recently urged a full acknowledgment of mestizo identities in the South, the process of *mestizaje* has in fact been important in the region for much longer than is commonly recognized. Trivial to some and sublime to others, one of the best examples of this process is cowboy culture. Modeled on the Mexican *vaquero* and including borrowed Spanish terms such as burro, bronco, mesa, rodeo, and corral, cowboy culture is clearly the product of mingled traditions. For many southerners, mestizo consciousness may today remain at the level of an appreciation for cowboys and perhaps Tex-Mex cuisine such as burritos, chimichangas, and tacos. In the future, as intermarriage and immigration rates continue to rise, more children — whether their parents have married across ethnic lines or not — will face the task of integrating their various cultural inheritances. More hybrid forms will undoubtedly emerge as these children continue to creatively assert their mixed southern cultural identities.

DONNA F. MURDOCK
University of the South

Gloria Anzaldúa, *Borderlands/La Frontera: The New Mestiza* (1987); Suzanne Bost, *Mulattas and Mestizas: Representing Mixed Identities in the Americas, 1850–2000* (2003); Arthur D. Murphy, Colleen Blanchard, and Jennifer A. Hill, eds., *Latino Workers in the Contemporary South* (2001); Alejandro Portes, ed., *The New Second Generation* (1996); Marcos McPeek Villatoro, in *Cultural Diversity in the U.S. South: Anthropological Contributions to a Region in Transition*, ed. Carole E. Hill and Patricia D. Beaver (1998).

Mexicans

Until the mid-20th century, the majority of Mexicans in the South lived in Texas; those born in the state are known as "Tejanos." The first U.S. Census of Texas in 1850 counted 14,000 Mexican Texans, making them one of the oldest Hispanic populations in the region. From the 1930s on, Mexican migrant farmworkers came to southern states seasonally and left. In the 1970s, however, Mexicans began settling permanently in the South, a trend that accelerated dramatically in the 1990s.

The 2000 census revealed this demographic revolution. Counties in North Carolina, Arkansas, Georgia, Tennessee, South Carolina, and Alabama are now home to the country's fastest-growing Hispanic (predominantly Mexican) population. Some are urban, such as Mecklenburg County, N.C. (Charlotte had more than 1,000 percent growth); and some are rural, such as Gordon County, Ga. (with more than 1,500 percent growth). Most of the South's Mexican Americans are foreign born, young, undocumented, speak little English, have little education, and come from both old migration states such as Jalisco and Michoacán and new migration streams from Veracruz and Oaxaca.

New Mexican immigrants in the South tend to do the jobs others will not do — dangerous, labor-intensive, monotonous, low-paying work. Men find work in poultry or pork processing plants, in nurseries, in construction, and in the service industry. Women often work picking or packaging produce, in factories, or in domestic service. Fear of immigration officials makes them vulnerable to exploitation from employers or landlords (often one and the same). Families most frequently live in apartment complexes and trailer parks alongside low-income blacks and whites. Some Mexicans own their own homes and businesses and bring compatriots to their new communities to work. Increasingly, immigrants are employed by other Mexicans in restaurants, specialty stores, and businesses established to serve increasing Mexican populations. Some young, unmarried men still find seasonal labor and return to Mexico, but dramatic numbers of single young people and married couples with children are choosing to become southerners.

Mexican children attend local schools and may act as the family translator. The number of Spanish-speaking children in southern public schools has soared. By 2007, 10 percent of all

Mexican carrot worker, Edinburg (vicinity), Tex., 1939 (Russell Lee, USDA Historic Photos Collection)

schoolchildren in the fastest-growing southern states were Hispanic (mostly Mexican). Especially in rural districts, teachers of English as a second language are in high demand.

Mexican Americans are predominantly Catholic. In the South, most areas had very small Catholic churches, if any, a few years ago. In 2002, Catholics had surpassed Methodists to become the second-largest religious denomination in Gwinnett, Cobb, De-Kalb, Fayette, Rockdale, and Clayton Counties in Georgia. In North Carolina, historic piedmont denominations like Quakers and Presbyterians dwindled while Catholic Church membership increased by nearly 90 percent. The increases come despite the fact that very few Catholic churches have bilingual priests. Southern Baptists and Pentecostal denominations have increased their Latino congregants by recruiting Latino ministers to serve the Mexican population and offer English classes, health clinics, and legal assistance. Many are responding to this outreach, and some scholars have suggested this is because Mexican Catholicism is populist and personal—very different from Anglo versions of Catholicism and similar to the evangelical and Pentecostal Christianity practiced in the South.

Mexicans have brought their distinctive traditions to the South, such as the annual feast of Our Lady of Guadalupe in early December (the feast honors the appearance of the patroness of the Americas to Juan Diego, an Aztec, near Mexico City in 1531). Most celebrations include parades of people singing *las mananitas* (devotional songs to Mary) and feature a girl dressed as the Virgin and a boy dressed as Juan Diego in a peasant's tunic, both surrounded by roses, which Mary caused to flower at her winter appearance. The parades end with a predawn Spanish-language Mass. Other Catholic traditions include the Christmas *La Posada*, a choral procession led by children dressed as Joseph and Mary, who wander from house to house looking for lodging. Participants drink *ponche navidena*, a hot punch made with baked guavas, sugarcane, and *tejocotes* (a fruit).

El Día de los Muertos (the Day of the Dead, celebrated near Halloween) also has religious overtones. Mexicans visit the graves of loved ones to pray, and they create altars at home to honor dead relatives and friends with candles and tokens of their lives. Mexicans eat *muertitos*, pastries shaped like a dead body with crossed arms, and *calabazas*, a pumpkin candy. New and old Mexican immigrants celebrate Mexican Independence Day on 16 September. Events feature fireworks, simple foods such as tamales and spicy pork tacos, and parades. Many Mexican American associations use such public events to share their culture with their new communities.

Mexican music plays an important role in all celebrations. Even after many years in the United States, Mexicans remain attached to traditional Mexican regional music such as *ranchero* and *grupero*, eschewing more mainstream Latin pop. *Norteño* music, which features the accordion and polka rhythms, is also popular at community events.

(The style developed through Mexican American contact with German immigrants in Texas.) Spanish-language radio stations now broadcast throughout the South, and most play regional Mexican music rather than Latin pop. At the fiestas that now occur in the majority of the South's large cities, such music may alternate with country western. As new immigrants become southerners, we can expect new cultural fusions like the *norteño* music, Tex-Mex cuisine, and Tejano identities developed by the oldest communities of Mexican Americans in the South.

ANGELA MOORE ATKINS
University of Mississippi

Jane Kitchen, *Hispanic Magazine* (January–February 2002); Rakesh Kochar, Roberto Suro, and Sonya Tafoya, *The New Latino South: The Context and Consequences of Rapid Population Growth* (Pew Hispanic Center Report, July 2005); Arthur D. Murphy, Colleen Blanchard, and Jennifer A. Hill, eds., *Latino Workers in the Contemporary South* (2001); James Peacock, Harry L. Watson, and Carrie R. Matthews, *The American South in a Global World* (2005); Clara E. Rodriguez, *Changing Race: Latinos, the Census, and the History of Ethnicity in the United States* (2000); Javier Serna, *Raleigh News and Observer* (13 December 2004); Thomas A. Tweed, *Southern Cultures* (Summer 2002).

Minorcans

Descendants of an 18th-century Proprietary colony, the Minorcans (or "Menorcans") have long been the population base of St. Augustine, Fla. In 1768 more than 1,400 Mediterraneans sailed to British east Florida to farm a 40,000-acre indigo plantation 75 miles south of St. Augustine. Governor James Grant reported of their arrival: "I believe this is the largest Importation of White Inhabitants that was ever brought into America at a time." Including Italians, Greeks, and others, they became known as "Minorcans" because the majority came from the island of Menorca (Minorca) in the Balearic Islands off the coast of Spain.

Suffering from starvation and political oppression in their homelands, these indigenous people were willing to indenture themselves in the expectation of eventually owning their own lands. They were disappointed. Without adequate food, and dwelling in hastily built palm huts in an unfamiliar, mosquito-infested wilderness, some 600 men, women, and children died within two years, temporarily exhausting the Catholic Minorcan priests' supplies of anointing oils. An unsuccessful revolt brought a detachment of soldiers to the New Smyrna plantation, which became a virtual concentration camp.

Partly because of the American Revolution, the indigo enterprise collapsed by 1777, but folk memory credits its demise to the Proprietors' failure to honor the indenture contracts and their harsh treatment of Minorcans. In a dramatic exodus, Minorcans marched overland in the summer heat to the sanctuary of Spanish St. Augustine, where they initially settled on land between the fort (Castillo de San Marcos) and the plaza, a section called the Minorcan Quarter. Allowing them to adapt to the Florida environment, their plantation "internship" also aided their

A Minorcan family poses in 18th-century whipple headdresses beside a statue erected on the 200th anniversary of the arrival of Minorcan colonists to St. Augustine (Photograph courtesy of John W. Griffin)

occupational development as farmers, mariners, fishers, and craftspeople. Clustering in family enclaves as they had in their homelands, they resumed their religious and social customs.

Their fortunes improved during the second Spanish period (1784–1821), but once the United States acquired Florida, their way of life began to erode. By the mid-19th century, the Minorcan dialect of Catalan was used only at home, and the traditional Carnival suffered from disapproval by the religious and secular authorities. However, the *formadjadis*, the colorful Easter eve serenade, continued into the 20th century. Minorcans embraced a statue of the Virgin Mary, called the Hurricane Lady because she was given to a local family by seamen nearly wrecked in a storm. She remains on display at the Father Miguel O'Reilly House.

About 10,000 people of Minorcan descent still live in St. Augustine, while a gradual migration all over the United States accounts for an unknown number. Families remain close and largely Catholic, and only after World War II did substantial exogamy occur. A few Minorcans now occupy positions of prominence, but a majority cluster in the building trades. Moneymaking is often secondary to other values, leading town newcomers to decry the lack of a work ethic. A local bumper sticker proclaims, "Three weeks late is one week early in St. Augustine."

With a flood of retirees impacting their home area, Minorcans' traditional culture is rapidly changing. However, adaptable and independent, descendants still maintain some of the old ways. The fall season finds family groups at the beach seining for the schooling mullet or on hot summer nights gigging for flounder from locally made boats. Minorcan clam chowder and the local shrimp dish *pilau* (pronounced "purlo") — both made tongue-lashing hot with the local datil peppers — the smoked mullet, and the *formatjadis* pastries please locals and visitors alike. Gopher tortoise stew, flavored with a claw or two to startle the unwary, is no longer served in restaurants because of the protected status of the animal.

The Minorcan imprint on St. Augustine today is subtle but pervasive. Minorcan workers built many of the city's colonial houses (such as the Llambias House and the Segui-Kirby Smith House), which are ideally suited to a warm, humid climate with south- and west-facing loggias and upstairs balconies overhanging the narrow streets. Visitors to the downtown plaza's Confederate monument will find almost all the names to be Minorcan. Every spring a Menorcan Heritage Day is open to the public, and some Minorcan celebrations continue, in altered form, in the two-week Easter Festival.

The *Mullet Wrapper*, the newsletter of the Menorcan Cultural Society, attests to the persistence of a relaxed way of life with the announcement under the letterhead, "Published when we get around to it."

PATRICIA C. GRIFFIN
St. Augustine Historical Society

Patricia C. Griffin, *Mullet on the Beach: The Minorcans of Florida, 1768–1788* (1991).

Monacans

"Monacan" refers to an indigenous group first encountered by an English contingent under Captain Christopher Newport in 1607 near the falls of the James River. British colonial officials also used the name to refer to the easternmost Monacan town on the James (present-day Manakin, Va.). The name has also referred to a larger confederacy, or alliance of Siouan-speaking tribes that once dominated western and piedmont Virginia. Groups such as the Manahoac, Tutelo, and Saponi may have also been a part of this alliance.

Agrarian peoples, the Monacan settled in towns along major rivers in Virginia's piedmont and westward into the Blue Ridge Mountains. Monacan towns were probably linked by a matrilineal kinship system and common language and consisted of round wigwams of birch or other durable barks.

Colonial and subsequent records reveal little of Monacan history, partly as Monacan groups moved inland to avoid European contact. Perhaps aggrieved that the Monacan dominated the Virginia copper trade, the chief of the Powhatans informed Captain John Smith that the Monacan were his enemies.

By the early 1700s the autonomy of Monacan groups had significantly weakened because of frequent migration between Virginia and North Carolina to contend with Iroquois raids and hostile settlers. By 1715 most had settled around Fort Christanna in Brunswick County, Va., where they placed themselves under the tenuous protection of colonial authorities and served as a buffer between colonists and so-called hostile tribes. By the 1740s many had migrated northward out of Virginia and were adopted into the Cayuga Nation under the auspices of the Iroquois Confederacy, in which vestiges of Tutelo-Saponi tradition remain.

Monacans remaining in Virginia, particularly in the vicinity of Amherst County, were often required to register as free people of color. Many had intermarried with non-Indians, and Virginia miscegenation laws classified them as "mulattos" regardless of the continued existence of cohesive communities identifying as Indians. After the Civil War (which brought about the elimination of the legal category of "free colored"), Virginia miscegenation laws were increasingly informed by the emergent pseudoscience of eugenics. Nearly all Virginia Indians were denied access to public education until the 1960s, and the Monacan in particular were often pressed into servitude under a peculiar "race"-based system of debt peonage on Amherst County orchards and tobacco farms until the mid-1960s. St. Paul's Episcopal Mission, established in the heart of the Monacan community at Bear Mountain in 1908, did afford local Indians up to a sixth grade education until they were integrated into county schools in 1963. Still, the first Monacan did not graduate from public high school in the county until 1971.

With the coincidence of public school integration, the civil rights movement, and changes in the local economy (notably, the demise of the orchard industry through strict enforcement of minimum-wage laws), the Monacan began to assert greater autonomy as individuals and as a distinct Indian community. In 1989 the Monacan gained state recognition as an Indian tribe and became officially known as the Monacan Indian Nation.

While several tangible forms of traditional Monacan culture seem to have been lost, the tribe has made many unique adaptations that mark it as an ethnically distinct entity. Recalling their years of tenant farming on local orchards, Monacan women now make fruit preserves as a symbolic staple of the tribal diet. Those who attend St. Paul's Episcopal Church have altered the service to emphasize communal prayer and charismatic expression. Others have engaged in cultural and linguistic revitalization initiatives, resurrecting old Tutelo songs recorded early in the 20th century and performing these at tribal gatherings and ceremonies—including the annual homecoming in October, repatriation ceremonies for ancestral remains, and the spring powwow. With proceeds earned during the tribe's first annual powwow in 1993, the Monacan began to buy back ancestral land on Bear Mountain. Currently, there are approximately 1,100 enrolled members, although only one family lives on the nearly 200-acre tribal land base. The annual powwow remains the largest source of tribal corporate income; however, the tribe has started to market traditional items, including honeysuckle gift baskets with fruit preserves. Such ventures offer an important segue as the tribe pursues federal recognition.

SAMUEL R. COOK
Virginia Polytechnic Institute and State University

Samuel R. Cook, *Monacans and Miners: Native American and Coal Mining Communities in Appalachia* (2000); Peter W. Houck and Mintcy D. Maxham, *Indian Island in Amherst County* (1993); James Mooney, *Bureau of American Ethnology Bulletin* 22 (1894); Heriberto Dixon, *American Indian Culture and Research Journal* (2002); Jeffrey Hantman, *American Anthropologist* (September 1990).

Moravians

The Moravians, or *Unitas Fratrum* (Unity of Brethren), are a Protestant denomination with roots in pre-Reformation Europe. The church went into hiding because of persecution before and during the Counter-Reformation and the Thirty Years' War. In 1722 a group of Moravians took sanctuary on the estate of Count Nicholas Ludwig von Zinzendorf in Saxony, forming the community of Herrnhut. From here the *Unitas Fratrum* reorganized.

Attempting to expand their missions to the native people of North America, the Moravians founded a settlement near Savannah, Ga., in 1733. They abandoned this short-lived settlement in 1740 after refusing to bear arms in border disputes between the Spanish and English. From Georgia they moved to Pennsylvania and founded the town of Bethlehem, which continues to be the headquarters of the northern province of the Moravian Church in America.

In 1752 the Moravians headed south again and were given a land grant for nearly 100,000 acres by John Lord Carteret, second Earl Granville in what is now Forsyth County, N.C. In the 18th century this land was in the middle of the unsettled Backcountry. They founded the settlement of Wachau, or Wachovia, named for the estate of Count Zinzendorf's family, and established their first town, Bethabara, meaning "House of Passage," in 1753. During the French and Indian War (1754–63) the palisade surrounding Bethabara served as a refuge for Moravians and non-Moravians alike. In 1759 settlers founded a second, agricultural community called Bethania. Three other Moravian congregations and communities were established on the Wachovia tract in the late 18th century: Friedberg in 1754, Hope in 1760, and Friedland in 1770.

Planned prior to its establishment in 1766, Salem became the central trading town and economic center for the area. A series of town boards controlled Salem as a theocracy. One example of church control involved the ownership of town lots: the church retained ownership of the lot, with individuals owning only the improvements on the lot.

In the 19th century, Salem and the surrounding Moravian settlements began to move away from their 18th-century congregational ideal. Changes in their policy regarding slavery show

Mother and child decorate a Moravian Christmas pyramid at Old Salem in North Carolina (Collection of the Wachovia Historical Society, photograph courtesy of Old Salem, Inc.)

a shift in attitude toward that of their slaveholding neighbors and the abandonment of the values of the original congregation. In the 18th century the church itself was permitted to own slaves, but the community was largely racially integrated, with European Americans and African Americans eating, worshipping, and being buried side by side. During the 19th century, gradual changes allowed individuals to own slaves and led to the construction of a separate church for African Americans. Additionally, changes in the social,

political, and economic structures occurred with the formation of social clubs, participation in political rallies and elections, and the establishment of Moravian textile mills and banks for capital. In 1831 the community also separated from its pacifist beginnings to form the Salem Light Infantry Company as part of the North Carolina militia. Although the church was losing social and economic control over the congregation throughout the 19th century, the decisive change in Salem came in 1856 with the end of the lot system.

After this date, residents owned their lots in addition to the improvements.

A strong belief in the importance of education for both boys and girls is a fundamental part of the Moravians' heritage. The town of Salem had schools for both sexes in the 18th century. In 1802 the community opened a girls' boarding school known as the Salem Female Academy. The institution has operated continuously since that time and now maintains both a preparatory school, Salem Academy, and a four-year women's college, Salem College.

The Moravians remain widely known today for their contributions to music. Early in their history in America, they enjoyed concerts of European music and contributed through composition to chorale music. Worship services were followed by "love feasts" (the sharing of sweet buns, coffee, and fellowship). The Easter Sunrise Service is also a Moravian tradition. Winston-Salem, N.C., is the headquarters of the southern province of the Moravian Church in America. Other churches are active in Georgia, Florida, Maryland, and Virginia. Old Salem Inc., a living history museum, preserves the 18th- and 19th-century lifestyle of the Moravians in North Carolina.

SARAH BAHNSON CHAPMAN
Old Salem, Inc.

Sarah Bahnson Chapman, *Bright and Gloomy Days: The Civil War Correspondence of Captain Charles Frederic Bahnson, a Moravian Confederate* (2003); C. Daniel Crews and Richard Starbuck, *With Courage for the Future: The Story of the Moravian Church, Southern Province* (2002); Adelaide Fries, Stuart Thurman Wright, and J. Edwin Hendricks, *Forsyth: The History of a County on the March* (1976); William J. Murtagh, *Moravian Architecture and Town Planning: Bethlehem, Pennsylvania, and Other Eighteenth-Century American Settlements* (1998); Penelope Niven and Cornelia Wright, *Old Salem: The Official Guidebook* (2000).

MOWA Choctaws

The MOWA Choctaw are a state-recognized Indian tribe who occupy lands in Alabama that were held by their Choctaw ancestors in the early 1800s. They adopted the acronym "MOWA" to indicate their geographic location in Mobile and Washington Counties. After the Treaty of Dancing Rabbit Creek in 1830, most Choctaw people relocated to Oklahoma. Descendants of some who chose to stay on their traditional sacred lands became the MOWA. Because they stayed, however, they lost access to Choctaw relocation funds and lived in a foreign society, which failed to acknowledge their Indian identity in increasingly biracial social categories. Through spatial, economic, and social separation, they have become a social enclave that is, while clearly a persistent Indian community, not federally recognized.

A governmental Indian school was first constructed in Mount Vernon, Ala., in 1835. Denied access to other public education, the MOWA Choctaw valued the educational opportunities afforded by Protestant Indian missions. The first Indian Mission school was named Coonshack (probably after *Koonsha*, one of the Choctaw clans).

This was also the name of the Indian mission church, which was built in a canebrake near brush arbors used for Indian ceremonial activities. Both the log church and school were built in 1850. The school bell was used as a means of communicating major events within the community; through a code of rings, the community could be made aware of births, deaths, and emergencies. The old school bell today is located in the cemetery of Reeds Chapel Church near the Reeds Chapel Indian School.

Another goal of the Protestant missions was to educate and make lay preachers of the MOWA Choctaw. George Reed was the first recognized MOWA Choctaw minister. Beyond religious assimilation (which was perhaps strategic), the MOWA retained many of their cultural traditions and identity through isolation. Contemporary oral history records places of ceremonial gatherings. A traditional stomping ground is near the current MOWA Choctaw tribal building in Mount Vernon. The MOWA maintained the Choctaw language through the 19th century. Although Choctaw who resisted Removal were expected to assimilate, neighbors of the MOWA continued to identify them as Choctaw. During the Civil War, a regiment from Mobile County was known as the "Choctaw Regiment."

The modern-day MOWA live in 10 kin-based subdistricts established through family landholding and inheritance patterns. Many such holdings came to have their own small Indian churches for which they are now named. All 10 districts have rep-resentation in the current MOWA Tribal Council.

The community has a high frequency of Marinesco-Sjogren Syndrome, a rare autosomal recessive genetic disorder that affects muscular coordination and other functions. They are the only population in the United States to have this syndrome. Today, the MOWA number close to 6,000, many of whom live near McIntosh, Ala. Their annual powwow, held during the third week of June, incorporates family reunions.

RICHARD STOFFLE
University of Arizona

Jacqueline Anderson Matte, *They Say the Wind Is Red: The Alabama Choctaw—Lost in Their Own Land* (2002).

Muskogees (Creeks)

The Muskogee people—also known as the "Muscogee," "Mvskoke," or "Creek"—are native to the southeastern states. Anthropological evidence indicates a Mississippian culture origin. However, their oral history describes a migration from the west by members of four Muskogee-speaking "ceremonial towns": Cusseta, Coweta, Abihka, and Tuckabatchee. Hunters and farmers, the Muskogee lived comfortably in permanent settlements, each near its ceremonial "square ground" within the Alabama, Coosa, and Chattahoochee river systems.

The disruption following European contact in 1539 led other tribes to join the Muskogee for security in a loose confederacy. Each of more than 50 towns maintained a separate identity and governance and sometimes spoke its own dialect. In the late 1600s, English colonists began to call Muskogees "Creeks," perhaps a shortened name for the people living along Ochese Creek.

Located on the French, Spanish, and British colonial frontier, the Muskogee actively participated in the 18-century South Carolina deerskin trade. When English and Scottish traders married Muskogee women, their Anglo-Muskogee children, often literate, bilingual, and familiar with both parents' cultures, sometimes became influential brokers in trade and diplomacy. When the deerskin trade declined about 1800, the Muskogee became livestock and cotton farmers, sometimes using African slave labor. These adaptations caused observers to classify the Muskogee as one of the Five Civilized Tribes.

By then, the Muskogee Confederacy was divided into Upper and Lower Creek factions based on geographical location, cultural change, and internal politics. Observers considered Lower Creeks, centered at Coweta, as "progressive" compared to Upper Creeks, who were generally more traditional and less receptive to Anglo-American ways. The Red Stick War (1813–15), a Muskogee civil war, reflected these differences. It merged into the War of 1812, and Chief William McIntosh of Coweta helped General Andrew Jackson defeat the traditionalist Red Sticks at the battle of Horseshoe Bend (1814). Some dissidents joined other Muskogees in Florida. They evolved into the Seminole tribe.

In the early 1800s Anglo-American pressure greatly reduced the old Muskogee homeland—Georgia and Alabama and parts of Tennessee, South Carolina, and Florida. The Muskogee divided bitterly over exchanging their remaining Alabama lands for new lands in the Indian Territory (Oklahoma). Lower Creeks began a voluntary migration west in 1827–28, following the execution of McIntosh for signing a federal Removal treaty. The remaining 22,000 Muskogees and their 900 slaves were evicted by 1836. About 40 percent died during the Removal and resettlement.

The relocated Muskogee Nation extended across the Indian Territory from the Arkansas River to the Texas Panhandle. The Lower Creeks settled in the Arkansas River Valley, and the Upper Creeks settled farther west along the Canadian River Valley. Until 1856 they shared their lands with the Seminole. By the 1850s they had established farms, businesses, a national school system, square grounds, and Christian churches. Their 1858 constitution continued traditional confederacy government based on town representation.

An 1861 Confederate alliance drew the Muskogee Nation into the American Civil War. Removal-era hostilities reemerged, splitting the nation in half and driving many into exile. For four years Muskogee men, with their former slaves, fought each other and their Indian neighbors as Union or Creek Confederate soldiers. By 1865 the nation was devastated, impoverished, and nearly deserted. About one in four Muskogees died of wounds or disease in military and refugee camps. The

Reconstruction Treaty (1866) forced the Muskogee Nation to free its slaves, adopt them as citizens assigned to three freedmentowns, and cede 3.25 million acres—half of its land—to the federal government.

By 1867 the Muskogee Nation had a new constitutional government and its citizens were rebuilding. Meanwhile, railroad construction and the flourishing cattle industry drew many non-Indians to Muskogee lands. The nation struggled to maintain its sovereignty and unity, but old hostilities and resistance to change periodically flared into violence. The Muskogee escaped allotment of their communal lands until 1899, but a federal mandate ended their national government in 1906 and they became American citizens. A small federally appointed administration concluded the nation's affairs; a major oil boom (1900 to the 1930s) complicated the process.

Muskogee sovereignty reemerged in 1971 with the reestablishment of the Muscogee (Creek) Nation, headquartered in Okmulgee, Okla. Today, the nation operates several enterprises and services in 11 Oklahoma counties for its approximately 55,000 enrolled members. Some former Muskogee Confederacy towns have achieved independence. In Oklahoma, Alabama Quassarte Tribal Town, Kialegee Tribal Town, and Thlopthlocco Tribal Town are federally recognized; the Yuchi (Euchee) Tribe of Indians has applied for federal recognition. The Poarch Band of Creeks, located near Poarch and Atmore, Ala., are descendants of Muskogees who escaped Removal. The Alabama-Coushatta Tribe of Texas is made up of descendants of immigrants who arrived just before 1800.

MARY JANE WARDE
Oklahoma Historical Society

Angie Debo, *The Road to Disappearance: A History of the Creek Indians* (1941); Kathryn E. Holland Braund, *Deerskins and Duffels: Creek Indian Trade with Anglo-America, 1685–1815* (1993); Grant Foreman, *The Five Civilized Tribes: Cherokee, Chickasaw, Choctaw, Creek, Seminole* (1934); Arrell Morgan Gibson, *Oklahoma: A History of Five Centuries* (1980); Michael D. Green, *The Politics of Indian Removal: Creek Government and Society in Crisis* (1982); Mary Jane Warde, *George Washington Grayson and the Creek Nation, 1843–1920* (1999).

Natchez

The Natchez are a Native American people whose ancestral homeland centered on the present-day city of Natchez, Miss. Like other native peoples of the South, the Natchez live today in eastern Oklahoma, having been forced west as a result of the U.S. government's Removal policies of the 1830s. The meaning of their name is unknown but, as first recorded by the French, the standard spelling "Natchez" represented a pronunciation similar to that preserved among Indian people in Oklahoma, often rendered in English as "Notchee."

Early European explorations of the region triggered significant social and demographic changes for the Natchez, whether or not they actually came into direct contact with the 16th century expeditions. By the time the French established their colony on the lower Mississippi in 1699, the Natchez polity had already been reduced in size by disease, warfare, and slavery—all introduced by European exploration, trade, and settlement to their east. Under these conditions, the Natchez retained their influence in part through the incorporation of a number of other remnant groups dislocated during this period.

The Natchez fascinated French observers, as they possessed a complex, hierarchical social structure that included a set of ranked social classes and detailed rules governing royal marriage. Political leaders also led a complex religious system, and the Natchez were the last southern Indian group to continue to utilize earthen mounds in their ceremonial life. Archaeologists have therefore relied heavily on sources dealing with the colonial Natchez in their interpretation of the precontact Mississippian societies of the Southeast. Unlike many of their neighbors, the Natchez maintained clear social and cultural continuities with the complex chiefdoms that existed throughout the region at the time of first European contact.

Especially after 1718, the land-rich Natchez suffered severely in their dealings with the French, who aimed to acquire land in the Mississippi Valley. In 1729 a final period of conflict erupted through which the Natchez were ultimately either killed, enslaved, or dispersed in groups that settled north and eastward among the Chickasaw, Creek, and Cherokee (all allies of the English and beyond direct French control).

Even scholarly specialists in Native American affairs often share the popular view that the Natchez disappeared in the wake of these colonial conflicts, but this is not true. Rather than assimilating completely into those neighboring groups with whom they took refuge, the Natchez maintained their language and ethnic identity. When the United States forced the majority of southeastern Indian people westward to what was then designated Indian Territory (present-day Oklahoma), the Natchez accompanied the Creek and Cherokee into exile. Although the Natchez today lack political autonomy and are distributed among, and subsumed within, one of these two tribes, "Notchee" identity is still preserved into the 21st century, both as family knowledge among Natchez descendants and among activists who have begun seeking to establish a formal political body to represent the Natchez community. Into the late 20th century the Natchez maintained their own ceremonial ground where they performed an annual round of tribal ceremonies. Today some people of Natchez heritage participate in similar ceremonies at Cherokee or Creek ceremonial grounds. Others attend local Indian churches alongside Christians from these neighboring groups.

Since Removal, the Natchez living among the Creek and Cherokee have had an influence disproportional to their small numbers. In the late 19th and early 20th centuries, they played an influential role in the maintenance and revival of traditional ceremonial life among the western Cherokee. They provided a social bridge between the Cherokee and Creek, with whom they shared cultural and political boundaries. Although it is now a moribund tongue, Natchez continued to be spoken into the 20th century. Collaborating with anthropologists and linguists, the last speakers enabled the partial documentation of this important southern language.

Natchez people have lived throughout the southern Cherokee and Creek Nations, but the area most closely identified with the Natchez today is around the town of Gore in Sequoyah County, Okla.

JASON BAIRD JACKSON
Indiana University

Patricia Galloway and Jason Baird Jackson, in *Handbook of North American Indians, Volume 14: Southeast*, ed. Raymond Fogelson (2004); John R. Swanton, *Indian Tribes of the Lower Mississippi Valley and Adjacent Coast of the Gulf of Mexico* (1911); Robert K. Thomas, *The Origin and Development of the Redbird Smith Movement* (1953).

Occaneechi Band of the Saponi Indians

Located primarily in the Alamance County communities of Pleasant Grove and Mebane, N.C., the 600 members of the Occaneechi Band of the Saponi Indians are descendants of a number of Siouan-speaking tribes that once occupied the North Carolina and Virginia piedmont. The first mention of the Occaneechi in the historical record occurred in 1670, when a German physician named John Lederer visited them at their town on the Roanoke River in Virginia, where they exerted enormous influence on the region's trade and religion. Historian Douglas Rights described them as "a strong tribe, fierce

and warlike, and their power was feared by neighboring tribes. So great was their influence that the religious ritual of the Indians for miles around was in their tongue. They controlled the Backcountry trade, forcing traders to pass through their island gateway to the hinterland of the piedmont, and compelling the westward Indians to transport their furs via Occaneechi Town."

Contact with colonial settlers, however, shifted the balance of power by the late 17th and early 18th centuries, and in the 1710s the Occaneechi joined forces with a number of local tribes, including the Eno, Tutelo, Saponi, and Cheraw in what some historians have called the Saponi Confederation. A 1713 treaty created a reservation community at Fort Christanna in Brunswick County, Va., and a subsequent treaty signed in 1715 designated members of the confederation as the Sapony tribe. During the late 18th century, families moved from Virginia into the area of Orange County, N.C., known as "Little Texas" and established new Indian communities. From there, they migrated to the west into the area called "Alamance." Census records from the 1830s recorded a population of between 250 and 300 people, comprised primarily of Occaneechi, Eno, Saponi, and other Siouan-speaking peoples. This community was known for many years as the Occaneechi Band of the Saponi Nation and it is widely regarded by tribal historians as the most important link to the historic Occaneechi tribe. In 1984 a contingent of Little Texas families organized themselves as the

Eno-Occaneechi Indian Association; in 1995 the tribal council changed the organization's name to the Occaneechi Band of the Saponi Nation. Census records from the 1990s show a population of between 550 and 600 members, most of whom are employed in a mix of agriculture and manufacturing.

Beginning with the Eno-Occaneechi Indian Association's organization in the 1980s, tribal members began an ongoing effort to document the group's historical link to the colonial-era Occaneechi, and they have initiated various programs designed to reinvigorate and maintain tribal culture. The tribe sponsors an annual powwow near Mebane, hosts language classes, and has opened a reconstructed Occaneechi village near Hillsboro, N.C. Much of this effort has been aimed at satisfying the criteria for state recognition established by the North Carolina Commission of Indian Affairs. Claiming that the tribe had failed to demonstrate a direct and compelling connection to a historic tribe, the commission denied their request in 1995. Three years later, administrative law judge Delores O. Smith supported the tribe's application. On 2 February 2002 the North Carolina Commission of Indian Affairs granted the tribe formal recognition.

CLYDE ELLIS
Elon University

Clyde Ellis, *Our State* (November 2000); John Lawson, *A New Voyage To Carolina*, ed. Hugh T. Lefler (1984); James Mooney, *Bureau of American Ethnology Bulletin* 22 (1894); Theda Perdue, *Native Carolinians: The Indians of North Carolina* (1985); Douglas L. Rights, *The American Indian in North Carolina* (1957); Thomas E. Ross, *American Indians in North Carolina: Geographic Interpretations* (1999); John R. Swanton, *The Indians of the Southeastern United States* (1946), "Early History of the Eastern Siouan Tribes," in *Essays in Anthropology Presented to A. L. Kroeber*, ed. Robert H. Lowie (1936).

Ozarkers

For the last two centuries the Ozark region, which includes sections of Arkansas and Missouri and smaller portions of Oklahoma and Kansas, has been home predominantly to native-born European Americans whose ancestry and cultural antecedents derive from Appalachia and the British Isles. Like those of southern Appalachia, images of the Ozarks have focused on the region's ruralness, comparative isolation, and Anglo-Saxon population, but since the middle of the 20th century the region has become more urban and ethnically diverse.

When Europeans first entered the Ozarks, the region was dominated by the Osage, with other Native American groups (the Illinois, Caddo, and Quapaw) living or hunting in the region's periphery. French settlers first built permanent settlements on the west bank of the Mississippi River in the mid-18th century, but their influence was rapidly displaced by the arrival of American settlers just decades later.

These Americans were typical frontier people of the upper South. Much has been made of the Ozark region's Scots-Irishness, but it is difficult to ascribe frontier, Ozark characteristics to one ethnic group. While most European American settlers in the Ozarks could trace their lineage to Northern Ireland, the crucible of the Appalachian and trans-Appalachian frontiers, through which most Ozark settlers passed, did much to burn away ethnic distinctiveness and forge a new identity.

The majority of settlers brought an evangelical Protestantism honed by the Second Great Awakening on the southern frontier. Methodists and Baptists held sway, but they were joined by Cumberland Presbyterians and devotees of Alexander Campbell, Barton Stone, and other leaders of the early 19th-century Christian Restorationist movement whose followers came to be known as the Disciples of Christ. Episcopalians, Presbyterians, and Congregationalists were generally found only in larger towns. In the mid-19th century German settlers brought Roman Catholicism and Lutheranism, and in the 20th century Holiness and Pentecostal movements thrived.

In contrast to most American settlers who followed the westward-moving frontier, German immigrants to the Ozarks in the mid-19th century made a conscious attempt to preserve their Old World culture. They established close-knit farming communities, often sent their children to religious schools, and continued to speak the German language well into the 20th century. Because of community agricultural practices, such as viticulture and the transgenerational retention of German-owned land—and of conscious celebrations of ethnic folkways, such as Maifests—the descendants of German settlers have preserved an ethnic distinctiveness that is unusual in the Ozarks.

A relatively small number of people of African ancestry have lived in the Ozarks almost as long as those of European ancestry. In the antebellum era hundreds of slaves and free blacks called the region home. In the late 19th and early 20th centuries, isolation, the lack of economic opportunities, and occasional racial violence contributed to a shrinking black population in the Ozarks. African Americans constitute only about 1 percent of the region's population in the early 21st century.

While the miniscule African American population has undoubtedly limited its impact on Ozark history and culture, scholars have found traces of African American influence in music. According to folklorist W. K. McNeil, the existence of elements and songs of African American musical tradition— as well as tunes and songs from non-Scots-Irish, European traditions—is one of the three significant traits distinguishing Ozark folk music from Appalachian folk music. Although once thought to be identical to that of Appalachia, the folk music of the Ozarks has a significant body of indigenous ballads.

Given the Appalachian ancestry of most Ozark residents and the obvious similarities in topography and folk culture between the two regions, the Ozarks have often been considered a cultural extension of the eastern mountains as "Appalachia West" or "Little Appalachia." While the comparison is not always exact, many Ozark customs and folktales are local adaptations of older traditions brought from Appalachia. Foodways resemble those of rural Appalachia, and, until the last third of the 20th century, hog killings, the making of sorghum molasses, and corn shuckings were important communal activities.

The earliest Anglo-American settlers introduced the single-pen log house to the Ozarks, and this type of dwelling, along with the offshoot double-pen (dogtrot) log house, remained the dominant architectural style into the mid-19th century. The modest means of most Ozark families meant that the typical home before World War II was comparatively small, but the I-house (a two-story, one-room-deep structure) was not uncommon, especially in more prosperous areas.

The cultural and ethnic composition established in the Ozarks in the 19th century remained comparatively undisturbed until the development of retirement communities in the 1960s. Incomers were mostly from the Great Lakes and Plains states, but in the 1990s thousands of Hispanics made their way to the region. By 2003 Latinos accounted for almost one in five residents in Rogers and Springdale, two of northwestern Arkansas's largest towns. This recent wave of immigration to the region promises not only to alter long-standing demographic patterns, but also to challenge traditional notions of what it means to be an Ozarker.

BROOKS BLEVINS
Lyon College

Brooks Blevins, *Hill Folks: A History of Arkansas Ozarkers and Their Image* (2002);

Russel L. Gerlach, *Immigrants in the Ozarks: A Study in Ethnic Geography* (1976); W. K. McNeil, *Ozark Country* (1995); Milton D. Rafferty, *The Ozarks: Land and Life* (2001).

Poarch Creeks

The Creek Nation ceded the last of its homelands to the United States by treaty in 1832. Individuals were supposed to be "free to go or stay as they please" (7 Stat. 366), but most were removed to Indian Territory during the 1830s and 1840s. Those who managed to stay were those Creek "mixed-bloods" loyal to the United States during the Creek War of 1813–14 who were living in the area around present-day Escambia and Baldwin Counties of southwestern Alabama.

By the end of the 19th century most of the scattered individual Creek Indians who had avoided removal were assimilated and no longer identified as Indians. There was, however, one group of Creek-descendant families living a few miles north of the present-day town of Atmore, Ala., at a place white settlers named "Poarch." The group was locally acknowledged as an "Indian" community, numbering nearly 200 people in the U.S. Census of 1900.

The core of the Poarch Creek land base was an allotment to a Friendly Creek named Lynn McGhee under the treaty that concluded the 1813–14 Creek War. McGhee's lands remained in federal trusteeship until 1924, but the community received no federal services. The Poarch Creek suffered land losses, extreme poverty, and discrimination during the first half of the 20th century. By the mid-20th century only fragments of native Muskogean language and custom survived. The Poarch Creek were thoroughly anglicized, Christianized, and acculturated.

Following World War II, one of Lynn McGhee's descendants, Calvin McGhee, led a major movement to improve educational opportunities for the Poarch Creek, to press a land claim against the United States, and to improve community life and advance cultural pride. Under Calvin McGhee, the Poarch Creek led the way in forming the Creek Nation East of the Mississippi. The land claim and McGhee's popularization of Indian identity stimulated many people long assimilated into the general population to declare their Creek ancestry. Eventually, there were many spin-off groups of self-styled "Creeks" in Florida, Alabama, and Georgia. Such groups continue to exist. Interest in Plains Indian–style powwows, which McGhee spurred, continues. The Poarch Creek annual Thanksgiving Day powwow, established in 1970, has grown into a major event, attracting thousands.

After McGhee's death in 1970 (two years before successful settlement of the land claim), the Poarch leadership had already begun to dissociate itself from the larger Creek Indian land-claims coalition in order to concentrate on local needs of the historic Indian community near Atmore. Their most ambitious goal was to obtain federal acknowledgement of their community as a sovereign Indian tribe. Finally, in 1984, the United States acknowledged the Poarch Band of Creeks as a sovereign Indian tribe under federal law—

the only Creek Indian group so identified east of the Mississippi and the only federally recognized tribe in Alabama or Georgia.

With federal recognition, many new opportunities came to the Poarch Creek. They had already begun to make significant gains in health care, senior citizen services, job training, and many other areas, but with federal recognition the Poarch Creek had all the benefits of tribal sovereignty and federal programs for which only recognized tribes are eligible. Today, tribal membership numbers approximately 2,000. The Poarch Creek have an expanding base of tribal trust lands and have developed an array of economic enterprises, including high-stakes bingo halls. Likewise, tribal government has established a full range of health and social services.

Some Poarch leaders have become prominent in American Indian affairs nationally through the National Congress of American Indians, the National Indian Health Board, the National Indian Gaming Commission, and in other arenas. Although the first Poarch community members to graduate from high school did so only in the late 1950s, by the early 2000s the tribe had many college graduates, including some from such prestigious institutions as Harvard and Duke Universities.

Along with their political and economic achievements, the Poarch Creek have also sought to strengthen their distinctive cultural heritage. Starting from an almost self-invented powwow "chanting" and dancing, through the years the Poarch Creek have fully adopted the established intertribal styles of the powwow trail. Since at least the 1980s, some Poarch people have tried to recapture their distinctly Creek language, religion, and traditions through contacts with Oklahoma Creek, despite the sometime strained political relations between the two tribal governments. A number of Poarch Creeks have participated in stomp dances at modern-day Oklahoma Creek Indian ceremonial grounds, and there are a few Oklahoma Creeks who are frequent visitors to Poarch. Some Poarch Creeks have become experienced enough to "lead" the distinctive calls associated with Oklahoma Creek stomp dances. Others are attempting, with the approval of the Poarch Tribal Council, to establish their own stomp ground on their reservation in Alabama.

From their obscure beginnings and long history of neglect and marginalization, the Poarch Creek appear to be well on their way to becoming a successful example of American Indian tribal revitalization and cultural restoration.

ANTHONY PAREDES
National Park Service

J. Anthony Paredes, ed., *Indians of the Southeastern United States in the Late 20th Century* (1992), in *Anthropological Research: Process and Application*, ed. John J. Poggie Jr., Billie DeWalt, and William Dressler (1992); Frank G. Speck, *America Indigena* (1947).

Powhatans

A paramount chiefdom of approximately 30 Algonquian-speaking tribes led by Wahunsenacawh (Chief Powhatan) occupied Virginia's coastal plain when the English arrived in 1607. The Powhatan tribes were sedentary horticulturalists (most with riverine adaptations), and nearly all were affiliated with complex political structures. The John Smith map of 1612 is the earliest known document indicating tribal names and village locations in what came to be the Commonwealth of Virginia. However, the rapid English settlement of the colony and the importance of tobacco as a cash crop resulted in a demographic shift, with Europeans controlling the majority of Powhatan lands by 1700.

As signatories to colonial treaties, Virginia tribes were among the first native groups to be granted small tracts of reservation lands, although most tribes lost control of these lands by the early 1800s. However, the Mattaponi and Pamunkey tribes still hold two of the 17th-century reservations, thus making these reservations among the oldest in the United States.

The Acts of Assembly for October 1649 indicates that the freedom of movement of native people was restricted by the colonial government, and other colonial documents suggest that enslavement of Indians occurred in Virginia. The 1677 Treaty of Middle Plantation guaranteed civil and property rights of Virginia Indians and required Indians to pay annual tribute to the governor in lieu of property taxes. The presentation of tribute, typically of deer or other game, by the reservation-holding tribes continues to the present day.

Pressures to assimilate to non-Indian society in the 17th and 18th centuries led to the demise of traditional religious practices and the loss of native language. During the Great Awakening, many Virginia Indians converted to Christianity. Indian Baptist churches were, and remain, an important focus of support and tribal identity for the Virginia native community. Farming, fishing, and the wood and pulp industries were the Powhatans' primary 20th-century economic activities.

In 1924 Virginia's General Assembly passed the Racial Integrity Law requiring all segments of the population to be registered at birth in one of two categories: "white" or "colored." Indian communities resisted the legislation by sending their children to church-sponsored schools rather than to segregated public schools. Some left the state seeking better educational and employment opportunities. Interestingly, anthropologist Frank Speck did fieldwork among the Powhatan tribes during the 1920s just as the state was denying the existence of Indians in the state with the newly enacted biracial legislation.

A period of openness on matters of native identity and history began with the repeal of the Racial Integrity Law in 1968 and the growing civil rights movement, and between 1983 and 1989 the Commonwealth of Virginia granted state recognition to eight Virginia tribes. Seven of these — the Mattaponi, Pamunkey, Chickahominy, Chickahominy Eastern Division, Nansemond, Upper Mattaponi, and Rappahannock — are descendant communities from the original Powhatan tribes. The eighth is the non-Powhatan Monacan Nation. In 1983 the state established the Virginia Council on Indians to act as an advisory board on matters pertaining to the state's native population. Since 1999 six of the nonreservation tribes have sought federal recognition.

While more than 22,000 residents of Virginia indicated they were of American Indian ancestry on the 2000 U.S. Census, approximately 3,000 of this number are from Virginia's eight state-recognized tribes. (Others are from elsewhere in the United States and the Americas.) The majority of state-recognized tribes have tribal centers located on or near ancestral lands, and several maintain tribal museums. Six of the state-recognized tribes hold annual powwows. Potters employing traditional ceramic designs sell their art at the Mattaponi and Pamunkey reservations.

The 2004 opening of the National Museum of the American Indian in Washington, D.C., has brought renewed interest in the history and traditional culture of the Powhatan tribes.

DANIELLE MORETTI-LANGHOLTZ
College of William & Mary

Helen C. Rountree and Randolph Turner, *Before and after Jamestown: Virginia's Powhatans and Their Predecessors* (2002); Helen C. Rountree, *Pocahontas's People: The Powhatan Indians of Virginia through Four Centuries* (1990); Sandra Waugaman and Danielle Moretti-Langholtz, *We're Still Here: Contemporary Virginia Indians Tell Their Stories* (2000); Danielle Moretti-Langholtz, *In Our Own Words: Voices of Virginia Indians* (video, 2002).

Puerto Ricans

According to the 2000 U.S. Census, 3,406,178 Puerto Ricans live in the United States, with 22.3 percent of them residing in the South. Texas is home to nearly 70,000 Puerto Ricans. Virginia has over 41,000, and both Georgia and North Carolina have Puerto Rican populations of over 32,000. Florida, however, has the largest concentration of Puerto Ricans in the South and the second-largest in the United States. A recent and continuing trend of Puerto Rican migration to Florida, both from the urban Northeast of the United States and the island of Puerto Rico, began in the 1970s. Termed by Puerto Rican activists as the "Florida phenomenon," these migrants find central Florida particularly attractive because of its good schools, inexpensive housing, and climate. The 1990 census reported Florida's Puerto Rican population at 241,000; by 2000, 482,000 Puerto Ricans lived in the state, with concentrations in Orlando, Miami, and Hialeah. Predominantly Democrats, Puerto Rican Floridians are beginning to become an active political presence through their growing numbers.

Puerto Ricans relocating to the mainland might simultaneously be considered immigrants and migrants because of the complex relationship between the United States and Puerto Rico. Since the United States claimed Puerto Rico as unincorporated territory in 1898, there have been three significant phases of Puerto Rican immigration to the mainland: the Pioneer Migration (1900–45), the Great Migration (1946–64), and the Revolving-Door Migration (1965–present). In each phase, Puerto Ricans have worked as migrant farm laborers in the South, especially harvesting crops such as peaches in Georgia and South Carolina. While Puerto Ricans began to establish permanent communities in the South before the 1960s, their numbers have increased significantly in the phase of revolving-door migration.

Puerto Rican communities maintain an active presence in the South through Spanish-speaking media and Latino organizations that celebrate the diverse influences that shaped Puerto Rican island culture (the indigenous *Taino* and Spanish and African heritages). In terms of religion, Puerto Ricans traditionally practice Roman Catholicism, although recent trends indicate that many former Puerto Rican Roman Catholics are converting to Pentecostal and charismatic churches. A number of Puerto Ricans have brought the religious practice of Santeria to the South, a religion that incorporates both the symbols of Roman Catholicism and Yoruban religions brought from Nigeria. As in voodoo, Catholic saints in Santeria have a double identity as African spirits. While some practitioners of Santeria consider themselves Roman Catholics, Santeria is practiced outside the church space and has its own priests, rituals (such as animal sacrifice), music, dancing, theology, and laws. A number of Santeria churches have been established in Florida, including the South Florida Church of Lukumi Babalu Aye in Hialeah.

Puerto Ricans have also brought traditional foodways, music, and dance that reflect the diverse roots of Puerto Rican culture. Puerto Rican cuisine offers a spicy mix of fruits and vegetables with rice and meat in dishes such as *pernil* (roast pork shoulder), *pastels* (green banana and meat patties wrapped in plantain leaves and boiled), and *arroz con gandules* (yellow rice with pigeon peas). Two key ingredients in Puerto Rican cooking are *sofrito*, a mixture of onions, peppers, olives, and spices, and *achiote*, which can be bought at supermarkets in Puerto Rican communities in the South. Restaurants, such as El Bohio in Palm Bay, Fla., La Casona in Tampa, Fla., Antojitos Criollos en Atlanta in Acworth, Ga., and Gran Sabana in Durham, N.C., offer Puerto Rican cuisine in a southern setting.

Puerto Ricans, like Cubans, have also brought salsa music and dance to the South. Salsa music can best be described as a combination of Latin American rhythms that reflect Spanish and African roots, jazz improvisation, and 1940s big band influences. The tremendous popularity of salsa music and dancing has inspired the opening of dance studios that offer salsa lessons, as well as clubs (such as Paracas in Tampa) that provide a forum for new dancers and an audience for Puerto Rican recording artists and radio stations.

Puerto Rican communities in the South organize numerous events to celebrate Puerto Rican heritage. One famous event, the Puerto Rico Cultural Parade and Folklore Festival, is celebrated on the last Sunday in April in the National Historic District of Ybor City, Fla. This parade features musical performances, dance, and papier-mâché masks of traditional Puerto Rican folk characters (such as *Vejigantes*, *Sanqueros*, and *Cabezudos*), which represent a fusion of African, Spanish, and Caribbean cultures. Other annual southern Puerto Rican festivals include the Puerto Rican Patron Saint Festival in Pinellas Park, Fla. (a celebration of the various patron saints of Puerto Rican cities) and the Puerto Rican Parade of South Florida in Orlando.

FRANCES ABBOTT
University of Mississippi

Maria Gonzalez, *Puerto Ricans in the United States* (2000); Ramon Grosfoguel, *Colonial Subjects: Puerto Ricans in a Global Perspective* (2003).

Quapaws

The Quapaw (Kappa) are the southernmost branch of the Dhegiha Sioux, a family that includes the Omaha, Osage, Ponca, and Kaw (Kansa) American Indian tribes. In 1673 the expedition of French explorer Louis Jolliet and Jesuit missionary priest Jacques Marquette found the Quapaw on both sides of the Mississippi River in present-day Tennessee, Mississippi, and Arkansas

According to oral tradition, all Dhegiha Sioux had migrated west together from the lower reaches of the Ohio River. All but the Quapaw crossed the Mississippi and continued westward. The Quapaw turned down the east bank of the Mississippi River, continuing south to their 17th-century locations. The date of this migration is much debated, but there is a strong possibility that the Indians Hernando de Soto encountered in 1541 at the towns of Pacaha and Casqui were Quapaw. Other 18th- and 19th-century European names for the Quapaw included forms of the word "Arkansas" (such as "Akansea"), as well as *Beaux Hommes*, "Bow Indians," "Arc" or "Ark," and "Ozark" (*Aux Arc*).

In the 18th century the Quapaw were generally hostile toward their southeastern Indian neighbors—the Chickasaw, Natchez, Tunica, and Koroa. They were staunch allies of the French and helped maintain a hold on the French route along the Mississippi between New Orleans and St. Louis. When the French arrived, the Quapaw lived in four towns—Kappa, Tongigua, and Tourima on the Mississippi and Osotouy on the lower Arkansas River. Epidemics caused a drop in the population from an estimated 6,000 Quapaws in 1680 to around 2,000 by 1780. The towns combined and settled near Arkansas Post, a small French fort on the Arkansas River. The Quapaw fought with the French against the Chickasaw and other allies of Great Britain, served the Europeans as guides, and were traders. They traded corn, deer hides, bearskins and grease, beaver pelts, and bison hides and suet for utensils, guns, metal tools, and alcoholic beverages. Sometime in the mid-1700s they sent beautifully painted hides to the French king. These pictographic missiles, some of which may still be found at the Musee de l'Homme in Paris, showed scenes of hunting and warfare and the animal "crests" of the Quapaw clans and chiefs. When France ceded Louisiana to Spain in 1763, the Quapaw continued to be of strategic importance on the Mississippi River—evidenced by the fact that the Quapaw received 16 percent of the goodwill presents distributed to Indians in New Spain. Following the 1803 Louisiana Purchase, the Quapaw developed relations with the United States that were similar to those they had maintained with France and Spain.

The United States recognized the Quapaw claim to all the territory west of the Mississippi bounded by the Arkansas and Canadian Rivers on the north and the Red River on the south. By 1818, however, their territory had been reduced to a small reservation south of Little Rock and Arkansas Post. In 1824 they were asked to give up all of their land and move to the extreme southwest corner of present-day Arkansas, across the Red River and onto lands reserved for the Caddo Indians. Proud of the Quapaw reputation for never having shed the blood of white men, they acquiesced, signed a treaty, and threw their tribe on the mercy of the government. Chief Hekathon's plea for just treatment was eloquent, but the tribe was forced on their own "Trail of Tears" during a terrible winter march.

The stay on the Red River proved short, as floods and epidemics split the tribe apart. Some returned to squat in the swamps of Arkansas, while others found refuge among Indian tribes along the Canadian River in Indian Territory (Oklahoma). Finally, in September 1834 the U.S. government granted the Quapaw a reservation of their own in the northeast corner of Indian Territory. The tribal headquarters and powwow grounds are today located on former reservation land near Quapaw, Okla.

Tallchief became the last hereditary chief in 1874. His daughter Maude Supernaw, until her death in 1972, continued to exercise the right to bestow clan names upon Quapaw children. Given in the Quapaw language, these names were different in meaning from their English names.

Political and economic affairs of the tribe were shared between the U.S. Bureau of Indian Affairs and an elected Quapaw chief and council between 1892 and 1956. At that time an elected business committee took over all tribal affairs, including lands and leases. The tribe now owns an industrial park, bingo hall, and convenience store. Each Fourth of July, a general council of all adult Quapaws who can trace their ancestry to the 1890 tribal roll meets at the tribal grounds near Quapaw, Okla., during a three-day public powwow.

GLORIA A. YOUNG
University of Arkansas

W. David Baird, *The Quapaw Indians: A History of the Downstream People* (1980); Gloria A. Young and Michael P. Hoffman, in *Handbook of North American Indians, Volume 13: Plains*, ed. Raymond DeMallie (2002).

Romanies

The Romani people are well represented among southern ethnic minorities. Romanies—popularly, though inaccurately, called "Gypsies"—maintain their distinctive language and way of life while remaining outside mainstream society. All Romani groups trace their ultimate heritage to 9th- or 10th-century India, but subsequent westward migration into Europe and from there to the Americas has scattered the original population, giving rise to a number of distinct ethnic subdivisions. In the South several of these subdivisions are represented, particularly the Romanichals, who came from the British Isles, and the Vlax (the *x* pronounced like *ch* in German *achtung*), who arrived later from southeastern Europe.

The first Romanies to reach the Americas came with Christopher Columbus on his third voyage in 1498 and were from Spain. The first to reach North America were probably those banished to serve in the Virginia plantations by Oliver Cromwell in 1664. The transportation of British Romanies to the American colonies continued sporadically until the mid-1800s, and the French began similar deportations to Louisiana after 1700. Spanish shipments to the same territory followed a proclamation issued in 1749; Romanies came as redemptioners from Germany to Pennsylvania, New York, and New Jersey following the Thirty Years' War, and some of them eventually made their way south. The Vlax Romanies began coming to America in the middle of the 19th century, when 500 years of Romani slavery in the Balkan states ended.

Romanichals live throughout the South, probably numbering between 50,000 and 100,000. Particularly large communities are found in Texas, Arkansas, Georgia, Louisiana, Kentucky, and the Carolinas. Almost all own homes and land and at the same time participate in a variety of occupations, such as horse raising, blacktopping, roofing, and paving. Others involved in these occupations follow an annual migratory business circuit and move from campground to campground, living in motorized trailers. The Vlax Romanies arrange marriages and have little to do with the Romanichal population, whom they outnumber by perhaps five to one.

Romani culture requires that social contact with non-Romanies, whom the Vlax call *gadjé* (singular, *gadjó*) and the Romanichals call *gorjers*, be kept at a minimum. Part of their desire for separation stems from their ideology of "clean" and "polluted" states related to personal hygiene, sexual behavior, and food preparation. All outsiders are considered unclean (*marimé* in Vlax and *mokadi* in the Romanichal dialect). To avoid contact with the *gadjé* in the past, one man was often called the "Gypsy king" by the media, and he negotiated with the *gadjé* community, but Romani communities do not actually have kings or queens. Women dress modestly, keep their legs covered, and cover their heads if married. Otherwise, Romanies avoid calling attention to ethnic identity and emphasize keeping a low profile.

Negative stereotypes of "Gypsies" have fostered historical and contemporary prejudice against Romanies at both the popular and administrative levels; consequently, Romanies have had little motivation to draw attention to their ethnicity. One Mississippi law stated that "gypsies . . . for each county . . . shall be jointly and severally liable with his or her associates (to a fine of) two thousand dollars" (State Code, 27-17-191). Another law in Georgia required

that "upon each company of gypsies engaged in trading or selling merchandise . . . $250 is to be collected" (Acts & Resolutions, 1927, Pt. 1 [ii].56). As a consequence, while Romani culture in the South is vigorous and in little danger of disappearing, the general public is hardly aware of it.

In recent years two independent movements, one sociopolitical and the other evangelical, have begun to bring changes within the Romani American population. The former has resulted in the creation of a national website called Patrin, the purpose of which is to bring news of national and international Gypsy-related matters to the Romani population, and the establishment of the Romani Archives and Documentation Center at the University of Texas at Austin. A number of ethnic organizations have also been created, such as SKOKRA and the U.S. Romani Alliance. The Christian evangelical movement has also led to the establishment of a newsletter, *Romany Fires of Revival*. While many Romanies are devout Eastern Orthodox Christians or Catholics, Protestant Romani churches, both Vlax and Romanichal, are now found in many southern cities, including Atlanta and Houston.

IAN HANCOCK
University of Texas at Austin

Irving Brown, *Gypsy Fires in America: A Narrative of Life among the Romanies of the United States and Canada* (1924); Ian Hancock, *The Pariah Syndrome* (1987), *We Are the Romani People* (2001); Andrew A. Marchbin, "A Critical History of the Origin and the Migration of the Gypsies" (Ph.D.

dissertation, University of Pittsburgh, 1939); Anne Sutherland, *Gypsies: The Hidden Americans* (1986).

Russians

The first Russians to inhabit North America carried out Imperial Russia's colonial endeavors in Alaska and California in the late 18th century, but Russians have played several key roles in southern history. Ivan Vasilevich Turchaninoff (John Basil Turchin), who served as a colonel in the army of Russia's czar Nicholas I before immigrating to the United States in 1856, became a brigadier general in the Union Army. His Eighth Brigade was based in Elizabethtown, Ky., and fought in Civil War campaigns in Tennessee and Georgia. St. Petersburg, Fla., was cofounded in 1888 by Peter Dementev-Demens (1849–1919), a railroad builder who named the city for his Russian birthplace.

The 2000 U.S. Census lists 2,652,214 persons with Russian ancestry living in the United States. These include both recent immigrants and first- and second-generation Russians born in the United States to immigrant parents or grandparents. The 2000 census also indicates that at least 706,000 persons over the age of five in the United States speak the Russian language at home. Historically, Russian immigrants formed communities around major cities, especially New York, but now such places as Sunny Isles Beach in South Florida are becoming known as "little Moscows." According to the 1990 census, 44 percent of persons

claiming Russian ancestry lived in the Northeast, while just 18 percent lived in the South. However, by 2000, more than 400,000 persons of Russian heritage lived in southern states, especially Florida (201,500), Texas (56,500), Virginia (45,000), and Georgia (32,000). Active resettlement programs for Russian Jews have been initiated throughout the South, including locales such as Houston and Chapel Hill, N.C. The largest populations of persons claiming Russian ancestry are in the southern cities of Houston, Atlanta, and south Florida's Miami, Boca Raton, and Sunny Isles Beach.

Russians in the South work in all spheres of the economy, including the science and health care sectors, education, computer technology, the arts, service industries, and private business. Most Russian immigrants are well educated but may find the skills they acquired in the Soviet educational system difficult to apply in certain spheres of American science and industry.

Cultural programs, including concerts, films, art exhibitions, and other performances, help Russians in the South maintain a sense of community. Cities such as Atlanta and Miami frequently host exhibitions of Russian artists and concerts of popular Russian musicians. Video stores near Russian neighborhoods stock recently released Russian films. Russian and Russian-Jewish cuisine is a focal point for many communities of Russians in the South, and many southern cities boast an array of Russian specialty shops, restaurants, and cafés with nightly Russian music and advertisement signs in the Cyrillic alphabet. In communities with significant populations of new Russian immigrants, local stores now stock traditional Russian foods, vodka, and Ukrainian chocolates. Many southern communities are now even seeing the growing popularity of Russian and Turkish steam baths.

Russians mark special days, particularly birthdays and New Year's Day, with lavish celebrations, usually in private homes and featuring Russian cuisine such as buckwheat pancakes, stuffed cabbage rolls, and salted herring. Russian Orthodox Christmas celebrations begin on 7 January in accordance with the old Julian calendar. Banned after the 1917 Russian Revolution, the holiday was not openly observed again in Russian until 1992. Russian southerners also may have the traditional Holy Supper on Christmas Eve—a meatless meal that begins with a symbolic porridge called *kutya*, which is eaten from a common pot. (The grain of the porridge represents hope, and the poppy seeds and honey used for flavor guarantee happiness and nights of untroubled sleep.) Christmas trees may be adorned with colored eggs, but these are more common at Easter, when they are made in two types: *pisanki* (ornamented and painted in two to four colors) and *krashenki* (unornamented and painted in one color). Decorated eggs are often given as Easter gifts.

The Russian Orthodox Church is central to the identity of Russians in the South. Sizable parishes include the Joy of All Who Sorrow Russian Orthodox Church in Cummins, Ga. (outside Atlanta), St. Vladimir's Orthodox Church in Houston, and St. Vladimir Church in Miami. St. Nicholas (the patron saint of Russia) is also a popular dedication for Orthodox churches. Russian Jews are active in the congregations of synagogues throughout the South. While many Russian communities have historically formed around synagogues, Jewish community centers, and churches, today many Russians also utilize community-building resources such as the Internet.

SARAH D. PHILLIPS
Indiana University, Bloomington

Dan N. Jacobs and Ellen Frankel Paul, eds., *Studies of the Third Wave: Recent Migration of Soviet Jews to the United States* (1981); Paul R. Magocsi, *The Russian Americans* (1989); Viktor Petrov, ed., *Russkie v Istorii Ameriki* [Russians in American History] (1988); Dennis Shasha and Marina Shron, *Red Blues: Voices from the Last Wave of Russian Immigrants* (2002); Vladimir Wertsman, *The Russians in America: A Chronology and Fact Book* (1977).

Salzburgers

Late in 1731 Count Leopold von Firmian, the Roman Catholic prince-archbishop of Salzburg, Austria, told the 20,000–30,000 Lutherans in Salzburg that they must accept Catholic doctrine or be expelled. Many of those who left settled in German towns and provinces. Others, under the leadership of Pastor Samuel Urlsperger, pietist Lutheran pastor at Augsburg, secured a welcome to go to George Oglethorpe's new colony of Georgia. The Society for the Promotion of Christian Knowledge in England also supported the Salzburgers' immigration to Georgia. Leaving Rotterdam, Netherlands, on 8 January 1734, they reached Savannah on 12 March 1734. Other groups followed from 1734 to 1752.

Salzburgers were initially expected to adapt themselves to the English colonial lifestyle, but they preferred to settle outside the Savannah limits in order to retain their language and customs. Thirty miles northwest up the Savannah River, they established Ebenezer (a biblical name that means "stone of help"). Ebenezer was modeled after Savannah and divided into "tythings," a sort of neighborhood that promoted familial living. Each tything had 10 households. The spiritual and secular leaders were Pastor Johann Martin Boltzius and Pastor Israel Christian Grounau, both of whom came to Ebenezer in 1734. The Ebenezer location was unfortunate: it had poor soil, malaria, and low-lying land that was prone to flooding. One-third of the group died in 1736.

In that year the Salzburgers moved to New Ebenezer, situated higher on the banks of the Savannah River. There, each family received a town lot and farmland. The new settlement was very successful agriculturally. Salzburgers introduced the first sawmill and silk mill in Georgia and the first gristmill and rice-stamping mill in the colonies. New Ebenzer also had the first Sunday church school and one of the first public schools in the southern colonies.

The Salzburgers also established the first orphanage in the American colonies at New Ebenezer in 1737. Pastor Boltzius modeled the project after his own orphanage in Halle, Germany, the center of German Lutheran pietism. (Credit for the first American orphanage is frequently and inaccurately attributed to George Whitefield, who established the Bethesda Orphanage near Savannah, Ga., in 1740.) The orphan house served as a refuge for the poor, widows, and the infirm and feebleminded, as a hospital for the sick, and as a school for children. Until a church was built, it also was used for all religious services, including daily evening worship for the whole settlement. The orphan house is now a museum.

Jerusalem Lutheran Church was first constructed as a frame building in 1741 and replaced in 1767–69 by one of the first brick structures in Georgia. With 21-inch thick walls and handmade bricks of local clay, some of which still bear fingerprints, the church is still in use today.

After the death of Boltzius in 1765, New Ebenezer went into decline. The British occupied and burned much of the town during the Revolutionary War and used the Jerusalem Church as a hospital and stable. Damaged by the war, New Ebenezer was never the same again.

In the post-Revolutionary period, New Ebenzer native John Adam Treutlen was elected as the first governor of Georgia in 1777. In 1782 the Georgia legislature met in New Ebenezer, which served as the first capital of Georgia for a short time. In 1830 the town, except for Jerusalem Church, burned, and during the Civil War General William T. Sherman used the church as his headquarters. Today, the church, a cemetery, and one house (built in 1755) are all that remain.

In 1925 the Georgia Salzburger Society was created to promote Salzburger heritage, and it still publishes a newsletter quarterly. Common surnames in the area today are Zeigler, Metzger, Seckinger, Lastinger, and Treutlen. Each Labor Day, Salzburger descendants have a heritage festival with a *markt platz* (a German-style marketplace selling farm products and crafts that were sold in the 19th century), heritage displays and lectures, posters about skills and trades Salzburger ancestors needed to survive in colonial Georgia, and traditional foods. Many participants dress in dirndls or other traditional attire. As the Huguenots wear a uniquely shaped cross, the Salzburgers adopted Martin Luther's symbol of the swan in 1734, and descendants now wear swan pins.

DONALD S. ARMENTROUT
University of the South

George Fenwick Jones, *The Georgia Dutch: From the Rhine and Danube to the Savannah, 1733–1783* (1992); George Fenwick Jones, *The Salzburger Saga: Religious Exiles and Other Germans along the Savannah* (1948); Carl Mauelshagen, *Salzburg Lutheran Expulsion and Its Impact* (1962); Mack Walker, *The Salzburger Transaction: Expulsion and Redemption in Eighteenth-Century Germany* (1992).

Sapponys

Formerly the Indians of Person County, the Sappony (or "Saponi") Indian tribe is one of North Carolina's small tribes with state, but not federal, recognition. Person County's most significant precolonial Indian tribes included the Saponi, Tutelo, and the Occaneechi. The Sappony likely descend from these and other tribes. Some members are "triracial" (of Indian, European, and African origins). The Sappony once spoke a dialect of a Siouan language that was similar to those of the neighboring and related Tutelo and Occaneechi. Like these tribes, they also had settlements in Virginia.

About 1,000 persons claim tribal membership today. Most older members reside in the High Plains community of northern Person County, while a few live across the state line in Halifax County, Va. Many of the younger tribal members have settled elsewhere in North Carolina and the United States.

Early explorers noted that Indians moved freely within the region. Traveling in the mid-17th century, John Lederer made contact with the Occaneechi, Saponi, Tutelo, Eno, and other tribes that were relocating their villages to escape the warring Iroquois. In 1670 the Saponi moved from southwest of what is now Lynchburg, Va., to the junction of the Staunton and Dan Rivers, where the Occaneechi were already settled on one of three islands. The Tutelo later joined them. By the early 1700s the three tribes had moved south into North Carolina. The Occaneechi briefly settled on the Eno River in Orange County, and the Saponi and Tutelo located along the Yadkin River in Davidson County. For security reasons, they moved again across the Roanoke River and closer to Anglo settlements in Virginia, where later travelers met them.

According to William Byrd, the Saponi and Tutelo villages were located in the path of the Iroquois and Catawba Indians, and this prompted their move into North Carolina. Byrd found no settled Indians in the area of what is now Person County during his trips in the early 1700s.

Half a century later, in 1755, Governor Dobbs listed 14 men and 14 women of Saponi background in Granville County, which included present-day Person County. Some Sappony now claim descent from the 19th-century Cherokee "Green Martin" (*Sa-mi-u-sdi*, as he was called before he took the name "Green"). In 1850 Green moved in with a Person County Indian community and married the daughter of its largest landowners, William Epps (a Cherokee) and Nancy Stuart (of the Powhatan Confederacy). The Martins had seven children whose descendants are linked to the Sappony people. However, the present generation retains no living memory of cultural traditions or speech from those particular Indian ancestors.

Separate educational institutions helped maintain a sense of Indian identity. In the late 19th century two acres of land donated by Green Martin became home to an Indian school. A second school was constructed several years later, located east of the original. In 1904 Diotrion W. and Mary Epps deeded land for a third school in which the Indian children of Person County, as well as those living in Virginia, enrolled. A new school was built in 1925.

An all-Indian high school, High Plains School, opened in 1948 with 24 students and closed only with integration in 1961.

Religious faith has also kept Sappony communities tightly knit. The first independent Indian church formed in 1830 at the High Plains settlement. Baptist, Holiness, and Methodist denominations are prevalent, although since the late 19th century many have wished to create an all-Indian Methodist conference.

For many years Person County depended upon agriculture, primarily tobacco, as the major source of employment and income. Most Indians now work in some type of industry rather than farming.

In 1913 the North Carolina General Assembly designated the group as the "Indians of Person County," regardless of their clouded genealogy. Although not referencing a tribal name, the bill did state that the Indians had been known as "Cubans." State recognition was unintentionally rescinded during the 1970s. In May 1997 the General Assembly passed another bill officially recognizing the Indians of Person County. In 2003 the General Assembly approved a name change to "Sappony."

The Sappony are currently seeking federal recognition as American Indians. Living in distinct communities with a history of their own educational institutions and churches, the Sappony have maintained a sense of their own Indianness as they continue to adapt to changing social and economic conditions. Their current participation in powwows signals their Indian identity to both other Native Americans and to their non-Indian neighbors, who have always regarded them as different. A seven-member council governs the tribe and appoints the chief. Each council member represents one of the seven major surnames of tribal members. The Sappony have an annual gathering on Labor Day weekends.

THOMAS E. ROSS
University of North Carolina at Pembroke

Madelin Hall Eaker, *The Heritage of Person County*, vol. 2 (1983); Douglas L. Rights, *The American Indian in North Carolina* (1947); Thomas E. Ross, *American Indians in North Carolina: Geographic Interpretations* (1999); Ruth Y. Wetmore, *First on the Land: The North Carolina Indians* (1975).

Scots, Highland

Highland immigration to the South was most dramatic in the colonial period. Highlanders fleeing the late 18th- and 19th-century "Clearances" more commonly went to Canada. Colonial immigration to the South is often romantically portrayed as a government-enforced exile of Jacobites. The last Jacobite Rising to replace a Stuart on the British throne ended with the 1746 defeat at Culloden of Prince Charles Edward Stuart. Fewer than 200 Jacobites were transported to the American colonies. While shiploads of political prisoners may not have swarmed southern shores, the social, political, and economic aftermath of Culloden drove Highland emigration patterns. When high rents became unbearable, "tacksmen" — military leaders who also leased land to clan members for their chiefs — often organized their clansfolks' exodus. Highlanders frequently immigrated communally in groups of hundreds at a time and resettled together.

North Carolina attracted more Highland Scots in the 18th century than any other state. Some may have arrived by 1729, but large-scale immigration began about 1732, increased in the 1760s, and peaked in 1774–75 before being temporarily banned. The majority (estimates vary between 15,000 and 30,000) came to North Carolina's Cape Fear Valley, including the Jacobite heroine Flora MacDonald and the Gaelic poet John MacRae (Iain MacMhurchaidh). The "Mayflower" of the Cape Fear Scots was a ship called the *Thistle* that sailed in 1739 with 350 passengers, mostly from Argyllshire. Later Highlanders came from Ross, Sutherland, and the Isle of Skye. A much later group, organized by the British Napier Commission, arrived in 1884.

Most immigrants were Presbyterians, but it was not until 1758 that the first Gaelic-speaking minister, James Campbell, arrived with the simultaneous founding of Barbecue, Longstreet, and Bluff churches. English replaced Gaelic as a primary language by the mid-19th century. In the late 20th-century a few elderly descendants of 18th-century Highlanders, some still farming land settled by their immigrant ancestors, could repeat Bible verses in Gaelic. Others actively study the language and compete in Gaelic singing competitions called *mòds*.

Descendants of Cape Fear Valley Highlanders were pioneers in Alabama, Tennessee, Mississippi, and Texas,

Scottish Americans in 19th-century and ancient Celtic dress at the Loch Norman Highland Games near Charlotte, N.C., 1994 (Celeste Ray, photographer)

and they settled "Argyle" in Florida's Panhandle in the 1820s. Colonel John McKinnon, a signer of the Florida state constitution, was among them, as were McLeans, McCaskills, Gunns, and MacBrooms. Several early settlers have memorials in the Euchee Valley Presbyterian Church Cemetery and are otherwise remembered at Argyle's annual Highland Games.

Highlanders also contributed to the settlement, politics, and place names of Georgia. In 1736 trustees for the colony of Georgia solicited hundreds of Highlander families (Mackays and Mackintoshes predominant among them) to settle the pine barrens of the Georgia coast and protect the fledgling colony from Spanish invasion. Under military governor James Oglethorpe, the Highland Rangers and the Highland Independent Company of Foot guarded the settlement first called New Inverness, then Darien, until it was disbanded in 1749. In the 1750s Highlanders moved out from the settlement to raise cattle and begin the lumber business that would remain the focus of Darien's industry until the Civil War. The town of Darien (population 1,800) in McIntosh County holds a "Scottish Day" in March, and a living history unit called the "Oglethorpe Highlanders," set about 1742, reenacts the settlement period.

In contemporary Scottish heritage celebrations, descendants of Lowland Scot and Scots-Irish immigrants also embrace a Highland vision of Scottish identity engendered by Sir Walter Scott long after their ancestors left Scotland or Ulster. Today, descendants of various Scottish ethnic groups commemorate their heritage by joining societies modeled on the Highland clan system and donning "clan tartans" largely invented in the 19th century. Southern states were the first to adopt state tartans, and before Tartan Day (6 April) became a national holiday, Tennessee declared one in 1996, followed by North Carolina in 1997. Currently, about half of

American Scottish-related societies are southern based, and more than one-third of America's almost 250 annual Highland Games and festivals occur in the region — the most prestigious being the Grandfather Mountain Highland Games near Linville, N.C. (founded 1956). In addition to standard athletic, bagpiping, and dance competitions, Highland Games in the South have a regional style, often devoting time for religious services and showcasing barbecue or Lowcountry boils, fiddling, clogging, or calf roping depending on the subregion of the South in which they occur.

CELESTE RAY
University of the South

Duane Meyer, *The Highland Scots of North Carolina, 1732–1776* (1961); Michael Newton, *We're Indians Sure Enough: The Legacy of the Scottish Highlanders in the United States* (2001); Anthony Parker, *Scottish Highlanders in Colonial Georgia: The Recruitment, Emigration, and Settlement at Darien, 1735–1748* (1997); Celeste Ray, *Highland Heritage: Scottish Americans in the American South* (2001), *Transatlantic Scots* (2005).

Scots-Irish

The Scots-Irish from Ulster were one of the largest immigrant groups to arrive in the North American colonies in the 18th century. Traditional estimates suggest 250,000 arrived before the American Revolution; recent scholarship has revised that number to 130,000 for the period from 1680 to 1815. Ulster immigration continued well into the 19th century. In 18th- and 19th-century America, these immigrants were identified as "Irish," "Protestant Irish," or "Scotch-Irish," and only rarely as "Scots." They have been called "Ulster-Scots" in Britain and Ireland in recent times and "Scots-Irish" in America since the 19th century. The complexity of their origins created ambiguity about their name.

Their ancestors were predominantly Border people from Lowland Scotland and northwestern England. They were an overwhelmingly Protestant (mostly Presbyterian), impoverished, and English-speaking people who sought a better life in Ulster when King James I established the "plantations" of Ulster in 1609 to consolidate Britain's conquest of Gaelic Catholic Ireland. The frontier environment of Ulster recast the culture of this immigrant community in the 17th century. The Ulster experience of tenantry, disenfranchisement by a landowning Anglican elite, and hostility from the Irish Catholic majority redefined them. The Scots-Irish immigrants who left Ulster for America in the 18th century were no longer in any sense simply "Scots."

Trade routes and geography combined to lead most Scots-Irish immigrants to the South. They moved from the Delaware Valley southwest along the Great Wagon Road into Virginia's Shenandoah Valley and the Carolina piedmont. Periodically, smaller numbers of Ulster immigrants arrived at southern ports such as Charleston, Savannah, and Wilmington. Concentrations of Scots-Irish settlements grew in several places along inland routes. In such "cultural hearths" — Lancaster and York Counties, Penn., Rockbridge County, Va., and the region between the Yadkin-Pee Dee and Catawba Rivers in the Carolinas — they were exposed to powerful new cultural influences. There they demonstrated a remarkable adaptability to new physical environments and to a wide range of ethnic influences, including those of other Europeans, Native Americans, and African Americans. From those cultural hearths they launched further migrations into the South, settling in later generations throughout Appalachia and west and southwest to the Ozarks and the Gulf Coast region.

The cultural adaptability of the Scots-Irish has made them difficult to identify. They did contribute to a rural cultural synthesis that characterized the southern Backcountry, including settlement patterns marked by a preference for dispersed single-family homesteads rather than nucleated villages; a mixed agriculture that emphasized open-range livestock grazing and summer herding to upland pastures; and distinctive language use, storytelling, and musical traditions. Backcountry culture also included a distinctive Presbyterianism that arose in Ulster and was characterized by an enthusiasm for evangelical open-field gatherings, or "holy fairs." These elements of their old-country traditions were especially well-suited to the southern Backcountry. At the same time, change and adaptation were an essential part of the Scots-Irish experience. Presbyterianism provides such an example. The Presbyterian insistence on a seminary-trained clergy and active participation in the synodal structure of the church hindered the faith in more remote communities such as those in Appalachia and the Ozarks. Nevertheless, even there the Scots-Irish carried their Ulster Calvinism into their new Baptist and Methodist churches. In much of the southern Backcountry, Presbyterianism endured as a marker of the Scots-Irish presence.

The Scots-Irish are a subject of myth within American immigration traditions. Many Americans proudly claim Scots-Irish ancestry with only a vague notion — too often shaped by uninformed stereotypes of Celticness, independence, clannishness, violence, and love of place — of what that legacy entails. For many recently, Highland Scots imagery has mistakenly come to represent Scots-Irish identity.

H. TYLER BLETHEN
Western Carolina University

CURTIS W. WOOD
Western Carolina University

H. Tyler Blethen and Curtis W. Wood Jr., *From Ulster to Carolina: The Migration of the Scots-Irish to Southwestern North Carolina*, revised ed. (1998); H. Tyler Blethen and Curtis W. Wood Jr., eds., *Ulster and North America: Transatlantic Perspectives on the Scots-Irish* (1997); David Hackett Fischer, *Albion's Seed: Four British Folkways in America* (1989); James G. Leyburn, *The Scots-Irish: A Social History* (1962); Patrick Griffin, *The People with No Name: Ireland's Ulster Scots, America's Scots-Irish, and the Creation of a British Atlantic World, 1689–1764* (2001); Celeste Ray, ed., *Transatlantic Scots* (2005); Marianne S. Wokeck, *Trade in Strangers: The Beginnings of Mass Migration to North America* (1999).

Seminoles and Miccosukees

Descended from late prehistoric-era moundbuilding cultures of the interior Southeast, the Seminole and Miccosukee people were settled in the major river drainages of Georgia and Alabama by the era of European colonial contact in the 17th century. Depopulation and shifting settlement patterns initiated by European contact in the 1540s changed aspects of traditional native culture. By the 1700s many native groups were actively involved in an English-based deerskin trade connecting them to European economic and political networks.

By mid-century, as Spain, France, and England struggled for control over the Gulf Coast, bands of Creeks (as they were then called) began moving south into the Florida peninsula. Florida's native people, decimated by European disease, slave raids from the Georgia and Carolina coasts, and the destruction of the Spanish missions, were now few in number and living in isolated swamp refuges. The Creek transplanted their farming way of life to the Florida hammocks and began herding cattle across the prairies of the old Spanish ranchos. Distancing themselves from the politics of the Creek Confederacy and taking on their own identity, they became known as the Seminole, from the Spanish word *cimarron* for "wild one" or "runaway."

When Florida became a territory of the United States in 1821, General Andrew Jackson quickly implemented plans for removing the estimated 5,000 Seminoles and attacked Seminole towns deep in the Spanish colony, striking as far south as the Suwannee River. Between 1817 and 1858 the U.S. government engaged in three wars with the Seminole. The most consequential of these, the Second Seminole War (1835–42), resulted in the forced removal of nearly 4,000 Seminoles to Indian Territory in what is now Oklahoma (where many of the 12,000 members of the Seminole Nation of Oklahoma now reside). By 1860 fewer than 200 Seminoles remained in Florida in the deep fastness of the Big Cypress Swamp and the scrub forests around Lake Okeechobee. A farming way of life was replaced by a hunting-fishing-gathering subsistence more suitable for life in the south Florida swamps. With the possible exception of the Pine Island Ridge settlement, towns did not exist. People lived in small clan camps occupied by families related matrilineally. By the end of the 1800s, tentative contact with settlers and traders in the areas of present-day Miami and Fort Myers brought food and manufactured goods to the Seminole in exchange for animal pelts, alligator skins, and bird plumes. Missionaries and government agents soon followed, and the Seminole again were inevitably drawn into the affairs of the outside world.

The contemporary Seminole and Miccosukee people are descended from those few survivors of the Seminole wars remaining in Florida after 1858. By the 1920s some Seminoles began moving onto federal reservation lands set aside for them between 1907–11 in Collier, Martin, and Broward Counties. By 1950 the reservation Seminoles were participating in a number of government programs and filed a land claims suit under the conditions of the Indian Claims Commission Act of 1946. One faction further pushed for federal recognition, which was approved in 1957 with the formation of the Seminole Tribe of Florida, now based in Hollywood, Fla. Another group living along the Tamiami Trail (U.S. 41), who had not supported the land claims suit, organized separately as the Miccosukee Tribe of Florida and was granted federal recognition in 1962. Seminole tribe members speak two distinct native languages: Mikasuki and Creek-Seminole (Muscogee). Members of the Miccosukee tribe are predominantly Mikasuki speakers.

Today, the 2,600 members of the Seminole Tribe of Florida and the 500 Miccosukees are striving for economic self-sufficiency through a mixed strategy based on gaming, agriculture, tourism, and diversified corporate interests. Both groups maintain a strong connection to their cultural past. The traditional Green Corn dance still occurs in early summer. The dance emphasizes purification and social harmony and reinforces clan bonds. Participants congregate in clan camps organized around the dance circle. Among the Seminole, eight clans now exist, although according to both written and oral sources there were more in the recent past. The present clans are Snake, Wind, Tallahassee, Otter, Bird, Little Bird, Panther, and Bear. Seminoles stress exogamy in the selection of marriage partners.

While Seminoles and Miccosukees viewed formal education as an intrusion of the outside world just a generation ago, it is now a top priority. Boosted by casino revenues, tribal education initiatives fund programs spanning preschool through college, with scholarships covering tuition, books, and housing. Challenges still remain, but an increasing number view education as a path to economic independence without sacrificing their cultural identity. Seminole and Miccosukee pride in identifying as the "unconquered people" bodes well for their cultural survival.

BRENT R. WEISMAN
University of South Florida

James W. Covington, *The Seminoles of Florida* (1993); Harry A. Kersey Jr., *An Assumption of Sovereignty* (1996); John K. Mahon and Brent R. Weisman, in *The New History of Florida*, ed. Michael Gannon (1996); William C. Sturtevant, in *North American Indians in Historical Perspective*, ed. Eleanor Burke Leacock and Nancy Oestrich Lurie (1971); Brent R. Weisman, *Unconquered People: Florida's Seminole and Miccosukee Indians* (1999).

Shawnees

The Shawnee are a Native American people with a complex history spanning the whole of the southern United States and much of the Ohio River Valley region. By the end of the 20th century, the Shawnee were universally fluent in English, but some tribal members also continued using their tribal language. The Shawnee language belongs to the Algonquian language family. The name Shawnee derives from their own ethnonym, which means "person of the South."

At the time of contact with Europeans, the Shawnee homeland was in what are today the states of Ohio and Kentucky, but during the colonial era the Shawnee ranged widely over eastern North America and lived in association with many other groups, including the Iroquois, Delaware, Yuchi, Creek, Kickapoo, and Caddo. At least since European contact, the whole of the Shawnee people have never lived in a single contiguous settlement. During the 18th century Shawnee settlements existed in the present-day states of Alabama, Georgia, South Carolina, Ohio, Pennsylvania, Missouri, and Indiana. In the 19th century American expansion policies pushed the Shawnee west, where they settled in present-day Ohio, Missouri, Kansas, Oklahoma, Arkansas, and Texas. In the later 19th century the Shawnee settled permanently in what is today Oklahoma. The "Eastern Shawnee" are found near the town of Miami in northeastern Oklahoma. The "Loyal Shawnee" reside in the vicinity of White Oak and Vinita, where they are settled on land obtained from the Cherokee Nation. The "Absentee Shawnee" live near the towns of Shawnee and Little Axe. (The designation "absentee" refers to those not living on the Shawnee reservation in Kansas when it was allotted.)

Historically, the Shawnee shared a basic economy with other Native American groups from eastern North America. Hunting and farming supplemented participation in the European fur trade, through which the Shawnee obtained manufactured goods. Like other southeastern Indian groups, the

Shawnee long participated in a frontier-exchange economy in which there was considerable cultural, social, and economic exchange—not only between the Shawnee and their native allies, but also between these groups and the European and African populations found on the southern, and later western, frontier. For example, much that is distinctive about southern foodways can be traced back to this world of cultural exchange. As a token of their aboriginal southern heritage, the Shawnee possess at least 15 different forms of cornbread, one of which is the centerpiece of the annual "Bread Dance" ceremonies. They also continue to grow tribal heirloom varieties of corn and to grind cornmeal by hand.

Given their complex settlement history, traditional Shawnee social organization is difficult to characterize. Familial interactions revolved around a patrilineal "Omaha" type kinship system. Individuals also belonged to a special kind of "clan" or "name group" based on the "Indian" name one is given at birth. Finally, in addition to belonging to one of three modern tribes, Shawnees live in local settlements established around a ceremonial life.

The traditional religion of the Shawnee is based on a yearly cycle of ceremonies linked to the change of season, the yearly round of economic activities, and a gendered division of labor in which men are closely associated with hunting and warfare and women are responsible for horticulture and domestic activities. Ceremonies combine daytime rituals with all-night social dances. All communal rituals serve both as a thanksgiving for the bounty provided by the Shawnee Creator and the natural world and as a petition for continued well-being.

In addition to communitywide ceremonies, Shawnee families observe a number of rituals domestically, including first-fruits feasts, ancestral memorials, and baby namings. Some Shawnees have adopted various Protestant faiths, and many others have taken up the beliefs and practices of the Native American Church or Peyote Religion as a compliment to traditional ceremonialism.

Living today on the western margins of the American South, the Shawnee are socioeconomically integrated into the modern United States, but they also are among the most culturally conservative American Indian populations in the region. They impressively preserve their own language, religion, community order, and customs despite centuries of forced relocation and policies aimed at either destroying them or forcing them to abandon their heritage for European traditions. The famous Shawnee chief and orator Tecumseh galvanized the opinions of many American Indian peoples against such colonial policies in the early 1800s, and the Shawnee today remain important advocates for the preservation of distinctly native ways of life.

JASON BAIRD JACKSON
Indiana University

Charles Callender, in *Handbook of North American Indians, Volume 15: Northeast*, ed. Bruce G. Trigger (1978); James H.

Howard, *Shawnee! The Ceremonialism of a Native American People and Its Cultural Background* (1981).

Spanish

Spain was the first European power to establish and impose a culture upon the aboriginal inhabitants of the American South. In 1513 Juan Ponce de Leon sighted a land mass he named *La Florida*. A series of ambitious explorations and expeditions brought Spanish settlers and missionaries to the American Southeast, the gateway to North America. Expeditions by Pánfilo de Narváez (1528) and Hernando de Soto (1539) explored large portions of Florida and the Southeast, bringing contagious diseases to some of the region's most populous Indian settlements. Imported Andalusian cattle and pigs thrived in the New World.

Spanish explorers reached as far north as Virginia, and the Spanish presence contributed to the founding of St. Augustine, Mobile, and Pensacola. A vigorous Franciscan missionary system shaped early attitudes and relationships toward Native Americans and African slaves. Spain was ultimately unsuccessful in maintaining its empire, ceding Louisiana (which it had gained in 1763) to France in 1800 and Florida to the United States in 1821. Another legacy of the modern South, Texas, remained a part of the Spanish borderlands until Mexican independence in 1821.

Despite the inability to sustain settlements in the United States, Spanish culture infused the South with a distinctive spirit. Spanish ways influenced the legal systems, land-use patterns, traditions of self-government, and economic affairs of Louisiana, Texas, and Florida. Ranching, with its colorful traditions, owes much to Spanish customs. Spain's Roman Catholicism provided the first European religious influence on the southern landscape. New Orleans, after the fire of 1788, was rebuilt in the Spanish design, characterized by wrought-iron grillwork, shaded patios, arcades, and fountains. The Spanish also added to the cosmopolitan nature of Louisiana, most notably in the Delta, where Isleños from the Canary Islands farmed in settlements such as New Iberia. Today, the Spanish language in Louisiana survives on the Delacroix Islands.

Spanish settlements were rare on the eve of the Civil War; only Louisiana claimed more than 1,000 Spanish immigrants. Beginning in the 1850s, the pace of Spanish emigration quickened because of economic, political, and diplomatic developments, as Spain wished to increase its loyalist population abroad. Key West emerged as a significant refuge during the Ten Years' War in Cuba (1868–78). A number of Spanish cigar manufacturers relocated their beleaguered factories in Key West, creating a thriving American institution with the skills imported from Cuba and Spain.

Later, during the mass influx of "new" immigrants between 1890 and 1921, relatively few Spaniards entered the United States, and even fewer migrated to the South. Spain encouraged emigration to its own colonies, especially Cuba, and Florida became a safety valve in times of political turmoil for Hispanics on that island. Tampa, Fla., evolved into the greatest Spanish American enclave outside of New York City. In 1885 Spanish manufacturers Vicente Martínez Ybor and Ignacio Haya, after considering offers from Galveston, Mobile, and Pensacola, chose Tampa as the new center for their cigar industry. Ybor City, organized as a company town in 1886 and soon incorporated into Tampa, attracted thousands of *tabaqueros* (Spanish, Cubans, and Italians), called "Latin" in the vernacular. By 1900 over 1,000 Spanish workers—many in highly skilled positions—had settled in Tampa, providing the organizing genius for the city's 100 cigar factories. In contrast, the next-largest Spanish center in the South was New Orleans, with 493 Spaniards. By 1920 almost 4,000 Spaniards (and 5,000 Cubans) had created a cohesive Latin culture in Tampa.

Spanish immigrants left a rich legacy of organizations. In 1887 Spanish doctors organized La Iguala, the first of many medical cooperatives in Tampa; these group enterprises aroused antipathy from the American medical establishment. Spaniards also erected magnificent clubhouses to house their mutual aid societies, Centro Español and Centro Asturiano. These societies provided complete medical care with the erection of modern hospitals amid a thriving cultural milieu. During the Spanish-American War in 1898, the U.S. Army took over Centro Español. During the New Deal, the Centro Asturiano housed America's only WPA Spanish-language theater. The stringent immigration quotas imposed in 1924 severely curtailed the Spanish population flow to America, an act especially injurious to the Spanish because of the imbalance of men over women.

A small but forceful group of Spanish anarchists coalesced in Ybor City between the 1890s and 1920s, serving as social critics and intellectual leaders. They supplied a class ideology that helped shape a labor consciousness of lasting power. Moreover, through their clubs, newspapers, educational work, and debating forums, they articulated a leftist orientation to the social problems of the day. By the 1920s the radical edge of the Ybor City labor movement had dulled. The labor wars of attrition had taken their toll, as had vigilante police tactics, especially evident during the long strikes of 1901, 1910, and 1920 and the Red Scare (1918–19).

The South's trajectory has come full circle in the new millennium. A region once part of New Spain has again witnessed an astounding upsurge of *hispanidad*. The South's Hispanic population (principally Mexican outside Florida) exploded in the 1980s and 1990s. Hispanic population growth was especially dramatic in states that had historically hosted relatively few immigrants. North Carolina's Hispanic population grew by almost 400 percent in the 1990s, only slightly higher than Arkansas (337 percent) and Georgia (300 percent).

GARY R. MORMINO
University of South Florida

Gilbert Din, *The Canary Islanders of Louisiana* (1988); R. A. Gomez, *The Americas* (July 1962); Gary Mormino, *Land of Sun-*

shine, *State of Dreams: A Social History of Modern Florida* (2005); George Pozzetta and Gary Mormino, *The Immigrant World of Ybor City* (1987); *Southern Folklore Quarterly* (1937–41); David Weber, *The Spanish Frontier in North America* (1992); Glenn Westfall, *Don Vicente Martínez Ybor, the Man and His Empire* (1987).

Swiss

As many as 10,000 Swiss may have settled in the South in the colonial era. By 1790 the descendants of Swiss colonial immigrants are thought to have numbered 389,000. Immigration continued throughout the 19th century, and 1920 census estimates revealed that 1.019 million Americans were of Swiss descent. Later in the 20th century, Swiss professionals pursued careers in industrial or research centers and have settled in significant numbers in southern towns such as Spartanburg, S.C. Over 86,000 southerners indicated Swiss as their first ancestry in the 2000 census.

The first known Swiss on southern soil was Diebold von Erlach, a member of the French Huguenot expedition establishing Charlesfort (in present-day South Carolina) in 1563. In 1607 some "Switzers" served as craftsmen at Jamestown, and in 1687 Jean François Gignilliat of Vevey, Switzerland, received a 3,000-acre land grant from the South Carolina Proprietors. In 1709 Baron Christoph von Graffenried established New Bern, N.C. In 1732 Jean Pierre Purry founded Purrysburg 20 miles upriver from Savannah, Ga., and brought some 450 people to the Carolinas, among them the portrait painter Jeremiah Theus. Johannes Tobler settled in new Windsor and led about 100 Swiss to South Carolina. John J. Zubly [Züblin] from St. Gallen, a pastor in Savannah, Ga., served as Georgia delegate to the Second Continental Congress, but he opposed independence. Between the 1750s and 1780s the French Swiss Henry Bouquet, the brothers Prévost (Jacques, Augustin, and Marc), and Frédéric Haldimand were high-ranking officers in British service. Three insightful novels by Carol Williams of Lexington, S.C., feature 18th-century Swiss immigrants in the Congarees.

In 1817 the Virginia lawyer William Wirt, born to Swiss immigrants in Bladensburg, Md., became U.S. attorney general. In 1848 French-Swiss "Plymouth Brethren" formed a religious community in Knoxville, Tenn. Among numerous Swiss who served in the Confederate army during the Civil War was the three-time congressman from Tennessee, Brigadier General Felix K. Zollicoffer, whose family hailed from Canton St. Gallen. Henry Hotze was born in Zurich, grew up in Mobile, Ala., and was an effective propagandist of the southern cause in Europe. In 1865 Henry Wirz from Zurich was appointed commandant of Georgia's Andersonville Prison for Union soldiers and later was executed by the U.S. government on controversial mistreatment charges. In the 1880s Peter Staub of Bilten, Canton Glarus, a businessman and three-time mayor of Knoxville, Tenn., promoted the settlement Gruetli-Lager in Grundy County,

Thoni descendants dedicating a historical marker to an ancestral Swiss immigrant in Grundy County, Tenn. (Photograph courtesy of Lynda Harper, archivist, Grundy County Swiss Historical Society)

which by 1886 counted some 330 Swiss. In 1881 two Swiss entrepreneurs initiated Bernstadt, a settlement in Laurel County, Ky., which by 1888 was home to about 1,000 people; other Swiss went to East Bernstadt, Grünheim, and Crab Orchard in Lincoln County. Cities such as Louisville, Ky., had in 1889 some 900 Swiss who, like those in other cities, founded benevolent and social associations whose members congregated in the "Swiss Park" from about 1850 to the 1990s.

The U.S. Census counted 134 Swiss in Texas in 1850 and 453 in 1860. Jacob Boll (1828–80) worked as a botanist who identified 32 Texas species of extinct vertebrates. In Dallas, which in the late 1880s counted some 200 Swiss, Benjamin Lang served as a post–Civil War mayor and U.S. district commissioner. Getulius Kellersberger (1821–

1900), in Texas since the late 1840s, was a noted engineer and surveyor who served in the Confederate army. George H. Hermann (1843–1914) of Houston and Henry Rosenberg (1824–93) of Galveston were successful businessmen and philanthropists, while the Italian Swiss Cesar M. Lombardi (1845–1919) was a Houston grain merchant and publisher. Edward W. Eberle (1864–1929), born of Swiss parents in Denton, northwest of Dallas, became superintendent of the Naval Academy in 1915 and was involved in the U.S. Navy's modernization efforts.

Historically, most Swiss throughout the South lived so-called ordinary lives, but a good number of their descendants are actively involved in shaping the South's vibrant culture. Today, Swiss organizations exist in many large cities across the South, including Nashville,

Tenn., Sarasota, Fla., Houston, Tex., Charlotte, N.C., and Spartanburg, S.C. — many of which have popular "fondue evenings" and Swiss musical and dance performances.

LEO SCHELBERT
University of Illinois at Chicago

John Paul von Grüningen, ed., *Swiss in the United States* (1940); Adelrich Steinach, ed., *Swiss Colonists in 19th-Century America* (in German, 1889; with new introduction and indexes by Urspeter Schelbert, 1995); Leo Schelbert, ed., *America Experienced: Eighteenth and Nineteenth Century Accounts of Swiss Immigrants to the United States* (2004); Herman E. Baumann, *Baldwin County's Bit of Switzerland* (1999).

Syrians and Lebanese

Arab immigrants from Syria and Lebanon first began to arrive in America in the late 1870s. About 25 percent settled, either initially or eventually, in southern states. Almost exclusively Christian, these early Arab immigrants included a few Protestants and mostly sects affiliated with the Roman Catholic Church (Maronites, Melkites, and Chaldean Catholics) and with Eastern Orthodox churches. The persecution of Christians in the Muslim Ottoman Empire encouraged emigration, as did economics, the desire to escape military duty, and the lure of America.

Most Syrian and Lebanese immigrants were unskilled and subsisted in their native land on small family farms. The modified plantation system they encountered in the South, characterized by tenancy and sharecropping, was completely alien. Many hoped to

make money and return to their homeland and were not interested in settling on farmland. The preferred occupation of these early immigrants was peddling household goods from farmhouse to farmhouse. Peddling required little capital and minimal command of English. The South's vast rural areas, lacking easy access to stores, provided a ready market, as did the coal-mining towns of Kentucky, Virginia, and West Virginia.

By the 1890s peddlers had become suppliers and, eventually, shopkeepers. By 1910 Syrian and Lebanese communities thrived in places such as Beaumont and Texarkana, Tex., Valdosta, Ga., Lake Charles, La., Vicksburg, Miss., and Roanoke, Va. A *Syrian Business Directory* of 1908 listed approximately 50 Arab-owned businesses in Alabama, 60 in Georgia, 65 in Mississippi, over 100 in Virginia, and over 150 in both Louisiana and Texas; over 70 percent of these businesses were grocers and dry goods stores.

As Arab immigrants became more settled and visible, they encountered considerable prejudice. In 1907 Alabama congressman John Burnett, protesting the influx of immigrants, declared, "I regard the Syrian and peoples from other parts of Asia Minor as the most undesirable, and the South Italians, Poles, and Russians next." In Georgia (1909) and South Carolina (1914 and 1923), court cases challenged the right of Syrians and Lebanese to naturalization.

In response to prejudice, and to preserve their heritage from the forces

The Ellises, a first-generation Lebanese American family, mother with children, Port Gibson, Miss., 1921 (Photograph courtesy of James G. Thomas Jr.)

of assimilation, Syrians and Lebanese began to form local clubs and associations. In 1931 over 400 representatives from dozens of these clubs throughout the South created an umbrella organization, the Southern Federation of Syrian Lebanese American Clubs. The federation's annual convention became an important political venue for discussing common concerns and a social venue for those seeking suitable spouses. Along with the local club, the church served as the center of social and cultural life for Syrians and Lebanese. Although most were Christians, the early immigrants were members of uniquely Middle Eastern sects, and thus tended to build their own churches instead of joining established ones; this also allowed them to conduct reli-

gious services in their own language. Under pressure to assimilate, however, some left their "ethnic" churches in the mid-20th century for Roman Catholic or Protestant congregations, and many Syrians and Lebanese changed or modified their names; for example, "Tannous" became "Thomas," "Elias" became "Ellis," and "Haddad" became "Smith."

By the 1970s the grandchildren of the early Syrian and Lebanese immigrants identified as Americans and southerners. Exogamy has become common, and the primary links to a Syrian or Lebanese heritage are church affiliations; foodways such as *kibbe* (baked ground lamb), *tabouleh* (a bulgur wheat salad), and stuffed grape leaves; and the use of a few Arabic words of endearment. The Southern Federation of Syrian Lebanese American Clubs remains active and as of 2006 had affiliated clubs in every southern state.

A new wave of immigration from the Middle East began in the 1970s, motivated by civil war in Lebanon, general regional conflict, and a relaxation in U.S. immigration laws. Many of these new immigrants are Muslims. Some come to attend universities and later decide to stay. Many are professionals or academicians and tend to settle in locales such as Houston, Miami, Atlanta, Birmingham, and the suburbs of Washington, D.C., in Northern Virginia.

Noted southerners of Syrian or Lebanese ancestry include Dr. Michael Debakey, renowned heart surgeon; U.S. congressmen Nick Rahall (West Virginia) and Chris John (Louisiana); Joe Robbie, former owner of the NFL's Miami Dolphins; Bobby Rahal, professional race car driver; Joseph Jamail, prominent Houston defense attorney; Robert C. Khayat, chancellor of the University of Mississippi; Richard Ieyoub, attorney general of Louisiana; and Tommy Hazouri, former mayor of Jacksonville.

WILLIAM MARK HABEEB
Arlington, Virginia

Naff Arab-American Collection, Archives Center, National Museum of American History, Smithsonian Institution, Washington, D.C.; Eric J. Hooglund, ed., *Crossing the Waters: Arabic-Speaking Immigrants to the United States before 1940* (1987); Gregory Orfalea, *Before the Flames: A Quest for the History of Arab Americans* (1988); Afif Tannous, *American Sociological Review* (June 1943).

Texans

While on the South's western border, Texas (particularly the eastern half of the state) has a southern history. Some Texans identify with the South, but all Texans have a distinct identity within the region and the nation. The modern history of Texas traditionally dates from 1822, when settlers from the Upper South began to take advantage of the Spanish and then the Mexican governments' offers of free land to farming families who would settle in this outermost part of Mexico. By 1835 Texas was heavily populated with these white southerners and their slaves, who together outnumbered the native Indian groups and the pockets of Mexican settlers at the forts of Bexar and Nacogdoches.

In 1836 the six-week Texas Revolution made the former colony of Mexico an independent nation. The trauma of the deaths of those defending the Alamo and the final victory over the Mexican president Santa Anna at the battle of San Jacinto became defining moments for Texans. Part of the "heroic" westward expansion of the times, early Texas history fostered a unique identity within the South.

During the years when Texas was a separate nation under the larger-than-life president of the republic, Sam Houston, Texans developed a strong sense of identity that endures to the present. At his presidential inauguration, George W. Bush tellingly read the famous letter by William B. Travis.

Travis was commander of the Alamo and his letter, addressed "To the People of Texas and All Americans in the World," declared he would never surrender or retreat and ended with the vow, "Victory or Death."

The history and identity of Texans have become fixed in the American imagination and mythologized in history books, novels, and films (*The Alamo, Hud, The Last Picture Show, Giant, Urban Cowboy,* and *Lonesome Dove* are among the most memorable Texas-themed movies). The sometimes fierce sense of difference from other Americans that Texans profess is one that newcomers to the state readily adopt as they become part of the Texas culture. Often this means taking on the cowboy persona—an antimodernity, antiintellectual attitude that extols love of sky and spaciousness, closeness to the land, willingness to "go it alone," and common sense folk knowledge. Texan identity is also based on a wry, ironic sense of humor combined with blunt speech, exaggeration, and bluster. Humorous writers such as J. Frank Dobie, William Brammer, Molly Ivins, Larry L. King, and Kinky Friedman and politicians such as Sam Houston, Lyndon Baines Johnson, and Ann Richards have all played up a Texan identity with self-deprecating jest and hyperbole.

Besides Anglo-Protestant Texans, Mexicans have been the most influential cultural group in Texas. They share Catholicism with the many Irish, German, and Czech immigrants to the state. Many Hispanic Texans speak Spanish or "Tex-Mex" (a hybrid of Spanish and English), eat Tex-Mex cuisine (tamales, tortilla soup, and chili), and wear Mexican-derived *vaquero* (cowboy) hats and boots. In Texas politics, patron-client relationships are the norm, and the Mexican style of storytelling and exaggeration has become a Texas tradition.

While immigrants from the Upper South brought slaves with them to Texas, Mexicans there were opposed to slavery. After Texas independence, slavery was a primary reason why the United States was reluctant to make Texas a state. Texas acquired statehood in 1845, seceded from the Union in 1860, and fought with the Confederacy. Texan slaves learned of the Emancipation Proclamation on 19 June 1865, and the date is now celebrated with "Juneteenth" festivities by Texans of all ethnic backgrounds and by African Americans across the country. After the Civil War, poverty was widespread, and Texas was more isolated from the United States. The coming of the railroad at the end of the 19th century provided a small boost to the state, but it was the early 20th-century discovery of oil that catapulted it into prominence nationally and internationally and added the "Texas oil man" dimension to stereotypical Texan identity.

The pre–Civil War cattle industry remains a strong part of the Texas economy and identity. Owning a "ranch" is a personal statement of Texanness. Seemingly every Texas politician has one, although many would-be ranchers are derided as being "all hat, no cattle."

Texans are a diverse group that includes a large Mexican population,

African Americans, descendants of English, Irish, and Scottish southerners, and those of direct immigrants from Ireland, Germany, and Czechoslovakia. The product of a unique creolization, the Texan identity remains distinct within the South and the nation and is an identity to which recent immigrants from around the globe still assimilate even in an age of multiculturalism.

ANNE H. SUTHERLAND
University of California, Riverside

Molly Ivins, *Molly Ivins Can't Say That, Can She?* (1992); Don Graham, *Giant Country: Essays on Texas* (1998).

Tigua Indians of Ysleta del Sur Pueblo

The Tigua Indians of suburban El Paso, Tex., present one of the most remarkable cases of ethnic persistence on the American landscape. The modern Tigua are descendants of Tiwa-speaking Indians from Isleta Pueblo on the Rio Grande in central New Mexico. Following the Pueblo Revolt of 1680, refugees and captives from Isleta accompanied retreating Spaniards downriver to El Paso del Norte, where a new pueblo and mission were established. The new settlement was called Ysleta del Sur, and the inhabitants received a land grant from the king of Spain in 1751.

Since that time, while generally assimilating into the regional Hispanic culture, the Tigua have also preserved a distinct Native American identity. They have always maintained their own government, using Spanish titles such as *cacique* (chief) and *capitán de guerra* (war captain) in the manner of the Pueblo Indians. A *tusla*, or ceremonial lodge, has always been at the heart of the community. During the 1800s the Tigua served as Indian scouts, fighting alongside Mexicans and Texas Rangers to defend the area from Kiowas and Apaches. Well into the 20th century they continued to dry farm and hunt deer and rabbits in the surrounding desert while gardening in their irrigated mission neighborhood.

Anglo speculators defrauded the Tigua of much of their original Texas lands after the Mexican War. Because Texas was part of the Confederacy when Lincoln granted land patents to various tribes along the Rio Grande, the Tigua did not receive federal protection. Maneuvers to transfer titles, involving disregard of the Spanish grant and the ultimately illegal incorporation of Ysleta between 1871 and 1874, left the Tigua destitute. By the early 1900s tribe members had congregated in an area a few blocks east of the old pueblo. This neighborhood became known as El Barrio de los Indios, though the Tigua grew somewhat less visible as Indians, having adopted the Spanish language and Mexican American dress, foodways, and wage-work patterns.

Ysleta was annexed by the city of El Paso in 1955, and the impoverished Tiguas faced onerous property taxation. They responded with a campaign to secure protection as a surviving Indian tribe, achieving state recognition in 1967 and federal status the following year. Arguments for their Indian identity rested on continuing Puebloan traditions. The *cacique* kept a white rooster caged in front of his house, analogous to the traditional chief's emblem of a captive eagle. The community held ceremonies honoring a kachina spirit called *Awelo* (from Spanish *abuelo*, meaning "grandfather") and the patron of the New Mexico pueblo, Saint Anthony. Tigua households had *hornos*, Puebloan bread ovens, in their yards. There were still traces of matrilineal clans and the Tiwa language. A stylized sun pictograph at Hueco Tanks, a syenite formation in the desert northeast of Ysleta used as a campsite by many tribes, was attributed to the Tigua and cited as further evidence of their native heritage.

Under state and then federal trusteeship, the Tigua built a reservation, transforming Ysleta with modern housing and a tourist complex, which became the showcase for retained, revived, and newly imported customs, including dances and pottery making. They began efforts to restore the Tiwa language. The tribal rolls grew as individuals who previously did not acknowledge Indian ancestry emerged to claim a Tigua identity.

Acting as a sovereign nation, the tribe opened a casino in 1994. Revenues from the operation reached $60 million per year, and the reservation became a major employer and economic generator for El Paso. Litigation that the tribe had begun to restore land losses was suspended as the Tigua were able to buy tracts outright, from lots around the old pueblo to a huge game ranch near Valentine, Tex. Tribe members enjoyed annual per capita distributions and developed a superb community infrastructure, including cradle-to-grave social services, civic buildings, restaurants, a chain of convenience stores, and an upscale housing complex in the neighboring town of Socorro. A challenge to Indian gaming from the state of Texas, however, led to a U.S. Supreme Court decision against the Tigua in February 2002, and the casino was shut down. Their economic future is uncertain, but some 1,200 Tiguas still benefit from recent gains, and their Indian identity appears secure.

DANIEL J. GELO
University of Texas at San Antonio

Rex Gerald, in *Apache Indians III*, ed. David Agee Horr (1974); Nicholas P. Houser, in *Handbook of North American Indians, Volume 9: Southwest*, ed. Alfonso Ortiz (1979); Bill Wright, *The Tiguas: Pueblo Indians of Texas* (1993).

Travellers

Although they are often referred to as "Gypsies," the Travellers have quite separate origins from Romani people. Travellers have formed communities across the South from Florida to Texas and maintain social networks between them. Travellers sometimes refer to each other as "Pavee" and to non-Pavee as "country people." To varying degrees, they retain their own form of speech, which they call the "Cant" and which some scholars call "Gammon." The Cant is a derivative of the argot of Travellers in Ireland (often called "Shelta" in Ireland), which has an English-based syntax and a core vocabulary from Irish Gaelic.

Some theories suggest that Travellers are descended from Irish "spalpeens," landless and seasonally migrant farm laborers who took to the road perma- nently because of evictions, poverty, and famine. Many Irish Travellers were metalworkers and were called "Tink- ers" (now a highly pejorative term) because of the sounds of tinsmithing. They sold tin mugs and repaired tin ware and other objects, performed odd jobs such as cleaning chimneys, and became famed as horse dealers in Ire- land (some of the same livelihoods they pursued in the South). Travellers may have come to the South as indentured servants prior to 1800, but the majority descend from Irish and Scottish Trav- eller families who came to America in the 19th century. They arrived mostly in Boston, New York City, and Pittsburgh and then made their way south after the Civil War. Today, the more affluent Travellers may visit Ireland or import Irish goods and Catholic icons for their homes.

Travellers are generally Roman Catholic and often give generous dona- tions to their local parishes. Women may attend Mass every morning, and men go on Sundays, although they may remain outside talking and enter the church only to take Holy Commu- nion. Priests play an important role mediating between exclusive Traveller communities and the outside world. Murphy Village near North Augusta, S.C., is named for a 1960s Catholic priest, Father Joseph Murphy, who helped the Travellers acquire land and settle.

In Murphy Village many Travellers have built sizable homes in a distinctive architectural style with multiple gables and large windows. While the older

generations and women stay in Murphy Village, men travel across the country in the spring and summer as pavers, roofers, lightening rod installers, barn painters, or landscapers. They some- times have regular, seasonal customers, but they are also widely known for scamming the unsuspecting and even banking institutions. When children are not in school, many Traveller families still go on the road together. Travellers based in Forth Worth, Tex., leave for the road at Eastertide with large mobile homes and return again in Septem- ber or October. The community has now purchased a mobile home park, and some Travellers have built houses nearby. For the community based out of Memphis, Tenn., the traveling sea- son may last from Easter until October or November. The same pattern takes place in large communities in Atlanta and Dallas.

Travellers are endogamous, mar- riages are often arranged, and a dowry is still expected. Murphy Village is home to about 545 families, all of whom have one of just 13 surnames. More than 200 families have the surname Carrol; the next-largest group is named Riley, followed by Sherlock. Other common surnames include Costello, Carpenter, Gormon, Lewis, McNalley, O'Hara, Roche, Sheedy, Joyce, and Hartnet. Until recently, divorce was quite rare. A strong emphasis on community and extended family means that the elderly are always given care within the home and that hundreds, or thousands, of Travellers from multiple communities attend funerals, weddings, and chris- tenings. While young people frequent local restaurants and shopping malls and enjoy active social lives, they do not as often mix with "country people," as many leave public school by the eighth or ninth grade, when boys generally join their male relatives on the road. To avoid outside influences, many are homeschooled. Some Catholic parishes offer GED programs especially for Traveller teenagers. A few southern Travellers have left their communities to become medical doctors and academics.

Travellers are the subject of rumor and exposé television shows such as *Dateline* and *20/20* (which focus on their scamming activities) and several works of fiction. The gritty 1997 film *Traveller*, written by Jim McGylnn, tells the story of a young man's return to a North Carolina community from which he is descended. The 2004 work of juvenile fiction by Kim Ablon Whitney, *See You down the Road* (about a young woman considering abandoning the Traveller life), begins in Florida. While they are magnanimous with the "country people" they befriend, their unsavory interactions with outsiders are what characterize public perceptions of Travellers. Except for the work of Jared Harper in Georgia, their lives have not been ethnographically documented in the South and much about their communities remains veiled.

CELESTE RAY
University of the South

George Gmelch, *The Irish Tinkers* (1977); Ian Hancock, *American Speech* (Fall 1986); Jared Harper, "The Irish Travellers of Georgia" (Ph.D. dissertation, University of Georgia, 1977), in *The Not So Solid South: Anthropological Studies in a Regional Subculture*, ed. Kenneth Morland (1971); Jane Leslie Helleiner, *Irish Travellers: Racism and the Politics of Culture* (2000); May McCann, Séamas O Síocháin and Joseph Ruane, *Irish Travellers: Culture and Ethnicity* (1994).

Tunica-Biloxi

The Tunica-Biloxi Tribe of Louisiana is the result of a 20th-century merger of historically distinct tribes, the Tunica and remnants of the Biloxi, Avoyel, and Ofo (all of the Mississippi Valley). The Tunica was the larger of the groups prior to their merger in the 1920s and spoke a different language from the Biloxi (the last Tunica speaker died in the 1930s). Although their initial contact with Europeans may date to Hernando de Soto's mid-16th century expedition, the first documented reports of definitive European contact with the Tunica date from 150 years later, with the mission work of French priests François de Montigny and Antoine Davion and their accompanying layman Jean-Baptiste La Source.

By this time, the Tunica had migrated south from the region in which they may have encountered de Soto and were residing in villages near where the Yazoo River meets the Mississippi. Davion established a mission and worked with the tribe for 20 years. This connection helped foster a close relationship with the French that would last throughout the colonial period. During the 18th century the Tunica were important allies for the French in their wars with the Natchez and other Mississippi

Valley tribes. By the time of the Louisiana Purchase (1803), the Tunica had again moved, this time into present-day Louisiana on the Prairie des Avoyelles, near the current location of Marksville, where they would largely remain into the early 20th century.

Much less is known of the Biloxi tribe, which spoke a language in the Siouan language family and whose ancestral lands were located on the eponymous Biloxi Bay on the Mississippi Gulf Coast. The French were again likely the first Europeans to contact them when, in 1699, the explorer Pierre Le Moyne, Sieur d'Iberville, and his brother Jean-Baptiste Le Moyne, Sieur de Bienville, visited one of their villages. Increasing pressures from both French colonialists and other native tribes, particularly the Choctaw, led to a number of westward movements during the 18th century. By the end of the century the Biloxi had also settled near Marksville in Avoyelles Parish and at Bayou Boeuf in Rapides Parish, near Alexandria. Over time, the tribes came under French, English, and Spanish colonizing powers, eventually facing the challenge of resisting assimilation into American society.

Proximity and persistent population loss on the part of both tribes led to their merger in the 1920s under the leadership of Elijah Barbry. The population further declined during the Great Depression, when perhaps half of the tribe left to find work in Texas. The last chief, Joseph Pierite (whose family was considered Biloxi), revived the campaign for official government recognition in the 1960s. The Tunica gained state recognition in 1975 and federal recognition under the U.S. Department of the Interior in the 1981, officially becoming the Tunica-Biloxi Tribe of Louisiana. The united tribe resides on a 740-acre reservation south of Marksville with an estimated population of near 1,000 members. The Tunica-Biloxi were one of the first American Indian tribes to operate a tribal museum with an artifact preservation program. The program came about through the need to conserve the "Tunica Treasure," native and European items from the colonial period taken from Tunica graves and kept at Harvard University with poor conservation. The Tunica regained the treasure only after litigation that set precedents for the later Native American Graves Protection and Repatriation Act.

Under the guidance of current chairman Earl J. Barbry Sr., the Tunica opened Paragon Casino and Resort, Louisiana's first land-based casino, in 1994. The casino employs over 1,700 persons and helps the tribe maintain self-sufficiency.

BENJAMIN D. MARSEE
University of Tennessee

Jeffrey Brain, George Roth, and Willem J. de Reuse, in *Handbook of North American Indians, Volume 14: Southeast*, ed. Raymond Fogelson (2004); Hiram F. Gregory, in *Native America in the Twentieth Century*, ed. Mary B. Davis (1994); Michelle K. Moran, in *The Gale Encyclopedia of Native American Tribes*, ed. Sharon Malinowski and Anna Sheets (1998); Kenneth Shepherd, in *The Gale Encyclopedia of Native American Tribes*, ed. Sharon Malinowski and Anna Sheets (1998); John R. Swanton, *The Indian Tribes of North America* (1952).

Turks

Since World War II, Turks have come to the United States predominantly for higher education, aided by immigration policies that favor elite professionals and skilled laborers over unskilled workers. High unemployment in Turkey since the 1960s, waves of economic crises and political strife, and negative reception of Turks in Western Europe have brought many Turks to the United States. Ethnic Turks have also immigrated from all the Turkic countries (Azerbaijan, Kazakhstan, Kyrgyzstan, Turkish Republic of Northern Cyprus, Turkmenistan, and Uzbekistan). Between 185,000 and 210,000 ethnic Turks had come to live in the United States by 1995.

In the South, Turks have created state and regional cultural associations in Florida, Georgia, and Washington, D.C. Members of many of these associations meet to share food, network, enjoy performances of Turkish music, or watch soccer games. At some gatherings, non-Turks are welcomed, and prizes of Turkish dolls, fabrics, or crafts may be raffled in aid of a community cause. Turkish groceries, cafés, and restaurants have now opened in southern locations as diverse as Cary, N.C., Chesapeake, Va., Newport, Ky., Dallas, and Atlanta. Since many Turks come to the South for higher education, Turkish student associations have been established near colleges and universities in Alabama, Florida, Georgia, Kentucky, Maryland, North Carolina, South Carolina, Texas, Virginia, and Washington, D.C. These associations promote Turkish culture and the maintenance of Turkish identity through public celebration of secular Turkish national holidays, Turkish-language classes, patronage of Turk-owned businesses, and organization of support for Turkish musical groups, films, athletes, and diplomats.

Most Turks in the South are Muslims, and some southern mosques are associated with the American Muslim Turkish Association. Muslim religious holidays, such as Seker Bayrami and Kurban Bayrami—the two holidays that mark the end of Ramazan (Ramadan) and the end of the Hajj, respectively—are usually celebrated privately, although the cultural associations often serve as ways for people to meet each other for more intimate gatherings. The celebration of the Children's Day National Holiday (23 April) in Atlanta, sponsored by the Turkish American Cultural Association of Georgia, consists of performances of several children's groups from the area who represent Turkish and other world cultures. Displays of Turkish folk arts, foods, and history line the hallways of the elementary school where the celebration is held, along with displays celebrating the cultures of other students who attend the school.

In private get-togethers, Turks are likely to invite guests from other cultures and take pride in being generous hosts. Foods served often include Turkish specialties such as *Çerkez tavu u* (Circassian chicken with walnuts), *böreks* (pastries) filled with meats or spinach and feta cheese, and Turkish tea as well as American-style hamburgers and southern pecan pie.

Most immigrants from Turkey to the South have arrived since the 1960s and have aligned themselves with light-skinned peoples in the racial status quo. In Atlanta, for example, Turks have primarily settled in European American middle- and upper-class neighborhoods to the north and northeast of downtown, but they do not live in ethnically segregated neighborhoods. Correspondingly, the activities of Turkish cultural associations primarily appeal to the middle- and upper-class immigrant populations from Turkey. Public presentation of Turkish identity reflects the Turkish national cultural ideal of an upper-class, western-oriented lifestyle. Thus, southern cultural associations may aid many Turks in making initial contacts with each other and maintaining communities in which to speak their language and share their experiences in a new land, but they may also distance other ethnic Turks who do not necessarily identify with the western image of Turkish identity that such associations project.

PATRICIA FOGARTY
Emory University

Tuscaroras

The Tuscarora are one of at least four Indian nations (the other three being Cherokee, Meherrin, and Nottoway) with Iroquoian linguistic affiliations that originally migrated out of northern Appalachia into Virginia and the Carolinas during the late prehistoric period. Archaeological evidence suggests that the ancestral Tuscarora first settled in northeastern North Carolina about 900–1000 A.D. These early

Tuscarora peoples eventually displaced or absorbed the Indian societies they encountered in the region between the Roanoke and Neuse River Valleys by 1200–1400 A.D. The Tuscarora inhabited their southern homeland for nearly a millennium before they were ultimately driven out of the South in the face of war and colonial oppression between 1713 and 1803. Today, most federally recognized Tuscaroras live on the Tuscarora Reservation in New York, where they retain their cultural identity, speak their native language, and continue to practice elements of social or political customs that have ancient roots.

Unlike many historically known Indian nations in the South, the Tuscarora were not culturally associated with southeastern Mississippian societies. Historic Tuscarora cultural practices were more closely associated with the Woodland societies of the Mid-Atlantic region. Tuscarora settlements in North Carolina included palisaded villages and dispersed farmsteads located along rivers and tributary streams, as well as seasonal hunting and fishing camps. Tuscarora subsistence practices included a mix of hunting, fishing, and agriculture, with maize, squash, and beans as major crops. Wild floral resources were seasonally gathered and included, among other items, leafy greens and herbs, berries and fruits, tubers, nuts, and goosefoot or amaranth seeds ground for flour. Hunting efforts focused on white-tailed deer and other mammals, especially during the fall and winter seasons, but Tuscarora communities relied most heavily on aquatic resources such as turtles, freshwater mussels, and fish throughout the year. The subsistence focus on farming and fishing in an environment rich in wild resources enhanced the development of a nearly sedentary society with a ranked social structure well before the period of European settlement in eastern North Carolina.

Contacts with armed European settlers and traders after 1650 led to the European enslavement of Tuscarora peoples, bitter trade disputes, and colonial encroachment of Tuscarora settlement lands and hunting territories. Conflicts between all indigenous inhabitants of eastern North Carolina and European settlers erupted well before the end of the 17th century. While the region's coastal Algonkian chiefdoms were significantly diminished from disease and warfare by 1700, the Tuscarora remained a populous sociopolitical entity that was relatively unaffected by war or European diseases until 1711. Tuscarora influence in colonial affairs during the early 1700s was due to their sizable warrior population (1,200–1,500 armed men) and their strong cultural and political ties with the powerful northern Iroquois Confederacy (the Five Nations).

Tuscarora hegemony over eastern North Carolina ended in March 1713 when the Tuscarora, in the wake of the Barnwell Expedition (1711–12), were defeated by an expeditionary force of some 1,000 South Carolina militiamen and Indian mercenaries at the Battle of Neoheroka Fort, the last major engagement of the Tuscarora War (1711–15). There, Colonel James Moore's well-armed force of Indian auxiliaries besieged the fortification near the Tuscarora community of Neoheroka and killed or enslaved some 900 Tuscarora men, women, and children. The defeated Lower Tuscarora fled to New York, where they eventually became the Sixth Nation of the Iroquois Confederacy in 1722.

The Upper Tuscarora communities, situated between the Roanoke and Tar-Pamlico Rivers, remained neutral during the Tuscarora War and stayed in North Carolina for a time. In 1717 these Upper Tuscarora communities, pressured by Catawba Indian raiding parties, congregated on a small reservation. Punctuated migrations beginning in 1713 ended in 1803, when the Indian Woods Reservation was abandoned and the last politically cohesive community of Tuscaroras in North Carolina dispersed.

While most of the North Carolina Tuscaroras chose to resettle in New York during the period of the Tuscarora diaspora (1713–1803), some individuals and familial groups removed to other English colonies. Some relocated to environmentally marginal areas in North Carolina, and other small groups settled in Virginia, Pennsylvania, and South Carolina, where they intermarried with other ethnic groups and eventually disappeared into the fabric of history and legend. In the 1960s and 1970s, several North Carolina groups distinguished themselves from the Lumbee and reclaimed Tuscaroran identities. Four groups in and around Robeson County have petitioned unsuccessfully for federal recognition. The Tuscarora Nation East of the Mountains, the Tuscarora

Tribe of North Carolina, the Tuscarora Nation of North Carolina, and
the Tuscarora Nation of Kau-ta-noh
now have a combined population of
approximately 3,000 to 5,000 members.

CHARLES L. HEATH
*University of North Carolina at
Chapel Hill*

Douglas W. Boyce, in *Handbook of North
American Indians, Volume 15: Northeast*,
ed. Bruce G. Trigger (1978); John E. Byrd,
*Tuscarora Subsistence Practices in the Late
Woodland Period* (1997); David Landy,
in *Handbook of North American Indians,
Volume 15: Northeast*, ed. Bruce G. Trig-
ger (1978); John Lawson, *A New Voyage to
Carolina*, ed. Hugh T. Lefler (1984); E. Law-
rence Lee, *Indian Wars in North Carolina,
1663–1763* (1963); Thomas C. Parramore,
North Carolina Historical Review (July 1982,
October 1987); David S. Phelps, in *The
Prehistory of North Carolina: An Archaeo-
logical Symposium*, ed. Mark A. Mathis and
Jeffrey J. Crow (1983).

Vietnamese

Between 1800 and 1973, an estimated
6,000 Vietnamese lived in the United
States. This small figure changed when,
after the fall of Saigon in April 1975,
the U.S. government granted political
asylum to South Vietnamese refugees.
Many first arrived at resettlement centers in the South, such as Fort Chaffee,
Ark., and Eglin Air Force Base, Fla.
Local churches sponsored Vietnamese
individuals and families to resettle in
their communities. Many Vietnamese
with ties to the former Saigon regime
chose to live in the Washington, D.C.,
area. This began the huge influx of professional and middle-class Vietnamese
immigrants into Northern Virginia. As
a result of American military involvement in Southeast Asia, many southern
servicemen came home with Asian
wives, and many Vietnamese already
had relatives living in the South who
sponsored their relocation there.

Today's Vietnamese American population is likely to be 25 to 40 percent
higher than the 1,122,528 recorded in
the 2000 U.S. Census. Close behind
the West Coast with the second-largest
Vietnamese population in the country,
the South has a Vietnamese population of 335,679 according to the census,
or 30 percent of the total number of
Vietnamese Americans. If one adds
the 43,709 in the Washington, D.C.,
area—considered by the census to be
an eastern metropolitan area despite
its deep roots in southern culture and
history—then the already sizable number of Vietnamese southerners becomes
even larger.

The South's warm climate and continued economic prosperity during
the last several decades attracted Vietnamese refugees seeking a better life
after 30 years of bitter war. In addition to the Washington, D.C./Northern
Virginia area, the Vietnamese community has tended to congregate around
Houston, Dallas–Fort Worth, Atlanta,
and New Orleans. Other substantial
Vietnamese communities in the South
include Tampa and Orlando, Fla.,
Beaumont–Port Arthur, Tex., Charlotte
and Gastonia, N.C., and Rock Hill, S.C.

The French Catholic tradition of
New Orleans and southern Louisiana

is a strong draw for the Vietnamese given their long colonial relationship with France. Roughly 30 percent of all Vietnamese southerners are Roman Catholic. Moreover, the French-style architecture of traditional houses in the Creole country reminds Vietnamese people of the homes and buildings they left behind in their homeland. Like native New Orleanians, the Vietnamese love their strong-drip café au lait and crusty French bread. French cooking has enhanced the complex and subtle flavors of Vietnamese cuisine, and a popular Vietnamese lunch or snack is their own rendition of po' boys made with fried soft-shell crabs, grilled pork, or pâtés stuffed with carrot strips, cilantro, and jalapeños. Today, New Orleans brims with Vietnamese restaurants. But as the Vietnamese become American southerners, they are assimilating the local southern culture while adding their own flavors.

Vietnamese culture emphasizes strong family ties and community awareness. Although the majority of non-Catholic Vietnamese practice a form of Mahayana Buddhism derived from China, all Vietnamese are steeped in the ethics and values of Confucianism with its focus on duty, obligation, and filial piety. Vietnamese tradition puts a premium on respect for the elderly. The reverence for education is exceedingly strong, and Vietnamese parents push their children to achieve a good education. The Vietnamese find the southern emphases on sense of place, family, and community appealing cultural parallels.

The Gulf Coast proved popular for Vietnamese fishers arriving from seaside villages during the early 1980s. There they pooled resources to buy shrimping and fishing boats. Lacking the education and urban skills of the first wave who came to the United States after 1975, these second-wave immigrants tended to be economic rather than political refugees. In Gulf Coast port towns, where Vietnamese shrimpers settled in significant numbers, there were unfortunate tensions as the Ku Klux Klan tried exploiting the fears of native-born southern shrimpers who felt their way of life was being threatened by newcomers. Today there is a general acceptance of the Vietnamese, and both native and Vietnamese shrimpers together face severe competition from underpriced shrimp from China and Vietnam.

The Vietnamese in the South can be found mostly in suburban communities and have constructed shopping malls in Houston, New Orleans, Atlanta, and Falls Church, Va., to cater to their growing communities. Many work as professionals in southern universities, medical facilities, scientific labs, and high-tech companies found in North Carolina's Research Triangle Park and Tennessee's Oak Ridge area.

Today, the Vietnamese American community represents the third-largest Asian community in the United States. The increase in intercultural marriages and the globalization of American foodways also mean that Vietnamese restaurants and shops are becoming popular among other southerners. The

Vietnamese are one of the latest waves of newcomers to the South who are successfully introducing their own unique ingredients into the southern cultural gumbo.

ALPHONSE VINH
National Public Radio

Nathan Caplan, John K. Whitmore, and Marcella H. Choy, *The Boat People and Achievement in America: A Study of Family Life and Cultural Values* (1989); David Haines, *Refugees as Immigrants: Cambodians, Laotians, and Vietnamese in America* (1989); Kali Tal, *Southeast Asian-American Communities* (1992).

Waccamaw-Siouans

Located primarily in North Carolina's coastal plain in Bladen and Columbus Counties, the Waccamaw-Siouan tribe traces it roots back to the 17th century. In the 1670s John Swanton noted that elements of the tribe were reported to be on South Carolina's Pee Dee River in the company of the Winyaw and Pedee tribes. By 1700 John Lawson, the celebrated explorer who traveled much of the Carolina Backcountry, reported that the tribe known to locals as the "Woccon" (apparently another name for the Waccamaw) was not far from the Winyaw and a number of other Siouan-speaking tribes in the vicinity of the Neuse River.

While the original Waccamaw homeland was along the modern border between North and South Carolina, the warfare and unrest accompanying the movement of the colonial frontier brought such havoc to the Waccamaw and neighboring tribes that numbers of Indian people migrated to the North

Carolina coastal plain during the 17th and 18th centuries. Swanton suggested that a number might have allied with the Catawba (who were themselves an amalgamation of displaced native people) by the middle of the 18th century, but he thought that the largest numbers had moved north along the Lumber River in what is now North Carolina. Historian Douglas Rights came to a similar conclusion, writing that as early as 1715 "the Siouan tribes, Waccamaw, Peedee, Winyaw, Cape Fear, and other native tribes of the region . . . could find a natural inland retreat to the swampy regions of the Robeson County area, where they would be more secure than in the exposed neighborhood of the [white] settlements." Thomas Ross, who has written the most comprehensive survey of the tribe's history, believes that the Waccamaw were pushed out of South Carolina before 1600 and settled at the confluence of the Pee Dee and Waccamaw Rivers. In 1705 some elements moved north to the Lower Neuse River; they stayed there until 1718, when they moved to the Black River area. Two years later they moved yet again to the Lumber River, remaining there until 1733, when they settled around Lake Waccamaw and Green Swamp. They have remained in that locale to this day. County land records suggest that the Waccamaw-Siouan have held clear title to lands on Lake Waccamaw and Green Swamp since 1800.

While the Waccamaw-Siouan were invariably described in 19th-century census records as "free persons of color," they were also widely considered to be Indian people. As with a number of other southeastern tribes, the Waccamaw-Siouan used education to shield the tribe from some of the worst effects of Jim Crow legislation and the social segregation that Indian people experienced through the 1960s. As early as 1885, tribal members built and ran their own schools, funding them on a subscription basis. At least four all-Indian schools were opened in Buckhead between 1885 and 1934. In the early 1950s several high schools for Indian students also opened, including the Waccamaw Indian School, which was in operation between 1954 and 1969. These schools became crucial in the maintenance of tribal identity, and many Waccamaws viewed the era of desegregation with mixed emotions as it meant the loss of one of the tribe's most cherished institutions.

In 1970 the Waccamaw-Siouan began a powwow that continues as a two-day event that merges pan-Indian elements with local cultural traditions, symbols, and identity. The event is intertribal and includes a community parade to the powwow grounds and the selection of a "Miss Waccamaw" to represent her people at local, regional, and state gatherings.

The state of North Carolina officially recognized the Waccamaw-Siouan tribe in 1971, by which time the tribe had nearly a half-century's experience of governing itself. W. J. Freeman was the recognized chief from 1924 until 1949. The Waccamaw-Siouan Development Association was created in 1971 with an elected five-member board that oversees programs in job training, housing,

and community service. The tribe is currently governed by a tribal council and chief according to procedures established in 1978. Efforts to secure federal recognition have so far failed.

CLYDE ELLIS
Elon University

John Lawson, *A New Voyage To Carolina*, ed. Hugh T. Lefler (1984), *A Vocabulary of Woccon* (1998); Patricia Lerch, *Waccamaw Legacy: Contemporary Indians Fight for Survival* (2004); C. J. Milling, *Red Carolinians* (1969); James Mooney, *Siouan Tribes of the East* (1894); Theda Perdue, *Native Carolinians: The Indians of North Carolina* (1985); Theda Perdue and Michael Green, *The Columbia Guide to American Indians of the Southeast* (2001); Douglas L. Rights, *The American Indian in North Carolina* (1957); Thomas E. Ross, *American Indians in North Carolina: Geographic Interpretations* (1999); Ruth Wetmore, *First on the Land: The North Carolina Indians* (1975).

Waldensians

North Carolina's first Waldensians (also known as the Waldenses) were French-speaking Italian Protestants who settled Valdese, N.C., in 1893. The Waldensians were pre-Reformation Protestants who traced their religious ancestry back to at least the 12th century. Theirs is one of the oldest Protestant traditions in existence. Persecuted as heretics for centuries in France and Italy, Waldensians took refuge in Switzerland, returning to the Cottian Alps on the French-Italian border in 1689, where they were bound to the land for centuries. In 1848 King Charles Albert issued the Edict of Emancipation, which permitted Waldensians to live anywhere in the Duchy

Waldensian descendants playing bocce (Photograph courtesy of Jules Bounous/Waldensian Heritage Museum)

of Savoy and gave them permission to own businesses and attend public schools and universities.

In the first few decades after freedom, their numbers grew. In the late 1800s Waldensians established colonies in other parts of Europe and in South America. Some created small enclaves in New York City, Chicago, Missouri, Texas, and Utah. They established their largest colony in North Carolina in 1893, when 222 Waldensians moved to what would become Valdese.

Many Waldensians began farming as soon as they arrived, and three served in the U.S. military during the Spanish-American War just five years later. Others left for service work in northern cities, while some moved to nearby towns and worked in textile mills. Some of those millworkers re-

turned and opened textile and hosiery mills in Valdese, creating industries that became central to the town's economy. While many Valdese businesses, even the bakery, are no longer owned by those of Waldensian descent, the nonprofit Waldensian Heritage Wines Winery opened in 1989 and is staffed by volunteers interested in keeping the traditions of Waldensian wine making alive.

The Waldensians repeated many of the features of their Italian lives in North Carolina. They emphasized the centrality of their church in Valdese's first constitution and organized Le Phare Des Alpes, a mutual assistance society for Waldensian immigrants. Settlers adapted their Alpine rock-building traditions to their North Carolina homes, barns, and communal bake ovens. Other Old World traditions the Waldensians brought to the South include a predominantly French patois, foodways, and the game of bocce.

Since 1967 a summer outdoor drama, *From This Day Forward*, has told the story of Waldensian persecution and migration. A Waldensian Museum (opened in 1974) also explains Waldensian social and religious history and displays household items, clothing, carpentry tools, books, and family Bibles brought to North Carolina from Italy. After trips to Italy, local historian John Bleynat helped reconstruct just over a dozen Italian buildings and monuments related to Waldensian history in Valdese as part of "The Trail of Faith." He and other community members give tours (especially for schoolchildren) in which they explain the architectural traditions of the Waldensians both in Italy and North Carolina, describing how each structure relates to the Waldensian past.

In 1897 townspeople began building a substantial Romanesque-style church that resembled the churches of their home valleys. They constructed the church out of rocks gathered from local fields and quarries, applied traditional stucco, and dedicated the building on 4 July 1899. While approximately 2,000–2,500 people in the general area of Valdese are of Waldensian descent, the church is now Presbyterian and its membership is only 49 percent Waldensian. Through exogamy and out-migration, other descendants have joined different congregations or moved away from the region, but Waldensian heritage remains an important part of congregational life.

On the second Saturday in August, Waldensian descendants celebrate the "Glorious Return" of their ancestors in 1689 from exile in Switzerland to Italy. The annual festival includes a church service, a street festival, a bocce tournament, and a traditional meal at the church's "Pioneer Hall" featuring *soutissa*, a sausage with cinnamon, nutmeg, garlic, and allspice. On 17 February of each year, the community gathers for a meal, a lecture, and French hymn singing in memory of their 1848 emancipation. In honor of their ancestors who lit bonfires on the mountaintops around their valleys after hearing of the Edict of Emancipation, the Waldensians conclude the event with a bonfire on the church lawn. Throughout the months of February and August, the church congregation sings at least one French hymn each Sunday. For commemorative events, a few women still don the traditional costume of a plain dark dress and kerchief (called a *cuffio* in the Waldensian dialect). To accommodate ongoing local and touristic interest in their origins, the Waldensians doubled the size of their local museum in 2005.

ELIZABETH CAMPBELL
Greensboro, N.C.

CELESTE RAY
University of the South

Elizabeth Campbell, "Everlasting Rocks: Conversations about the Rock Buildings of Valdese, North Carolina" (M.A. thesis, University of North Carolina at Chapel Hill, 1998).

West Indians

For thousands of black emigrants from the British West Indies, assimilation to the South was complicated by the need to adapt to patterns of racial stratification in addition to cultural differences. A flow of West Indians became regular after the Civil War and was directed primarily toward Florida, where over 2,000 lived in 1880. They formed one stream in a growing migration from the British West Indies that carried newcomers to Michigan, New York, and Massachusetts. Because of its proximity to the island homelands, Florida was a major point of entry from which West Indians fanned out to settle in neighboring states. By 1900 over 7,500 immigrants (37 percent of the foreign-born black population) lived in the South-Atlantic and South-Central states. As the influx continued, the West Indian population in the South-Atlantic states alone grew to nearly 13,000 by 1930.

A sizable proportion of the newcomers were skilled workers, and most had sufficient schooling to read and write English. Other young adult males came to take jobs in agriculture and construction during the labor shortages of World War I. Over 3,200 laborers from the Bahamas arrived to work on government construction projects in Charleston, S.C., and on the truck farms of Florida's east coast.

Although the West Indian population in the South grew substantially in the early 20th century, West Indians were migrating in greater numbers to the cities of northeastern states such as Massachusetts and New York. Industrial and commercial jobs were more available there than in the South, where the proportion of West Indians employed in rural jobs was 10 times higher than in the Northeast. The percentage of black immigrants who lived in the southern states shrank from 37 percent in 1900 to 15 percent by 1930.

The communal life of West Indians in the South was profoundly affected by proximity to the home islands. The West Indian community of Florida provides a valuable case study. The relative ease of going home from the peninsula produced a high rate of return migration. A third of all departing black aliens in the 1920s left from Florida.

The migratory flow between the West Indies and Florida kept alive attachments to home island traditions. Many West Indians worshipped as Episcopalians and revered the British royal family. A study of West Indian immigrant life indicated that the cultural forms persisting strongly after migration were customs relating to death and burial, courtship and marriage, spiritualism, folk narratives, and a semitropical diet. The West Indians stressed and displayed proudly their English traditions, partly to differentiate themselves from native southern blacks and to impress southerners with their cultural sophistication. Unwilling to exchange an identity as a British subject for American citizenship under Jim Crow laws, West Indians in Florida became naturalized at one-half the rate at which West Indians in New York were becoming citizens.

Even during the post–World War II economic expansion and lessening of racial discrimination, West Indian immigrants avoided permanent settlement in the South. The West Indian population in the South grew only 8 percent from 1960 to 1970, while in the Northeast it more than doubled in size. Unlike the communities of the Northeast, those in the South contained a much higher proportion of transient males, which produced a gender imbalance that limited endogamous family formation. In 1960, while the sex ratio was nearly even among West Indians in the Northeast, West Indian males in the South outnumbered females by three to one. The difficulties of maintaining permanent employment and finding marriage partners may have discouraged newcomers from flocking to the South. Also, West Indian immigrants may have wanted to avoid the pressure of merging with the southern black community and so chose to settle in Boston or New York City, where they could be identified as another immigrant group. Still, by 1970 over 17,000 West Indians had made their homes in the South, and in the subsequent decades newcomers arrived on the currents of legal and illegal migration from the Caribbean.

New immigrants continue to negotiate their way through American ideas of race. They both identify with, and distance themselves from, African Americans and often maintain close-knit relationships with other West Indians. Immigrants from Jamaica, Guyana, Trinidad, and the Bahamas continue to socialize with Caribbean social organizations (which may also include immigrants from coastal Honduras, Cuba, and Haiti). According to the 2000 U.S.

Census, the largest number of West Indians in the South are in Florida (almost 500,000, or 3 percent of the state's population), followed by Georgia with 45,380 and North Carolina with almost 16,000.

REED UEDA
Tufts University

Milton Vickerman, *Crosscurrents: West Indian Immigrants and Race* (1998); Thomas Sowell, *Race and Economics* (1975); Reed Ueda, in *Harvard Encyclopedia of American Ethnic Groups*, ed. Stephen Thernstrom, Ann Orlov, and Oscar Handlin (1980).

Wichitas

The Wichita people call themselves *Kitikitish*, which roughly translates to "raccoon-eyed people." This designation refers to the traditional practice among the Wichita of tattooing their faces and upper bodies. The term "Wichita" may be derived from the Choctaw term *wia chitoh*, or "big arbor." The Choctaw term is probably in reference to the traditional architecture of the Wichita, especially their arbors for drying corn and their large, beehive-shaped, grass-thatched houses.

Known today as the Wichita and Affiliated Tribes, the historic Wichita were actually distinct bands that spoke different dialects of the Wichita language. These bands were united by their language, religion, and shared traditions, but they maintained distinct and separate identities. The tribe today consists of the Wichita, Tawakoni, and Waco bands, as well as members of the Keechi tribe. Although a completely separate tribe with their own language and traditions, the Keechi became affiliated with the Wichita while in Texas and have maintained a close relationship with them ever since.

The Wichita's traditional homeland is a vast territory ranging from Kansas through Oklahoma and into Texas. Their command of such a vast territory is but one of the reasons the Wichita may be considered one of the most important tribes on the southern Plains. The Wichita worked out a particularly successful adaptation to this environment by combining horticulture and life in settled villages with extended hunting and trading expeditions throughout the Plains and adjacent areas.

The Wichita have always maintained strong relationships with other Caddoan-speaking tribes, such as the Pawnee to the north and the Caddo to the southeast. After their removal from Texas in 1859, the Wichita, Caddo, Keechi, and Delaware tribes were settled on a reservation on the north side of the Washita River in Caddo County, Okla. Following the allotment of reservation land to Indian people at the turn of the 20th century, white settlers occupied the remaining land. Allotment—along with other policies of the U.S. government, Christian missionaries, and attendance at boarding schools—have all had detrimental impacts on the traditional culture of the Wichita people. Even so, Wichita people are actively working to preserve their traditions and pass them on to future generations. For example, a series of classes, coordinated with a local university, provide a place for

elders and young people to gather and discuss Wichita history, culture, and language. The Wichita tribe maintains its governmental headquarters and tribal dance ground, where an annual powwow is held each August just north of Anadarko, Okla.

RHONDA S. FAIR
University of Oklahoma

Robert E. Bell, Edward B. Jelks, and William W. Newcomb, *Wichita Indian Archaeology and Ethnology: A Pilot Study* (1967); George A. Dorsey, *The Mythology of the Wichita* (1995); Elizabeth A. H. John, *Storms Brewed in Other Men's Worlds: The Confrontation of Indians, Spanish, and French in the Southwest, 1540–1795* (1975); Muriel H. Wright, *A Guide to the Indian Tribes of Oklahoma* (1968).

Yorubas

The Yoruba who came to the American South hailed primarily from the southwestern region of Nigeria. Their central city of origin is Ile Ife, followed by Oyo, Benin, Ibadan, and a range of smaller village settlements throughout the southwest region of Nigeria. It was not until recent times that Yoruba gained recognition as an ethnic identity that encompassed religion, language, food, and shared history. Prior to the 1700s Yoruba people self-identified as citizens from the city-states of Oyo, Benin, or Ibadan under the domination of the Oyo Empire.

With Oyo dominance as the preeminent state, the characteristics of what would become Yoruba identities and cultural practices took shape. This included the formation of new standards for Oyo-Yoruba identity, including the development of the cluster of Kwa-speaking peoples who developed common Oyo-language standards, foodways, and cultural and religious practices. Over time, however, with the increasing spread of Fulani-Islamic influences from the north (through warfare) and the encroachment of European colonial powers from the south, the urban centers became zones of warfare, slave trapping, and raids. The Oyo Empire crumbled by the early to mid-1800s, and the height of slave raids and the export of captives led to the dispersal of Kwa-speaking people who would eventually be classified as "Yoruba" — a Hausa word that described the people of the state of Oyo and was given wider circulation by the 1840s by Christian missionaries.

The first wave of Yoruba-related settlements in the Americas took place in the late 16th to 17th centuries, when Yoruba-Dahomean captives were brought as slaves to Brazil, Cuba, Haiti, and Trinidad. One of the Kwa languages included Lukumi, and with the movement of African slaves to the Americas the slaves popularized a language system known as Lukumi and religious practices known diversely as a form of orisa worship or Vodou. The second distinct wave of arrivals to the Americas was a small number of Lukumi-speaking captives brought to the American colonies for sale in slave auctions. With the growth of a plantation economy, increasing numbers were transported to the American South. In New Orleans there were marked numbers of Lukumi-speaking, Vodou-practicing slaves, some of whom were

formerly living in Haitian plantations. However, it was not until the 1960s and 1970s that voluntary immigrants from three distinct groups of recognizably Yoruba people began settling in the American South.

The first significant group included a small number of black American revivalists who, in the spirit of the Black Power movement, moved from the American North to the South and developed a religious movement toward the reclamation of African, specifically Yoruban, religious traditions. The second group moved from Cuba and Puerto Rico and settled in southern Florida, especially in cities such as Miami and Fort Lauderdale. Characterized as "Afro-Cubans" with a joint African-Yoruba and Cuban heritage, they migrated after the Cuban Missile Crisis of 1962 and settled by the thousands, continuing the celebration of Afro-Cuban cultural, social, and religious practices. Finally, the third group represented some thousands of Yoruba immigrants directly from southwestern Nigeria who had immigrated to the American South in search of a better life. These recent arrivals have settled in cities such as Atlanta and Savannah, Ga.; parts of North and South Carolina; Houston and Austin, Tex.; Nashville, Tenn.; and Jacksonville, Fla. Unlike the second group, they are mostly Christian, and many still hold Nigerian citizenship, claiming a Yoruba identity in the United States. Although adapting to "things American" whenever possible, they maintain some of their national cuisine, traditional ceremonies, and social practices; live in extended families; and still encourage endogamy and Yoruba-language competency for their children. Nevertheless, many have pursued an American education, developed professional careers, and participate in the development of Yoruba cultural life in the South through celebrations of births, rituals of death, Nigerian Independence Day events, Yoruba drumming traditions and folk music (prominent in Afro-Latin and Caribbean music styles), and various festivals.

Today, all three groups continue to represent different aspects of what constitutes "Yoruba" in the Americas and how Yoruba life, in its diversity, can be lived in the 21st century.

KAMARI MAXINE CLARKE
Yale University

Kamari M. Clarke, *Mapping Yoruba Networks: Power and Agency in the Making of Transnational Communities* (2004).

Yuchis

The Yuchi Indians (also known as the "Euchee," "Uchi," or "Uchee") are perhaps best known as inhabitants of some of the many autonomous towns (*tvlwv*) that coalesced to form the Creek Confederacy in the South during the 18th century. They are now part of the Creek or Muscogee Nation of Oklahoma. Writers in the 17th and 18th centuries referred to the Yuchi under numerous ethnonyms, including the "Chisca," "Rickohockans," "Tomahitan," and "Westo." Not until 1715 and their participation in the Yamasee War do they appear under the ethnonym "Yuchi."

The Yuchi traded slaves and deer-skins with the English and allied with Governor James Oglethorpe for the protection of the early Georgian settlement of Savannah. The Yuchi also played a part in the survival of the Austrian Salzburger settlement at Ebenezer, Ga. With the continuing encroachment of the English, the Yuchi moved farther west, settling along the Chattahoochee and Flint Rivers in western Georgia and allying themselves with Lower Creek towns. For negotiation purposes, the U.S. government recognized them only as one of the many Creek towns that comprised the confederacy.

Unlike the other confederacy towns that resided in a central location with one ceremonial fire, the designated "Yuchi Town" maintained several settlements and ceremonial grounds. During their brief tenure with the Creek in Georgia, the Yuchi lived in three separate residential villages. This residence pattern persisted after their removal to Indian Territory.

In the 1830s, unwilling to cede their eastern lands and be removed to Indian Territory, the Yuchi fought with other Creek towns and later with the Seminole. Labeling the Yuchi as hostile, the federal government forcibly removed them without funds or goods to assist them in their new homeland. The Yuchi settled in the northwest section of Creek lands in Indian Territory, geographically removed from most of their Creek neighbors. Again, they resided in three geographically close but separate areas with ceremonial grounds active in all three locations. The three Yuchi stomp grounds (religious geographical areas) are Mother Ground, or "Polecat" (near Kellyville, Okla.), Duck Creek (near Glenpool, Okla.), and Sand Creek (near Bixby, Okla.). These ceremonial grounds, with sacred fires brought from the Southeast, still serve as central meeting places for religious and social activities. The Yuchi continue their stomp dance tradition as part of their religious obligations and hold Green Corn ceremonies each summer. Individuals either belong to a stomp ground or a Christian church (usually Methodist) or may fluctuate between them at different periods in their lives.

Their residence patterns, ceremonial activities, and language use helped maintain Yuchi identity. Language distinguished the Yuchi from their neighbors. The language is an isolate and unrelated to the Muskogee language of most Creek towns. Until the 20th century the majority of Yuchi used their own language for most communication needs. However, fewer than 20 people still speak the Yuchi language today. Early subsistence practices entailed women working the fields and men hunting. Gendered division of labor continues, but most Yuchi people hold wage-labor jobs. Women and men compete against each other in Yuchi-style football games during the summer. Such gatherings may be followed by an evening meal of fried pork, fry bread, *sofke* (corn soup), fried potatoes, and fried corn. While 19th-century marriage patterns tended strongly toward endogamy, by the 1990s marriage with other groups was increasing as young people left their home areas to attend colleges and join the workforce. The Creek Nation has recently recognized the Yuchi Indian tribe as distinct from the Creek, but the tribe has yet to secure federal recognition. Continuing to thrive in Oklahoma, members of the Yuchi tribe may be commonly heard to remark, "I am Yuchi, not Creek."

PAMELA WALLACE
Sam Noble Oklahoma Museum of Natural History

J. Joseph Bauxar, *Ethnohistory* (Summer 1957); Verner W. Crane, in *American Anthropologist* (July-September 1918); Jason Baird Jackson, *Yuchi Ceremonial Life: Performance, Meaning, and Tradition in a Contemporary American Indian Community* (2003); Mary Lynn, "A Grammar of Euchee (Yuchi)" (Ph.D. dissertation, Indiana University, Bloomington, 2001); Frank G. Speck, *Ethnology of the Yuchi Indians* (1909); John R. Swanton, *Early History of the Creek Indians and Their Neighbors* (1922); Pamela S. Wallace, *Ethnohistory* (Fall 2002), "Yuchi Social History since World War II: Political Symbolism in Ethnic Identity" (Ph.D. dissertation, University of Oklahoma, 1998).

INDEX OF CONTRIBUTORS

Page numbers in boldface refer to articles.

"symbolic" or "convenience," 3; as a
political identity, 5
Ethnogenesis, 2
Europeans, 1, 10, 11, 34, **41–56**, 197; demo-
graphics of, 7, 9
Evangeline (Longfellow), 11

Falls Church, Va., 245
Fante, 10
Fayette County, Ga., 191
Filipinos, 24, 25, 26, 75, 79
Filippakis, Ioannis, 149
Filmer, Robert, 142
Finns, 29
First Seminole War, 100
Fischer, David Hackett, 142
Fitzhugh, George, 142
Flatonia, Tex., 139
Florence, Ala., 43, 50
Florida: demographics of, 9; Seminoles in,
11, 224; Afro-Cubans in, 16, 93; farms in,
17; foreign-born whites in, 18; "Ameri-
can" ancestry in, 19; foreign-born
residents in, 20; Cubans in, 21–23, 66,
137–38; Nicaraguans in, 23–24; Puerto
Ricans in, 23, 66, 210; Indians in, 25,
166; Koreans in, 25, 181; Filipinos in, 26;
Arabs in, 27; Haitians in, 28, 154, 155;
Nigerians in, 29; American Indians in,
34, 35, 40; Spanish in, 41, 42; French in,
43, 144; Jews in, 46–47, 175, 176; Germans in, 48, 147; Irish in, 50; Welsh in,
50; Cornish in, 51; Italians in, 53, 173;
Greeks in, 54, 149; Russians in, 55, 215;
Greater Senegambians in, 58, 59; Mexicans in, 66; Latinos in, 69; Asians in,
73; Alabama-Coushattas in, 95; Black
Seminoles in, 99, 100; Cambodians in,
109; Conchs in, 131; Czechs in, 139; Guatemalan Mayans in, 150; Minorcans in,
192–93; Moravians in, 198; Muskogees
in, 200; Turks in, 241; West Indians in,
250, 251; Yorubas in, 253
Florida Keys, 130–31
Fon, 1, 10, 63, 64

Foodways, southern, 8, 9, 11, 12, 90. *See
also* individual ethnicities
Forsyth County, N.C., 196
Fort Bragg, N.C., 79
Fort Chaffee, Ark., 244
Fort Charles, S.C., 143
Fort Christanna, Va., 194, 203
Fort Lauderdale, Fla., 47, 155, 169, 173, 253
Fort Maurepas, 43, 143
Fort Myers, Fla., 225
Fort St. Louis, La., 143
Fort Worth, Tex., 24, 54, 55, 69, 71, 238
Frank, Leo, 17, 177, 178
Fredericksburg, Va., 43, 50
Freeman, W. J., 247
Free Moors, 15
French, 1, 11, 29, 43, 104, 119, **143–45**, 202,
212, 213, 239, 240
French and Indian War, 196
French Creoles, 135, 136
French Haitians, 64
French language, 7, 106–8, 132, 133, 144,
162
Frenenu, Ézè Nri, 164
Friedberg, N.C., 196
Friedland, N.C., 196
Friedman, Kinky, 235
Fulbe, 58, 63
Furman University, 79

Gaelic, 1, 7, 170, 220, 237
Gainesville, Fla., 46
Galveston, Tex., 177, 229, 231
Galveztown, La., 111
Gambia, 1
Gastonia, N.C., 244
Gates, Henry Louis, 86
Gates County, N.C., 184
Gatschet, Albert, 173
Geechee, 10–11, 152
Genealogy, 3
Georgia, 46; demographics of, 9; Gee-
chee/Gullahs in, 10, 152, 153; annual
income in, 17; farms in, 17; Afri-
cans/African Americans in, 18, 19, 57,

McIntosh, William, 200
McIntosh County, Ga., 222
McKinnon, John, 221
McNeil, W. K., 205
Mebane, N.C., 203, 204
Mecklenburg County, N.C., 66, 189
Meherrins, **184–85**, 242
Melungeons, 14, 15, **185–87**
Memphis, Tenn., 17, 46, 68, 78, 146, 167, 238
Mende, 10
Mennonites, 38
Mercer County, Ky., 48
Mestizos, 23, **187–89**
Mexicans, 20, 21, 25, 66, 102, 188, **189–92**, 235
Mexico, 19, 65, 66, 68, 69, 70, 71, 100–101, 234
Miami, Fla., 23, 27, 28, 47, 48, 54, 66, 70, 93, 94, 137–38, 148, 155, 181, 187, 210, 215, 216, 225, 234, 253
Miami, Okla., 226
Miami Beach, Fla., 179
Miccosukees, 40, **224–26**
Michigan: foreign-born whites in, 18; Arabs in, 27; West Indians in, 250
Mikasuki language, 11, 100, 225
Miles, Emma Bell, 83
Mills, James, 156
Mina, 64
Minorcans, 42, 172, **192–94**
Mississippi, 9; demographics of, 9; Italians in, 17, 53, 172, 173; Africans/African Americans in, 18, 19, 58, 97; Mexicans in, 21; Asians in, 24; Vietnamese in, 26; Mississippians in, 33; Choctaws in, 40, 126–28, 175; Irish in, 50; Highlanders in, 51, 220; Greeks in, 54; Czechs in, 54, 139; Alabama-Coushattas in, 95; Chickasaws in, 119–20; Chinese in, 122–23; Koreans in, 181; Quapaws in, 211; Gypsies in, 214; Syrians and Lebanese in, 232
Mississippian peoples, 33, 94, 199, 202
Mississippi Delta, 7; Chinese in, 25, 76, 122–23

Mississippi Masala (film), 73
Missouri: Germans in, 147; Irish in, 170; Ozarkers in, 204; Shawnees in, 226; Waldensians in, 248
Mobile, Ala., 13, 17, 27, 49, 135, 146, 178, 228, 229, 230
Mobile County, Ala., 198, 199
Mocsary, Adam, 162
Monacans, **194–96**, 209
Moncks Corner, S.C., 102
Montagnards (Vietnamese), 78
Montana: farms in, 17; foreign-born whites in, 18
Monteagle, Tenn., 86
Montgomery, Ala., 95, 176, 178
Moore, James, 243
Moravians, 23, 44, 45–46, **196–98**
Mordecai, Abraham, 176
Morganton, N.C., 68, 87, 151, 158
Mountain people. *See* Appalachia
Mount Airy, N.C., 28, 87
Mount Vernon, Ala., 198, 199
MOWA Choctaws, **198–99**
Mozambique, 64
Multiculturalism, 6
Murfree, Mary Noialles, 83
Murphy, Joseph, 238
Murphy Village, S.C., 238
Muscogee, 225
Music, southern, 7. *See also* individual ethnicities
Muskogean language, 34, 94, 117, 119, 121, 133, 159, 207
Muskogees, 11, 39, 100, **199–201**, 254

Nacogdoches, Tex., 234
Nago (Yoruba), 58, 64
Nansemond, 156, 209
Napoleonville, La., 172
Nash, R. C., 161
Nashville, Tenn., 19, 25, 27, 29, 43, 68, 146, 173, 231, 253
Natchez, Miss., 201
Natchez Indians, 103, 119, 126, **201–3**, 212, 239

Race, concept of, 4–5
Racial Integrity Law of 1924, 16
Rahal, Bobby, 234
Rahall, Nick, 234
Raleigh, N.C., 71
Raleigh-Durham, N.C., 68
Rapides Parish, La., 103, 240
Rappahannock, 209
Reagan, Ronald, 47
Reconstruction Treaty, 201
Red Bones, 14, **102–4**
Red Stick War, 200
Reed, George, 199
Reed, John Shelton, 39, 89–90
Removal, 11, 34, 35, 100, 113, 114, 116, 120, 127, 156, 173, 174, 198, 200, 202, 212, 225
Ribault, Jean, 143
Richards, Ann, 235
Richardson, Alfred, 156
Richardson, Jerry, 156
Richardson, Lonnie, 156
Richardson, W. R., 156
Richmond, Va., 17, 25, 27, 43, 47, 69, 146, 148, 181
Richmond-Rosenburg, Tex., 139
Ridgeville, S.C., 102, 103
Rights, Douglas, 203, 246
Riviera, Fla., 131
Roanoke, Va., 181, 232
Robbie, Joe, 234
Robeson County, N.C., 182–83, 243, 246
Rockbridge County, Va., 223
Rockdale County, Ga., 191
Rock Hill, S.C., 112, 244
Rodgers, Jimmie, 7
Rodriguez, Albita, 138
Rodriguez, Nina, 57
Rogers, Ark., 205
Rolfe, John, 16
Romanians, 55
Romanichals, 213, 214
Romanies, **213–14**, 237
Roots (Haley), 3
Ros-Lehtinen, Ileana, 138
Rosenberg, Henry, 231

Rosenberg, Tex., 175
Ross, Thomas, 246
Rouge, Eugenia Soulier, 126
Rucker, "Sparky," 86
Ruff, Willie, 7
Russell, Julia Lowry, 183
Russia, 29
Russians, 55–56, **215–16**

Sabine Parish, La., 103
St. Augustine, Fla., 41, 42, 44, 54, 147, 172, 192–94, 228
St. Bernard Parish, La., 42, 111, 112
St. Charles Parish, La., 47, 64
St. Cosme, Jean Francois, 125
Saint-Domingue, 63, 154
St. Helena Island, S.C., 154
St. John Parish, La., 47
St. Johns Island, S.C., 153
St. Joseph Day alters, 53
St. Louis, Mo., 212
St. Mary Parish, La., 125
St. Patrick's Day, 50, 168
St. Petersburg, Fla., 215
Salem, N.C., 196–98
Salvador, Francis, 176
Salvadorans, 24
Salzburgers, 44, **216–18**, 254
Sampson County, N.C., 129
San Antonio, Tex., 26, 27, 66, 123, 172
San Miguel de Gaundape, S.C., 41
Santa Anna, 234
Santees, 9, 14, 15, 103
Santeria, 210
Sapelo Island, Ga., 153, 154
Saponi, 156, 157, 184, 194, 203, 218, 219
Sapponys, **218–20**
Sarasota, Fla., 48, 232
Savannah, Ga., 17, 43, 45, 46, 49, 50, 51, 75, 168, 170, 171, 172, 176, 177, 178, 196, 217, 223, 230, 253, 254
Schwerner, Michael, 177
Scotland, 1
Scotland County, N.C., 182
Scots, 34, 44, 51–52, 220–22, 238

Scots, Highland, **220–22**

Scots-Irish, 19, 47, 52, 84, 142, 204, **222–24**

Scott County, Miss., 173

Scott County, Va., 185

Seadrift, Tex., 79

Sea Islands, 10–11, 57, 64, 152

Secada, John, 138

Second Seminole War, 100, 225

See You down the Road (Whitney), 239

Seminoles, 11, 34, 35, 36, 40, 94, 127, 200, **224–26**, 254; Black Seminoles, **99–102**

Senegal, 1, 58, 64

Senegambia, 1, 59, 61, 63

Sequoyah, 119

Sequoyah County, Okla., 203

Séraphin, Fred, 28–29

Seven Years' War, 119

Shawnee, Okla., 226

Shawnees, **226–27**

Sheftall, Mordecai, 176

Shenandoah Valley, 147, 223

Sherman, William T., 218

Sicilians, 17, 172

Sierra Leone, 1, 58, 59, 61, 64

Singer's Island, Fla., 131

Siouans, 34, 112, 194, 203, 218, 240

Slave trade, 57–64, 98–99, 152, 164, 253

Slavonians, 17

Smith, Delores O., 204

Smith, John, 194

Smith, Lee, 83

Smoaks, S.C., 102

Sneedville, Tenn., 186

Socorro, Tex., 237

Somali, 19

Somalians, 29

Southampton County, Va., 165

South Asia, 25

South Asians, **72–82**. *See also* Asians

South Carolina, 14; demographics of, 9; Gullahs in, 10, 152, 153; Brass Ankles, Santees, and Turks in, 14, 15, 102–3; annual income in, 17; Africans/African Americans in, 19, 57, 63; American Indians in, 34, 39, 40; Huguenots in, 44, 161–62; Irish in, 49; Cornish in, 51; Scottish in, 51; slave trade in, 63–64; Latinos in, 65–66; Asians in, 73; Indians in, 73; foodways of, 78; and Barbadians in, 98, 99; Black Seminoles in, 100; Catawbas in, 113; Cherokees in, 117; French in, 143; Guatemalan Mayans in, 150; Haitians in, 154; Hmong in, 157–58; Naturalization Act of 1697, 161; Jews in, 176; Hispanics in, 189; Muskogees in, 200; Puerto Ricans in, 210; Shawnees in, 226; Swiss in, 230; Turks in, 241; Tuscaroras in, 243; Waccamaw-Siouans in, 246; Yorubas in, 253

Southern Appalachia: and mountain people, **82–88**; religion of, 83; foodways of, 84; music of, 84

Southern Baptist Convention, 79

Southerners, **89–91**

Southern Highlander and His Homeland, The (Campbell), 83

Southern Regions of the United States (Odum), 17

Spain, 93, 137, 177, 192, 213, 228

Spanglish, 188

Spanish, 1, 11, 41–42, 100, 135, 161, 173, 213, **228–29**

Spanish-American War, 41, 248

Spanish language, 65, 70, 94, 111–12, 188, 189, 191, 192, 228, 235

Spartanburg, S.C., 230, 232

Speck, Frank, 209

Springdale, Ark., 205

Sri Lanka, 25

Stanly, John Carruthers, 165

Staub, Peter, 230

Staunton, Va., 47

Stone Mountain, Va., 186

Strike at the Wind! (outdoor drama), 183

Stuart, Jesse, 186

Stuart, Nancy, 219

Sudanese, 19

Summerville, S.C., 102

Sumter, Thomas, 15

Sunny Isles Beach, Fla., 215

Tuckabatchee, 199
Tullahoma, 9
Tunica, 14, 39, 212, 239
Tunica-Biloxi, 40, **239–40**
Turchaninoff, Ivan Vasilevich, 215
Turkey, 14
Turks, 14, 15, 29, 179, **241–42**
Turnbull, Andrew, 172, 178
Turner, William H., 98
Tuscaroras, 156, 184, **242–44**
Tuscarora War, 7
Tutelo, 194, 203, 218, 219
Tutelo-Saponi, 195

Ukraine, 29
Ukrainians, 87
University of Florida, 25
University of Mississippi, 234
University of North Carolina at Pembroke, 182, 183
University of Texas at Austin, 214
University of the South, 141
Upper Mattaponi, 209
Urlsperger, Samuel, 216
Utah: Waldensians in, 248

Valdese, N.C., 45, 53, 87, 172, 247, 248–49
Valdosta, Ga., 232
Valentine, Tex., 237
Vardy, Tenn., 186
Vásquez de Ayllón, Lucas, 33, 41
Venice, Fla., 53
Vicksburg, Miss., 27, 232
Victoria, Tex., 55
Vietnamese, 24, 25, 73, 75, 78, 79, 80, 81, **244–46**; Montagnards, 78
Vietnam War, 108
Villatoro, Marcos McPeek, 188
Vinita, Okla., 226
Virginia: miscegenation laws, 13; eugenicists in, 15–16; Asians in, 24, 73; Koreans in, 25, 181; Filipinos in, 26; Arabs in, 27; American Indians in, 34, 39; English in, 42, 141–42; Germans in, 42, 47, 48, 145, 147; French in, 43, 143; Huguenots in, 44; Cornish in, 51; Scottish in, 51; Greeks in, 54; Africans in, 63; Igbo in, 65, 165; Latinos in, 69; Redbones in, 103; Cambodians in, 109; Indians in, 166; Italians in, 173; Meherrins in, 185; Melungeons in, 185–87; Monacans in, 194–95; Moravians in, 198; Powhatans in, 208–9; Puerto Ricans in, 210; Romanies in, 213; Russians in, 215; Sapponys in, 218; Scots-Irish in, 223; Syrians and Lebanese in, 232; Turks in, 241; Tuscaroras in, 243; Vietnamese in, 244
Vlach, John Michael, 10
Vlax Romanies, 213, 214
Von Erlach, Diebold, 230
Von Graffenried, Baron Christoph, 48
Von Zinzendorf, Nicholas Ludwig, 196
Voodoo (Vodou), 9, 28, 64, 155, 253

Waccamaw, 39
Waccamaw-Siouans, **246–47**
Wachovia, N.C., 196
Waco, Tex., 54, 251
Wahunsenacawh, 208
Waldensians, 45, 87, **247–49**
Walk toward the Sunset (Hunter), 186
Walloons, 43
Walterboro, S.C., 102, 103
Warren County, N.C., 156, 157
Washa, 125
Washington: foreign-born whites in, 18
Washington, D.C., 29, 68, 181, 234, 241, 244; as part of southern region, 4
Washington County, Ala., 198
Waxhaw, 113
Weber, Max, 5
Welsh, 29, 50, 86
Wends (Sorbs), 54
Wesleyan College, 124
West, Tex., 55
West Africa, 9, 10, 11
West Central Africa, 63–64
West Indians, **250–51**
West Indies, 10, 98, 165, 250

West Palm Beach, Fla., 54, 148, 155, 181

West Tampa, Fla., 93

West Virginia: as part of southern region, 4; "American" ancestry in, 19; Germans in, 48; African American miners in, 96; Syrians and Lebanese in, 232

Whatley, Thomas, 173

White Oak, Okla., 226

Whitney, Kim Ablon, 239

Wichitas, **251–52**

Wilkesboro, N.C., 78

Wilkins, Michael, 183

Williams, Carol, 230

Williams, Cratis, 85

Wilmington, N.C, 223

Winston, N.C., 184

Winston-Salem, N.C., 45, 198

Winyaw, 246

Wirt, William, 230

Wirz, Henry, 230

Wisconsin: foreign-born whites in, 18; Kickapoos in, 179

Wolof, 1, 58, 63

Wood, Peter, 7, 98

Wyoming, farms in, 17

Yamacraw, 44

Yamasee, 99

Yamasee War, 7, 254

Ybor, Vicente Martínez, 16, 173, 229

Ybor City, Fla., 16, 21, 53, 93, 137, 138, 173, 229

Yeamans, John, 99

York County, Pa., 223

Yoruba-Dahomeans, 253

Yorubas, 1, 29, 58, 64, **252–54**

Yuchi (Euchee), 201, 226, **254–55**

Yulee, David, 176, 178

Zboray, Theodore, 162

Zedillo, Ernesto, 68

Zollicoffer, Felix K., 230

Zubly, John J., 230

Zydeco music, 7, 136